Nature, Culture and Religion
at the Crossroads of Asia

Some Books from Social Science Press

Reflections on Cambridge (HB)
ALAN MACFARLANE

*Religious Division and Social Conflict:
The Emergence of Hindu Nationalism
in Rural India* (PB)
PEGGY FROERER

*India's Economic Future: Education, Technology,
Energy and Environment* (HB)
Edited by MANMOHAN AGARWAL

*The Politics and Culture of Globalisation:
India and Australia*
Edited by HANS LÖFGREN AND
PRAKASH SARANGI

*'Good Women do not Inherit Land': Politics of
Land and Gender in India* (HB)
NITYA RAO

*New Mansions for Music: Performance, Pedagogy
and Criticism* (HB)
LAKSHMI SUBRAMANIAN

*Writing History in the Soviet Union: Making the
Past Work* (HB)
ARUP BANERJI

*Political Theologies: Public Religions
in a Post-secular World* (HB)
Edited by HENT DE VRIES AND
LAWRENCE E. SULLIVAN

Regulation, Institutions and the Law (HB)
Edited by JAIVIR SINGH

*Globalization and the Millennium Development
Goals: Negotiating the Challenge* (HB)
Edited by MANMOHAN AGARWAL AND
AMIT SHOVON RAY

Cultural History of Medieval India (PB)
Edited by MEENAKSHI KHANNA

*The Enigma of the Kerala Woman: A Failed
Promise of Literacy* (HB)
Edited by SWAPNA MUKHOPADHYAY

Cultural History of Modern India (PB)
Edited by DILIP M. MENON

Delhi: Ancient History (PB)
Edited by UPINDER SINGH

*Unbecoming Modern: Colonialism, Modernity
and Colonial Modernities* (HB)
Edited by SAURABH DUBE AND
ISHITA BANERJEE-DUBE

*Literature and Nationalist Ideology: Writing
Histories of Modern Indian Languages* (HB)
Edited by HANS HARDER

*The Sundarbans: Folk Deities, Monsters
and Mortals* (HB)
SUTAPA CHATTERJEE SARKAR

The Many Worlds of Sarala Devi: A Diary
SUKHENDU RAY
&
The Tagores and Sartorial Styles (HB)
MALAVIKA KARLEKAR

*After the Iraq War: The Future of the UN and
International Law* (HB)
Edited by BERNHARD VOGEL, RUDOLF DOLZER AND
MATTHIAS HERDEGEN

Social and Economic Profile of India (HB)
(In full colour)
PEEYUSH BAJPAI, LAVEESH BHANDARI AND AALI SINHA

India and China in the Colonial World (HB)
Edited by MADHAVI THAMPI

*Everyday Politics of Labour: Working Lives in
India's Informal Economy* (HB)
GEERT DE NEVE

Viramma: Life of a Dalit (PB)
VIRAMMA, JOSIANE RACINE AND JEAN-LUC RACINE

*Lived Islam in South Asia: Adaptation,
Accommodation and Conflict* (HB)
Edited by IMTIAZ AHMAD AND HELMUT REIFELD

*Reforming India's Social Sector: Poverty,
Nutrition, Health and Education* (HB)
Edited by K. SEETA PRABHU AND R. SUDARSHAN

*Human Security in South Asia: Energy,
Gender, Migration, and Globalisation* (HB)
Edited by P.R. CHARI AND SONIKA GUPTA

*Religion and Personal Law in Secular India:
A Call to Judgment* (HB)
Edited by GERALD JAMES LARSON

Trade, Finance and Investment in South Asia (HB)
Edited by T.N. SRINIVASAN

Forthcoming

*Telecommunications Industry in India: State,
Business and Labour in a Global Economy*
DILIP SUBRAMANIAN

*Unruly Hills: Nature and Nation in India's
Northeast*
BENGT G. KARLSSON

Nature, Culture and Religion at the Crossroads of Asia

Edited by
Marie Lecomte-Tilouine

SOCIAL
SCIENCE
PRESS

Published by
Esha Béteille
Social Science Press
69 Jor Bagh, New Delhi 110 003

© Social Science Press 2010

All rights reserved. No part of this publication may be reproduced, stored in a retrieval system, or transmitted, in any form or by any means, without the prior permission in writing of Social Science Press, or as expressly permitted by law, or under terms agreed with the appropriate reprographics rights organization. Enquiries concerning reproduction outside the scope of the above should be sent to Social Science Press, at the address above.

You must not circulate this book in any other binding or cover and you must impose this same condition on any acquirer.

Not for sale outside India, Pakistan, Nepal, Bhutan, Bangladesh, Myanmar, Sri Lanka and Maldives.

Distributed by
Orient Blackswan Pvt. Ltd.
Bangalore   Bhopal   Bhubaneshwar   Chandigarh
Chennai   Ernakulam   Guwahati   Hyderabad   Jaipur
Kolkata   Lucknow   Mumbai   New Delhi   Patna
www.orientblackswan.com

ISBN: 978-81-87358-46-6

Advisory Board
T.N. Madan
Dipankar Gupta
Jonathan Parry
C.J. Fuller
Veena Das
Bibek Debroy
Kaushik Basu
Abusaleh Shariff
Alaka Basu
Pratap Bhanu Mehta

Set in Giovanni Book 10.5/13
Typeset by Eleven Arts, Delhi 110 035
Printed by De Unique, Delhi 110 018

Contents

Introduction   2
    Marie Lecomte-Tilouine

PART I   HINDUISM, BUDDHISM, ISLAM AND SHAMANISM

At the Articulation of Nature and Artifice: The Rite   32
    Charles Malamoud

Nature and Culture in Tibetan Philosophy   48
    Stéphane Arguillère

Allah, Saints and Men in Islam: Diverging Conceptions of Nature in Theology, Mysticism and Law   60
    Marc Gaborieau

Variations in Shamanist Siberia   86
    Roberte N. Hamayon

PART II   HIMALAYAN CASE STUDIES

To Be More Natural than Others: Indigenous Self-determination and Hinduism in the Himalayas   118
    Marie Lecomte-Tilouine

Subjectivity and Governance in the Himalayan Environment   156
    Ben Campbell

Political Aspects of the Territorial Cult among the Mewahang Rai   190
    Martin Gaenszle

'Wilderness of the Civilization': Knowledge and 222
Perception of the Jad Pastoral Community
   Subhadra Mitra Channa

Love and Vengeance in Indus Kohistan 244
   Claus Peter Zoller

Conceptions on Tibetan Relics 260
   Rachel Guidoni

Plant Growth Processes and Animal Health in 284
Northwest Yunnan
   Andreas Wilkes

Terrace Cultivation and Mental Landscapes in 318
Southern Yunnan
   Pascal Bouchery

The Sacred Confluence, Between Nature and Culture 344
   Chiara Letizia

Contributors 370

Index 374

Introduction

Marie Lecomte-Tilouine

Grazing the cattle from a high view point, Western Nepal
(Photo: Marie Lecomte-Tilouine)

The English text of the volume was revised by Bernadette Sellers (UPR 299, CNRS), and the workshop from which it originates was financed by the CNRS, France.

For those who wish to venture into the Himalayan region a number of Indian or Nepalese travel agencies offer 'nature and culture tours'.[1] A 'nature tour' includes trekking or rafting, while a 'culture tour' offers tourists visits to temples or the opportunity to attend festivals. The activities in each category come as no surprise and attest to a broad distinction or categorization now commonly used. Yet interestingly, parallel to the growing use of these categories, they have been the object of heavy criticism over recent decades.

The definition of man as a cultural being as opposed to wild categories of living creatures has long been essential in Western philosophy. This definition was first challenged by the discovery of features in the realm of nature that were once exclusively associated with 'human' culture or civilization. With the discovery of the new world and the wars of religion in Europe, the notions of barbarity and civilization were first relativized from a moral point of view. They were later fully re-evaluated in view of the complexity of 'primitive cultures'. More recently, the notion of 'animal culture' in Ethology has contributed to further blur the limits of what is cultural and what is natural. Similarly, ecologists have emphasized the essential part of human action in many ecosystems hitherto considered natural and have underlined this dimension as being 'anthropogenic environments'. On the other hand, a less widespread school of thought, notably represented by socio-biology, has explored the natural part of culture or the influence exerted by the environment on human societies. Consequently, we are led to consider that animals and landscapes are more cultural than we thought, while humans are more natural.

The boundary separating the two domains of reality called 'nature' and 'culture' in Western languages is therefore subject to considerable interplay on one side and various upheavals on the other. At the same time, several anthropologists have recently shown that these categories are far from universal,[2] and have

---

[1] See for instance *visitnepal.com* or the website of the Nepalese Ministry of Culture, Tourism and Civil Aviation.
[2] Strathern, 1980; Descola, 1992.

argued that their use introduces an ethnocentric bias in the understanding of non–Western societies.[3]

This position raises several issues concerning first, the legitimacy of the use of a concept unknown in a culture to describe its reality, and second, whether or not it may throw light on the culture being studied. In fact, this is also true of numerous notions and concepts which are commonly used in Social Anthropology,[4] and more generally, of the use of a particular language to describe a human reality which is not formulated in it. Yet, before reaching this dead end, another problem emerges that is becoming increasingly difficult to set aside in current anthropology: it involves the introduction of new ideas or the modification of local concepts in most human societies, due to the influence of Western languages through globalization. This striking phenomenon occurs when in some parts of Social Anthropology, the tendency is to privilege the study of groups least contaminated by other cultures or to select only seemingly 'genuine' material.[5] This has resulted in a paradoxical situation with regard to the 'nature and culture' issue. Indeed, we now face a situation whereby traditional subjects for anthropological study, i.e., groups calling themselves Indigenous Peoples, have started organizing themselves politically on the basis of their specific link to nature (whether or not they have borrowed the concept),[6] and to oppose the groups and institutions whom they accuse of having deprived them of their land and rights. This opposition is expressed by the very opposition of nature and culture, but this dichotomy is denied as being part of the Indigenous Peoples' world conception.

[3] Descola and Pálsson, 1996.

[4] Thus, an important field of study in Anthropology, namely kinship, lacks its exact translation in many languages.

[5] On this subject, see A. Bensa, 2006.

[6] See B. Campbell (2005: 286) on the encounter between the modernist objectification of the environment and its effects on local understandings of people's environmental relations, particularly the case of the Gujjars (northern India), who 're-invented' themselves as a 'forest people' when threatened by the establishment of a forest protected area (Gooch [1998] quoted in Campbell 2005: 286).

Following a long and complicated history of the uses and understandings of an expression such as 'children of nature', for instance, a point has been reached where, when an aboriginal poet recalls, 'Children of nature we were then',[7] an anthropologist speaking of the same people asserts,[8] 'Children of nature they are not.' Of course, when placed in their contexts of enunciation, the former explains that they were happier before colonization, while the latter seeks to show that the people he studies are of a complex culture. Yet, the question remains that the debate regarding nature in Social Anthropology seems out of phase, even in contradiction with contemporary Indigenous Peoples' statements.

Numerous publications emanating from all over the world, including Europe, attest to the existence among Indigenous Peoples of a political trend using an opposition or dichotomy 'nature versus culture', even if, in many cases, the dichotomy is ascribed by Indigenous Peoples to groups from whom they are willing to distance themselves. To take one example among many, Katerina, an advocate for the Macedonian Indigenous People's rights, claims:[9]

> The indigenous peoples ... sprang from the land they live on. [T]hey feel they belong to the land ... They are Nature's children ... Their survival, their culture, their way of life is viewed by themselves as the natural life cycle. [By contrast, Greek] society is not a naturally occurring phenomenon but a man-made one, its survival depends on codes and rules that must be adhered to.

With its appropriation by Indigenous Peoples the expression 'nature's children' has obviously acquired a new meaning, which is both responsive and political. Although it was criticized by many Westerners as aiming to infantilize them or sometimes

[7] A poem by Noonuccal, quoted in A. Shoemaker 2004.
[8] K. Ackerman: 'The Dreaming, an Australian World View', *www.udel.edu*.
[9] Katerina: 'Concerns', *The Macedonian Digest*, Feb. 2006, *www.maknews.com*. I purposely chose a European example, but the same arguments can be found on all continents among groups who have adopted an Indigenous Peoples identity.

used as in Diderot's argument, whereby all human beings as 'children of nature' have the same rights, its present usage in the first person brings about a reverse appropriation of nature, and signifies greater legitimacy. Katerina, the above-quoted author, formulates the idea explicitly, by evoking the Indigenous Peoples' love for the nature they inhabit, and the concern for its preservation:

> Conquerors understand how to 'own' something but not how to 'love' it. This is the main difference between conquerors and indigenous people, who are less hostile, less aggressive, more tolerant and peaceful, as they are generally more concerned with the preservation of what they truly love.

Along with Indigenous Peoples portraying themselves as nature's children, they now also commonly use the notion of 'indigenous mentality' (as well as Indigenous knowledge and spirituality). This is close to Lévy-Bruhl's much criticized 'primitive mentality', since it is defined as ignoring dichotomy and linearity.

These self-definitions have a clear utilitarian or political aspect: they are indeed often formulated to obtain specific rights, such as autonomy (as in the example quoted above) or a privileged status.[10] This dimension, however, does not nullify their value, as this is equally true of all definitions to varying degrees. On the other hand, the question as to whether or not these self-definitions correspond to a reality in people's practices is the subject of quite a different debate, which we deliberately set aside here since it does not fall within the scope of Social Anthropology. It particularly concerns Ecology, in its attempt to evaluate the compatibility of Indigenous Peoples and the preservation of biodiversity.

---

[10] To quote one example among thousands, the Indigenous Peoples of the Kamchatkan Region claim (when demanding to have their region recognized as Territories of Traditional Nature Use): 'Aboriginal mentality should be known and taken into consideration; ... who else, if not the indigenous inhabitants as genuine children of nature would be vitally interested in the preservation of biodiversity of these inimitable landscapes?' *Indigenous Peoples' World—Living Arctic*, No. 14, 2004 (English translation from Russian), *www.npolar.no*.

With the development of Indigenous intellectuals dealing with their group's self-determination, Social Anthropology has acquired *de facto*, a dialogical form, not only during the data collection phase, as has always been the case, but also following the reconstruction of these data. One example of this with regard to the Indigenous Peoples of the Himalayan region—the focus of this study's context—emerged during the workshop which prompted the publication of this volume. While one Western scholar developed the idea that the categories of nature and culture were unknown in the group he was studying, my neighbour, a foreign-educated Nepalese scholar of the same 'tribal origin', raised her eyebrows, and whispered to me: 'of course we have these notions...'. Her reaction reminds us that denying certain concepts to a particular group of population may displease its members. Besides the fact that it may naturally be felt as a lack of some sort, it also appears to suggest that the concepts of nature and culture being used by the Indigenous Peoples as their main political argument is a borrowed one.

This idea is sometimes clearly formulated. Thus, after quoting a young Kanak woman who said: 'We come out of nature ... and that's what makes our culture, that's what sets us apart,' an anthropologist offers the following interpretation:

> The concept of nature/culture derives from a Western worldview (Descola and Pálsson 1996; Escobar 1999). Thus, in defending a privileged relationship to their natural surroundings, Kanak necessarily adopts Western terms and ideologies.[11]

This borrowing may in turn be interpreted as a sign that its users are not genuine representatives of the people they belong to, and it therefore contributes to discrediting the recent reflection carried out by Indigenous intellectuals. Indeed, it conveys the idea that their argument is fallacious, given that together with their specific link to nature, Indigenous Peoples all over the world choose to present themselves as guardians of ancient and

[11] L.S. Horowitz, 2001: 244–5.

authentic traditions, even when using Internet to sell their products or when active in international organizations.

Among the recent attempts to render the complexity of such a diffused notion as 'nature', A. Escobar's suggestion (1999) to account for the coexistence of various constructions of nature within an individual is worth noting. Escobar distinguishes the numerous overlapping landscapes a social activist would have in mind as 'the organic landscape of the communities', the 'capitalist landscape of the plantations', and the 'technoscape'. These constructions, he notes, do not form distinct autonomous entities, but are relational and co-produce each other. He hereby pinpoints what appears to be the fundamental dimension of the formulated definitions of the group's relationship with nature, in which the relational or even reactional dimension indeed seems determining. This, for the simple reason that this relationship itself is part of a self-determination process, which in turn is constructed in opposition to some other group taken as the referent *alter ego*.

The relational dimension of the conception of nature is well illustrated by one of the most striking aspects of Indigenous Peoples' self-determination, namely their similarity, even though they emanate from an extraordinary variety of groups in terms of languages, social organizations, environments, etc. The fact that they all developed similar ideas about nature and culture at the same period of time not only means that they influenced each other within international organizations, through printed matter, etc., but also that they all found themselves in the same colonial or semi-colonial situation, and in the same marginal and subaltern position within it. Indigenous Peoples' focus on nature/culture concepts, which are not actually formulated in their indigenous languages (even when they have had no experience of Western colonization), is still puzzling. In this respect, Roberte Hamayon's suggestion that among Siberian peoples, nature and culture may be viewed as 'implicit categories', which used to be formulated differently in the past, according to various groups' practices *and* self-definitions, provides a path for further exploration.

The study of conceptions and the way they are expressed through language and practices necessarily includes a historical dimension, which is both decisive and difficult to document in the absence of written testimonies. It is striking that even in one region of the world such as Nepal, where no foreigner was allowed until 1951, where until 1990 religious converts were punished by prison sentences, and where many villages are still difficult to access, people, languages and ideas have always circulated widely. There, the relationship between the mother tongue and the Nepali language among Indigenous Peoples represents a first stumbling block in trying to apprehend the latter's worldviews. Indeed they often master several languages, and Nepali, the national language, has become a *lingua franca*, if not the mother tongue, of many Indigenous Peoples. In addition, a growing proportion has access to English via education. Parallel to this widened and composite knowledge, new actors, such as Indigenous scholars, have emerged and given shape to newly constructed world-views. These have been formulated over the last two decades in a vast set of literature devoted to ethnicity, elaborated by urbanized members of the various Indigenous Peoples, whose ideas form a bridge between the global world and the groups they represent and in turn, influence. In spite of the fundamental role played by this type of material, this is not yet sufficiently taken into account in Western analyses, which are usually based on written texts only concerning philosophy or great religions, and on rituals, myths or oral narratives as regards contemporary non-Western societies deprived of a literate 'Great Tradition'.

Before the recent means of disseminating ideas thanks to world capitalism and globalization, religions influenced—and still do—a great diversity of populations to varying degrees. The adoption of the world-views conveyed by these colonizing ideologies, as well as the specific distortions they have been subjected to, have been significant in Asia. The Himalayan region proves to be a most interesting place for observation to address these questions, as it forms a crossroads where three great religions and a multitude of shamanist and animist practices converge.[12] In

---

[12]We have not considered recent Christian influence, which is mainly found in North-East India.

addition, groups with different languages and ways of life coexist in a great diversity of environments due to the various altitudes and the contrasted climates on the two southern and northern slopes of the range. It is particularly difficult for just one specialist to undertake the task of comparison and generalization in such a context.[13] Perhaps its complexity has kept this region somewhat removed from the recent debate concerning categories of nature and culture, as exposed for instance in the remarkable volume by P. Descola (2005), who offers a typology of the various kinds of human relationships with nature.

To address the Himalayan diversity without over-simplifying it, the present volume offers different scales and angles of study. The first part gathers distant points of view, insofar as they are based on non-contemporary textual traditions or on comparative studies on the four main religious streams which were, and still are, influential in the Himalayan range: Hinduism, Buddhism, Islam and Shamanism. This set of studies serves as a framework for the second part, made up of case studies and reflections based on more localized ethnographies of contemporary groups living in different regions of the Himalayan range, from Northern Pakistan in the West to Southern China in the East.

The nature/culture opposition encompasses several sets of dualities: the contrast between a cyclical time ruling nature and a linear time ruled by events (history), between the regular and the unforeseen (laws versus contingency), between the spontaneous and the fabricated, the innate and the acquired or transmitted, the raw and the refined, the wild and the domesticated, what can be appropriated and what cannot, what is common to all living beings and what is specific to human beings.[14]

The philosophical and religious worldviews in each of the four great religions which have been dealt with in these pages develop some of these oppositions.

---

[13] And the local complexity may explain that most studies dealing with this region focus on ethnography, to the detriment of generalization and theorization, which are difficult to extend across various contexts.

[14] A. Roger and F. Guéry eds, 1991.

The Hindu tradition possesses categories close to nature and culture in the Sanskrit terms *prakriti* and *samskriti*, which are still used in modern Indo-Aryan languages. Both *prakriti* and *samskriti* are expressed with the notion of action, *kriya*. *Kriya*, the action, also designates the rite. Built on this root, *prakriti* or nature is both what is pre-acted and a productive form, while *samskriti* or culture literarily means perfection. As their common root suggests, both 'nature' and 'culture' were created by ritual action. Charles Malamoud explains this in his opening contribution on how the categories of nature and culture revolve around each other in ancient Indian normative and poetic texts. Malamoud explores these categories through the theme of the retreat into the forest. Presented in the normative treatises as a means of access to a purer or stronger form of being, a stay in the forest is the third stage in life and even more so in the fourth stage during which the individual abandons social life and sacrificial rites. The aim is to quash desire in order to obtain liberation. However, Malamoud shows that poetic creation blurs these conceptions and presents a paradoxical situation in which the individual undertakes ascetic practices in the forest not to dampen but to fulfil his desire. Furthermore, he depicts utopian societies of ascetics who have solved the contradiction between the requirements of social life and respect for nature (a contradiction which is illustrated by the fact that sacrificial offerings are by definition cultivated vegetal and domesticated animals). Moreover, some poetic works describe an osmosis with nature which is obtained not by putting an end to ritual activities but by total devotion to them.

Charles Malamoud's observation echoes Roberte Hamayon's remark on the concept of nature in Siberia, which, she says, is quite different within the same population if one considers a particular type of material, such as ritual or actual hunting practices. More generally, it strongly parallels the coexistence since Greek antiquity of two contrasted human relationships with nature in Western thought, as highlighted by Michel Hadot.[15] The author characterizes the two opposed approaches to Heraclitus' formula,

---

[15]*Le voile d'Isis. Essai sur l'histoire de l'idée de nature,* Paris: Gallimard, 2004.

'Nature loves to hide', as on the one hand, the Promethean approach, which is linked to experiment, curiosity, science, and violence, and which promotes man's domination over the natural realm; on the other hand, the Orphic approach, which includes mysteries, secrets, art and respect, and which is based on harmony and fusion.[16] Michel Hadot's fascinating study examines the underlying tension between these two approaches in the Western world, which could not be revealed by examining just one type of material. And, in view of the warm reception of the idea that Westerners are distinct from the rest of humanity because they alone distinguish between nature and culture we cannot but agree with Per Binde (2001: 26) who notes that the models used in Anthropology are constructed in opposition to supposed Western conceptions that are 'seldom discussed in depth'. Binde warns: 'It would be unfortunate if another sharp dualism were to be introduced: that between conceptions of nature in the West and the non-West.'

Charles Malamoud shows that in ancient India, 'man, because he performs rites, builds a "made-up" world, which is thus distinct from the given or natural one'. However, Vedic texts hold a double discourse on action: sacrifice is on the one hand rendered possible by ritual knowledge, which is acquired, and thus cultural, yet man does not *perform* sacrifice, he *deploys* it, as a continuation of the initial sacrifice which created the world. In this schema: 'It is rite which precedes nature and society and determines them both.' This is why rituals act on both registers in this tautological worldview where 'the rite reveals and deploys nature, which is itself already instituted by the founding sacrifice'.

The following chapter, by Stéphane Arguillère, focuses on the notion of time in Tibetan Buddhist philosophy. In this tradition,

---

[16] Per Binde (2001), identifies three views of nature within the Roman Catholic Tradition: first, as 'matter' opposed to the 'spiritual' (i.e. man should dominate nature as the spirit dominates the body), second, as related to the divine (and therefore to be respected as part of creation), and third, as the realm of supernatural forces (i.e. catastrophes as divine messages, etc.).

as in Western thought, there exists a distinction between linear and cyclical time. However, although culture is conceived as a linear time which emerged from the cyclical time of nature in Western philosophy, in Tibetan Buddhism, the cyclic and the linear are not related to nature, history and culture in the same way. Indeed, human beings are not separate from other beings, but are encompassed within the broad category of sentient beings, which includes animals and humans, as opposed to non-sentient things. For sentient beings, there exist two distinct temporalities: the wandering in the repetitive time of the *samsara* and a linear progression towards liberation, *nirvana*. Nevertheless, this opposition displays an inversion of Western conceptions, because the cyclic has to be produced while the linear path to *nirvana* is immediate. As S. Arguillère notes, the cyclic *samsara* may thus be assimilated to nature, not to a nature that is opposed to culture, but instead to 'transnature', or metaphysis.

Similarly, the contribution by Marc Gaborieau recalls that Arabic has several equivalents for nature but none for culture. God is the main agent of both the natural world and human destiny: therefore 'nature is opposed not to human agency, but to God's omnipotence'. The various schools of Islam have developed quite different ideas related to nature. Arabic philosophy views God as a remote creator, whereas in apologetic theology, god is omnipotent and everything is a miracle. The regularity observed in natural phenomena is attributed either to the role of the saints, who fulfil human desire (for rain in particular), or to God's regular habits. God's omnipotence is the sole source of legislation, and the only real agency in cosmological events and human actions. Culture is therefore not what refines nature, since the world was made perfect by God, but rather a degeneration, which is not designated by any name.

The last contribution in the first part, by Roberte Hamayon, deals with Shamanism in its alleged place of origin: Siberia. We have chosen to place this unwritten religion on the same footing as Hinduism, Buddhism or Islam for the prominent role it plays in the Himalayan regions and to draw a model from Siberia because of the similarities between Himalayan Shamanism and Siberian Shamanism.[17] Roberte Hamayon observes that all Siberian peoples have borrowed the concepts of nature and culture from the Russian. Today they claim to be 'children of Nature' and to be 'in harmony with nature', be they urbanites or not, a claim which may be interpreted as a refusal to yield to any power. For R. Hamayon, nature may be described as an implicit category, which was expressed by 'wilderness' by the Siberian peoples before they adopted the Russian language. As she demonstrates, the notion of wilderness itself is also relative since hunters and herders' shamanic practices respectively display an inversion in relation to natural resources and the environment. In fact, even self-determination as hunters or herders is a deliberate choice, rather than being determined by activities.

The Ehirit-Bulagat herders, a native population of Buryat, emphasize the riches of the forests and the lakes rather than their wilderness. Their hunting season is opened by epics, which narrate the hero's quest for a spouse whom he receives after much difficulty from his 'rich' father-in-law.

Hunters, on their part, open the hunting season with a long shamanic ritual which stages a hunt, and which ends with the shaman's marriage to a spirit, who is described as the daughter or sister of the Master of the Game.

In both cases, the wedding is a hunting metaphor, and is made possible through an alliance with the spirits or with the in-laws. However, the relationship is reversed in the two cases as the herders' starting point is alliance, whereas the hunters' is the hunt.

For hunters, men and animals are part of the same food chain. Their souls and spirits are similar and are to be found in the bones, which are always kept intact for reproduction. Yet their relationship is not fully reciprocal. Men try and take more than they give. They delay payment of their debts by trickery, which they say they borrow from animal tricks, and which they then combine with their human nature. Thus, 'Shamanism is a type of "culture" that takes its shape from "nature", but ... with the

---

[17]John Hitchcock, 1967.

result that man's behaviour permanently differs from that of the animal being imitated.'

The first contribution to the second part takes up Roberte Hamayon's remarks in the Himalayan context. Marie Lecomte-Tilouine explores the recent claim of the Indigenous Peoples of Nepal that they belong to nature, as opposed to Hindu groups who, they say, colonized their territories. She documents the construction of this new identity and the opposition, expressed through an opposed relationship to nature, which forms its basis. The indigenous relationship to nature is positively characterized by harmony, fusion and participation, while the Hindus' relationship is viewed as negative and distant: a distance which goes from the transformation of nature to the non-intervention in nature. These ideas, though newly formulated within an international context, play a fundamental local political role for they do not oppose the dominants' views, but bring about their reversal, through the reification of a vision projected onto 'tribal groups' by the Hindus since ancient times.

Ben Campbell reacts to this approach, which uses the discourse of indigenous activists and intellectuals as anthropological material, and warns against their biases. By discussing A. Agrawal's concept of environmentality and E. Viveiros de Castro's perspectivism, B. Campbell's concern, through the exploration of a group of Tamangs in Nepal, is to characterize a relationship to the non-human, similar to animism, which illuminates villagers' resistance to nature protection. To this end, he suggests introducing the notion of 'environmental subjectivity', which includes both human-environment relatedness and the way the environment is made an explicit category. The task is re-constructive since environmental subjectivity is not a body of knowledge, but fragments, which, when put together, may allow for analysis by anthropologists.

In Nepal, worship of earth-gods by Tibeto-Burmese speaking groups often seems modelled on a reaction to political dominance, once their territories have been invaded by foreign groups.[18]

---

[18]See Lecomte-Tilouine, 1996.

Martin Gaenszle's study shows that among the Mewahang Rais, 'political power derives from the subjugating power of the "civilizing" process' over 'the territorial forces of nature and wilderness', which are embodied in the divinities of the soil. Interestingly in this case, the worship of these divinities not only excludes latecomers (though the Kulunge Rais settled 'seven generations ago'), but also the 'illegitimate' first settlers, the Sampange Rais. The Sampange Rais were troubled and killed by the local divinity, whereas the Mewahangs, who had proper ritual knowledge to worship it, chased them away and settled there under the protection of the god. This ritual order persists even today, but tends to have become secondary with the development of new territorial cults, which are less exclusive, and in which newly empowered patrilines are integrated. Like most 'Indigenous peoples' in Nepal, the Rais have developed the cult of earth-gods whom the Hindus themselves neglect, though the latter have established their political power over their whole territory. This suggests more generally that the various indigenous groups placed in a similar position of 'subjugation' developed similar answers to counter it, namely by emphasizing their exclusive relation to the local environment, and by ritually constructing the environment as a territory.

The world conception of the Jads, a small group of Tibeto-Burmese speaking people inhabiting the region located at the source of the Ganges, equally seems strongly influenced by the socio-political relations they maintain with a dominant Hindu population. However, instead of developing exclusive ritual links with the figures embodying their territory, the Jads choose to hide and keep their distance from the dominant culture. Subhadra Channa shows that except for the separatists who adopted Buddhism as a clear way to oppose the dominating Hindu world, the Jads do not have a named religion and use all kinds of ritual specialists. They have developed a tendency to keep their distance both mentally and physically from the Hindu world. Instead of altering their culture and knowledge in response to their negative perception by the dominant Hindu population, the Jads conceal them, just as they conceal their habitat when settling to the south, near the Hindus. The Jads view themselves as being close to unspoiled nature, i.e., altitude pastures and forests. However, a clear distinction is made among them between the males, who are more closely related to this domain where they spend some months with their herds, and the women, who must be careful not to anger spirits when venturing into the forest and are not allowed to spend the night there. The Jads valorize their own environment, which they view as nature, and devalorize culture, which they understand as being that of the dominant Hindus.

In the region of Kohistan (Northwest Pakistan), recent Islamization has led to a ban on regional traditions, such as the singing of epics and performance of shamanic rituals. However, Islamization has not affected, in the same manner, the different categories of the landscape, which are highly contrasted. Thus the high mountains, which form other worlds inhabited by fairies and giants, have not been Islamized. Kohistanis use these remote places for rendezvous with their lovers. Claus Peter Zoller uses the nature-culture opposition as implicit knowledge, and as a hermeneutic strategy or tool, which offers a possible way of reading the Kohistani practices of love. In this context, love is a liminal experience, which is 'legal' only in the wilderness and excluded from the settlements where respect, but not love, prevails between husband and wife. The married lovers meet secretly in the high meadows where their love is bereft of any social consequence as it is strictly platonic. All Kohistanis have lovers, yet this has to remain strictly secret, otherwise they will be killed by their kinsmen and transformed into fairies. If love enters the settlement which is the sphere of respect, it creates wilderness within society: killings and rapes, with no emotional restraint and a total lack of control over actions. There is thus a 'close correspondence between the oppositional notions of culture and nature on the one hand, and the Kohistani practices of secret love affairs and vendettas on the other,' says Zoller. Somehow, wilderness here serves as the framework of pre-Islamic elements whereby Kohistani society gave a particular shape to their Islamization. Surprisingly enough, it has resulted in an institutional game of playing with fire, where the forbidden values of the wilderness are so attractive that one risks his life for it.

Tibetans are mainly known through their vast religious textual tradition, yet, as Rachel Guidoni shows, present-day Tibetans share common knowledge about relics which find few echoes in this written corpus, even though relics play an essential role in Tibetan religious life. Although relics are highly thought of, their spontaneity or naturality is crucial; if they are the product of some artificial procedure or intention, they are devalued. Except for holy scriptures, any sacred source may produce relics, which manifest the virtues of both its emitter and of its receptor. Relics are usually pearl-shaped whitish balls emitted by the body of holy persons (whether dead or alive) and are commonly found in sacred places which also produce them. They are carefully kept in dark places where they are said to grow and multiply, or even to move. While Buddhist philosophy groups together the various kinds of sentient beings, as far as relics are concerned, a clear distinction is drawn. Indeed, like humans, animals may also generate relics, but these are black, and if kept by humans, they lead to hell.

The last three contributions focus on socio-cosmological models which preside over different scales and domains of human societies and their environment in the Himalayan region. These represent broad explanatory systems in which energy flows circulate along networks structuring living beings, their settlements, environment and the whole cosmos alike. The all-encompassing nature and the circularity of these explanatory models do not allow the determination of any starting point from which they can be constructed, but highlight a conception of the universe and all its components as being ruled by the same phenomena and in relation to each other. This material blurs both scales and categories by focussing on processes and networks, in which humans are included but which they also reproduce.

The practices of pastoralists from Yunnan are based on two alternative explanatory models of the processes that affect plant growth as well as the health of animals and humans. Andreas Wilkes shows that the same explanatory models were found relevant in experiments on exotic fodder technologies and on methods to control weed infestation in alpine meadows. These ideas underlie villagers' understandings of the value of these new technologies and their plans regarding their use. They also explain why they attempt to maintain the productivity of their herds of cattle by the specific custom of feeding meat to cows.

Pascal Bouchery's study focuses on the models governing the irrigation system and the conception of the social and physical environment among the Hanis of Yunnan. The author shows that their similarities are striking. The local environment is seen as being crossed by two types of energy flows: the first ones originate from the mountain tops (the realm of the gods) and follow their 'paths', from one summit to another, down into the valley; the second ones follow the streams from their sources, which are the habitat of deities named 'water owners'. Human settlements are located on these flows, or even better, at their place of convergence, to benefit from their energy, exactly in the same way that the parcel of land achieves its degree of fertility from above through irrigation channels, into which manure is thrown. Like the energy flow, the irrigation system is oriented downwards and its flux should never be interrupted: a principle which is regulated by social laws and carefully monitored. In this conception, human techniques closely parallel the world's perception and both are fully interlinked.

The energy networks among the Hanis recall the visible and invisible networks which cross the cosmos, the earth and the human body in Hinduism. Chiara Letizia shows that the common structure of these networks is made up of threads and knots representing passages. The structure relies both on the physical world and on the imaginary, since invisible elements are also part of the networks. Humans circulate along the river network, and towards holy confluences, which represent passages or *tirtha*, in the same manner as air is said to make a pilgrimage through the human body, along its channels and *cakras*, and to make ablutions in its interior holy passages (*tirtha*). In this vision therefore man is both 'pilgrimating' the world and 'pilgrimated' from within. He does not differ from his environment.

Himalayan Hindu and Indigenous Views on Nature and Culture

Some remarks on the Hindu world in its relation to these populations in Central Nepal will provide an understanding of the context dealt with in this set of contributions dealing primarily with indigenous groups inhabiting the Himalayas, as well as the data for investigating the reactive dimension of the conception of nature and culture. The specific Hindu social organization in a caste hierarchy is generally presented as being fully independent of a historical process of settlement and of any territorial dimension, though the caste with the greatest numerical strength, and/or the caste owning the largest part of land in a given locality or region is recognized as the dominant caste. In the Hindu Himalayan context, caste organization was imposed on all groups during the Middle Ages as a common framework, and spread its correlated ideas on purity and hierarchy. However, in this context, these notions are not fully exempt of the geographical setting and especially of the criterion of autochthony. Autochthony, which is closely associated with wilderness and nature, distinguishes the 'elders' within local societies. In many regions, and especially in Western Nepal, the first settlers maintain a specific political or ritual status and role, even if they are of a low caste. In the hilly regions inhabited by both caste and tribal groups, the elders are usually found among the latter and are viewed as more savage and closer to nature than the former. They often claim to have emanated from nature, to be the local 'men of origin'. Low-caste groups play an analogous role in the Indian Western Himalayas, where they are seen as autochthonous in comparison with the upper castes who describe themselves as latecomers.

At first sight, the autochthony criterion, as a source of prestige and of ritual or political prerogative, reveals a worldview that is independent of the functioning principles of the caste organization based on the pure and impure. Alternatively, it may be that this dimension has been neglected in the way social anthropologists have theorized about this organization. Indeed, in the Hindu myth of the creation of the social hierarchy, the most eminent class, that of the Brahmans, is also the first-born. Hence pre-eminence is expressed by (or co-extensive with) primacy. However, Hindu social order is not maintained by mere abstract principles, and the Hindu myth of the creation of kingship offers another, more complicated scenario, where an evil and barren Hindu king, then a tribal king, are respectively killed and expelled before a good Hindu king is enthroned by the Brahmans. Absolute eminence is thus aptly transcribed by absolute anteriority in the Hindu myth of human creation, yet ruling over a territory and society—or kingship—is the result of a series of adjustments dealing with different pre-existent categories of beings.

In present-day practices, when they have not been killed or expelled, autochthonous groups of Nepal are recognized as having a right over the territory. This is often expressed in rituals but has nothing to do with the criteria of purity, and even transgresses it. This phenomenon is not restricted to the Himalayan area. The Brahmans of the village studied by Jean-Luc Chambard (1994: 69-70) in Central India, for instance, are said to have eaten the half loaf of bread offered by the Chamar impure caste, the original inhabitants of the place, in order to be able to settle on the same territory. Though not absent in the Gangetic plain, the chronology of settlement is more systematically used to describe and explain local power struggles, as well as ritual organization in the Himalayan area. This fact is explained locally by the late coming of Hindu groups to territories already occupied by numerically important autochthonous groups. Whatever the reason, one of the consequences of this right is that Himalayan Hindu kings are closely associated with those who represent autochthony: they have wild counterparts, the Raute or Kusunda hunter-gatherers with whom they maintain a fraternal joking relationship, or they themselves are seen as the offspring of local tribes. The Hindu king thus partakes in the wilderness, and he may freely intermarry with tribal women. When seen as being good, the king is viewed as a god who indulges in the accumulation and redistribution of wealth and pleasures; when evil, he is to be slaughtered like a dog. The Brahman, on the other hand, is an ascetic god and when guilty, he becomes an untouchable to be expelled, not an animal to be killed. Whereas the Brahman thus crosses the social hierarchy along the pure-impure axis, the Hindu king evolves along another axis ranging from civilization to wilderness.

Geographic rooting is not only fundamental for Hindus with respect to settlement chronology, but also regarding their 'culture'. High-caste Hindus inhabiting the Himalayas frequently express a feeling of having migrated from a civilized place, northern India, towards a more savage region, the Himalayan Mountains. This statement comprises numerous dimensions, since wilderness is a complex and paradoxical notion for Hindus. On the one hand, it is clearly characterized by social un-differentiation and this feature is usually negatively connoted: a wild place is inhabited by *ajat* people, or people with no caste. This feature is attributed to all inhabitants by the environment, and high-caste individuals inhabiting remote Himalayan areas express the idea that their immersion in the wilderness has made them just as wild as the autochthons. Yet, on the other hand, *ajat* people, 'normally' ranked as impure, are not seen as such when wild. Indeed, wilderness forms a kind of parallel world, where people deprived of *jat* are seen as wild alter egos of their civilized counterparts, not as belonging to the bottom rung of the social hierarchy. This is expressed by the pure status in the Hindu hierarchy conferred on all local groups throughout the Himalayan range, despite their culinary or other social habits that are so 'disgusting' in the Hindus' eyes. It is also expressed, most remarkably, by the treatment of the most savage among the local groups, the Kusunda, Raute or Raji hunter-gatherers, who are regarded as Kshatriyas of a strange kind: the kings of the forest. In the case of animals, wilderness even confers an additional degree of purity: thus the boar is eaten by Kshatriyas, though the pig is not, and wild chickens are eaten by Brahmans whereas domestic ones are not, etc.

In Nepali, wilderness (*jangal*) is a relative notion designating a 'less domestic' space than the point of reference: for instance, the outside when speaking from the inside of a house or uncultivated places when speaking in a cultivated field, with the forest as its extreme manifestation. It also has an absolute definition for the Hindus, as the space where rice cultivation is impossible. High-caste individuals explain that they cannot settle above the geographic rice cultivation limit or they would be 'wild'. This is significant because rice is an absolute necessity for their life-cycle rituals, or *samskar*, especially the ritual of the first solid food offered to a child, and the death rituals. They refer to the essence of what they call 'culture', *samskriti*, which is defined by *samskar*. Shantiraj Sharma, the Brahman author of a booklet on the culture of the Khas-Kirat people, highlights the relationship between *samskriti* and *samskar* and defines the relationship between nature and culture in the following passage:

> The word *samskriti* [culture] was built around *samskar*. Now the word *samskar* has two meanings. The first one is the following: when man is born, he is similar to other animals. Animals, as men, search for food, sleep, are afraid, copulate, feel maternal love, the heat and the cold, protect themselves and their race. This is why Vedic texts called *shudra* [name of the lowest social class] the beings who possess only these low attitudes: these people deprived of *samskar* remain in their wild form. After birth, the different *samskar* rituals purify man of his animal aspect and raise him to a higher stage. Raising man from the wild or the animal stage, *samskar* offers him civilization (*sabhyata*).
>
> There is another meaning of *samskar*: the form and design that the potter gives to raw clay, once cooked, cannot be erased, and it is the same with molten metal. Once cooked, the form no longer changes. In the same way, the memory of the *samskar* left by the beliefs and observances in our ancestors' spirit, remains indelible. These *samskar* of the spirit are called *samskriti*, (culture). The Hindu Aryas of the plains attach great importance to contacts, to purification rules, to purity. In hot areas where one perspires, washing oneself and one's clothes daily is unavoidable. If not, not only would one's body smell, but insects and vermin would also take residence and transmit diseases. Gradually, this usage became registered as a *samskar* consisting in washing and cleaning. Purity became associated with cleaning. Because of this, if they cannot wash, the Hindu Aryas of the plain develop allergies. They attach importance to washing, even

in the mountains, even when the weather is cold. This is their natural and mental *samskar*. However, the fresh air of the mountains has all the power to purify: there, water is not necessary but once a mental *samskar* is built, one cannot erase it by simple reasoning. Those who live on the mountain tops do not wash, do not clean their clothing or the pots in which they eat; they are not concerned with purity and impurity (*jutho-choko*), as they take pleasure in eating leftovers or dried meat. This is their geographical culture (*bhaugolik samskar*). In the *samskar* of the mountainous nature, there is no disgust relating to food, and people do not develop allergies. The mountains erase dirtiness, and this is why such peoples are not affected by vermin. Cold air, snow and frost ensure their natural destruction. Then why adopt the *samskar* of the Hindu Aryas of the plain [in the mountains]? (Sharma, 1995: 6–7).

For this author, culture therefore has a dual basis: it is both geographical (i.e., conditioned by environmental factors) and mental, or, as he explains, inherited. From a natural origin, culture, once registered in the mind, becomes disconnected from the environment. It is a progressive process similar to the cooking of clay or the melting of metal, which is perpetuated from generation to generation (until one Brahman realizes that it is meaningless in the new environment). Another distinct part of culture, called 'civilization' here, is opposed to wilderness, and acquired by the lifecycle rituals, which to varying degrees, refine the different categories of human beings, who are all born equally wild.

Santiraj Sharma's views are illustrated by actual education practices in rural Nepal: children (be they tribal Magars or upper-caste Hindus) are told by their parents to keep their distance vis-à-vis wild counter-models: not to behave like monkeys (by chewing on corn on the cob) or like wild beasts (by eating pieces of meat before they are cooked). Education is akin to domestication. Though the process of cultural refinement is presented as definitive in the image of cooking used by Shantiraj Sharma, Nepalese villagers often express the idea that, when in contact with wilderness, living beings return to this state. Among animals for instance, domestic species are viewed as still akin to their wild counterparts. The dog does not bark at the jackal, its cousin, but lets it kill poultry. A chicken or a piglet released into the forest is said to become wild in this environment. Human beings also carry with them the dangers of the wilderness and hunters or those who venture into wild places for ritual purposes ritually get rid of them before returning to the village; babies are not to be handled by anyone coming from outside unless the person rids themselves of the dangers from the outside by placing their hands over a fire; and finally, Himalayan peasants who rarely wash their bodies, as Shantiraj Sharma recalls, carefully wash the earth off their feet so that it does not enter the house.

For Hindus, high places are wild for they do not offer full conditions for maintaining their cultural norms. The Nepalese Hindu government took into account this dimension and adopted less stringent rules in remote areas because it was considered impossible to behave in the same manner as in other parts of the Hindu kingdom. Interestingly enough, liberal rules for remote places did not only involve food, but also sexual practices. Perhaps it was on the basis of this principle that regulations for low-ranked groups were less strict than for upper-castes. They performed fewer *samskars* and were thus less refined; their wild behaviour was more acceptable, if not normal: they simply had to avoid polluting others.

In the hills of central Nepal, most people speak Nepali, a language in which the categories of nature and culture are often used in an oppositional way. For instance, it is used in the characterization of divine stones, to distinguish the worthiest ones, *prakritik* or natural, from those that were created by man. Various factors confer the status of a natural form of a god on a simple stone: physical factors (i.e., its appearance, its abnormal weight, its displacement), or external factors such as a revelatory dream. Unexpected encounters with divine *prakritik* icons, their selection, their valorisation and their worship form a major part of central Nepal's religious life. They are the only venerable icons, and if man-made representations of gods are added they have mostly, a decorative purpose. The idea that a ritual can confer permanent divinity on a man-made representation is not common in this region; the process is used by Brahmans, but only temporarily, and at ephemeral shrines (*jagge*).

Gods generally manifest themselves through the natural world comprising some objects and phenomena that are considered divine, and qualified as natural, *prakritik*. Once acknowledged, they are set up in ultra-natural spaces, guarded by a wall where men are not allowed to intervene: no digging, ploughing, building or taking, not even dry wood or leaves. In these places set apart, wilderness forms the gods' temple, showing the sacred character conferred on unspoiled nature.

Puzzled by this conceptual field combining the divine and 'naturalness', as opposed to human and civilized, one day I quite simply asked a villager, a Chetri (or Kshatriya): 'what is cultural—*samskritik*—and what is natural—*prakritik*?' He indicated at once his nearby field and answered: 'Here there is wheat. Man sows seed here: it is cultural. But afterwards, it grows: this is natural.'

This answer is interesting coming from a peasant because, as such, he knows that a seed borne away by the wind or a bird can germinate on its own, whereas man helps his wheat to grow by undertaking a series of operations: manuring, weeding, ploughing and other tasks. Thus sowing can be seen as natural and the growth of the plant as resulting from cultural operations. However, my interlocutor had radically separated these two processes from each other, according to the required degree of human intervention: without man, he added, a strong concentration of cereals cannot grow in a given place. On the other hand, germination and growth may prove excellent in a fertile place, without man having any part to play in it.

The example of the field shows that, for a peasant from central Nepal, the nature versus culture opposition does not translate the distinction between what occurs *de facto* with no human intervention and what does not, but between what *can* occur naturally and what *cannot*. The distinction relates to the possibility of a phenomenon occurring, not to the real conditions of its occurrence. In sowing seed, man's intervention is a determining factor, whereas in its germination and growth, this is secondary.

This conception is not idiosyncratic, since it is expressed in numerous myths about the foundation of villages in central Nepal, where hunters, seeing land ploughed by wild boars, sow seed and return a few months later to evaluate the yield. If there are large ears of grain, they know that the land is fertile and therefore settle on the spot. In this widespread account where even the preparation of the soil is not the product of human intervention, sowing indeed represents the founding cultural gesture, the result of which predicts future human settlement.

This scenario is literally opposed to another type of founding account narrating the transformation of 'wilderness' into 'auspiciousness' (*jangal ko mangal*), and thus a real transformation of the nature of nature by man. This transformation is narrated by high-caste Hindu groups, when referring to the clearing of land to establish new settlements,[19] or metaphorically, when evoking the establishment of the Hindu order and laws.[20] Thus when King Prithvi Narayan Shah conquered Kirtipur, though a highly urbanized area, he is said to have rendered the wilderness of Kirtipur auspicious, by felling trees. Interestingly, the description of the conquering process is presented as a hunt with the enemy kings as deer. The Hindu royal conquest thus literally parallels the settlement of hunters on a wild space they clear, followed by the auspicious transformation of the territory into a cultivated and irrigated place.

It might be rapidly concluded from these few elements that we are faced with two groups: one (the Indigenous Peoples), closely related to nature, has a selective attitude toward its environment, both in the establishment of its gods, and in its settling process; the other (the Hindu upper castes living in a wild environment) accepts and recognizes this attitude, but encompasses it within their transformational capacity towards the natural realm and the supernatural one. This capacity is nonetheless limited in their

---

[19] See for instance the family history of Motilal Malla (2045 VS: 1-6), which relates the migration of 500 families from Baglung to Surkhet-Dailekh in 1831, and describes how they cleared land and made canals.

[20] See the chronicle edited by D. Vajracarya, (2019 VS: 117). For another mention of this process in Nuwakot, see p.196.

understanding: temporally limited in the case of the gods, who are invoked in some object or symbol for the time of the ritual only; spatially limited since the high caste's ability to transform the wilderness into auspiciousness is only made possible by cultivating rice. The absence of rice prevents them from following their culture, especially their crucial *samskar*, or lifecycle rituals. As a matter of fact, it is possible to correlate the settlements of high-caste Hindus with rice cultivation throughout the Himalayas.

However, the situation is even more complicated; since rice, being a cultivated plant, is considered something of a pollutant, it must not be offered to the purest deities who only accept wild food, just like ascetics. The wildest regions are thus considered the purest because they are less contaminated by human activity. Yet, they are not compatible with the life of a householder, whose duty is to perform *samskar*.

Here the valorization of untouched nature coexists with the need for transforming space into a properly cultural zone, i.e., a cultivated one. The paradox is formulated in the literally opposite meanings attributed to the expression, *jangal ko mangal*. This usually denotes the clearing of forest for settlement and can be translated as 'from wilderness: auspiciousness'; it is also sometimes used to laud the beauties of nature, in which case it has the opposite meaning of 'the auspiciousness of the wilderness'.[21] This inversion of the terms reveals a field of tension between ideas that co-exist among the Hindu population of the Himalayas, and within which the indigenous groups have managed in various ways to preserve a distinct identity.

References

Ackerman, Kenneth. nd. 'The Dreaming, an Australian World View'. www.udel.edu.

---

[21] See for instance the poem entitled 'jangalko mangal' by Dilliraman Dhakal (2040 VS: 12–13).

Bensa, Alban. 2006. *La fin de l'exotisme. Essais d'anthropologie critique.* Toulouse: Anacharsis.

Binde, Per. 2001. 'Nature in Roman Catholic Tradition'. *Anthropological Quarterly* 74 (1): 15–27.

Campbell, Ben. 2005. 'Changing Protection Policies and Ethnographies of Environmental Engagement'. *Conservation and Society* 3 (2): 280–322.

Chambard, Jean-Luc. 1994. 'Les violences d'un village hindou'. In D. Vidal *et al.* eds. *Violences et non-violences en Inde.* Collection 'Purushartha' 16. Paris: EHESS. pp. 61–80.

Descola, Philippe. 1992. 'Societies of nature and the nature of societies'. In A. Kuper ed. *Conceptualizing Society.* London: Routledge. pp. 107–26.

⸻ 2005. *Par-delà nature et culture.* Paris: Gallimard.

Descola, P. and G. Pálsson, eds. 1996. *Nature and Society: Anthropological Perspectives.* London: Routledge.

Dhakal, Dilliraman. 2040 VS (1983). *Nepalko prakritik saudarya ra Shah vamshako den* [*Natural Beauty of Nepal and the Shah Clan's Contribution*]. Kaski: author.

Escobar, Arturo. 1999. 'After Nature: Steps to an Antiessentialist Political Ecology'. *Current Anthropology* 40: 1–30.

Hadot, Michel. 2004. *Le voile d'Isis. Essai sur l'histoire de l'idée de nature.* Paris: Gallimard.

Haudricourt, André-George. 1964. 'Nature et culture dans la civilisation de l'igname: l'origine des clones et des clans'. *L'Homme* 4: 93–104.

Hitchcock, John. 1967. 'A Nepalese Shamanism and the Classic Inner Asian Tradition'. *History of Religions* 7 (2): 149–58.

Horowitz, L.S. 2001. 'Perceptions of Nature and Responses to Environmental Degradation in New Caledonia'. *Ethnology* 40 (3): 237–50.

Katerina. 'Concerns'. *The Macedonian Digest.* February 2006. www.maknews.com.

Lecomte-Tilouine, M. 1996. 'Le culte de la déesse-terre chez les Magar du Népal'. *Diogène* 174: 24–39.

Malla, Motilal. 2045 VS (1988). *Surkhet-Dailekhko serophero* [*The Environs of Surkhet-Dailekh*]. Birendranagar, Surkhet: G.B. Malla.

Roger, A and F. Guéry eds. 1991. *Maîtres et Protecteurs de la Nature.* Seyssel: Champ Vallon.

Sharma, Shantiraj. 1995, *Khas-Kirat samskriti* [*Khas-Kirat Culture*]. Silgadhi: Nepali Sahitya Pracar Samiti.

Shoemaker, A. 2004. *Black Words, White Page: Aboriginal Literature 1929–1988*. Melbourne: ANU E Press, *http://epress.anu.edu.au*.

Strathern, Marilyn, 1980. 'No Nature, No Culture: The Hagen Case'. In C. MacCormack and M. Strathern eds. *Nature, Culture and Gender*. Cambridge: Cambridge University Press. pp. 174–222.

Vajracarya, Dhanavajra, ed. 2019 VS (1962) *Pandit Sundaranandavicarit triratna-saundarya-gatha*. Kathmandu: Nepal Samskritik Parishad.

PART I
HINDUISM, BUDDHISM, ISLAM AND SHAMANISM

At the Articulation of Nature and Artifice
The Rite

Charles Malamoud

Osmosis with nature, western Nepal (Photo: Marie Lecomte-Tilouine)

This article originally appeared as 'À l'articulation de la nature et de l'artifice: le rite'. *Le Genre humain* 12, *Les usages de la nature*, 1985: 233–46. English translation by M. Lecomte-Tilouine.

Ancient India

The forest hermitage (in Sanskrit *tapovana*, literally 'wood of asceticism', or *dharmâranya*, 'forest of observance') is a favourite theme in Indian literature, especially in Sanskrit literature.[1] In the two great epics, the *Mahâbhârata* and the *Râmâyana*, in the dramas (several of which borrow their subject from one of these epics), in the 'Antiquities', the vast collection of cosmological legends that are the *Purâna*, in folktales, novels, and learned poetry (*kâvya*), the evocation of forestial loneliness and of the men and women who undertake a retreat there, be it voluntary or not, forms an essential ingredient. In these texts, the retreat into the forest is usually presented as a means of access to a purer or stronger form of their being.

Poetic creation impetuously illustrates the prescriptions of the normative treatises (*çâstra*), which teach what life of men should be. It also somehow blurs its contours, as we will see. These codes, among which the most famous is the book of the *Laws of Manu*, state and explain the observances which constitute the socio-religious

---

[1] An absolute or even relative chronology of ancient Indian texts is obscure. The history of India is such that the margin of incertitude spreads over several centuries. It is commonly accepted that the two epics, each presenting various recensions, may have been composed in the centuries which immediately preceded the beginning of the Christian era. The various *Purâna* were composed between the 4th and the 14th centuries of our era. The most ancient works of Indian theatre known to us are attributed to Bhâsa, who is asserted, by conjecture, to the 4th century of our era. Kâlidâsa, the most brilliant and famous author of all Sanskrit literature is better known. Tradition at least presents him as a subject of King Candragupta II. Thus he is said to have lived in the 4–5th centuries. For the *Laws of Manu*, one oscillates between the 2nd century BC and the 2nd century AD.

The *Veda* belongs to a much older period. It includes two parts: 1) a collection of hymns and prayers, in the form of poems; its composition is usually estimated to range between the 15th and the 10th centuries BC; 2) treaties, mostly in prose, which expose the doctrine of sacrifice: the *Brâhmana* and their prolongation, the Vedic *Upanishad*. This second part of the *Veda* texts was constituted between the 10th and 5th centuries BC.

norm (*dharma*) of Brâhmanism and Hinduism.[2] (In the epics, some didactic developments, in the form of narratives placed in the mouth of such or such character, represent verbal versions of these *dharmaçâstra*).

This norm, as it is known, states that the life of man is divided into four stages. Man, or more precisely the Twice-Born, i.e., the man born in one of the three superior classes (*varna*), at the end of his childhood acquires a second birth by an initiatory rite (*upanyana*). He then must be a 'brahmanical student' (*brahmacarin*) devoted to chastity and to the service of the master with whom he studies the Veda. Then comes the second stage: the Twice-Born gets married, lights his sacrificial fires and carries on the life of a 'householder' (*grihastha*). This is an eminently social period, devoted to procreation, economical activity and the celebration of rites. Upon old age, the Twice-Born is supposed to leave the village, and, alone or accompanied by his wife, become a *vânaprastha*, 'one who leaves for the forest'. He then ceases to work and accumulate material goods, his relations with people loosen, and he imposes upon himself all kinds of new restrictions about food, and more generally, about corporal pleasures. But he continues to offer sacrifices (as far as it is compatible with his distance from

[2] The religious system exposed in the *Brâhmana* and in the treatises such as the *Laws of Manu* forms what is called Brâhmanism. Hinduism, the religion practised by the majority of Indians today, derives from it. Its basic texts are the *Bhagavad-Gîtâ* (one part of the *Mahâbhârata*) and the different *Purâna*. Between Brâhmanism and the many various forms of Hinduism, the effective differences are numerous; the principal one being that in Hinduism, there are divine images, temples, and places of pilgrimage. Theology and the general conception of the relations between man and divinity are greatly determined by these features. But these differences are not such that one could determine an assumed rupture between these two phases or aspects of the Indian religion that are Brâhmanism and Hinduism. The *Veda* is still the ultimate reference, and to use an expression of Madeleine Biardeau, Brâhmanism is the orthodox core of Hinduism. The work of Madeleine Biardeau, *L'Hindouisme, anthropologie d'une civilisation*, Paris, Flammarion, 1981 (a revised and augmented version of *Clefs pour la pensée hindoue*, Paris, Seghers, 1972), is a masterful presentation of all the problems indicated by its title, which is, in itself, the enunciation of a thesis.

the village and with his impoverishment), and devotes most of his time to rituals, to thought collection and meditation.

This third stage is normally the last one. However, the texts consider that the Twice-Born may engage in a fourth one, the stage of 'renouncement' (*samnyâsa*). The break is then radical: the 'renouncer' abandons any kind of social life. He lives alone and practises extreme austerities. He abandons the rites through a rather spectacular ritual and from then on, the sacrificial fires he used to take care of burn inside his own body. Ascetic fervour may produce a double effect: it confers formidable powers. The ascetic heat (*tapas*) accumulated in the body can be transformed into a kind of splendour (*tejas*) which allows any being, including the gods, to be burnt or at least, neutralized. But this kind of power made possible by forceful mortification, characterizes the ascetic who has not truly abandoned desire. For the true 'renouncer', strictly speaking, *tapas* (combined with an obsession not to harm life and complete attention focused on breath control) is overall the means of exterminating his affective and corporal being. It is also the means of reducing the residue of his *karman*, i.e., the set of actions he performed in this life or in his preceding ones, which condemns him to be indefinitely reborn as long as the effects of his actions are not exhausted and the movement which, under the pressure of desire leads him to act, is not redeemed. The renouncer's austerities aim at the annihilation of desire and *karman*: it is under this condition and by this path that man may obtain liberation (*moksha*), or the possibility to escape the unceasing cycle of rebirth. It must be specified that according to the Brâhmanic doctrine, strictly speaking, 'renouncement' is only accessible to men and, in principle, restricted to Brahmans.

The Forest of Utopia

Such is the theoretical scheme of the succession of life stages. However, whereas normative texts forcefully declare that one must go through the first three stages before committing oneself to the fourth, and underline the features which distinguish the extreme 'renouncer' from the simple hermit, literary texts present a much richer and nuanced description. In these texts, men, and sometimes women, undertake a kind of training in the forest, not to put an end to their lives, but to experience exile or to practise austerities which may help them fulfil a wish. The trials that they impose upon themselves combine hermit and 'renouncer' practices in various ways. The setting is the forest, terrifying at times, pleasing at others, but always filled with animals, and always favourable to romantic encounters.

In India, the 'woods of asceticism' are the simple and perfect form of utopia. And the utopian kingdom is foremost the one where there are numerous hermitages enjoying peace which nothing can trouble.[3] Their utopian nature is owed first to the fact that they are, *par excellence*, the residence of *vânaprastha*. The status of these people in the third stage of their existence is remarkable for harmoniously combining features of 'mundane life' and other features which characterize solitary life, as if they were compatible. The hermit lives far from the village, in this non-social place which is the forest. Usually, it is to form a pacifist, pure, and homogenous society in the forest with other hermits or couples of hermits. Herein there is no real work division and even, it can be said, no distinction between the ones holding power and those subjected to it. At most, one may notice that in the ideal image reflected in poetry and drama, these 'âshram' are gathered around a particularly revered spiritual master, a *rishi*, or inspired 'seer' who received the revelation of the Veda and transmitted it to men.

The traveller lost in the forest realizes that he is near a 'wood of asceticism' by the following signs:

> The deer are confident here, they come and go without fear...
> The trees, whose branches are full of flowers and fruits, are maintained with love. No cultivated field around. No doubt: it is a hermitage. Smoke rises above numerous hearths.[4]

---

[3] See for instance, the description of the reign of Dilîpa, in the first chant of the *Raghuvamça*, by Kâlidâsa. (French translation by Louis Renou, 1928).

[4] Bhâsa, *Svapnavâsavadatta*, act I, 12. A much more flourished and detailed description of the same characteristics may be found in *Raghuvamça, loc. cit.*

The hermits merge with the wilderness and gradually become its ally in a gentle way, without renouncing their social being. Resolved contradiction: they perform rites, celebrate sacrifices, and at the same time, succeed in keeping nature intact by not splitting the earth with the plough.
The forest offers them what is necessary to live and to make offerings. A wonderful paradox, if we consider that by definition, vegetal offerings are cultivated cereals (as well as animal victims which must be domestic animals). It is the very presence of hermits which determines this good will of nature:

> For having lived in contact with hermits, the beasts became tamed... The banks of the Tamasâ (the Tenebrous) are not desolated, for hermits inhabit there. Tenebrous, it dissipates darkness...[5]

Râma and Sîtâ, back from exile, contemplate with emotion some paintings in which the painter has represented their past adventures and the forest which was the theatre of their trials and love. Râma exclaims:

> Here, on the banks of these mountain creeks—in these forests of retreat whose trees shelter hermits—where the householders devoted to the duty of hospitality, their senses calmed down, live in their houses and cook handfuls of wild rice.[6]

Later, Râma returns to this place:

> Here it is, this forest—I see it again now... This is where we have lived for a long time, hermits and householders together, rejoicing in our duty and enjoying the pleasures of this world... Here are these mountains where peacocks were crying, and these wooded plains with their intoxicated deer—and there, with their

---

[5]*Raghuvamça*, XIV 75 sq.
[6]Bhavabhûti, *Uttararâmacarita*, act I, 25. This drama was translated in French and annotated (with the original text) by N. Stchoupak, Paris, 'Les Belles Lettres', 1935 (collection Emile Sénart).

bamboo of harmonious murmurs and their clumps of dark blue rush, the river banks.[7]

Ascetic Prowesses of the Divine Princess

Other texts, though of the same inspiration, go further: friendship between man and nature is transformed into a kind of osmosis. And this 'naturalization' of man is not determined by the cessation of rites, as in the case of the 'renouncer', but, on the contrary, by a will to devote oneself entirely to them. An example is provided by Kâlidâsa's *Kumârasambhava*.[8] Actually, the character described in this vast mythological poem is not a mortal but a divine princess, Pârvatî, whose destiny is to marry Shiva. In any case, emotions and ascetic achievements, as well as the behaviour of Pârvatî, conform to the stereotypes of 'those who leave for the forest'. The fact of her being a woman makes the marvellous and utopian nature of this lifestyle even more conspicuous. In her retreat, Pârvatî harmoniously combines rite and nature. She also displays, like many other Indian heroines, the contrast of a tender and delicate body, accustomed to luxury and the commodities of palaces, with the rough austerities to which she submits herself. Târaka the demon threatens to destroy the world. No one but a son of Shiva may get rid of him. However Shiva is absorbed in meditation from which nothing can distract him, especially not amorous thoughts. The love god (Kāma) himself tries to pierce him with his arrow in order to create a quake of desire. But Shiva punishes him by reducing him to ashes with a single glance. Princess Pârvatî wants to be the one who will receive Shiva's semen and give the world a saviour. To force Shiva to come out of his yogic concentration and to get him to make love to her, Pârvatî relies on the power of austerities. She takes the vow to live alone in the forest until Shiva takes her as his spouse.

[7] ibid. act II, 22 sq.
[8] *The Birth of Kumāra (Kumārasambhava)* by Kâlidâsa V, 8 and 11–25.

There was no way of changing her resolve. She removed her necklace[9] the rows of which brushed against the sandal wood paste (which perfumed her chest). She donned reddish bark, the colour of early dawn, which tore open under the pressure of her breasts. Her hand no longer touched her lips, now free of any trace of red. Finished too the game with the ball, which used to become red on rubbing against the make-up covering her breasts. (Now) her fingers were slit by clutching *kuça* grass blades and rosary beads. Engaged in austerities, she placed these two things into two (recipients) as a wage, to take them back later: to the thin creepers she entrusted the grace of her gestures; to the deer, her wavering gaze. Without ever flagging, she made shrubs grow with the flow from her jug (from her breasts, so it seemed), as it fell on them. Guha[10] himself would not have deprived them of this maternal touch, which they deserved as elders. Enticed by the wild grains Pârvatî offered them in her hands, the deer showed such trust in her that she was able to measure the size of her eyes against theirs, out of curiosity, in the company of her friends.[11] She was going about her ritual ablutions and making her offerings to the Jâtadevas fire.[12] For clothes on the upper part of her body, she wore (tree) skin; she recited sacred texts. In their desire to see her, the *rishi* approached her: a tender age is of no import for beings that observance has made mature. Animals hostile towards each other had shaken off their primal egoism; trees were honouring their guests with their most precious fruits; fires were lit inside the leaf huts. Thus lay the hermitage, a purification of the world.[13]

[9]This passage contains a pun in Sanskrit: 'necklace' is *hâra* and 'impossible to remove' *ahârya*.

[10]Guha is one of the names of the son that Pârvatî wishes to obtain from Shiva. Another name for this god is Kumâra (which appears in the title of the poem).

[11]Some Indian commentators are shocked that Pârvatî engages herself in such a frivolous occupation. They thus propose that Pârvatî is measuring her friends' eyes against those of the deer and not her own. See Mallinâtha's commentary in the edition by Nirnaya-Sâgara Press (second edition), Bombay, 1886, p. 79.

[12]The Jâtadevas fire is one of the sacrificial forms of the god Agni.

[13]Non-violence, hospitality and maintenance of (sacrificial) fires: by these (combined) three elements, the world is pacified, says Mallinâtha's commentary, *op. cit.*, p. 80.

(But) once she understood that the austerities and concentration that she had so far performed were not enough to obtain the desired fruit, she indulged in extreme mortification, with no concern for her delicate body. She, whom a simple ball game used to exhaust, now engaged in the *munis'* observances.[14] Her body was a gold lotus: delicate yet robust and overflowing with strength. In the pure summer season, this woman with a pure smile,[15] whose body is so thin in the middle,[16] went to stay in the middle of four blazing fires.[17] She triumphed over the brightness which destroys sight, fixing the sun without averting her eyes. As food, she had, without asking for it, only water, as well as the rays of the one whose essence is ambrosia and who is the lord of the constellations;[18] her way of life was truly no different from trees' means of subsistence. Severely burnt by the many fires, the fire moving in the sky and the one made up of pyres, Pârvatî, once the heat gone, was wetted by the new waters, and together with the earth, she exhaled a sigh of vapour, straight towards the sky... And while she was lying on the stone, having for home what was not a house, in the unceasing rain crossed by the winds, the nights were watching her with their eyes made of lightning, as witness, it seemed, to her extreme asceticism.

Here we are faced with the relation of a complex transmutation, which starts with a transposition: the red of the mundane ornaments, which is also the red of passion, is substituted by the red of the tree bark and by the one of the wounds caused by the

[14]The *muni* are ascetics who practise extreme austerities and also observe silence.

[15]Here again, we reproduce a repetition which is a pun in Sanskrit: 'pure' is *çuci*, but *çuci* is also the name of one of the three summer months and by extension, a poetical name for the entire season.

[16]Pârvatî has a thin waist, that is, in Sanskrit that she has 'a beautiful middle' (she is *su-maddhyamâ*), and she goes into the middle of the fires (she is *madhya-gatâ*).

[17]The four fires, one in each cardinal direction, and a fifth one, the sun.

[18]This is the moon, a male figure, in India. The moon god is identified with the god Soma, and the lunar celestial body is considered as the recipient of *soma*, the liquor of immortality.

kuça grass blades. This grass is used to strew across the surface of the sacrificial area, to carry the flame from one hearth to another, to make purificatory bundles. The rosary, made up of wild beads, takes the place of the man-made necklace. The metaphors become reality: Pârvatî's body (and especially her arms) is compared to lianas, as is the case for all young women. But then Pârvatî transfers part of her being to the real lianas of the forest and the affinity founded on analogy takes the shape of a substantial continuity. Taking care of young trees would be an activity too similar to gardening and too marked by the heterogeneity of man and vegetation if this nourishment were not assimilated at once to breast-feeding. In a first stage, Pârvatî takes a bark cloth; bark, which is the cloth of trees, is also their skin. Thus, to show the progress of Pârvatî's naturalization, the poet later says that she wears the tree's skin and not bark, conveying the idea that this added element has become a part of her organism—as it is for a tree. In a symmetrical way, nature is pacified around her, becomes hospitable for men, and, we might say, is ritualized.[19] From this dual movement, the hermitage is born, which purifies the world by its mere existence. The neighbouring *rishi*, disregarding the rule by which youngsters must pay a visit to elders and not the contrary, come to admire the hermit princess.[20] Far from being scandalized, they are amazed on seeing her offering sacrifices and studying the Veda, activities normally forbidden to women. In Pârvatî, a surplus of rite and surplus of nature occur together. She crosses a new threshold by submitting herself to this extreme practice of the forest hermit's programme as prescribed by Manu: 'In summer let him expose himself to the heat of five fires, during the rainy season live under the open sky, and in winter be dressed in wet

---

[19]By offering its fruits and flowers to the guests, the forest performs the rite of hospitality in due form for them.

[20]According to some commentators (cf. vol. II of the Trivandrum edition, 1913, p. 178), the mere sight of this hermit princess had the effect of destroying evil. There are several ways to be 'mature', and they vary with the different texts. For instance, one can be mature by age, by the absence of passion, by conduct, by knowledge. Pârvatî is mature by her conduct.

clothes, (thus) gradually increasing (the rigour of) his austerities.'[21] What is remarkable in the case of Pârvatî is that she does not seek to affirm herself against herself by confronting nature. She endures the fate of the trees and earth, she is dried up, nourished and vivified with them, she follows their pace, obeys their existential principle.

Fabrication of the Natural

We shall now leave the mythological settings of rite, and the poetical games they induce, to go back to the *Brâhmana* texts. Here the rites are not the details which bring colour and body to a myth. On the contrary, it is myth which is evoked, with more or less pertinence, and usually with a kind of lightness, to justify or illustrate a ritual prescription. The general idea emerging from these texts is that rite (always analysed as a more or less attenuated form of sacrifice and always tied to the ideal schema of sacrifice) is conceived and recognized explicitly as a violent intervention against a pre-existing matter, the oblatory material. In the same way that the victim is put to death, the vegetal offerings are killed by crushing or grinding before being offered to the gods, and one operates a kind of destruction in the corpus of speech by reciting prayer formulas.[22] This violence must be veiled, denied, or at least compensated by propitiation or reparation procedures. The latter are artifices in the sense that they form an autonomous construction, superimposed on the general system of symbolic efficiency on which the rite is founded in Vedic India as elsewhere. Besides, though Vedic India knows neither temples nor divine images made by man, the rite is conceived as the very type of

---

[21] *Manu*, VI, 23. English translation by G. Bühler, Oxford, 1886 (reprinted Delhi, 1964).

[22] See Charles Malamoud, *Le Svâdhyâya, récitation personnelle du Veda*, Paris, De Boccard, 1977, p. 79 sqq (Publications de l'Institut de Civilisation indienne, fascicule 42).

action (*karman*), performed by man, that builds a 'made-up world', distinct from the given one, the natural world.

To our modern eyes, rite is classified as an institution: it is a component of culture and thereby a feature specific to a human grouping, which is organized and defined by its decision to detach itself from the state of nature. Shall it be deduced from this fact that sacrifice determines the setting-up of a 'made-up world'[23]—and the distance between 'made-up', 'constructed' and 'fake' being short—that, in Indian theory, rite is an apparatus invented or discovered by man to affirm that he is also something other than nature, that he is not immersed in it?

In fact, Vedic texts hold a double discourse on rite and notably on sacrifice. On the one hand, sacrifice is an action. When one offers it, something new is added to the world. To celebrate rituals is proper to human beings, to human society. Ritual knowledge is acquired. For humanity, it results from a series of revelations and for each human generation, from the transmission of knowledge, which may be done under certain determined conditions of social life. On the other hand, it is forcefully affirmed that man does not perform sacrifice, but deploys it.[24] By performing certain ritual actions, one reveals an implicit sacrifice, and in doing so, prolongs and repeats an initial sacrifice, which in Vedic cosmology corresponds to the very act of creating the world. This mythical scheme is prodigiously long-lived and fruitful.[25] At its origins, the universe is a giant who is uncreated or rather who is engaged in a system of 'reversible kinship links', through which he is created by a being, of which he is also the creator. Though he has 'one thousand heads, one thousand eyes, one thousand feet', the giant has a human shape, he is Man (*purusha*). This cosmic giant is sacrificed and dismembered by the gods. Each part of his organism

[23]*Çatapatha-Brâhmana*, VI, 2, 2, 27. English translation by J. Eggeling, Oxford, 1882–1900 (reprinted Delhi, 1963).
[24]See S. Lévi, 1898; second edition, 1966: 79.
[25]*Rig-Veda*, X 90. See the translation of this poem by L. Renou, 1956: 90–100.

gives birth to the elements constituting the universe: the sky, the intermediary space, the earth, the moon and sun, the cardinal directions, animals and the gods (who are thus distinct, it seems, from those who were already there to perform the sacrifice), and also the melodies, the liturgical and metric formulas on which the poems of the Veda are constructed. What about man? As a species, he does not result from creation: he is, we can imagine, anterior to this sacrifice and a contemporary of the victim, or rather, indistinguishable from the cosmic giant of whom he bears the name. But from this creative dismemberment are born the four social classes: the Brahmans, the warriors, the producers and the servitors.[26] Society is thus not second to nature[27] since both have the same origin and are constituted simultaneously. It is rite which precedes them and determines them both.

It is thus not surprising to observe that in the Brahmanic doctrine, the sacrifices celebrated by men, being an explicitation of the primordial sacrifice, have for object, both the cosmic and the social order (the alternance of days and nights, the constitution of the year, but also the domination of warriors over plebeians).

[26]We have here the listing of the four *varna*. The Sanskrit terms are: *brâhmana, kshatriya, vaiçya, çûdra*.

[27]Such is the doctrine presented by the *Rig-Veda* X 90, and which is maintained by ancient Brâhmanism. In the major texts of Hinduism, cosmology is complicated by the introduction of the idea of a cyclic time and a division of each cycle into four ages, each of them being characterized by a degradation and a decrease in *dharma*. See for instance, *Manu* I 79–86. Besides, some Purânic texts clearly expose that one shifts from an initial and perfect state (in which human society, divided into four *varna*, results as all the cosmos, from creation), to a society modified by the effect of Time and the development of human beings' capacity to suffer and to sin, as well as by the multiplication of the artifice. People start to build houses and fortresses, gather and settle in villages and towns, invent agriculture, and more generally, the means to fulfil their needs by their labour. By contrast, before Time became an active and deleterious force for them, people were only devoted to offering sacrifices and the gods gave them rain and food in exchange. Pure, virtuous, and happy, men used to come and go without having to settle anywhere. Cf. *Vishnu-Purâna* I 6, 1–26, quoted and translated in J. Muir, *Original Sanskrit Texts*, London, 1872, reprinted Amsterdam, Oriental Press, 1967, vol. I, p. 60 sqq.

Moreover, correspondences between elements of the cosmos and society are unceasingly highlighted. But when examining the detail of what the *Brâhmana* teach, we may note that their purpose is not simply to join these two registers and to show how they are combined. They also aim at showing that the artefacts made by man at ritual occasions are as natural as the plants or the body's organs.

Thus it is said about the pole (*yûpa*) to which the victim is tied before being immolated that it must be cut from a tree in such a way as to have an octagonal section and the height of the man who offers the sacrifice. It is therefore, without a doubt, a devised and made-up object. However, the pit into which the pole is to be fixed is filled with grass, 'so that the pole is not buried (in a pit) but established among the plants'.[28] Planted in this mass of vegetation, the pole is turned back into a tree, and in order for it to develop itself vigorously, one also puts a chip of wood into the pit, the first one to be detached when cutting the tree. Why the first? Because it necessarily comes from the external part of the tree, from the part holding the bark. And when trees are deprived of bark, they dry up. It is thus in the bark that the vigour of the tree resides.

To take another example, the man who is about to offer a sacrifice, after all kinds of ablutions and after having had his head shaved (and thus received the mark of 'culture') must wear a linen cloth 'to be complete',[29] says the text.

> In truth, it is his own skin that he wears when dressing with this cloth. (And, in effect, one must know that) the skin which is presently on the cow was on man at the origin. The gods decided that the cow, on whom everything depends on this earth, had to receive the skin which was on man in order to stand the rain, the cold, and the heat. And thus they flayed man and placed his skin on the cow... Because man, in fact, is flayed, this is why the smallest blade of grass hurting him makes him bleed. Gods placed on him this skin which is the cloth... One should take care to be well dressed in order to be completely draped in one

[28] *Çatapatha-Brâhmana* III 7, 1, 7 sq.
[29] ibid. III 1, 2, 13–17.

own skin. And man should not be naked in front of a cow. Because the cow knows that she is wearing man's skin and she would run away from fear that he takes it back.

Finally, here are the instructions concerning the king's dress during the royal consecration ceremony.[30] He is first given a kind of dress embroidered with designs representing diverse sacrificial utensils (vases, spoons, etc.) and one officiating priest says, speaking to the dress: 'you are the internal embryo membrane of kingship'. 'Thus,' says the text, 'he makes it such that the king is born from what is the internal membrane of kingship.' He is then given a shawl of wool to wear, which is assimilated to the external membrane. Finally a mantle is thrown on his shoulders: it is the matrix of kingship. Later in the text, these clothes are identified with another part of the organism: they were the milieu in which the embryonary life of his royal being developed itself; now that he is born as king, the clothes are truly his limbs; when giving them, the officiating priest 'puts him in possession of the limbs which are his, of the body he has by birth'.

What is said here of the king is, in fact, valid for all men. At least for those who belong to the first three classes of society (those who have access to the knowledge of the Veda, according to its prescriptions), the rites of passage which punctuate the various stages of their life, especially childhood, are conceived as being as many 'perfectionings'. The most important one, the 'initiation' is, as mentioned above, a second birth, which is 'cultural' or 'social', but which does not modify the situation created by 'natural' birth. Its role is to allow the 'Twice-born' to gain possession of his own nature, the one that was provided by his biological birth, but only as a necessary but not sufficient condition.[31]

---

[30] ibid. V 3, 5, 20–5.
[31] The 'perfectionings' are not added to nature, but 'qualify' it, i.e. they make manifest the qualities which allow a man to correspond to his definition when they are actualized. This recalls the passage of the *Râmâyana* (influenced by the *sâmkhya* philosophy, at least in its vocabulary), which later appears in Bhavabhûti's *Uttararâmacarita*, act VI, 31: 'By her very

The rite reveals and deploys nature, which is itself already pre-instituted by the founding sacrifice. Thus we can try to give a first meaning to the troubling tautology of the Upanishadic text, beyond any mystical interpretation: 'By what is one really a Brâhman?— That by what one is such, this is by that that one is such.'[32]

References

Bhavabhûti. *Uttararâmacarita*, translated into French and annotated (with the original text) by N. Stchoupak, *Uttararâmacarita: la dernière aventure de Râma*. Paris: 'Les Belles Lettres', 1935 (collection Emile Senart).

Biardeau, Madeleine. 1981. *L'Hindouisme, anthropologie d'une civilisation*. Paris: Flammarion.

Çatapatha-Brâhmana. English translation by J. Eggeling, Oxford, 1882–1900 (reprinted Delhi, 1963, Sacred Books of the East, XII, XXVI, XLI, XLIII, XLIV).

Lévi, Sylvain. 1898. *La Doctrine du sacrifice dans les Brâhmanas*. Paris. Second edition with a preface by L. Renou. Paris: P.U.F, 1966, (Bibliothèque de l'Ecole des Hautes Etudes, section des sciences religieuses, volume LXXIII).

Malamoud, Charles. 1977. *Le Svâdhyâya, récitation personnelle du Veda*. Paris: De Boccard, (Publications de l'Institut de Civilisation indienne, fascicule 42).

Muir, J. *Original Sanskrit Texts*. London, 1872, reprinted Amsterdam: Oriental Press, 1967, vol. I.

Renou, Louis. 1956. *Hymnes spéculatifs du Veda*. Paris: Gallimard (Collection UNESCO Connaissance de l'Orient).

Senart, Emile. 1934. *Brhad-Âranyaka-Upanishad*. Translated and annotated. Paris: 'Les Belles Lettres', (Collection Emile Senart, vol. 3).

The Laws of Manu, English translation by G. Bühler, Oxford, 1886 (reprinted Delhi, 1964, Sacred Books of the East, XXV).

---

nature (*prakriti*) Sîtâ was dear to Râma ... but she was increasing this love by her qualities.'

[32] *Brihad-Âranyaka-Upanishad* III 5, 1. For a detailed study of this passage, see its edition, with translation and notes by E. Senart, 1934: 48.

Nature and Culture in
Tibetan Philosophy

Stéphane Arguillère

Tibetans praying in front of a sacred mountain, Swayambhunath,
Nepal (Photo: Marie Lecomte-Tilouine)

The opposition of nature and culture implies an anthropology in which man would be a 'de-natured' or distorted being, who has been led astray from his original condition. The loss of the 'state of nature' is regarded as having opened to man the ways to a greatness of another order—the one that is conquered through *history*, within the realm of *culture*. It is only in the Age of Enlightenment, around the systems of Rousseau and Kant, that this nature/culture opposition was set up in a form that is recognizable to us. From then on, we get the complete picture, in which all of the following elements are brought together:

The idea of a *primordial condition* promoted as sane and good though crude, primitive, and characterized by cyclic repetition of the same, or, at least, by its stationary aspect.

A *discontinuity*, quite accidental and inexplicable (precisely because it does not follow on logically from the natural state), which makes a transition towards an uncertain future; a linear evolution that is no longer a circular repetition.

Some degree of *valorization* of this evolution, involving *inventiveness* and (in the classical version) the *cumulative progress* of culture, through which mankind overcomes both the limitations of nature and the dangers of the shapeless freedom of beings gone astray from nature.

Culture, then, is understood as a second nature, a spiritual rather than beastly one, not given, but constructed by man.

When carefully examined, this classical framework of the relationship between nature and culture might well appear as a secularized version of the central theme of Christian humanism. Innocence first, then the Fall, followed by Redemption which is not supposed to restore the original, edenic condition, but a salvation even greater than the state of the angels. In the history of ideas in the West, there is a transitional form between the religious version of the theme and that of the Enlightenment ideology: a secularized combination of the system focussed on Christian salvation and a concern for the development of the mind through culture. This can be found in the works of the Renaissance authors, especially Charles de Bovelles in the *Liber de Sapiente*. Interestingly, there is a high degree of superimposition of the Christian themes and conceptual elements borrowed from Neoplatonism in the works of these authors. It is in the tradition of this Neoplatonician philosophy of mind that the great post-Kantian idealism can be situated, especially Schelling's 'Nature-philosophy' and Hegel's philosophy of history. Our contemporary understanding of 'nature and culture' is, consciously or not, rooted in Hegel's thought. Even those who are consciously opposed to the Hegelian tradition are somehow bound to express their conceptions in a framework that was originally elaborated by Hegel. It seems as if he opened a dimension of thought within which we have no choice, so far, but to dwell!

It is quite ironical that the West is inclined to consider Asian thought as being imbued with mythology and thus being far from the transparency of 'purely rational' ideas. Western thought is oblivious of the historical and cultural *thickness* of its own concepts, which in most cases, consist of many accumulated ideological layers. This cursory reminder might not be utterly pointless as we try to apply these conceptual tools to Tibetan philosophy and thought.

Can we expect to find anything in the Tibetan world that would be more or less analogous to this opposition of nature and culture?

Let us first consider matters on a philosophical plane. It would sound odd, in a Buddhist context, to make a clear-cut opposition between the realm of nature and a field or range of the artificial, of the factitious, and, what is more, of *purely human factitious phenomena*. Actually, like most doctrines of Indian origin, Buddhism does not especially set mankind aside from the rest of nature. If there is any relevant difference in the Buddhist system, it is the one that distinguishes sentient beings (men, animals, and all sorts of gods, spirits and demons) from non-sentient beings (plants, minerals and artificial objects). It is extremely meaningful that animals are grouped with human beings rather than with plants. While plants or minerals are entirely given over to a form of passivity, to some unchanging natural determination, to which they cannot but mechanically adhere, animals, as well as humans, are regarded as being, to some degree, authors of their own destinies, architects of their future.

Both animals and human beings, as well as spirits, gods and demons, belong to the realm of *karman*, and that is a key notion to our problem. A being endowed with *karman*, in Buddhism, is conceived as being the maker, the author, of himself—so, one might be tempted to say, he is a cultural being.

Sentient beings, insofar as they are given over to *karman*, can be defined as beings that build up their own future condition through their present actions—which are only partly determined by their present state, itself conditioned by their own past actions. What is at work in such a device is definitely not a notion of freedom as 'free will', but a conception of the relative plasticity, malleability, of the sentient being. Their destiny is a series of metamorphoses, or rather an unceasing, ongoing metamorphosis carried out through imperceptible degrees. These neither happen according to the being's own liking, nor randomly, but in some sort of dialectics between the condition or state that is itself the result of his past actions and the way in which he reacts to the circumstances that befall him. Those reactions construct the *karman* that will condition his future existence.

Should we then invent a *broadened notion of culture* that would work for all sorts of sentient beings? And what would become of the idea of nature, if its boundaries are restricted to the vegetable and mineral kingdoms (not to say anything of the artificial devices)? Actually, the problem is still very badly formulated for on a purely philosophical level, it is clear that Buddhism, especially later Buddhism inherited by the Tibetans, is driven by a strong idealistic tendency: it considers the 'non-sentient' environment merely as the *scenery* in which sentient beings display their existence. So in a broader sense, stones and plants are not beyond the range of 'culture', as they are mostly projected by the *karman* of sentient beings, who are the 'contents' (*bcud*) of this 'container' (*snod*) world.

The natural environment is not a presupposition of culture, as Schelling or Hegel might have phrased it; it is not an underlying compost, on the basis of which culture would grow and blossom.

It is the opposite: it is merely the *caput mortuum* of the life of the mind, its dead and inert result.

Aristotle defines habit as being 'a second nature', meaning that once one has got used to behaving in some way, then this habit imposes itself with the same strength as a natural impulse would have. It would not be an exaggeration to say that, in Buddhism, there is no nature that would not be 'second'. Now, 'second nature' is as well a name for culture, insofar as it is a system of customs and constraints, not deriving from nature, but collectively elaborated by men.

It would appear that the line between the two concepts is becoming rather blurred.

Is it to say that Tibetan thought, inasmuch as it has become largely absorbed by Buddhist speculation, would be unable to attribute any meaning to such notions of nature and culture? Do we mean to say that, in answer to this question, Tibetan thought would merely cast light upon the presuppositions that the question involves? It is not quite so obvious. Actually, in the nature/culture opposition, there is also another aspect: that of the contrast between the 'becoming' of nature, supposed to be circular, non-historical and repetitive, and the linear, historical, progressive and cumulative 'becoming' of culture.

In Tibetan culture, we find an opposition between a more or less circular 'becoming' and a linear one: this is the one that we discover between the wandering in the *samsâra* on the one hand and the progression towards Liberation on the other hand. The condition of sentient beings in the cycle of existences is definitely characterized in Buddhist literature in terms that clearly connote vain and fruitless repetition—turning round. Conversely, the progression towards Enlightenment is described as having progressive levels, gradually rising, like the steps on a ladder, towards an ultimate goal.

The connection I would like to make between culture as a collective product of mankind and the spiritual 'becoming' of an individual may sound odd. But in fact, it is plain that the worldwide historical perspective assumed, for example, by Hegel (and also by Schelling) derives from the superimposition of the idea of the progress of Enlightenment, as found in eighteenth-century ideology, within Christian frameworks that were inspired by Neoplatonism.

It does not seem possible to set the nature/culture opposition in Tibetan thought upon the basis of the alleged historicity of culture: Tibet, despite its sustained interest in chronology (in which it differs from India), has in common with other pre-modern thoughts the fact that it does not know any notion of history, conceived as an ongoing process of series of revolutions in the fields of science, techniques, philosophy, art, religion, styles of life and modes of economic production, as well as social and political organization. When society is seen as a sphere within which, finally, there is forever 'nothing new under the sun', it is even more difficult to distinguish culture from nature.

In fact, there are societies that, despite their relative immobility ('non-historicity'), draw a strong line between nature and culture through rites of passage to adulthood and other such rituals. In such societies, no doubt the distinction is clear between the social, human and ritual and the natural, raw and beastly. Yet, in Tibetan society, there are no such rites that clearly mark the 'humanization' of the child, his or her parting from raw nature.

Now, to what extent can we characterize the *samsâra* as 'nature' and the cultivation of the path leading to *nirvâna* as culture?

As already seen, the *samsâra* is 'nature' merely through its repetitive and circular aspect. Otherwise, it is always thought of, in Buddhism, as coming close to the artificial, the contrived, the constructed, the *samskrta*, the resulting, and not as belonging to the sphere of the original and the given. What is more, it is not strictly repetitive, in the same sense as when we consider nature as defined by immutable laws and by the cyclical return of the same phenomena like seasons. The most satisfying definition of nature may well be the one that has been formulated by Kant: 'the whole of phenomena inasmuch as they are ruled by laws'.

Firstly, the notion of *law* in that sense, so narrowly tied with that of nature in Western thought, is unknown to Buddhism. And this is no accident: actually, this notion, despite the materialist and secularized form that it has taken in modern science, originates in theology. That is why we should not be surprised not to find it in Buddhism, which is a genuine form of Atheism. It is very plain that the idea of 'laws of nature' comes forth from the transposition of the *legal* register of discourse into the field of nature (combined with the old Platonician astonishment about the fact that *mathematical* truths, in terms of pure intellectual insights, actually apply to material objects). Nature has laws because it has a legislator and because this wise legislator governs it according to immutable decrees. One might add: if those laws can be expressed in mathematical formulas, maybe it is because the Creator's intelligence is not totally alien to the procedures of our intellect, however transcendental the divine mind may be in our imagination.

In Buddhist thought, there are definite facts of causality. Such and such a set of circumstances has occasioned the production of such and such an effect—*but Buddhists never conceived anything like laws ruling the process*, though all their ethics are based on the idea of regularities within the causation process (each time I act in passion, it ends in pain, etc.).

Secondly, the *samsâra* is nothing more than roughly repetitive or circular. It is not an eternal return of the same; it is rather an endless chain of insignificant variations, of irrelevant differences. If we consider the most consequential system of Indian Buddhist Philosophy, *Vijñânavâda* idealism, and if we wonder what, for the authors of the posterity of Asanga and Vasubandhu the stable elements, the constants in the *samsâra* could be, it is clear that they are none other than the *mere form of the process* that gives birth to the restless wandering in the *samsâra*, that is, the dependant arising, in each mind stream, of the eight consciousnesses (*vijñâna*). Mind (*citta*) does not have any general laws or any eternal structures; it is more like a machine which, like the 'desiring machines' in Deleuze's *Anti-Œdipus*, 'produce only themselves and work through breaking down' ('ne produisent qu'elles-mêmes et fonctionnent en se détraquant').

In the system of Buddhist Idealism, this device of self-production of the mind can certainly give birth to a phenomenal world that has laws and structures; but such laws and structures are merely epiphenomena or superstructures.

What is more—and at this point the question becomes highly interesting—it is the *samsâra* that tends to be invested with the values of the artificial, the compounded, the conditioned, the contrived, as opposed to the *nirvâna*, which, at least to some extent, bears the connotations of the natural, the timeless, the primordial. The *samsâra*, as a production of phenomena that are always new, though they do not evoke anything new, comes closer to culture. The *nirvâna*, in its primordial purity, devoid of vagaries, looks like nature in the sense of what is neither constructed and composed, nor distorted or warped. In Vasubandhu's *Abhidharmakosa*, it belongs to the list of the three 'unconditioned phenomena' or 'uncompounded dharmas' (*asamskrta*).

Here, we reach a thorny paradox, very embarrassing for Buddhist thought in general: it is annoying that this *nirvâna* should be at the same time immediate (natural, unconditioned, uncompounded) and resulting (as a fruit of the culture of the spiritual path). While the *samsâra* is an artificial nature, the nirvâna is an immediate resulting. Buddhist philosophy causes the narrow framework of the notions of nature and culture to shatter.

The Tibetans have been confronted with this problem, which the doctrinal development of Buddhism in India heightened century after century. It seems that Tibetan thought could be aptly described as having two main contradictory orientations: an orientation that tends to 'naturalize' Enlightenment, stressing its 'immediate' side, and another one that tends to 'culturalize' it, stressing its 'resulting' side. The first option is more or less instantiated by the *Mahâmudrâ* of the bKa'-brgyud-pas and more clearly by the *rDzogs-chen* of the rNying-ma-pas and of the 'para-Buddhist' religion of the Bon-pos. The second is symbolized by Sa-skya pandita in the thirteenth century and is illustrated throughout the dGe-lugs-pa school, Tsong-kha-pa's posterity. In between the two tendencies, a number of paradoxical figures can be found, such as Dol-po-pa Shes-rab rgyal-mtshan, the great doctor of the Jo-nang-pa school. He naturalizes Enlightenment (which he identifies with the Buddha-nature, eternally already present in everybody, as a jewel in its gangue) while, at the same time, he insists on the necessity of all the stages of the Path, understood not as a construction of Enlightenment, but as a destruction of the obscurations that cover it.

In the dGe-lugs-pa school, Enlightenment is very clearly understood as a product, no less artificial than the *samsâra*, a Buddha having a mind (*sems*, skt. *citta*) which is impermanent, produced from one instant to the next, *skad-cig skad-cig*, born from causes and conditions, etc. Enlightenment is not, according to Tsong-kha-pa, an eternal life, beyond duration; it is rather the perpetual movement of a mind that re-produces itself at each instant in an omniscient and happy state, likely to benefit all beings. The spiritual path is, somehow, the gradual and meticulous layout of this liberating machine—a Buddha. In that sense, in the practice of the dGe-lugs-pa school, culture is highly promoted, not only as a body of knowledge to be acquired, but also as a pattern of behaviour to be mastered and of meditative states that one should gain. Conversely, the idea of a peaceful surrender within the natural state is completely banned in the school; it is associated with laziness and with mental apathy, of sleep, fainting fits and coma. To phrase it otherwise, there is mostly, in this tendency, an opposition of a correct culture—that of the path which leads to the production of the *nirvâna*—and a perverted culture—linked to the restless wandering in the *samsâra*. There is no status for nature in the dogmas of the so-called reformed school, which have been dominant in Tibet since the seventeenth century.

Yet it is probably not an exaggeration to say that it is the other tendency that expresses the spontaneous orientation of Tibetan religiosity. It is very likely that the doctrinal subtleties of Sa-skya pandita and Tsong-kha-pa never penetrated deep into popular faith. On the other hand, the mystic doctrines of the bKa'-brgyud-pas, and even more so those of the rNying-ma-pas and the Bon-pos, though supposedly reserved for spiritual elites, are surely more in harmony with the naive representations of the Tibetan people. They can be found between the lines of texts for rituals performed by lay people themselves, such as the *bsangs* burnt offerings. The conceptions of the other tendency, on the other hand, are dry and abstract so that one hardly finds a refraction of them even in the dGe-lugs-pas' ritual literature. It would not be difficult to find rituals performed in the dGe-lugs and Sa-skya schools, where elements of representations specific to the rNying-ma-pas (and more or less common with the Bon-pos) are quite clearly expressed, and accepted not so reluctantly for their 'poetic' character (as fairly good 'metaphors' of a truth, the accurate presentation of what should be looked for in philosophical speculation). It is especially the case for everything connected to the cult of the guardian deites (*srung-ma*), *bsangs* rituals, as already mentioned, as well as the *g.yang-'gugs* rituals. That is why I am inclined to believe that the most basic and essential elements of Tibetan religious feelings are to be found mostly on that side.

In *rDzogs-chen*, whether in its rNying-ma form or in its Bon form, a state of primordial perfection is clearly mentioned, as well as a Fall from that state. The original condition is definitely valued with all the connotations of nature, the spontaneous, the unaltered or un-corrected, of the purity of the origins, and, also, of all the uncompounded or unconditioned aspects of *nirvâna*. The 'Fall' is actually presented as some sort of accident, even though a close examination of the texts and a reflection on the global logic of the system leads to the conclusion that such an accident could not happen. Finally, the *samsâra* that follows from it is really supposed to be on its way 'towards a future always new', as Plotinus says in the *Ennead* III, 7. Enlightenment, somewhat like the ultimate goal of Neoplatonician spirituality, is apparently conceived as a reintegration into the primordial, natural condition.

A configuration follows on from all that, in which the Natural, it seems, is a metaphysical eternal essence, source and destination of all beings, while all the empirical world (the Tibetan equivalent of Plato's 'sensible world') is artificial and somehow 'cultural', insofar as it is a product of the mind (*sems*, skt. *citta*). Yet, in fact, as soon as this characterization is established, it falls apart. In the doctrine of *rDzogs-chen* (whose articulation around Indian

Buddhism, on this point, is not devoid of difficulties), the phenomenal world—the mind (*sems*) and its perceptions (*snang-ba*)—is, in a way that cannot be precisely explained here, the display or the 'game' (*rol-pa*, skt. *lîlâ*) of the 'expressiveness' (*rtsal*) of the primordial Ground of Nature. Now, let us remember, in the word 'nature', there is the idea of 'birth', as in the Greek word *phusis* there is *phuein*, to grow, in the vegetable sense (*cf. phuton*). Nature, in fact, for the ancients, is not so much opposed to the field of culture as to the realm of the 'moveless and separated beings', according to Aristotle's phrase—beings who are at rest because they are fully equal to their essence. In a Neoplatonician context, nature, in this respect, is all that belongs to time, 'mobile image of eternity', as Plato says in the *Timaeus*—all that is the reflection or the shadow cast into matter by the essential realities and which is subject to some kind of urge for a return to this source.

Now, it is the same, *mutatis mutandis*, for the *samsâra* as it is conceived by the rDzogs-chen-pas: reflection and expression in space and time of this sort of intelligible world which they call the 'epiphany of the Ground' (*gzhi-snang*), the name for the *Dharmadhâtu* in the *rDzogs-chen*. So the *samsâra* is, in a new sense, nature, not a nature that can be opposed to culture, but a nature which has to be understood by contrast, if not with a 'supernature', at least with a 'transnature', a *metaphusis*.

What happens then, in such a context, to everything that for us belongs to 'culture'—social institutions, customs and traditions, beliefs and sciences—it seems all that is included without any marked difference within the sphere of nature. Lastly, this is also the tendency of one among the classical philosophers, the closest to Buddhism in many respects: Spinoza. In his *Treatise of Theologico-Political Authorities*, he follows Hobbes and anticipates Rousseau when he conceives the transition from the state of nature to the state of society in the form of a social pact or contract. What sets him apart from both Rousseau and Hobbes, is the fact that he clearly inscribes civil law, all the functions of society, in the general frame of the laws of nature, without any essential discontinuity. Society and culture are no more an exception to the laws of nature, for Spinoza, than biological phenomena are in complete rupture with physical phenomena. This does not mean, whatever the case, that the former are reducible to the latter. I similarly believe that it would be a misinterpretation to try and introduce a nature/culture opposition within Tibetan thought. It also follows that trying to interpret the elements of Tibetan 'culture' on the basis of our pre-notion of culture is certainly already an anthropocentric approach.

Allah, Saints and Men in Islam
Diverging Conceptions of Nature in Theology, Mysticism and Law

Marc Gaborieau

A Muslim glass-ornaments seller, or Curaute, Kathmandu, Nepal (Photo: Marie Lecomte-Tilouine)

Nature and Culture Opposition in Islam

The opposition between nature and culture was popularized by Lévi-Strauss. In his *Structures élémentaires de la parenté*[1] he created the myth—which he did not however analyze—of the institution by men of a social rule, a social norm which made him leave the realm of animality or nature, to found a new realm, that of culture, which he identified as a social law, a manmade norm, the prototype of which is the prohibition of incest. In Lévi-Strauss' thought, the very concepts of nature and of culture are problematic; even more problematic is the opposition between them. Can this opposition be an operative tool? This may be doubted in the Western context where it appears—in its use by Claude Lévi-Strauss himself—as idiosyncratic, or at best brilliantly rhetorical.[2]

It is even more doubtful in the context of Islamic thought, as we can show in the three following proposals. We must first concede that—under the influence of Greek thought—there is among Muslim thinkers discussion of the concept of nature, for which they use words with a wide range of meanings. We will discuss two of them: *'âda*[3] and *fitra*, which are both often given as substitutes for *tabî'a*, a translation of the Greek *phusis*. But in the second place, it would be difficult to find an equivalent of 'culture' in as general a meaning as Lévi-Strauss uses: there is no general entry 'Culture' in the *Encyclopaedia of Islam (EI2)*, nor in the *Encyclopaedia of the Qur'ân (EQ)*. It is therefore impossible—this is my third proposal—to find the same general nature/culture opposition as in Lévi-Strauss.

This absence is not difficult to explain. Lévi-Strauss belongs to the current of modern sociological and political thought, inaugurated by Jean-Jacques Rousseau, in which man is the agent

---

[1] Lévi-Strauss 1949: Chapter 1; Pouillon 1967: 98–100.
[2] Lévi-Strauss 1964: 280–87.
[3] To transliterate letters specific to Arabic, the following conventions have been followed:
  '(French *accent aigu*) for the letter *'ain*, as in *'âda*
  underlining for the emphatic letters, as in *fitra*.

of his own destiny, creating human society and political institutions, and must therefore struggle against the natural world to establish his own order.[4] In addition, building such an opposition between nature and culture presupposes an evolutionist conception of the universe, in complete contradiction with fixist antique and medieval views. Islamic thought, on the contrary, belongs to the Medieval world where—in both Islam and Christianity, which shared many common features as we shall presently see—the main agent of the natural world as well as human destiny was God; whether man had any agency in his actions and in establishing the laws of social behaviour before God who was the omnipotent creator and legislator, was questionable, and indeed questioned (Boulnois 2002b). In encyclopaedias of the Western Middle Ages, for instance in the *Dictionnaire du Moyen Âge (DMA)*, as is the case in encyclopaedias of the Islamic world, one finds neither a general entry on culture, nor an opposition between nature and culture: nature is opposed not to human agency, but to God's omnipotence.

But I would be as abstract and as vulnerable to criticism as Lévi-Strauss if I were to speak of Islamic thought as an undifferentiated entity. It contains, on the contrary, many contradictory currents which differ according to the various intellectual disciplines, and even according to the various phases or schools in each of the disciplines. I will first echo here the views of classical apologetic theology *(kalâm)* of the Sunni orthodoxy—which seem to negate the very idea of nature—as they crystallized from the ninth to the eleventh century against the rational theology of the Mu'tazilites (Gimaret 1993) and the speculations of the philosophers *(falâsifa)*.

[4]However, in another aspect of his metaphysical thinking—for he is more of a philosopher than an ethnologist—he tried to abolish this distinction between nature and culture and merge the cultural world with the physical world (Bertholet 2003: 298–310; Lamouche 2004). This was particularly clear in 1963 when he announced that the aim of his study of American mythologies was to prove that the human mind 'was chained up and determined in all its operations' (Lévi-Strauss 1963: 630; 2004 reprint: 171). To my knowledge, Lévi-Strauss did not clearly address this inner contradiction of his thought which he tried to hide by pretending to work on a general theory of communication which encompassed both natural and cultural worlds.

I will then ask whether ideas comparable to our concept of nature do not creep back into religious and legal speculation first in the conception of the cosmos as seen through the lenses of mediaeval mysticism and popular piety, then in the conception of human behaviour as codified in Islamic Law. Are not Muslim thinkers thus reintroducing in these fields, in another way, a concept which had been negated in theology?

Since this volume is centred on the Himalayas and South Asia, I will as far as possible use material collected from among the Muslims of Nepal, particularly the bangle-makers of the Western Hills (Gaborieau 1993a). If unavailable, I will then look to Indian schools of thought, such as that of Deoband, the direct influence of which is attested among the bangle-makers (Gaborieau 1993b and in this chapter). Failing that, I will turn to other schools whose indirect influence is probable, such as the modernist rationalism of Sayyid Aḥmad Khân in the nineteenth century, or the comprehensive synthesis of medieval thought made by Shâh Walî Allâh in the eighteenth century. But to fill the gaps, and to make a coherent historical picture, I will have recourse to older medieval authors.

One of the questions I have been asked by the editor of this volume is: how much does the Islamic view of nature differ from the Hindu one? Are we to expect a clear opposition between the two views; as Louis Dumont (1966) would have it? Or are they analogous? We will bear this question in mind and try to answer it in the conclusion.

Islamic Theology versus Greek Philosophy: Nature or Allah's 'Custom'?

Muslim thinkers encountered our notion of nature in the early Arabic translations of Greek texts. To render the Greek concept of *phusis*, and more generally *natura rerum*, in scientific, philosophical and theological writings, they used words derived from the root *ṭ.b.'*, the most common one being the noun *ṭabî'a*. These terms do not etymologically express the idea of productive force, as do the words *phusis* in Greek and *natura* in Latin both of which refer to birth, but the notion of what is imprinted in something. The same root was also used for minting coins, and later for printing. As in Greek thought, it was associated in Islamic sciences and philosophy with the idea of productive force, of causality: the nature of a thing is an innate character which produces effects and explains events.

Now Koranic revelation has consistently put to the fore the notion of God's omnipotence and exclusivity: how can a causality inherent in the nature of things be conciliated with these attributes of Allah? There are two solutions: one given by philosophers, and the other given by theologians.

Nature in Islamic Philosophy

Philosophy *(falsafa)* in the Islamic world developed as a continuation of late Greek philosophy, the main works of which were translated early into Arabic (Arnaldez 1965). The 'philosophers' *(falâsifa* plural of *failasûf* = *philosophos)*, such as Avicenna (Ibn Sînâ, 980–1037) and Averroes (Ibn Rushd, 1126–98), perpetuated this Greek philosophical tradition in an Islamized fashion; they later transmitted it to Latin Christianity which in its turn, notably through Thomas of Aquinas, produced a Christianized version of the Aristotelian conception of nature (Solère 2002).

These Muslim philosophers interpreted Koranic revelation allegorically. They considered reason, as defined in Greek thought, as the guide; they continued to affirm that things had a nature, and that there was a causality inherent in them. The order of the cosmos and of human behaviour was regulated by this nature, without any direct intervention of God who was viewed only as a remote creator (Pingree & Haq 2000: 25–26). The first school of rational theology, that of the Mu'tazilites (Gimaret 1993) started in the eighth century, adopted the views of the philosophers on this question (Pingree & Haq 2000: 27a). Such rationalist views surfaced again in the apologetic theology of the nineteenth century, which tried to defend Islam from attacks by Western missionaries, as in the case of Sayyid Ahmad Khan (1817–98), the founder of the Aligarh Muslim University in India. He explicitly took his inspiration from Averroes to build a rationalist theology; counting himself as a 'theistic philosopher' and a 'naturalist' *(nacarî,* from English 'nature') (Troll 1978: 171–77, 191–202 and 215–22).

Another concept, of Arabic origin, existed in literature and in philosophy, which could be translated by nature: *fitra.* This time—in contrast to *tabî'a* which was coined to translate Greek texts—it is a real Koranic term (XXX: 29/30).[5] It is usually translated as primordial nature (Baljon 1986: 209) or, in French, primordial conception ('La conception originelle' in Blachère 1959: 432 and Gobillot 2000). We shall leave aside for the time being its original religious meaning, which is specifically Islamic and will be developed in the third part of the chapter; we will only consider its profane meaning. In lay usage, it was mainly applied to human nature, to the innate dispositions of men (Gobillot 2000: 112–29). It was used in that sense by the Jâhiz (780–869), a classical literary figure; and by the great philosopher al-Fârâbî (d.950). Later, in Avicenna's philosophy and in common language in Persian and Urdu, it came to mean the individual nature of a man, his character.[6] It could even mean the ethnical character as in the following passage of the Delhi divine Shâh Walî Allâh (1703–62):

> Every nation, every climatic region has its own *fitra* upon which its affairs are based. Thus it is part of the *fitra* of the Hindus to find the slaughter of animals repugnant and to believe in the eternity of the universe. It is of the nature of the children of Shem among the Arabs and of the Persian to permit the slaughter of animals and to believe in the createdness of the universe. Consequently a prophet sets out to see what kind of creeds and

---

[5] References to the Koran are given in Roman numerals for the suras, and Arabic numerals for the verses. Since the numbering of the verses is not the same in all the recensions of the Koran, I followed Régis Blachère's system of giving alternative verse numberings after a slash (Blachère 1957). As for the translations, I have either duly acknowledged existing ones when appropriate, or have made my own based on the Arabic text.

[6] Nowadays, *fitra* is even used in the sense of sexual orientation, as, for instance, in S. Kugle 2005: 14–15.

customs people maintain, and he sanctions and adopts what suits the refinement of souls, rejecting what injures them
(quoted and translated by Baljon 1986: 113).

This view of nature, whether it was expressed by the terms *ṭabî'a* or *fiṭra*, was problematic for believers who literally interpreted the Koran: if nature followed its own course as originally set by the Creator, there was no room for miracles, contrary to the letter of the scriptures which recount such extraordinary facts. This contradicted the notion of God's omnipotence. Though reluctantly, Medieval Muslim philosophers such as Avicenna conceded that God could make exceptions and change the laws he had created to honour prominent people like the prophets (Fakhry 1958: 100–03). Sayyid Ahmad Khan, having built a more radical but rather naive rationalism, went to the extreme view that there were no miracles at all, since God never changes the laws of nature he has established once and for all (Troll 1978: 177–91).

Occasionalism of Islamic Theology

Medieval Christian thought, at least in the larger current created by Thomas Aquinas, followed in the footsteps of Greek and Muslim philosophers in affirming that nature followed its own laws once it was created by God, although the possibility of miracles was preserved.

The main orthodox current of Muslim apologetic theology *(kalâm)* followed an opposite course (Gardet 1970; Gardet 2002: 199–212). Instead of emphasizing the regularity of the universe, it firstly accentuated God's omnipotence, which could change the course of events at any moment. A causation by created things would contradict His omnipotence, for He is 'the sole Being and the sole Agent... He is the creator of human acts, of which man is really the receiving subject' (Gardet 1970: 1144b; see also Arnaldez 1978). Theology therefore had to provide explanations that would not offend God's preeminence: it did not refuse a rational view of the universe, but it chose a theory which would not give it its own autonomy as did the philosophers' Platonician or Aristotelian views. To this aim, theologians *(mutakallimûn)* adopted an atomist philosophy: the universe was made of atoms linked together in a contingent way by the supreme will of God. The regularities we observe are constantly recreated by God: He is the only efficient cause of whatever happens in the universe, even human acts, which are each time created by Him, although man is held responsible, and punished or rewarded for them. There are no laws of nature, but only the divine habits (`âda*) of God, 'He who originated creation and repeated it, and He who gives you sustenance from the sky and from the earth' (Koran XXVII: 65/64). This way of thinking (Pingree & Haq 1993: 26–27) was systematized by the theological school of al-Ash`arî (d.935) (Gimaret 1990), which remains to this day the leading current, and is considered the best exponent of orthodoxy. A classical illustrator of this theology of continuous creation was al-Bâqillânî (d.1013) who brought to perfection this way of thinking associating atomism and occasionalism, the latter term meaning a philosophy according to which there is only one efficient cause, God, while the other occasional events which precede any fact are not its real causes (Fakhry 1958; Schmutz 2002: 233–234).

Miracles, in this theology centred on God's omnipotence, posed no problem: since Allah is continuously recreating the universe, He can change the custom (*'âda*) He usually follows when and where he pleases. This He does for two purposes (Gaborieau 1989: 218): proving the mission of a given prophet by confounding his adversaries, in which case this is called *mu'jiza* (Wensinck 1993); or distinguishing a saint, in which case it is called *karâma*, a word derived from the Greek *charisma* (Gardet 1978). But in both cases the supernatural mechanism is the same: it is a momentary deviation from God's custom, an abandonment *(kharq)* of it. The general abstract concept for miracle is therefore in Islamic theology: *kharq al-'âda*, abandonment of custom, which of course is exceptional and momentary in relation to the customary course of things. Paradoxically, it can be said that miracles are possible precisely because, in this theology of continuous creation, everything is a miracle. Alternatively, we could say that there are in reality no miracles, because everything is a miracle.

How do Muslims Deal with Regularities?

We now analyse the way Muslims have dealt with the regularities they encountered in their life. Since philosophy was disqualified as unorthodox, they had to compose with an occasionalist theology which denied the very idea of nature. Did they create substitutes for this concept? The question will be subdivided according to two spheres of reality.

The first one is the cosmos. When they have to deal with the natural world, especially in agriculture, are men directly confronted with the unpredictable will of God? Or are there intermediaries between men and God who impose a certain regular order on the cosmos, and whom men can deal with?

The second sphere is human behaviour where the absence of nature seems even more problematic in our eyes (Gardet 2002: 143). If there is no human nature and if man has no real power, who is the real subject of his acts? If there is no natural moral law in the sense of Christian medieval philosophy (Boulnois 2002a), are the norms only arbitrary laws edicted by God and not based on reason? Are we to expect any regularity in man's pursuits? If we are, there must also be in this sphere a substitute for nature. What is it?

These two spheres will be explored separately in the two remaining parts of this chapter.

Man and the Natural World

There are two ways of considering the relation of man to the vegetal and animal world. One, which I would call fundamentalist, takes into account only the oldest historical layers of Islam, by relying exclusively on the Koran and admitting only purified rituals of the Wahhabi type, where there are no intermediaries between man and God. The other includes intermediary worlds and beings which were created by mediaeval mysticism and popular religion.

Man, Vegetation, Agriculture: A Fundamentalist View

It has often been said that the vocabulary of commercial transactions has a preeminent place in the image of Islam presented in the Koran. This view is misplaced. The sacred book puts to the fore man's relationship with the cosmos, and in particular with the vegetal world and agriculture; this is the 'dominant motif': 'the life cycles of natural world, of plants and of animals are governed by the divine gift of water which an equally dependent human kind should acknowledge with appropriate expressions of gratitude' (Waines 2001: 43, referring to Koran XXXIV: 14/15). Three features should be emphasized.

First, the Koranic text, in prefiguration of the theory of continuous creation, insists on God's exclusive agency. He is the One who creates and sustains plants and animals; decides on fertility and infertility. In this way creation is a divine message, a kind of revelation: 'signs *(âyât)* for people who have intelligence' (Koran II: 159/164).

Second, God's most important instrument in sustaining this living world is water, the eminent symbol of life and fertility: 'God is the one who sent down water from the sky, and with it We [God] brought forth all manners of plants and foliage from which We bring forth clustered seed; and from the flowering date palm [come] accessible clusters of fruit. [We also brought forth] gardens *(jannât)* planted with grapes, olives and pomegranates in many similar and distinct varieties. When they blossom, look to the fruit when they bear fruit and ripen. These are surely signs *(âyât)* for people who believe' (VI: 99, translated by Waines 2001: 12). In Islamic tradition, the symbol of this creation and fertilization through water is the garden *(jannat)*, a term which means both paradise, and a man-made irrigated garden.

Third, it is man's duty to recognize from these signs God's supreme role in creating and sustaining the cosmos, and show proper gratitude. This he can do *inter alia* through the ritual of offering Him the first fruits of the harvest, and the firstlings of animals. The Koran (VI: 136/137 and 140/141) refers to such a setting aside for God of a portion of the cattle and grain produce in continuation of precedents in pre-Islamic Semitic ritual, although in Islam generally the offering of first fruits was replaced by the alm-tax, *zakât* (Chelhod 1955: 126–31).

This strict Koranic view, where God acts directly with no intermediaries, always remained in the background of the Islamic tradition. It resurfaced in reformed versions of Islam, vaguely labelled as Wahhabism, which since the nineteenth century have tried to do away with mediaeval piety, and have insisted on praying to God exclusively and offering the first fruits only to Him. Such was the case, for instance, among the Muslim Bangle-makers of central Nepal, who had been subjected to reformist propaganda of the Indian Deobandi school (Metcalf 1982) as I have shown elsewhere (Gaborieau 1993a: 91–99; 1993b): they had a special ritual offering of the first fruit of the harvest, which they called, in Nepali, *nuwâgî* or *nwâgî* (Sharmâ 2019: 586), which is used by the Hindus to designate the oblation of the first part of the new harvest to the deities.

Saints, Water and Harvests in Medieval Thought

This austere practice was a far cry from the traditional festivities which marked the new harvest, and were linked to saints who served as intermediaries between men and God in the dispensation of fertility. For it has long been believed that God did not immediately manage the cosmos, but delegated his prerogatives in this matter to Saints who formed an invisible hierarchy. This process was vividly described by Hujwîrî (d. *c.* 1070), who lived in Lahore (now Pakistan), in the first Sufi treatise ever written in Persian:

> God has saints (*awliyâ*, pl. of *walî*) whom he has especially distinguished by his friendship and whom he has chosen as the governors of His kingdom [...] He has made the saints the governors of the universe [...] Through the blessing of their

advent the rains fall from heaven, and through the purity of
their lives the plants spring up from the earth [...]
(quoted in Digby 1986: 62;
see also Gaborieau 1989: 218 and 226–29).

Medieval saints had their own specialization; some of them were precisely known for their cosmic role in granting harvests and fertility (Gaborieau 1983: 303–04). The most famous among them, in northern India and Nepal, is Ghâzî Miyân, whose cult I had the privilege of studying in Western Nepal (Gaborieau 1975 and 1996). It is remarkable that in these cults, as in the Koran, mastery over rain is the key to the control of vegetation and agriculture. In the Ghâzî Miyân festival in Western Nepal, this power is exercised through a big mast, actually a fir tree trunk, which is erected every year in front of the saint's shrine. He-goats are sacrificed at the foot of the mast on the day of the annual festival to ensure sufficient rain for the year to come. Should an exceptional drought occur before the next festival, then exceptional goat sacrifices are performed at the foot of the mast. Another saint, Guru Mastân Shâh, who protects devotees against hail, is usually propitiated along with Ghâzî Miyân.

As in the Koran again, gratitude has to be expressed for the crops. This is also done at the annual festival, which always falls in May according to the luni-solar calendar, and corresponds to the wheat harvest. The first flour made from newly-harvested grain must first be offered in thanks to the saint in the form of pancakes before the devotees can taste it themselves. This is indispensable if one wants to ensure the renewed favours of the saints for the coming agricultural cycle. This expression of gratitude ends with a festival where at a banquet, the meat of the goats and the wheat pancakes are served amidst great rejoicing, singing and dancing.

The Muslim character of the festival is marked by the representation of the saint by his tomb, not by a statue or a stone as among the Hindus. Nevertheless one cannot but be struck by the analogies between the propitiation of Muslim saints and the cult of Hindu deities. Indeed I have good reason to believe that this Ghâzî Miyân festival is a Muslim avatar of the antique Hindu veneration of the rain god Indra, who was also worshipped in the form of a mast in the spring (Gonda 1962: 404–05; Gaborieau 1996: 253).

To complete this analogy with Hindu rites, at least in the context of Western Nepal, mention must be made of spirit possession. A Hindu god, in addition to being represented by a statue, a stone or a mast, can also be temporarily incarnated in the human body of a medium through whose mouth he speaks directly to the devotees. Such instances are widespread in western Nepal (Gaborieau 1969). It is remarkable that at the Ghâzî Miyân festival this institution of spirit possession is also present: when devotees want to consult the saint directly—and not through the intermediary of his tomb or of his mast—he incarnates himself in the body of a medium and speaks to them (Gaborieau 1975: 312–13).

This example confirms the conclusion of the French Orientalist Garcin de Tassy (1794–1878)—who incidentally was the first scholar to study Ghâzî Miyân—that the 'saints replaced the multiple gods of the Hindus' (Garcin de Tassy 1869: 15; on this question see Gaborieau 1993: 410; 2000). In many respects Hindus and Muslims relate to the cosmos in analogous ways. These theological affinities also explain why Muslims can be eclectic by using, simultaneously or successively, both Hindu and Muslim rituals to deal with fertility (Gaborieau 1978: 41–44; 1993b: 123–27 and 147–51).

This complex organization of the cosmos, with the supernatural world of the saints controlling vegetation and fertility on behalf of God, may be said to be a substitute for nature. It does not offer complete regularity. It at least presents men with a certain kind of reliability, and offers procedures to deal with difficulties.

Human Domain and Innate Morality

We will now examine whether, in the domain of human behaviour, any substitute can be found for human nature, which would make Islam comparable to the Christian Middle Ages. At that time was there a conception of a natural law, considered as a reflection in humanity of God's will, which itself conformed to reason? God-given religious law would only perfect this basic law common to all human creatures (Gardet 2002: 142–43; Boulnois 2002a).

Absence of Human Nature in Mainstream Theology

If we only consider the mainstream doctrine of Ash`arî theology, the case would seem desperate for three reasons. On the one hand, legislation imposed on man by God is completely arbitrary; it is not based on reason or justice: man can only accept it, without trying to understand or even guess or deduce it. On the other hand, one does not find in man any innate disposition to obey God's law: he has only to submit to what is an external injunction. Finally, man is not the real author of his acts, which are at each moment caused by God. If we follow the logic of these speculations, there is neither natural law, nor human nature. It is only metaphorically that man can be said to be the author of his acts and accountable for them (Gardet 2002: 209). These tenets were reaffirmed in India at the end of the nineteenth century, by one of the founders and the main theologian of the traditionalist seminary of Deoband (Metcalf 1982), Muḥammad Qâsim Nânotawî (1833–77), in his refutation of Sayyid Aḥmad Khân's naturalist theology:

> Do not say that all the mandates of Islam are in conformity with nature [...] Man has had one power bestowed upon him as a (temporary) loan, but the relationship that obtains between this human power and God's power is that which obtains between your or my hand and a pen... (Nânotawî 1890: 69 and 71).

Fiṭra, a Substitute for Nature in Islamic Religious Sciences

But if we leave aside the logic of speculative theology and its astonishing conclusions, we discover that, in discussing human action from a legal point of view, Muslim thinkers start reasoning as if there were some common norms of behaviour innate in all human beings, Muslim or non-Muslim alike.

It is expressed by the term *fitra* (mentioned in another sense in the first part of this chapter), which is found in the Koran, in the oldest legal treatises as well as in the oldest compilations of Prophetic traditions since the second century of Islam. Its profane meaning, as we have seen, is quite clear. Its religious meaning, which we are now to study, is more mysterious. This word is derived from the root *f.t.r.*, which means to split, to open and hence to endow, to create (Macdonald 1965; Gobillot 2000: 7–10).

It appears twenty times in the Koran (Gobillot 2000: 10–14) in the nominal form *fitra*, and in verbs derived from it, the standard example being verse XXX: 29/30: 'Observe religion as a *hanîf*,[7] in conformity with the primordial nature (*fitra*) God has endowed (*fatara*) the men with. One must not change what God has created. This is the immutable religion, but people do no know it' (Translation mine; see Blachère 1957: 432). It is most often translated as primordial nature, or primordial religion. It has actually a wide range of meaning.

There is first a minimal meaning invoked to justify important observances, which are not obligatory in the Law of God, but are recommended for Muslims, and even often distinctive. These observances are enumerated in a tradition of the Prophet found in the collection of Muslim (821–875):

> Â'isha relates that the Prophet said: 'there are ten qualities of the prophets: clipping the mustachios so that they do not enter into the mouth, not cutting or shaving the beard, cleansing the teeth, cleansing the nostrils with water at the usual ablutions, cutting the nails, cleaning the finger joints, pulling out the hair under the arm-pits, shaving the hair of the privates, washing with water after passing urine, and cleansing the mouth with water at the time of ablutions. (Trans. Hugues 1885: 129).

---

[7] A follower of the primordial religion of humankind which is best represented by Abraham, the common ancestor of the monotheist religions (Hughes 1885: 161–62; Watt 1966).

These observances concern ritual purity and more generally hygiene; they are invoked to justify circumcision and excision which are not obligatory in the letter of the religious law. Not all of these observances are actually followed, as witnessed in the literature (Levy 1957: 252) and fieldwork: the bangle-makers of Nepal do not shave their arm-pits and pubis, and do not practise excision, putting exclusive emphasis on circumcision (Gaborieau 1993a: 174). In this restricted sense *fitra* may be translated with Reuben Levy *(loc. cit.)* as 'natural primitive religion'. Marcel Mauss rightly saw in it 'the very basis of Semitic religions',[8] or a heritage common to the Jews and the Muslims (Mauss 1998: 331).

Yet the term usually has a wider and deeper religious meaning. Its most common early occurrence is in the multiple versions of a tradition (Gobillot 2000: 18–22), known in no less than 25 recensions, which says: 'All children are born in the *fitra*: it is his parents who make him a Jew or a Christian'. It was quoted in the context of several problems. Some of them were legal ones, such as: what was the real religious affiliation of the children before the age of discretion? How should they be treated in matters of enslavement, funerals and inheritance? In the circumstances, when it was permissible to kill unbelievers, was it possible to kill their children under the age of discretion? Some others were theological and concerned the controversy of free will against predestination (MacDonald 1965; Gobillot 2000: 22–45). Here we do not have to go into the details of these controversies, but only to delineate the meanings of *fitra* which emerged from them. There were, broadly speaking, two main interpretations.

One was restrictive, meant to maintain the frontier and the hierarchy between Muslims and non-Mulims: *fitra* was not the same for everybody and for some, it might mean conformity with Islam and lead to salvation. For others, it means going astray and thus damnation. These views were established by theologians in order to found the doctrine of predestination.

[8]'les assises mêmes des religions sémitiques'.

The other was more liberal and considered that all men were alike and free at the time of their birth; they had the same innate dispositions to practise the same religion. It was not, in the long run, the most widely admitted. But it represents the moment when Islamic thought came nearest to our concept of human nature, and of a natural law all people are innately inclined to follow. This natural law is of course conceived as identical to Islam, in the same way as Catholics view Church law as being in consonance with natural law. This was beautifully expressed by the already quoted eighteenth century Indian divine, Shâh Walî Allâh; according to his ablest commentator his thoughts were as follows:

> The essential text for the establishment of what is to be qualified as 'true religion' is the Qur'anic verse which states that pure faith stands for what is consonant with man's innate character *(fitra)* created in him by God *(Qur'ân XXX, 29)*. The very mainstay of an upright worshipper is his *fitra*, for he knows that his God has deposited in it true knowledge and true consciousness of God. 'Anyone [, Shâh Walî Allâh says,] who denies the knowledge which God has put in man's innate character and on which the imposition of religious duties is based, is a zendiq [atheist]'. The *fitra* actually regards [, Shâh Walî Allâh says,] 'the *dîn* (religion) which does not change with the change of epoch, and on which all prophets are in agreement'.
>
> (Baljon 1986: 171; see also Hermansen 1996: 72).

Actually, according to a more recent commentator and translator, this *fitra*, was a 'substratum of beliefs and practices suitable to the basic constitution of all peoples he [Shâh Walî Allâh] terms the *'madhhab tabî'î'* [i.e. natural religion]' (Hermansen 1996: xxi, xxiii, 281, 285, 290, 341). It is remarkable that a similar broad and humanist interpretation of this concept of *fitra* appears in classical Chinese Muslim literature which developed in the sixteenth century in the Chinese language under the influence of Confucian notions (Murata 2000: 103 and 223–n.35).

Pre-eternal Determination of Human Destiny

For a more complete understanding of *fitra*, one must consider how Muslim thinkers imagine its origin. We are used to the Christian view according to which human destiny is at stake only after the creation of the world and the fall of Adam; the drama of sin and redemption is played in historical time. For Muslims this is not the case; creation of the world and of mankind is a secondary event. The primordial events occurred in a time before time, which actually is not time, but pre-eternity *(azal)*, i.e., eternity *a parte ante*. Sufis and popular piety hold that the Light of Muḥammad *(nûr muḥammadî)*, the perfect Prophet is the eternal principle of the creation of angels, prophets, saints and ordinary humans (Trimingham 1971: 208-09, 309): this belief was echoed among the bangle-makers of Nepal in the sermons pronounced by their religious leaders when they celebrated the Prophet's birthday. Such a conception is grounded in the Koran, according to which there was a primordial covenant *(mîthâq)* between God and all human beings still to be born who swore allegiance to their Creator (Hugues 1885: 61; Gobillot 2000: 46-70; *EQ*, vol. I, 2001: 26, 455-67).

The Koranic verse (VII: 171/172) reads: 'Your lord took from the backs of the children of Adam their offspring and made them testify against themselves. [God said,] "Am I not your lord?" They said, "Yes, we bear witness [to this]"' (Trans. *EQ*, vol. I, 2001: 26). This text is actually not very explicit: the event seems to take place after creation, and the word *mîthâq* does not appear. Yet early prophetic traditions and Koranic commentaries soon corrected the picture and came to agree that all the children to be born were taken from the back of Adam (and not his sons), that this pact was concluded in pre-eternity and that it was the primordial covenant *(mîthâq)*. They also agreed that this covenant was the origin of *fitra*; for instance an early commentator, Ibn ʿAbbâs (619-87), considered as the ancestor of Koranic exegesis, remarked after quoting the Koranic verse: 'All those who were to be born until the Day of Judgment were present. This is the *fiṭra* according to which Allah has created human beings.' (Quoted in Gobillot 2000: 46)

Did this covenant make all people equal before God? Liberal current among the Muʻtazilites, the Shiʻa and the Sufis tended to believe so. But the main trend of orthodox Sunnism, with its belief in predestination, held that everyone's destiny (belief or unbelief, salvation or damnation) was already fixed at the time of the covenant according to the quality of every man's response; this belief is mysteriously described in an early tradition ascribed to the middle of the seventh century, and reported by Ṭabarî, the father of Kuranic exegesis (839–923); it says that, at the time of the pact, Adam asked God to show him all his progeny to come. 'Then Allah placed Adam in front of them. The latter beheld them and saw among them rich and poor people, handsome and ugly ones, and exclaimed; "O Lord! Could not You create all of them equal?" Allah answered: "I love to be praised"'. The transmitter of this tradition added: 'There was in Allah's science, at the time of the pact, the knowledge that some of them would be faithful, the other renegades' (Quoted in Gobillot 2000: 48).

Let us, to conclude this part, assess the import of this theory of primordial nature and covenant on the question of human nature in Islam. Among liberal Islamic thinkers in the Middle Ages, as we have seen, there has been an attempt to consider *fiṭra* as a nature common to all people, who are free agents, all equal before God, Muslims and non-Muslims alike. This attempt has been recently renewed by a Tunisian scholar, Muhammad Talbi, as a basis of ecumenism, to enable Muslims and non-Muslims to speak as equals, partaking of the same human nature (Talbi 1998; Gobillot 2000: 1–5, 142–45).

There is still a long way to go to reconcile this modern view of human nature with mainstream orthodox Islam. This is for two reasons. One is that, in traditional Muslim views, people are not equal, neither socially (Gaborieau 1993a: 351–57), nor in the prospect of salvation, since the theory of predestination holds good. The second reason is that, since *fiṭra* results from a pact founded on the legislative power of God, it is not in its essence natural law, natural religion. Its nature is more that of a positive law. It remains thus characteristic of Islam where God-given law is always above and beyond rational and natural law (Gardet 2002: 141); *fiṭra* may well be the Islamic concept which is nearest to our notion of human nature, it is not an exact substitute for it. And we may conclude that in Islamic thought, there is no real nature in the human domain nor in the physical domain.

Conclusion

Let us now consider the implications of this statement. Our argument started from ways of thinking akin to antique and medieval Western thought, through philosophy and theology, to come progressively to two specifically Islamic religious sciences, exegesis and law, in which we encountered concepts which were not directly borrowed from Greek, and are specific to the Islamic tradition. Nowhere did we encounter concepts which were strictly equivalent to the western conception of nature. We only found inadequate substitutes. Even the notion of *fiṭra*, which comes nearest to our concept of human nature, cannot be exactly superposed on it.

The reason for this inadequacy is not so difficult to find. In Greek and in Western medieval thought, a conception of nature as a causative agent could be found because emphasis was laid on the autonomy of the world and of mankind. In Islam, on the contrary, God's omnipotence was placed in the foreground, both as the sole source of legislation, and as the real agency in cosmological events and in human actions. Currents which sought to emphasize autonomy of the cosmos and human agency, and thereby came nearer to our conception of nature, were marginalized.

We now come to another question: do Muslims characteristically differ from Hindus in their conception of nature? In social science there used to be a tendency to portray people of different religious affiliations as holding completely opposed world views. Such was the case for instance of the sociology of Louis Dumont (Dumont 1966) which I have criticized elsewhere (Gaborieau 1993a and 2002). The data studied in this chapter corroborate my previous criticism. If we keep to general metaphysical orientations, it is true that we encounter very different inspirations. Hindu life is regulated by *dharma* which is both the law of the cosmos and the law of mankind; men believe they live in harmony with the cosmos. Muslims on the contrary see themselves not as moved by the cosmos, but by the arbitrary omnipotence of a legislative God.

But we would be wrong to deduce from such metaphysical differences a difference in behaviour; or, to speak like Dumont, to deduce from diverging values, diverging social arrangements. In order to build a coherent argument, I had to found my argument in part on older Arabic texts. But I was careful to present, whenever available, Himalayan or at least Indian material. It is striking that these illustrations did not reveal opposed behaviour which could differentiate Muslims and Hindus. On the contrary the analogies were remarkable. In dealing with the natural world, the attitudes of the Hindus were quite comparable to those of the Muslims who only substitute Muslim saints for Hindu gods, or even worship Hindu gods. In the field of society, we have seen that the concept of primordial human nature, *fiṭra*, although deemed to be specifically Islamic, was accommodated by the Delhi divine Shâh Walî Allah to accommodate the Hindus in his world view, and to portray them as partaking in the same human nature. Although holding diverging metaphysical views, Hindus and Muslims behave in comparable ways toward nature.

It remains to be seen whether, in all this material, we can find data which could be construed as an opposition between nature and culture. In the domain of the cosmos, we did not really come across such an opposition: culture, in the form of agriculture, did not really come into opposition with natural forces or, to be more exact, to the saints who govern the universe according to medieval beliefs. Human efforts and propitiation of the saints were meant to help, not to contradict, the usual process of the natural world. The case is not the same for human nature. If we take it here in the sense of the most liberal interpretation of the concept of *fitra*, human nature is conceived as a kind of a primordial constitution, 'a "spiritual nature", which is common to all human beings prior to their acculturation', as James W. Morris puts it in a commentary of the great mystic Ibn `Arabî who died in Damascus in 1240 (Ibn `Arabî 1988: 548-n.113). In this perspective nature and culture are opposed. But the values attached to each of the terms are the reverse of what holds in western thought. In the latter case, culture is the noble term which comes to refine a wild nature in an evolutionist and optimistic view: perfection is expected to come at the end of history. Islamic thought, on the contrary, is pessimistic: perfection is in the beginning, that is to say in the past. The process of acculturation—unless it is adhesion to pure Islam—is necessarily a form of decadence, since the world is going from bad to worse, up to the end of the world. Acculturation is mainly conceived there as adhesion to a religious tradition, a religious law other than Islam, which can only subvert and degrade the natural religion innate in every man since the time of the pre-eternal covenant. What is valorized is nature, understood in this peculiar religious sense of a kind of primordial pure monotheist religion, not culture, which is described in a derogatory way.

References

Arnaldez, Roger. 1965. 'Falsafa'. In *EI2*, vol. II. pp. 769-75.
____, 1978. 'Khalk'. In *EI2*, vol. IV. pp. 981-88 (particularly § IV, 'Khalk in *kalâm*').
Baljon, J.M.S. 1986. *Religion and Thought of Shâh Walî Allâh Dihlawî, 1703-1762*. Leiden: E.J. Brill.

Bergeville, Gilles. 2002. 'Miracle'. In *DMA*. pp. 827-9.
Bertholet, Denis. 2003. *Claude Lévi-Strauss*, Paris: Plon.
Blachère, Régis. 1957. *Le Coran*. Paris: Maisonneuve.
Boulnois, Olivier. 2002a. 'Loi'. In *DMA*. pp. 842-4.
———, 2002b. 'Toute-puissance divine'. In *DMA*. pp. 1399-1400.
Chelhod, Joseph. 1955. *Le sacrifice chez les Arabes. Recherches sur l'évolution, la nature et la fonction des rites sacrificiels en Arabie occidentale*. Paris: Presses Universitaires de France.
Digby, Simon. 1986. 'The Sufi Shaikh as a Source of Authority in Mediaeval India'. In M. Gaborieau ed., *Islam et société en Asie du Sud/Islam and Society in South Asia*. Paris: EHESS, (Purushârtha n°9). pp. 57-77.
DMA = *Dictionnaire du Moyen Âge*. Claude Gauvard, Alain de Libera, Michel Zink, eds. Paris: Presses Universitaires de France, 2002.
Dumont, Louis. 1966. *Homo hierarchicus. Essai sur le système des castes*. Paris: Gallimard.
EI2 = *Encyclopaedia of Islam*, second edition, Leiden: E.J. Brill, 13 vols., 1960-2005.
EQ = *Encyclopaedia of the Qur'ân*, Leiden: E.J. Brill, 2001 sq.
Fakhri, Majid. 1958. *Islamic Occasionalism*. London: Allen & Unwin.
Gaborieau, Marc. 1969. 'Note préliminaire sur le dieu Masta'. *Objets et Mondes* IX (1): 19-50, (English translation in J.T. Hitchcock & R. Jones eds. *Spirit Possession in the Nepal Himalayas*, Warminster: Aris & Phillips Ltd, 1976, pp. 217-43).
——— 1975. 'Légende et culte du saint musulman Ghâzî Miyân au Népal occidental et en Inde'. *Objets et Mondes* XV (3): 289-318 (English translation in M. Waseem ed. *On Becoming an Indian Muslim: French Essays on Aspects of Syncretism*. Delhi: Oxford University Press. 2003. pp. 294-315).
——— 1978. 'Le partage du pouvoir entre les lignages dans une localité du Népal central'. *L'Homme*, XVIII (1-2): 37-67.
——— 1983. 'The cult of Saints among Muslims in Nepal and Northern India', in S. Wilson ed., *Saints and Their Cults: Studies in Religious Sociology, Folklore and History*. Cambridge: Cambridge University Press. 1983. pp. 291-308.
——— 1989. 'Pouvoirs et autorité des soufis dans l'Himalaya'. In V. Bouillier & G. Toffin, eds., *Prêtrise, pouvoirs et autorité en Himalaya*. Paris: EHESS. pp. 215-38 (Purushârtha 12).

_____ 1993a. *Ni brahmanes ni ancêtres: colporteurs musulmans du Népal.* Nanterre: Société d'ethnologie.

_____ 1993b. 'The Transmission of Islamic Reformist Teachings to Rural South Asia: The Lessons of a Case Study'. In H. Elboudrari ed. *Modes de transmission de la culture religieuse en Islam.* Cairo: Institut Français d'Archéologie Orientale. pp. 119–57.

_____ 1996. 'Les saints, les eaux et les récoltes en Inde'. In M.A. Amir-Moezzi ed. *Lieux d'islam. Cultes et cultures de l'Afrique à Java.* Paris: Éditions Autrement. pp. 239–54.

_____ 2000. 'Muslim Saints, Faquirs, and Pilgrims in 1831 according to Garcin de Tassy'. In J. Malik ed. *Perspectives of Mutual Encounters in South Asian History, 1760–1860.* Leiden: E.J. Brill, pp. 128–56.

_____ 2002. 'Incomparables ou vrais jumeaux? Les renonçants dans l'hindouisme et dans l'islam'. *Annales HSS* 1 janvier-février: 71–92.

Garcin de Tassy, Joseph. 1869. *Mémoire sur les particularités de la religion musulmane en Inde d'après les ouvrages hindoustanis.* Second rev. edition Paris: Labitte (first edition Paris, *Journal asiatique* and Imprimerie royale, 1831. English transl. M. Waseem. *Muslim Festivals in India and other Essays,* New Delhi: Oxford University Press, 1995. pp. 28–122).

Gardet, Louis. 1970. '`ilm al-kalâm', *EI2*, vol.III, pp. 1141–50.

_____ 1978. 'karâma'. In *EI2*, vol. IV. pp. 615–16.

_____ 2002 [first edition 1967]. *L'islam. Religion et communauté.* Paris: Desclée de Brouwer.

Gimaret, Daniel. 1990. *La doctrine d'al-Ash`arî.* Paris: Le Cerf.

_____ 1993. 'Mu`tazila'. In *EI2*, vol. VII. pp. 783–93.

Gobillot, Geneviève. 2000. *La Fitra. La conception originelle, ses interprétations et fonctions chez les penseurs musulmans.* Le Caire: Institut Français d'Archéoloie Orientale.

Gonda, Jan. 1962. *Les religions de l'Inde,* vol. I, *Védisme et hindouisme ancien.* Paris: Payot.

Hermansen, Marcia K. 1996. *The Conclusive Argument from God. Shâh Walî Allâh of Delhi's Hujjat Allâh al-Bâligha.* Translated by. Leiden: E.J. Brill.

Hugues, Thomas Patrick. 1885. *A Dictionary of Islam,* London (quoted from the reprint, Lahore: Premier Book House, 1964).

Ibn 'Arabî. 1988. *Les illuminations de la Mecque. The Meccan Illuminations.*

Selected texts translated by, and published under the direction of Michel Chodkiewicz. Houston: Rothko Chapel÷Paris: Sinbad.

Kugle, Scot. 2005. 'Queer Jihad. A View from South Africa'. *ISIM Review* 16 Autumn: 14-15.

Lamouche, Fabien. 2004. 'Parcours de Claude Lévi-Strauss. A partir d'une biographie récente'. *Esprit* 301, janvier (Special issue *Claude Lévi-Strauss, une anthropologie 'bonne à penser'*): 110-19.

Lévi-Strauss, Claude. 1949. *Les structures élémentaires de la parenté*. Paris: Presses Universitaires de France (Second rev. edition, Paris: Mouton, 1967).

―― 1963. 'Réponses à quelques questions'. *Esprit* 11: 628-53 (reprinted in *Esprit*, special issue *Claude Lévi-Strauss, une anthropologie 'bonne à penser'* 301, janvier 2004: 169-92).

―― 1964. *Mythologiques*, vol. I, *Le cru et le cuit*. Paris: Plon.

Levy, Ruben, 1957. *The Social Structure of Islam*. Cambridge: Cambridge University Press (1st ed.: *Sociology of Islam*, 2 vols. 1931 and 1933).

MacDonald, Duncan B. 1965. 'fiṭra'. In *EI2*, vol. II. pp. 931-2.

Mauss, Marcel. 1898. 'Vestiges du paganisme en Arabie', review of J. Welhausen, *Reste der arabischen Heidentums*, second edition, Berlin, 1897. *L'Année sociologique* 1 (reproduced in Marcel MAUSS, *Œuvres*, vol. 1. Paris: Editions de Minuit. 1968. pp. 329-32).

Metcalf, Barbara Daly. 1982. *Islamic Revival in British India: Deoband 1860-1900*. Princeton: Princeton University Press.

Murata, Sachiko. 2000. *Chinese Gleans of Sufi Light*. Albany: State University of New York Press.

Nânotawî, Muḥammad Qâsim. 1890. *Taṣfiyyat al-`aqâ'id*, Delhi (Quoted from the English translation by Peter Hardy, 'Assessment of Tenets'. In A. Ahmad and G. von Grunebaum eds. *Muslim Self-Statement in India and Pakistan, 1857-1968*. Wiesbaden: Otto Harrassowitz. 1970. pp. 60-76).

Pingree, D.E. and S. Nomanul Haq. 2000. 'ṭabî`a'. In *EI2*, vol. X. pp. 25-8.

Pouillon, Jean. 1967. 'L'œuvre de Claude Lévi-Strauss'. In C. Lévi-Strauss *Race et histoire*. Paris: Éditions Gonthier. pp. 87-127.

Schmutz, Jacob. 2002. 'Causalité'. In *DMA*. pp. 232-5.

Sharmâ, Bâl Candra, 2019 VS (1962). *Nepâlî shabda kosh*. Kathmandu: Royal Nepal Academy.

Solère, Jean-Luc. 2002. 'Nature'. In *DMA*. pp. 967–76.
Talbi, Muhammad. 1998. *Plaidoyer pour un islam moderne*. Paris: Desclée de Bouwer.
Trimingham, J. Spencer. 1971. *The Sufi Orders in Islam*. Oxford: Clarendon Press.
Troll, Christian W. 1978. *Sayyid Ahmad Khan. A Reinterpretation of Muslim Theology*. New Delhi: Vikas Publishing House.
Waines, David. 2001. 'Agriculture and vegetation'. In *EQ*, vol. I. pp. 40–50.
Watt, W. Montgomery. 1966. 'Ḥanîf'. In *EI2*, vol. III. pp. 165–6.
Wensinck, A.J. 1993. 'Muʿdjiza'. In *EI2*, vol. VII. p. 295.

Variations in Shamanist Siberia

ROBERTE N. HAMAYON

Nomadic hunters and wood cutters, Raute, Western Nepal
(Photo: Prem Shahi, 2002)

> Never let yourself be goaded into taking seriously problems about words and their meanings. What must be taken seriously are questions of facts and assertions about facts: theories and hypotheses, the problems they solve and the problems they raise.
>
> Karl Popper

'We are children of Nature'[1]—more generally, a close relation to Nature—is a current claim today among native peoples of Eastern Siberia. The songs and dances most of them perform during their national festivals called 'Games' consist of imitating birds and other animals with the aim of encouraging general reproduction. They convey the idea that humans belong to Nature, that they are indebted to it for their living and committed to preserve it,[2] which is currently summarized as 'children of Nature'. Following their elites, they are taking up this old stereotype of their own ethnography to flaunt their identity in the global world, which the end of the Soviet era has enabled them access. Apparently, they have easily and quickly appropriated the term Nature, which, however, has no equivalent in their languages.[3] They use it as if deeming it

---

[1] 'We are children of Nature [...] it feeds and warms us, its beauty rejoices us every day, without it we'd be nothing, without it there'd be no life', sentences recorded among the Evenks by A. Lavrillier (2000: 25).

[2] 'Imitating birds is our way not to disappear from this world', the Even scholar Alekseev writes (Alekseev 1993: 33). The songs of the Even express the idea that humans are part of nature, which they are born from. The round dance *heed'e* is for 'harmony with nature'. People imitate the mating dance of white cranes, miming their gaggling, moving their arms like wings. They also imitate young reindeer's troating. They consider larch-trees as sacred reindeer and put the corpses of their dead in their branches, a sign of their return to the bosom of nature. During the national festival, they stretch a rope between two larch-trees, seen as father and mother, then they hang to the rope as many tufts of reindeer neck overhair as there are families. Each tuft is supposed to fly away in a crane's shape. 'We shall live. Look how proudly these cranes fly. [...] Get your strength, forget all that is not fine and let us fly like cranes [...]' (Alekseev 1993 *passim* and 51).

[3] Schooling was general during the Soviet period and most people nowadays know Russian. They are aware that Nature and Culture are borrowed notions, and that their understanding and attached values may

appropriate to express a concept inherent in their own traditions although not explicitly, and meaning roughly 'what is not being acted upon by man', although its understanding is not one and the same throughout Siberia. In particular, it is as a 'religion' or a symbolic system based on 'Harmony with Nature' that they nowadays redefine their shamanism, another emblematic component of their post-Soviet identity. Thus, 'Harmony with Nature' is what they consider to be the very specificity of *their* 'cultures', however 'Nature' is defined.

Referring to 'Nature' is all the more important in these peoples' present-day identity claims, since they hold it to be inherent in shamanism: their country, Siberia, as the land where the term shaman originates, is entitled to serve as its representative. A proximity to 'Nature' is mentioned in many Western definitions of shamanism, though with certain nuances. At the time of Enlightenment, its use was aimed at banning the shaman's figure from the civilized world: appearing animal-like because of his ritual behaviour and attire, this figure was classified as wild, backward, unruly—therefore devilish. By contrast, romanticists discovered poetry, purity and greatness in this destitute magician's struggle with 'Nature'. In Russian and Soviet literature, closeness to 'Nature' was connoted negatively. Nowadays, the very idea of 'Nature' has acquired positive connotations with the recent political changes brought about by the fall of the Soviet regime and with the help of world-wide ecological trends. Moreover, due to the post-modern fancy for shamanism, this alleged link to 'Nature' is what best supports the idea that shamanism is

---

vary. Two terms convey the notion of Nature in Russian: *priroda* and *natura*, a very old borrowing of Latin origin; they are quite similar in meaning, but *priroda* would be more appropriate in the present context. The understanding of the notion of Nature conveyed by these two terms does not differ from the current one in the West, but that of the notion of Culture, *kul'tura*, does. Moreover, Siberian peoples have not appropriated the term Culture to a similar extent as that of Nature. They use it either to refer to education received at school—Culture in general—or to refer to each people's specific traditions—'their' own culture. Only the second understanding will be referred to in this chapter.

universal and authentic as a joint physical and spiritual expression of human 'nature', regardless of the cultural framework.

Whether associated or not with shamanism, 'Nature' appears in all types of Siberian self-portraits as aimed at the rest of the world, provided its precise meaning can be both kept unclear and as positively valued as possible. Now, if it implicitly concerns land such as untouched by man, along with the plant and animal species that live in it, 'Nature' is perceived as rich, pure and revitalizing rather than 'wild'. If it is about a way of life dealing with wildlife, it is seen as intrinsically and forever relevant to human health. If they use it in relation to an ideological view, they intend to point to its being balanced, sustainable and of world interest. With respect to a mode of behaviour, 'Nature' implies, for them, straightforwardness and reliability. Whatever the case, claiming to be close to 'Nature' is associated, in their mind, with genuineness and, above all, vitality.

Siberian peoples now use their shamanism and its constitutive closeness to 'Nature' as a source of self-esteem and self-confidence in today's global world, and a source of political legitimacy whenever political issues are at stake. Their shamanism deserves a privileged place amidst ecological trends. Now, hardly has 'closeness to Nature' or 'being a child of Nature' the same meaning for all those who use these expressions to define themselves. It depends on whether they live in urban or rural areas, talk to other natives or to foreigners, and, above all, on whether they belong to a people with primarily a hunting or herding tradition, while all peoples in this area actually practise more or less both lifestyles.

The last difference is highlighted by the example—among other possible examples—of two neighbouring peoples in the vast space of Yakutia. About 35,000 Evenks (Tungus) live scattered in remote areas hard to access,[4] while about 400,000 Yakuts are concentrated in large central plains. A century ago the Evenks used to depict themselves by referring to the forest. In his comment of the 1897 census, Patkanov praises the energy and liveliness of

---

[4]They are basically hunters and also keep small herds of reindeer to make their nomadic life easier.

these 'people made for living and dying in the forest *(taiga)*' (Patkanov 1906: 271–72). At all times, explorers of Siberia have selected their guides from among them, so renowned for their trailing skills. Even today, they are extraordinarily clever at finding their way around; children who grow up in the *taiga* carefully learn all the details of the hydrographical network: they should be able to go from Lake Baikal to the Arctic Ocean and from the Yenissei to the Okhotsk Sea by passing from one river to another (Lavrillier 2005). Their concept of *taiga* encompasses the watercourses that cross it—this is roughly what they have in mind when saying 'Nature'—and it also encompasses all that lives there, especially the wild animals they hunt for food, clothing, etc. (ibid.).

By contrast, the ideal dwelling landscape according to the Yakut pastoral tradition was and still is that of an *alaas*, a type of large clearing in the forest, whether natural or man-made, where meadows, hills and at least one watering place are found. A good *alaas* is expected to provide a herding unit (the Yakuts herd large flocks of cows and horses) a large encampment and enough pasturelands for them not to have to move far from their home, while allowing them to go and hunt small game in the surrounding forest from time to time (Maj 2009). Of course, such distinctions do not matter for their fellows living in the cities, who do not specify what they refer to when claiming 'harmony with Nature'.

Thus, 'Nature' is not the same from a hunter's and a herder's viewpoint. Now, it is the hunting life that is unanimously acknowledged as the source of the link to 'Nature' inherent in shamanism. This idea, first expressed by the early explorers (for instance, by J.G. Georgi who journeyed in Siberia from 1768–74), is a point of agreement between specialists such as Mircea Eliade (1951), Évelyne Lot-Falck (1953), Andreas Lommel (1967) etc. It is also one of several conclusions to my own works, except for one important aspect. As a matter of fact, the existence of forms of shamanism related to lifestyles other than hunting is largely agreed upon. This has led me to attempt to redefine the reference to 'hunting life' so as to account for the plurality of existing forms by common principles. In speaking of hunting as the backdrop to shamanism, I do not refer to the effective practice of hunting, but to the conception of the relation to the world that this way of life implies. It should be understood as the underlying ideology behind this way of life, likely to survive when fading out as an effective practice, as well as to revive regardless of it.[5] To throw more light on the idea of 'Nature' that characterizes the ideology of hunting life, I shall point out some differences with the representations linked to pastoral life according to Siberian data. These differences show a meaningful inversion of the conception of 'Nature' from one lifestyle to the other, along with a correlative inversion of relations to it, i.e., of the contents of the society's specific culture. I will attempt to throw light on the logical base of this reversal, which nonetheless does not preclude the common claim of being 'children of Nature'.

Thus, the understanding of what is referred to when speaking of 'Nature' is far from uniform among peoples who have similarly borrowed this concept, through Russian, from the international vocabulary and live in close contact with each other. They do not oppose systematically an abstract notion of 'Nature' to one of 'Culture', which is perceived in a more uniform way. Yet they specify their own cultures by reference to their own understanding of and relations to 'Nature', whatever these relations and understanding.

Many elements in Siberian ethnography incite me not to reject these categories, notwithstanding their now being under critical discussion in anthropology.[6] I shall briefly mention a few of them. All peoples, in particular those who both keep and hunt the same species—reindeer—systematically and radically distinguish the domestic one from its wild counterpart. The Yakuts describe their

[5]The claim of 'Harmony with Nature' does not imply the least nostalgia for a golden age really based on any hunting activity. Everybody is aware that it generates the dread of starvation. It refers to the ideology of hunting life, in that it is imbued with a taste for freedom and voluntarism and gives a large place to individual agency.

[6]I will not enter into this discussion in this chapter. I will only refer occasionally, on the basis of Siberian data, to certain arguments put forward by some scholars engaged in it (Ingold 2000, Descola 2005 and others).

horses as 'wild' and want them to conform to this ideal, although they actually breed them during the first years of their life (Ferret 2006). The Evenks change their nomadic routes every few years so that their reindeer do not have to walk trampled ground—whereby the same spaces are considered alternatively as wild and domestic (Lavrillier 2007). Such elements show that calling animals or spaces 'wild' depends on the way one relates to them, which may change over time. Therefore I shall consider 'wild' as a component of an implicit category, which in the framework of this chapter I will call 'Nature'.

However, the understanding and scope of this implicit category vary with specific cultures and with specific contexts within each society. As a matter of fact, besides variations between cultures and societies, we observe meaningful variations in relation to 'Nature' between different types of data: myth, ritual, informal speech, concrete practices or techniques, within a single society. The chapter on a hunting lifestyle will illustrate that taking into account the type, level and status of the data where the information is taken from allows us to grasp meaningful differences: the relations to wild animals such as expressed, for instance, by ritual staging differ radically from those implied by actual hunting. I shall try to stress the relevance of such variations to understanding why Siberian peoples have so easily adopted the terms 'Nature' and 'Culture' without attempting to define them precisely. At the risk of oversimplifying, I would like to argue that this variability is precisely what makes the pair methodologically valid for analysing Siberian data, although to a limited extent only. These concepts share the destiny of many others in social sciences, that of being at the same time criticized and extensively used for their convenience: their relative indefiniteness and flexibility are what determines their usability for a very broad first approach that always requires further refinement.

This chapter is not aimed at restoring the view of 'Nature' held by concrete historical societies of native hunters and herders in Siberia. This would hardly reflect the reality of this large space where hunting peoples, in most cases, also keep domestic animals and where none of the pastoral populations really refrains from hunting. In pre-Soviet times, they were all peoples of oral tradition[7] and had a non-doctrinal (shamanic) religious background. Moreover, their present situation, marked by decades of communist rule and sudden access to modernity, is too diverse to serve as a useful reference in our perspective. That is why this chapter deals with these societies taken in their state prior to the Soviet era, which—to a certain extent—is accessible thanks to extensive documentation gathered during the colonization of Siberia under the Tsars' Empire. Pieces of oral literature and field materials related to that time concerning the Buryat tribe of the Ehirit-Bulagat (who are at the basis of my argument) supplement published sources.

The name Buryat encompasses a set of groups that speak Mongol dialects and live on both sides of Lake Baikal. Many of them came here from Mongolia after the collapse of the Mongol Empire, bringing their pastoral culture with them. They will not be dealt with here. I will only deal with the Ehirit-Bulagats, who originate from the west side of Baikal. They are held to be the only native Buryat group of Buryatia. They are usually featured as forest hunters having long ago started to keep horses in order to enhance the effectiveness of hunting, and then developed cattle breeding. They adopted agriculture in the late nineteenth century, when pressure from farmers coming from central Russia intensified. Under imperial colonization, they maintained their organization as a set of territorial groups, and they remained strongly attached to shamanism while officially converting to Christianity.

At that time, hunting and herding still coexisted among them, and world views associated with both lifestyles intertwined. Nevertheless, variations indicate that the idea of 'Nature' is mainly ideological in both cases and inverted from one to the other. Whatever the geographical and historical constraints upon one

[7]Only the Buddhicized Buryats who live to the east of Baikal had a writing of their own before the advent of the Soviet regime: the Mongol writing, tied to the spreading of Buddhism propagated among them from the neighbouring country of Mongolia. The native elites educated in schools founded by the Orthodox Church began to record their traditions in Cyrillic writing in the late nineteenth century. Specific writings have been created for all languages of Siberia in the early Soviet period.

or the other way of life, claiming to be primarily hunter or herder (whereas practising both) seems to imply a part of deliberate choice. Not to mention that, according to our data, a major claim is 'herding with a hunter's mind (soul, spirit)',[8] which implies a double system of values. It is from a particular angle, that of the 'socialisation of Nature',[9] that I will attempt here to define such a part of deliberate choice, which the natives themselves consider to be a mark of their 'Culture'. I will therefore only set out some aspects of the Ehirit-Bulagat view and treatment of 'Nature', which will give rise to more general remarks about what the choice of living on hunting or herding respectively implies.

Rich: An Environment to Benefit from, a Father-in-law to Compel

'Rich', *bayan* (the long form of a widespread Altaic root), appears in many place names, starting with Baikal, 'Rich Lake'. In mythical narratives, it is often combined, as an epithet, with the word *hangay* used in the generic sense of forest.[10] As a proper noun, *Bayan Hangay*, 'Rich Forest', designates an entity that is at the same time, geographical and symbolic, the forest merging with the spiritual being that animates it. This is a generic 'spirit of the forest', featured as an elk with large antlers.

The root *hanga-*, the meaning of which is 'to satisfy one's hunger', underscores the way 'rich' should be understood. It describes a source of food as plenteous, which incites one to define forest

---

[8] This expression suits the Ehirit-Bulagat or Cisbaikalian Buryats particularly well and may be useful to distinguish them from the nomads of Transbaikalia whose pastoral practice is extensive, in the Mongol style (Hamayon 1990).

[9] The word *baygaali*, 'Nature', a neologism derived from *bayha* 'to be', is not a relevant concept in this respect.

[10] In Central Mongolia, a strongly pastoral country, the word *hangay* is purely geographic; it means 'wooded highlands' and has very positive connotations.

and water as two nourishing environments the Ehirit-Bulagat appreciate as such. What matters is their being rich—whether in game or fish. Their shape also does not matter—both are conceived of as horizontal, thick and adjacent to each other—and still less their location. Besides, the sources indicate that the forest, while being seen as a protective refuge for all those who live there, is not an object of ownership, at least as regards hunting large game (elk, reindeer), which is the only really valued type of hunting, based on tracking.[11] Tracking is perceived as a singular hence somewhat personal[12] encounter between a hunter and an animal, and it is respected as such from one end to the other of the Siberian taiga: any other hunter happening to cross the track should then turn round. Likewise hunters take care not to interfere when a bear prepares to eat a smaller animal: they respect its eating its prey and go away. In such a world view, humans define themselves as being on an equal footing with animals in their nourishing environment that everyone may benefit from.

Bayan also appears in the name of a major character in epic narratives: the hero's father-in-law. The main thread of the story is invariably the hero's search for a wife. 'Since my early years until my old age, I kept being a son-in-law', one of the heroes exclaims (Homonov 1964, 2, 13.637–13.638). Narratives start and end with this search, which is reputed the hardest of all campaigns a man should carry out and requires heroic determination to be

---

[11] By contrast, there are areas reserved for lying in wait and trapping (Hamayon 1990: 385–86 *et passim*). Fishing is not important among the Buryats at the period considered here. Watercourses matter mainly for transportation. Yet there were reserved areas for setting up fishing nets among the groups who also relied on fishing for food.

[12] This does not entail that the animal is seen as a singular 'person'. The animal remains representative of its species. It is never given a personal name, contrary to domestic animals. The extension of the notion of personhood to wild animals which Tim Ingold infers from the gloss of the Cree word for 'person' as 'he lives' (quoting Scott 1989: 195) would not be valid for Siberian data. Ingold (2000: 51) writes: 'personhood, far from being added on to the living organism, is implied in the very condition of being alive: the Cree word for 'persons' [...] can itself be glossed as 'he lives'.

achieved. The epic performance is submitted to very strict rules. It is imperative to sing epics during the hunting season: it is held to be a form of training for hunters who are to actually hunt just afterwards; as a ritual preparation for hunting, it is absolutely compulsory. It is strictly prohibited to sing epics during daytime and during the other half of the year, when hunting is forbidden. The epic performance is also held to be the appropriate ritual action aimed at 'preparing' for other hard campaigns (for instance, against epidemic diseases) or 'hard times'.

Now, hunting is hardly alluded to in epic narratives and it does not affect the unfolding of the story. The hero is a mounted man and he rides to go and get his wife-to-be. His horse is wild. He has had to go and capture it on a summit where it was grazing along with big cervids. He had also had to break it in. However, never is he described as treating it as a domestic animal, nor caring for the herds he is sometimes said to possess. The heroic search is not related to the breeding or herding activity. It is a long and winding quest, punctuated with obstacles that have to be surmounted. Its final phase is a series of apparently wanton trials imposed on the hero by his wife-to-be's father: 'Father-in-law! With which intentions do you make such a fanciful use of your power in regard to me?' (Homonov 1961, 1: 5197–201). The epic narratives insist on the fact that the hero must marry precisely this girl to the exclusion of all other possible girls, by virtue of the fathers' former agreement. Now, the stubborn father-in-law always has 'rich' in his name: Gazar Bayan Han 'Land Rich King', Dalai Bayan Han 'Sea Rich King' and even Bayan Hangay 'Rich Forest'.[13] He is 'rich' in having a daughter and reluctant to let her be taken away, as the forest is with regard to game.[14]

---

[13] Hamayon 1990: 234 and 761 n.8.

[14] The hero's horse and wife-to-be are said to be 'predestined' for him and only him. Nevertheless, this is not enough for him to 'obtain' them. He must also prove his personal value to have this right turned into reality. Likewise, hunting rights do not exempt the hunter from being clever and skilled. Significantly many heroes have *mergen*, 'clever archer', in their name. From a wider point of view, the analysis of the process may help to elucidate the practice called 'marriage by abduction'.

Searching for a Wife, Searching for Game

I deliberately use the notion of metaphor, whose relevance is also contested in the framework of the debate on Nature/Culture and, more generally, in recent cognitivist approaches to anthropology.[15] I do not refer to 'metaphor' as a specific rhetoric figure. I refer to the very process of metaphorization, in the broad perspective opened by Lakoff & Johnson (1980) about the metaphorical structuration of conceptual systems.[16] As a subject of ongoing research, it will only occasionally be commented on

[15]Tim Ingold aims at contrasting the view 'that hunter-gatherers' perception of the environment is embedded in practices of engagement, with the more conventional alternative that such perception results from the reconstruction of naturally given realities in terms of metaphors drawn from the ideal 'realm of culture.' (Ingold 2000: 10). The possible 'given reality' could be the reindeer's behaviour when it is aware of being pursued: it stands stock still instead of running away, which, among native hunters of Canada, gives rise to the view that 'the animal offers itself up, quite intentionally and in a spirit of will and even love towards the hunter' (Ingold 2000: 13). A similar idea of 'love' between the hunter and his prey is also widespread in Siberia; this is commonplace in informal representations and short stories, but no similar behaviour and feeling is mentioned for the hero's wife-to-be in the epics, which insist on marrying as part of a set of rules imposed on the future husband. This is metaphorical in that hunting wild animal species for food—however fundamental its experience is—is *conceived of in terms* of marriage alliance (see footnote 16 on metaphor as conceptualization). Just as a man should not, according to the epic model, behave as a woman's abductor, a hunter should not, according to the shamanic model, steal game, but make a prior agreement with the game holders. The status of 'husband' is what makes the hunter legitimate as such. Epics are all about the formalized relationship and not about the possibly associated feeling. This does not, of course, preclude that the bard, and more especially the hunters who listen to his performance, do not feel emotionally involved, since the group's life is at stake.

[16]Their definition of metaphor is quite simple: 'The essence of metaphor is understanding and experiencing one kind of thing *in terms* of another.' 'Metaphor is pervasive, not merely in our language but in our conceptual system [...] Metaphor is one of the most basic mechanisms we have for understanding our experience' (Lakoff and Johnson 1980: 210-211).

here, in relation to the present question, i.e., in order to account for the fact that preparing for hunting consists in a ritual performance focused on an extremely formalized search for a wife.

If we jointly consider the epic narratives and rules for performance, the search for a wife appears to be a wide metaphor for hunting, which is enough to justify that the epic season is also the hunting season. As a realm defined by rules, alliance is a suitable model for establishing the activity of hunting with a framework of prohibitions and prescriptions. The fact that the epic discourse is highly ritualized may also contribute to imposing on the hunters who are listening the absolute duty to respect rules, in the image of the hero.

But the question remains as to why searching for a wife should serve to conceptualize hunting—which entails likening not only marriage to hunting, son-in-law to hunter, but also woman to game (and, as an implicit consequence, sexual intercourse to eating). This is a puzzling question since the epic genre develops along with herding among the Buryats, whereas it is missing among neighbouring peoples who, having only domestic reindeer, remain more regularly defined as basically being hunters (Sel'kups, Evenks of the Yenissei etc.). Now, the latter ritually prepare for hunting by performing a shamanic ritual at spring.

This ritual, the only large periodical one, may last for more than one month for it is also a festival where small nomadic units gather after winter dispersal. It stages a representation of a hunt for a wild elk or reindeer, and, as a backdrop to it, that of a wedding: the 'wedding' of the shaman with a spirit's daughter (or sister) of that species, which is game *par excellence*.[17] She supposedly fell in love with him some time before and for this reason he trained to become a shaman. Only the ritual 'wedding' allows him to prepare for his community's hunting campaign. People expect that, once duly 'married', the shaman's 'spirit wife' will enable him to obtain 'promises of game' from her or, to adopt a more

---

[17] For details, see Hamayon 1990: 425–539. The relations staged in this ritual are strictly limited to spirits of species hunted for food. They never apply to fur game.

current expression, 'good luck at hunting' for the community. We thus have again a metaphorical cross-reference between hunting and marrying (from a male's point of view). However, the process starts with hunting—from man's relation to animals—in the case of the hunters' ritual, while it starts with marrying—from a social relation between humans—in the case of the herder's epic narrative. The difference lies in the realm referred to: 'Nature' in one case, society in the other.

Socializing without Humanizing the Animal, Playing the Animal while Remaining Human

This type of ritual performed by the neighbouring 'peoples of the forest' throws light on how a marriage quest is appropriate to symbolically 'preparing' for a hunting campaign. The way it is staged focuses on the alliance relationship rather than on the individual shaman's marriage.[18] Hardly is his wife's figure suggested. It is said that openly speaking of her would make her run away, which would put the shaman, and hence, the whole group, in great danger. The shaman's ritual 'marriage' is intended to give concrete expression to the alliance between the human community represented by the shaman, and the animal species which is its main game, represented by a spirit's daughter of this species. This is why, if the season is good, the community will solicit the same shaman to conduct the next ritual, during which he will have to 'marry' again. His successive 'marriages' are aimed at 'updating' the global alliance between humans and animal spirits.

Many elements in the organization of the ritual make the alliance relationship, as such, an obvious concern, starting with

[18] Like the 'spirit of the forest' with a reindeer or elk's appearance, the daughter is conceived of generically: each shaman, so to speak, has her as a wife. Again we may say that the concrete relation is perceived as personal, while the animal partner is not seen as a singular person, but as a representative of its species with which alliance is contracted. In societies where the shaman function is inherited, the shaman is supposed to ritually marry his line's spirit-wife, who 'always loves in the same line from generation to generation'.

task sharing between marriage partners, between men and women, etc. The whole atmosphere is permeated with joy and love, and the ritual is punctuated with various games—all in imitation of animal modes of behaviour.[19] However, the main feature is that the shaman portrays himself as 'husband', more precisely, as a human husband of an animal spirit wife. Everything is done to underscore this very special status of his: his attire, behaviour and the words that designate his movements and also, beyond them, the shamanic action itself. He wears a dress and boots made of a reindeer or elk's skin. On his head, he has a crown adorned with antlers, but it is made of iron and the adorning antlers are mere evocations of antlers, stylized rather than realistic. His voice seems to come from the back of his throat as if he were to bellow and snort, like a stag, then it develops into a human song with words. He jumps and prances, jerks and twists, moves his hips and shakes his head, but does not stay or walk on all fours. Metaphor always applies only partially.

The verbs used to name the shaman's ritual movements belong to the vocabulary of animal behaviour at the mating season. Some of them also mean 'to shamanize', 'to carry out a shamanic rite'. Three verbs are used in Buryat to describe the shaman's behaviour: *hatarha* 'to trot (reindeer)', *naadaha* 'to mate (birds and fish)', *mürgehe* 'to head butt (horned ruminants)', a verb which the noun *mürgel*, found in *böö mürgel* 'shamanism', is derived from. The Altaic root of the Tungus term shaman *saman* designates movements of the lower or back part of the body of some animal species. The Yakut *oyuu*—'to leap or jump about' as a reindeer or capercailzie, is found in the words for shaman and shaman ritual action.[20]

---

[19] The games *par excellence* are types of wrestling and jumping dances, echoing the way some species (namely cocks and horned ruminants) fight their rivals and prepare to mate.

[20] The idea of mating is sometimes clearly expressed by the way the drum is beaten. The one-sided drum is held vertically, with the open side on one's chest and the membrane outside. The outside membrane is tapped with the beater, from the bottom up. More rarely, the drum is explicitly held to represent the shaman's wife. Thus, among the Shors, a small group living in the Altai, the drum is placed standing on a chair between the

All in all, during the ritual, the shaman should look animal enough to make the idea of his union with his animal spirit 'wife' credible, but he remains a human being, standing and crowned with iron (which moreover evokes weapons), for only as a human is he able to represent and act on behalf of the human community in the realm of animal spirits. Conversely, in spite of her 'marrying' a human, his 'wife' must be portrayed as an animal so that she may give her husband access to the animal world. She is socialized without for all that being humanized.

The couple's relationship as expressed in these rituals stands on two planes. One plane is clearly physical. It is aimed at making obvious that contact with 'Nature' provides vitality.[21] The other plane is institutional. It opens a path towards understanding the basis of shamanism among these peoples, in particular, their conception of spirits. The 'alliance' the rituals are aimed at establishing (which I shall call 'shamanic alliance' from now on) implies that both partners belong to one and the same world. It also implies that, within this world, they are at the same time similar in status and dissimilar in essence, insofar as they belong to different species, as partners of exogamic marriage belong to different lines. And it finally implies that the 'natural' partner is ascribed such properties that they allow the human partner to communicate with it and, more importantly, to expect replies similar to his own from it.

Equal but Unlike Within the same World

'Peoples of the forest', 'children of Nature', hunting peoples say they feel at home in the forest like the wild animal species that live there. In their informal discourse, the huts of the former,

---

man, who has made it, and his wife. A scarf is wrapped around its frame, in the way Russian countrywomen do around their head. The shaman should 'abduct' the drum to marry it, according to Shor wedding tradition.

[21] The Ehirit-Bulagat, who do not carry out this type of ritual since they prepare for hunting by performing epics, practise another type of ritual to periodically 'animate' *(amiluulaha)* their shamans' ritual tools—which means both 'put a spirit into' and 'restore life or vital force to'.

covered with skins or barks depending on the season, are akin to dens, lairs or nests of the latter. The idea of equivalence reflects the experience that wild animals feed on each other, and for this purpose, track and trick each other. In their world view, humans conceive of themselves as one among other species in the forest, party to the food chain that ensures life for everyone. They may even stage a token of their contribution to the food chain e.g. by putting fish bones on paths where mice usually go. As if to prove they apply the logic of the food chain to themselves, they lay the corpses of their dead so that birds of prey and carrion eaters can eat them (Hamayon 2001).

The inclusion of humans in the food chain appears to be a crucial empirical element that can be considered, from an analytical point of view, as being at the root of the conceptual construction underlying the above-mentioned shaman ritual. This construction may be interpreted either as being aimed at allowing humans to coexist with other species within 'Nature' and to take advantage of this, or, in other words, as being intended to justify the very fact of living off hunting. It shows how the 'hunting life', the very notion of spirit and shamanism are tied to each other.

This construction is based on a very simple idea: to catch the animals they wish to eat, humans should arrange it so that the animal species accept to be involved in an exchange of food with them. There is therefore no global conception of 'Nature' behind this, which only applies to species hunted for food. From an analytical point of view, human interest is focused on the food that 'Nature' conceals and whose catching is not determinable, yet it also extends to other species: hunting species that are man's rivals—and species whose moves and calls indicate the presence of game that are man's helpers. It is clearly about a principle of symbolic action upon animals, and it implies conceiving animals as somehow similar to humans. The conception that prevails throughout Siberia can be expressed in this way: the bodies of animals are 'animated' by an intangible component (a 'soul') just as the bodies of humans are, while 'vital force' is necessary to feed it just as meat feeds the body. In ethnographic literature, the notion of 'spirit' is more currently used if speaking of animals, with the following nuance: an animal spirit is, so to speak, a generic soul tied to a species which is perpetuated through the generations (and not to a particular animal which is deemed to die). What matters is that human souls and animal spirits are thought to be similar (though not identical) in status and function, for this is what makes interrelations possible. Conceived along the lines of relationships between humans, relationships with spirits are expected to give access to animals, insofar as spirits supposedly infuse human-like feelings and intentions in animals.

Close to this conception lies the following idea. Souls are thought to be located in the bones. They are to be re-used from one generation to the next within the same human line or the same animal species after being somehow 'recycled' in the world beyond. According to this idea, on one hand, hunting species should only take meat from each other, and, on the other hand, bones should be kept intact so that a new individual of the same species may come to life. Bones of big game and human corpses are similarly displayed high in the open air, either in the branches of large trees or on a wooden platform resting on four poles about two meters high.[22]

Nobody ever neglects their duty resulting from being included in the forest food chain. Native people spell it out clearly, though in a quite different, informal, kind of speech: just as humans live on game, consuming the meat and vital force of animals, so they argue, do animal spirits when they feed on humans, devouring their flesh and sucking the vital force from their blood.[23] However,

---

[22]The name and shape of such a platform are the same for humans and large wild animals among the Yakuts and Buryats *(aranga)*; they slightly differ in Tungus. Significantly, this aerial type of funeral, which both the tsarist and Soviet powers had tried to eradicate, has recently reappeared— just one among other signs of a 'return to tradition' trend produced by the post-communist context (see Hamayon 2001).

[23]The idea that game is an 'unconditional gift' from the forest that Ingold draws from Bird-David is—at best—but a partial representation that does not reflect the whole conceptual system. This is refuted by another idea of the same native hunters as discussed by the same scholars, which

they do not explicitly and deliberately carry out the 'giving back', which they strive to reduce and postpone as long as possible.

We may then describe their view as implying a reciprocal and symmetric exchange between the realm of humans and that of game, in the shape of an everlasting mutual consumption that brings life and death to both. In this exchange, humans and game are alternatively partners (as souls and spirits)[24] and objects (as bodies). This applies to society itself, as a self-reproducing whole. The progressive loss of vitality linked to ageing, as well as death, is considered to be part of life's natural order. Sickness and death are not only a kind of payment to the spirits for the food that is given, but also the prerequisite for the provision of food for future generations.

However, at the level of an individual, insofar as one should eat before dying and be a hunter before becoming a quarry, this taking and giving back must be disconnected both in their carrying out and in time in order to allow individual life to happen. This is why everyone must produce offspring before dying, otherwise the exchange would not be perpetuated. According to tradition, an old hunter may go and 'give' himself back to the forest only when he has grandchildren.[25] A current practice aimed at delaying the deadly payment consists in feeding small wild animals kept captive at home or in smearing with fat small figurines made to represent such small wild animals, both known as *ongon*.

---

involves 'sharing'. 'Hunter-gatherers liken the unconditional way in which the forest transacts with people to the similarly unconditional transactions that take place among the people of a community, which in anthropological accounts come under the rubric of sharing.' (Ingold 2000: 44). 'Transaction' and 'sharing' imply that something is 'given' on both sides. We may think that what is unconditional is the principle of 'sharing'. This is what Siberian rituals are aimed at establishing. Unfortunately, the author gives no information about rituals and makes no distinction between 'representations' and other types of data.

[24] The spirits of game species are supposed to have flesh-eating species at their command to 'eat' human flesh.

[25] This is usually called 'voluntary death'. It seems to be a hunter's ideal death rather than the real occurrence.

It is believed that, if the *ongon* were not fed, the animal spirits would be still more eager to devour humans or would refuse them any piece of game.

Alliance Relationship as an Institutional Framework for Practical Use

Through the shaman's union with an animal spirit, these rituals establish institutional relations aimed at guiding the exchange of food. As a framework, the marriage alliance is the most constraining possible, since it determines an endless string: any man who marries a woman should give any daughter of hers to a husband, and so on. While the 'shaman marriage' expresses and supports alliance as an institutional framework of relations, its periodical updating guarantees its perpetuation. It is in this sense that the very idea of attributing spirits—i.e. subjectivity, intentionality, agency—to animals to make an alliance with them can be analysed as serving to legitimize hunting as such.

Comparative data may help stress what is at stake here. In his study devoted to the Kulung Rai of Nepal, Grégoire Schlemmer (2004) brings to light their conception of spirits of the forest or 'of the wild'. It is akin to that of the Siberian hunting peoples in many respects, with the exception of socialization. On the one hand, the Kulung Rai practise a ritual commemorating a primeval 'marriage' with the daughter of a spirit associated with 'Nature'. Yet this is a unique 'marriage', fixed in mythical times, and the ritual, performed by each household, has a strong domestic character; as if an alliance relationship had been established once and for all in bygone times, but with a spirit partner now fixed in houses and no longer associated with 'Nature'. On the other hand, the Kulung Rai have their soothsayers practise a kind of ritual aimed at repelling and chasing away any forest spirit, excluding any type of relationship with it. It is as though it were henceforth out of the question to set up new relations with the wild world for a society that no longer needs it to pursue its existence.

Moreover, the orientation of the Siberian 'shamanic alliance'—from human husband to animal spirit wife—is also paramount.[26] In Siberia, although women may also carry out shamanic rites, relationships between human females and male animal spirits are only conceivable in the form of imaginary love stories that never turn into marriage but always end in disaster. One may wonder whether such a male-oriented alliance with 'Nature' has something to do with the patrilineal rule in force in these societies. Be that as it may, it is tempting to transpose to Siberia a property of alliance that Ernst Kantorowicz brought to light with respect to English and French Medieval Kingships. This property, typical of many patrilineal societies observing exogamy, amounts to making the wife's goods inalienable and the husband responsible for them. Thus, by taking a wife from among wild species, the Siberian shaman would make himself responsible for his wife's goods—game—as inalienable. This might contribute to explaining why, in Siberian traditional shamanist societies, game cannot be sold (only furry animals can be sold and used individually), and why one should never take too much of it, never more than needed.[27]

Manipulating Reciprocity: Loyalty and Trickery

Whereas the 'shaman alliance' thread with its joyful and playful aspects largely predominates in the ritual, the other side of the coin is also featured, though in a quite different atmosphere. The end of this ritual stages the way the shaman carries out the duty of paying back for the promises of game he obtained during his long symbolic hunt. It is here that the antlers on his crown and the other elements that liken him to an elk or reindeer become particularly meaningful. After having appropriated this animal's male qualities, the shaman is now to copy its fatal destiny as quarry. For some time, he lies motionless on his back on a rug portraying a forest with wild animals, as if to offer his body to the spirits. In the mind of the audience, he is being

[26]For details, see Hamayon 1998.
[27]Kantorowicz 2000 [1989]: 802-17.

devoured by the animal spirits, part of his duty as a shaman. They eventually fear that he let himself be devoured for good and thus 'revive' him ritually.

Thus, from an analytical point of view, the shaman completes the whole exchange process on his own. His mimed 'self-offering' is intended to serve as a token of his community's future repayment to the spirits. It can be seen as a 'promise' of human vital force, as a guarantee that humans will respect the law of exchange fairly. As if to also convince his fellows that they will really have to pay, he proceeds with a delicate divinatory rite, which all of them attend with great emotion though in silence: under the guise of giving each of them indications as to their future, it concerns their life expectancy. Among the Yenissei Evenks for instance, the shaman shoots a miniature arrow through the smoke hole of the hut for each participant; the farther the arrow falls down outside the hut, the longer life will be. All are aware that some members of the community must die so that the others may go on living.

Still from an analytical point of view, the shaman's 'self-offering' also completes the alliance process: he can be considered to represent both a woman and a piece of game, whose statuses in the exchange relation are assimilated.

We may thus consider that this type of ritual encompasses the whole of the conceptual system and gives concrete expression to each of its articulations. Not only are the two key steps in the exchange process, taking and giving back, clearly distinguished; their simultaneousness would make human life impossible. Yet they are also dealt with in radically contrasting ways. Thus, the search—the explicit object of the ritual—lasts for the large majority of ritual time; divided up in a quest for a wife and a quest for game, it enhances the shaman's male status as the representative of humans in the animal spirit world; by unfolding in a lengthy and conspicuous manner in a cheerful and exuberant atmosphere, it is displayed as a metaphor of life. In a strikingly contrasted way, the last episodes only implicitly remind humans of the repayment duty: the shaman's role as a woman and a piece of game to be taken by the spirits is confined in motionlessness and silence, as a metaphor of death.

Shamanism in Hunting Life: 'Culture' Emerging from 'Nature'

This contrast reflects what appears to be a core principle in the shamanic handling of relations with animal spirits. While forcing the human partner to respect the law of exchange by losing vital force, the shamanic function is aimed at turning the exchange process to human advantage, in particular by trickery concerning the timing and amount of repayment. The art here is to delay and reduce human losses as far as possible. In other words, while claiming to be one among other species on an equal footing with animal species in 'Nature', humans impose their own social laws on animal spirits in order to put the exchange to the best possible use for themselves. In this light, shamanism appears to be a conceptual system peculiarly relevant to the topic in question by the 'Nature/Culture' pair, insofar as it is based on the claim that humans belong to 'Nature' and proceed by imitating animal species. By crowning his head with antlers, the shaman appropriates what is a weapon for the stag but makes merely symbolic use of it. He copies only those animal movements thought to be necessary for self-defence and reproduction, but still stands as a human does. The very fact of resorting to tricks is likened to luring modes of behaviour observed among animals.[28] Therefore, by drawing from the model of animals, shamanism does not violate the order of 'Nature'. The hunter's trickery is acknowledged as such. The playful framework is loyal to the spirits, leading as far as the

---

[28] I refer here to a widespread assumption, even though not many Siberian examples of it are found in literature about Siberia. Tricking is all the more acknowledged by hunting societies in that they observe similar behaviour among animals, in whose realm 'trickery and mimicry stand amongst the main engines of life' as remarked by two biologists, Nuridsany & Pérennou (1990: 8). The authors continue: 'Mimicry is a canvas woven by three protagonists: the model, the mime and the dupe. The model is the surrounding plant or mineral whose colour and shape the animal adopts in order to hide itself (camouflage). The mime is the one who imitates the model and benefits from the confusion it produces. The dupe is the keystone of the system and the source of its dynamics, as far as it guarantees the efficacy of trickery.'

eventual human losses: tricking, winning or losing are part of the rules of the game. The playful relationship with animal spirits is a positive experience and it is permeated with notions of pleasure, virility, freedom, fortune. More generally, the widespread use of the verb 'to play' to designate ritual action stresses how human and animal modes of behaviour are akin to one another.[29] Nor does 'playing' one's very best in order to win, as the shaman must do as the humans' representative, amount to violating the laws governing inter-species relations within 'Nature'. To take up the categories discussed here, we may say that shamanism is a type a 'Culture' that draws its shape from 'Nature', but consists in making use of animal behaviour patterns to human benefit, with the result that man's behaviour permanently differs from that of the animal being imitated.[30] In other words, while they objectively and explicitly assume the animal species to be on an equal footing with them, they subjectively and implicitly make full use of what they consider to be a human privilege, the faculty of conceiving— partially—'one kind of thing in terms of another'.

[29]'Playing' is a secondary meaning of many verbs that literally designate animal movements and a shaman's ritual gestures. See also Hamayon 1995, 1999–2000.
 [30]This entails a passing remark on the problems Siberian materials would pose for generalizing the perspectivist model that E. Viveiros de Castro and others elaborated on the base of South-Amerindian references. The Siberian form of shamanism implies that humans and spirit animals are similar (but not identical) in essence and equal in status, but excludes their being symmetrical to the extent that their perceptions could be reversible, for this would merely preclude the ritual action from operating. The shaman's marriage only socializes his animal spirit wife without making her into a human being or a person, which would render the established alliance relation useless. And the shaman only 'plays' with animal spirits according to his own rules that exclude their victory. I agree with Ingold on this point: '[...] the people themselves profess to be aware of but one world [...] This does not mean, of course, that they fail to differentiate between humans and animals. On the contrary [...] while humans may have sexual relations with certain other humans, and may kill and consume certain non-human animals, the consequences of categorical confusion [...] would be disastrous' (Ingold 2000: 49 quoting Scott 1989: 197).

Shamanism in Pastoral Life: 'Culture' Aimed at Domesticating Parts of 'Nature'

In all respects, pastoral life ties in with different relations to 'Nature', starting with geographical perceptions. Unlike the hunter's concern for the 'richness' of the forest, the herder's main concern is for pasturelands and nomadic routes, which are close to 'Nature' without actually belonging to it insofar as they are distinct from both the camps and the forest. However, the main landmarks are mountains or hills that overhang camps, pastures and routes. Even though covered with woods, they are not called *hangay*, but *hada* 'rocks' (whether really rocky or not) or, more rarely, *uula*. They are neither envisioned in a generic way nor personalized, but they are socialized, in that they are held to be involved in social relationships. In a herder's view, a mountain merges with the 'Mountain's Old Men' of the community, i.e. with their ancestors whose souls supposedly rest on the mountainsides and, from there, protect their flocks and pasturelands.[31] Thus, within 'Nature', they constitute a sub-category that remains implicit as such, but whose existence is evidenced by their being socialized as 'Old Men' or ancestors of specific descent lines. This sub-category may be characterized as well in terms of the naturalization of ancestors or the ancestralization of parts of 'Nature'.

The dead who cannot become ancestors for lack of descendants are significantly assigned *wild* sites as after-death rest places: lakes, sources, bushy groves ... that are peripheral to the herder's and the hunter's world.

On the whole, what matters for herders is spatial localization in the verticalized world of pasturelands, and hierarchy in social relations. They radically differentiate not only domestic animals from wild ones (especially when they both hunt and breed the same species), but also their respective meat: while game *obtained* from spirits is to be shared out, domestic meat *produced* thanks to one's ancestors' protection is owned personally. With respect

---

[31] E.J. Fridman 2004 also notes the Buryats' concerns for specific places *(locale)* associated with ancestors.

to rituals, they address ancestors with prayers and sacrifices—'playing' with them being considered as inconceivable. Now, on one hand, the logic of substitution engaged through sacrifice is deemed fair, in as much as domestic animals consist of bloody meat (like humans). On the other hand, it is also factually tricky and can be deemed deceitful, inasmuch as it consists in replacing a man by an animal—something more valued by something less valued. Such is explicitly the point of view of some groups who preserve a 'hunter's mentality' even while rearing animals, whereas no stockbreeder would consider the hunter's way of tricking animal spirits to be deceitful.[32] Contrary to the hunter's, the stockbreeder's trickery is not acknowledged as such. Along with offering substitutes to his ancestors, he can merely adopt an attitude of worship in order to disclaim any deceitful intention. From the hunter's point of view, the moral is: deception is reserved for human spirits, who are 'so stupid' (Hangalov 1958-1: 398-99 & 1960-III: 36, 43) as to let themselves be deluded.

Invention of Super-nature

The categories under discussion here may serve to formulate a few remarks in guise of a conclusion. The fact that Siberian peoples imagine spirits that animate the animals they hunt or herd, may be analysed in this way: what may be considered as their 'culture' consists in associating with 'Nature' a kind of symbolic double that may be called 'super-nature' and is aimed at establishing human-like relations with 'Nature'. It is through their, so to speak,

---

[32]The logic of substitution is likely to be indefinitely extended to new kinds of substitutes. In Buddhicized areas, sculptures of animals made of flour and covered with red paint meant to evoke blood are offered instead of real animals. Shamanist stockbreeders who are satisfied with sacrificing domestic animals denounce red-painted flour offerings, which, to their mind, are not edible food: either the deceitful giver is to be punished or the deities who let themselves be deluded in such a way are too stupid to be of any use.

'super-natural' double that natural beings or sites are socialized: wild animals through their spirits and mountains through ancestors' souls. In both cases, the establishment of a social relation with animal spirits or ancestors is a prerequisite to hunting wild animals in the forest or herding flocks on a mountainside.

I would like to argue that, apart from being tied to economic realities, the hunter's and the herder's ways of socializing 'Nature' also express 'cultural choices' that are part of their global relation to the world. The hunter, who objectively does not own any resources and therefore is totally dependent on his direct 'taking' from 'Nature' in order to survive, perceives himself as able to symbolically get the better of the 'super-nature' that animates it: this is what is ritually meant by 'playing'. Conversely, the herder, who, in conventional terms, has a 'productive' action upon 'Nature', or more exactly who possesses resources insofar as his ancestors have domesticated some species, perceives himself as being under his ancestors' domination: suitable ritual behaviour is worshipping. Their respective major concerns are inverted: what is paramount for the hunter is the life of the wild species, whereas for the herder, it is society's internal order. This explains that, as shown by the history of Siberia, small human groups disappear into the forest to escape from constraining human powers, even if it means being confined to the hard lifestyle of huntsmen. This may explain that one may practise 'herding with a hunter's mind', i.e. attempt to conciliate the choice of economic security with a taste for freedom, and from another perspective that, in the view expressed in the Ehirit-Bulagat epics, the hero's figure is not a leader's.[33] This might at last explain the present-day Western fashion that idealizes a fantasized shamanism 'close to Nature' like the hunter's.

This may also help to understand the present unanimous claim to be 'children of Nature' made by Siberian peoples while

---

[33] For this, having flocks is not enough, mastering social relations is also required (according to other versions of Geser's epic than the Ehirit-Bulagat); a leader's position can be reached only with the help of *tengeri* 'skies', a supernatural category hierarchically higher than ancestors.

being on the path to modernization, whatever their lifestyle, their view of and relation to 'Nature'. As a matter of fact, since a large part of them live in urbanized areas and are no longer involved in hunting and herding, they only have a very abstract and detached view of 'Nature', with very few practical consequences. The hunters' conception of supernatural mediators to negotiate with at least partly motivates this claim. When villagers and city-dwellers declare that shamanism and 'Harmony with Nature' are the basic principle of their own culture, they have in mind the set of attitudes this conception entails—which may also be interpreted as a refusal to submit to any power.

Epilogue

Although 'Nature' and 'Culture' may help characterize the analytical models drawn from Siberian data, these categories are nonetheless too vague, sometimes even misleading, to account for certain aspects of native conceptions. The hunting peoples of Siberia would not establish a 'shamanic alliance' with the spirits of species other than edible ones. Thus, not everything found in 'Nature' can be given the status of a spirit, unless via a misleading shortcut. Stones, trees, objects may be said to be 'animated' by the spirits they host temporarily or permanently (as the hills are by ancestors), but they do not have the properties required for spirits in the logic of these peoples' conceptual system. These properties, essential for communication with humans, are not only life (and therefore death) and subjectivity, but also (autonomous) mobility. Only humans and animals own all of these properties.[34] This precludes inferring a generalized animism of the natural world from the above definition of super-nature.[35]

[34] For this reason, plants cannot be assimilated to animals in a broad category of 'non-humans' as in Amazonia (Descola 2005).
[35] The spirits emanated from the souls of the deceased are clearly distinguished from those of living wild animals although they are also associated with 'natural' spaces.

References

Alekseev, Anatolii Afanas'evich. 1993. *Zabytyi mir predkov. Ocherki tradicionnogo mirovozzreniya evenov Severo-zapadnogo Verhojan'ja.* Jakutsk: Kif 'Sitim' Minist. po delam narodnostey Severa Respubliki Saha, 94 p.

Alekseev, Nikolai Alekseevich. 1975. *Tradicionnye religioznye verovaniya yakutov v xix—nachale xx v.* Novosibirsk: Nauka (Yakutskii filial) 1975, 199 p.

Descola, Philippe. 2005. *Par-delà nature et culture.* Paris: Gallimard.

Eliade, Mircea. 1951. *Le chamanisme ou les techniques archaïques de l'extase.* Paris: Payot.

Ferret, Carole. 2006. *Techniques iakoutes aux confins de la civilisation altaïque du cheval. Contribution à une anthropologie de l'action.* Thèse en anthropologie et ethnologie, École des Hautes Études en Sciences Sociales: Paris.

Fridma, Eva and Jane Neumann. 2004. *Sacred Geography. Shamanism among the Buddhist Peoples of Russia.* Budapest: Akadémiai Kiadó.

Hamayon, Roberte. 1990. *La chasse à l'âme. Esquisse d'une théorie du chamanisme sibérien.* Nanterre: Société d'ethnologie.

—— 1995. 'Pourquoi les "jeux" plaisent aux esprits et déplaisent à Dieu'. In G. Thinès and L. de Heusch eds. *Rites et ritualisation.* Paris/Lyon: Vrin. pp. 65–100.

—— 1998. 'Le sens de l'"alliance" religieuse: "mari" d'esprit, "femme de dieu"'. *Anthropologie et Sociétés* 22 (12): 25–48.

—— 1999–2000. 'Des usages de "jeu" dans le vocabulaire rituel du monde altaïque'. *Études mongoles et sibérienne*, special issue: *Jeux rituels.* 30–31: 11–45.

—— 2001. 'Nier la mort, simuler l'amour et rappeler la vie ou Le traitement funéraire du gibier abattu chez les peuples chasseurs de la forêt sibérienne'. In Liliane Bodson ed. *La sépulture des animaux: concepts, usages et pratiques à travers le temps et l'espace.* Liège: Université de Liège (Colloques d'histoire des connaissances zoologiques 12). pp. 107–28.

Hangalov, M.N. 1958–61. *Sobranie sochinenii.* Ulan-Ude: Buryatskii Institut Obshchestvenyh Nauk, 3 vols.

Homonov, M.P. 1961–64. *Abai Geser hubun. Epopeya (Ehirit-bulagatskii variant).* Ulan-Ude: Buryatskii Kompleksnii Nauchno-Issledovatel'skii Institut, 2 vols.

Ingold, Tim. 2000. *The Perception of the Environment. Essays in Livelihood, Dwelling and Skill.* London & New York: Routledge.

Kantorowicz, Ernst. 2000 [First edition 1957]. *Les deux corps du roi. Essai sur la théologie politique au Moyen âge* in *Œuvres.* Paris: Gallimard. Translated from: *The King's Two Bodies.* Princeton University Press.

Lavrillier, Alexandra. 2000. 'La taïga, berceau des Évenks. Les représentations de la nature chez un peuple altaïque de Sibérie'. *Boréales* 78-81: 25-44.

_____ 2005. *Nomadisme et adaptations sédentaires chez les Évenks de Sibérie postsoviétique: 'jouer' pour vivre avec et sans chamanes.* Thèse, École pratique des hautes études: Paris.

_____. 2007. Gestion duelle de l'espace à long terme chez les Évenks éleveurs de rennes et chasseurs des Monts Stanovoï: interférences ou cohérences des zones *sauvages* et *humanisées,* in S. Beyries et V. Vaté (dir.), *Les civilisations du renne d'hier et aujourd'hui. Approches ethnohistoriques, archéologiques et anthropologiques,* Antibes, éd. APDCA: 65-88.

Lommel, Andreas. 1967. *The World of the Early Hunters: Medicine-men, Shamans and Artists.* London: UK Evelyn, Adams and Mackay.

Lot-Falck, Évelyne. 1953. *Les rites de chasse chez les peuples sibériens.* Paris: Gallimard.

Maj, Emilie, 'Des tournants spatiaux: approche diachronique de la sémiotique du paysage en Sibérie', GéoCité [On line], Russie, Dossiers, updated: 12/11/2009, URL: *http://tice.caen.iufm.fr/revues/geocite/index.php?id=97.*

Nuridsany, Claude and Marie Pérennou. 1990. *Masques et simulacres.* Paris: Éd. du May.

Patkanov, S. 1906. *Opyt geografii i statistiki tungusskih plemen Sibiri na osnovanii dannyh perepisi naseleniya 1897 g. i drugih istochnikov.* St-Petersburg, Zapiski IRGO, XXXI, t.2.

Schlemmer, Grégoire. 2004. *Vues d'esprits. La conception des esprits et ses implications chez les Kulung Rai du Népal.* Thèse, Université Paris-X: Nanterre.

Viveiros de Castro, Eduardo. B. 1998. 'Cosmological deixis and Amerindian perspectivism'. *Journal of the Royal Anthropological Institute* 4: 469-88.

PART II
HIMALAYAN CASE STUDIES

To Be More Natural Than Others
Indigenous Self-determination and Hinduism in the Himalayas

Marie Lecomte-Tilouine

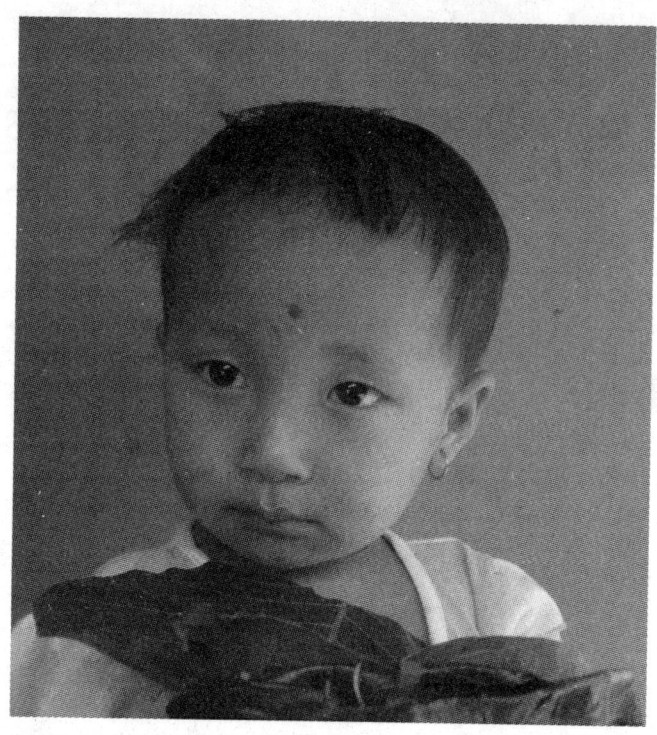

A Magar girl bringing leaf-plates for the ritual, Central Nepal
(Photo: Marie Lecomte-Tilouine)

To some extent, man's relationship with nature is built irrespective of it, and independent of the reality of actual practices. Within the context of present-day Nepal, this relationship between man and nature seems closely linked to the complex play of human relations in their construction of group identity. In particular, the Indigenous Peoples' symbolic relationship to nature, as expressed in their own printed writings, is obviously more closely linked to changes in their self-representation with regard to Hindu upper castes than to other types of changes in terms of economy or environment (disappearance of species, legislation on natural resources, etc.).

Broadly speaking, the way the Hindu upper castes and Indigenous Peoples defined their respective relationship to nature before the post-1990 Indigenous Peoples' revival can be defined as follows. The Hindu upper castes evoked their power to transform nature, and emphasized their ability to render a place auspicious by performing rituals, or a field fertile by irrigation. The worthiest crop grown was rice, which is the only crop accepted by major Hindu gods.[1] As for the ethnic groups who now define themselves as Indigenous Peoples (*adibasi*) or as Nationalities (*janajati*),[2] they referred, above all, to their contract with the spirits controlling nature, which allow them to legitimately exploit its resources.

With the 1990 people's movement and the introduction of multi-party democracy, popular protests and contesting views flourished. Hindu upper castes (Bahun-Chetris, or even Aryas, as they are now commonly called) started to be described as

---

[1] Within the numerous varieties of rice cultivated in Nepal, upper caste Hindus consider that dry rice, *gaya* or *pakhe dhan*, and high-altitude rice (*anga*, which is reddish) are not pure enough to be offered to gods. In some places, only the long maturing *jaran* variety of rice (which cannot reach maturity above 1,200 metres) may be used as ritual offerings. This clearly shows the link between low-altitude irrigated cultivation and Hindu culture.

[2] These two appellations were adopted in the 1980s by the ethnic minorities of Nepal to distinguish themselves from the rest of Hindu society in which they are integrated. I therefore refer to them as Indigenous Peoples or Janajatis in these pages.

harmful exploiters of nature and people. On the other hand, the Janajatis who had long been portrayed as naive savages by their Hindu neighbours, developed the idea that they were the guardians of nature, and promoted their 'indigenous spirituality' and 'knowledge'.

This reversal which came about over the last fifteen years and on which we will focus, is only roughly associated with a transformation in lifestyles, but it suddenly appeared within a new national socio-political context, forging ties with international organizations. The Nepalese Indigenous Peoples have been influenced by a global ideology and have become active agents in international indigenous rights movements. At the same time, they have constructed their own identity within the Hindu fold—a specific context in which the upper caste Hindus dominated them.

. Before 1990, Indigenous Peoples and Hindu upper castes' relationships with nature were reflected in the ritual functions assigned to each of these two groups. Since their encounter during the medieval period, when the Hindu groups migrated towards the Himalayan region, the Janajatis have maintained or more probably have been assigned a role of priest to the earth gods,[3] while the Hindu upper castes have mainly been used by the Janajatis as purifiers during the two most polluting stages of life: birth and death. During the same period of time, the Janajatis were relegated to or confined to the highlands while upper caste Hindus progressively cultivated the lowlands suitable for irrigated rice. However, this is a statistical outline and in reality, the hilly region of Nepal is composed of multi-ethnic and multi-caste settlements where it is difficult to draw any clear-cut boundaries between the groups, their practices and even their values, except concerning a few points.

The Hindu upper castes described their presence as an operator allowing the transformation of *jangal* into *mangal*, or wilderness into auspiciousness, but the Janajatis opposed their inalienable bond to the land. As a consequence, the former remained immigrants notwithstanding their ancient settlement on Nepal's

---

[3] M. Lecomte-Tilouine, 1996.

present-day territory, which, in most cases, dates back several centuries. However, it is likely that until recently, they continued to migrate within the Himalayan range to a much wider extent than the Janajatis. At any rate, Hindu upper castes still retain an image of themselves as clearers and irrigation entrepreneurs, wandering in search of suitable new places to be irrigated or improved. Until the 1970s, cultivation and irrigation were strongly encouraged by the authorities: they thus fulfilled the vows of Hindu kings and their representatives (the village headmen), who received extra revenues through taxes on newly-cultivated land (and especially on irrigated land where taxes were higher).

By way of illustration, a Nepali novel written at the end of the nineteenth century depicts this in a dialogue between the King of Pyuthan (Western Nepal) and a high-caste newcomer:[4]

> King Udayasan: Who are you and where do you come from?
> —O Great King, I am the headman Tanhausimha Thakur and those who came with me are Brahmans, Kshatriyas, Vaishyas, Shudras of the four births and thirty-six colours (*car jat, chattis varna*). Our village was located on the bank of the Kali Ganga, in the kingdom of Palpa. Our houses, rice-fields and dry fields were carried away by a flood. This is why we came to clear lands here. We will pay you taxes and will raise your cattle.

For a long time, cultivation remained synonymous with culture and civilization in the Nepalese hills. It is not surprising in this context that the founding King of Nepal (eighteenth century) used the most carefully tilled soil, the garden, as a metaphor to designate his kingdom.

Today, despite profound social and ritual differences, the way the environment is exploited in the same altitudinal belt hardly differs between the groups of diverse origins that make up the Nepalese population, and that usually cohabit in multi-ethnic villages. As shown by Philippe Sagant's study (1976), agricultural techniques and practices were very homogeneous in Eastern

[4] G. Joshi, 1965: 212.

Nepal in the 1970s. Nevertheless, Sagant's informants claim that terrace cultivation and the use of the plough were introduced by Hindu groups and adopted by the indigenous Limbus when they came in close contact during the nineteenth century.[5] A survey carried out at the end of the 1980s in a multi-ethnic village of central Nepal documented a uniformity of agro-pastoral practices between Hindu castes and local Janajatis (Magars).[6] There, the disparities between high castes, Magars and low castes were mainly related to wealth, since land, rice production and the number of heads of cattle (especially buffaloes) ran parallel to the social hierarchy. However, the high castes had a marked tendency to privilege irrigated rice, by frequently transforming a dry field yielding two crops into an irrigated field yielding only one. The Magars, on the other hand, had closer contact with the forest, because they raised numerous cows and goats which they led to the forest to graze; the high castes, on their part, invested more in buffaloes, which could be kept in sheds. However, the Magars' proximity with the forest did not corroborate their idea that they were less harmful to the forest than their high-caste neighbours, since grazing their cows and goats was more harmful to the forest's renewal than selectively cutting fodder from species that are plentiful and sparing the endangered ones, such as the *ningalo* bamboo.

The image of civilized and mobile Hindu groups bringing auspiciousness and rice civilization with them somehow lasted until the end of the partyless Panchayat period (1962–90) during which the 'development' of the country played a role analogous to government incentives to cultivate and irrigate land during the Shah and Rana periods (1769–1951). Indeed, development then also focused on irrigation, with huge amounts of money being spent on irrigation channels. This benefited lowland landowners, who, for the most part, were Hindu upper castes.

[5] Ph. Sagant's observation is corroborated by our study on the different types of ploughs in the Himalayan range (Dollfus, P., Lecomte-Tilouine, M, and O. Aubriot: 2001), which shows that the Indigenous Peoples of Eastern Nepal use the same type of plough as their high-caste neighbours.
[6] Lecomte-Tilouine, M. and C. Michaud, 2000.

From the point of view of the Indigenous Peoples of Nepal, they alone partake in nature and represent its oldest creatures. In a movement reciprocal to that of their own creation, they stress that their ancestors in turn fashioned nature through their work and fertilized it by their own corporal substances, their sweat and blood. They view themselves, therefore, both as 'sons of the earth' (*bhumiputra*) and as 'fathers of the earth' (*bhumipitra*). Through these expressions they associate identity with territory, and establish a genealogical link with their environment, which they conceive as an organic being with which they share common substance.[7] Anywhere outside the 'ancestral territory', they experience a feeling of ill-being, suggesting that the territory acts as a generator which fuels their sense of existence. Hindu people, on the other hand, do not maintain such strong links with a delimited space, like ancestral territory, but are loosely bound to a vast holy land, which covers the Himalayan range and India. They acquire rights over a specific place by conquest, which seals their ruler's alliance with the earth, the king being the *bhupati*, master/husband of the earth. As a spouse, Hindu earth is depicted as a weak female figure to be protected by the king.

Believing themselves to be the living representatives of the oldest human societies, and sharing the weakness projected by the Hindus over the natural realm, the Janajatis have the feeling that their culture is in danger of extermination. It is threatened by acculturation and still further, by the cultural genocide which the Hindus are accused of perpetrating. To remedy the situation, they evoke the duty of the Hindu king to protect Nature, asking for protection like endangered animal species, and for the nation to again become the garden of thirty-six human groups,[8] as when it was founded, and for each group to recover its own culture and territory of origin.

[7]This vital link is often mentioned. For instance, for K. Bhattachan (n.d.): 'Land, water, forest, and pasture are life and blood of Indigenous peoples.'
[8]This image of Nepal was formulated by its founding king, Prithvi Narayan, in his memoirs.

To Define Oneself as Indigenous

None of the sixty-one Indigenous Peoples officially recognized by the Nepalese government in 1997 declared themselves Hindu. It would have denied the very basis of what constitutes a Janajati group in their eyes: 'One's own language, religion, and costume'.

However, the 'own' of the Janajatis does not distinguish some from others, it being understood that they were all born from common Mongol or Kirant ancestors. In the same manner, their 'own' includes Buddhism despite its status as a world religion. In fact, the Janajati identity relies mainly on distancing themselves from Hindu people and their religion that form *the* referent of the Janajatis' self-determination. This referent was generally used in a positive manner until 1990, when it suddenly became negatively connoted in the new political context. This reversal was expressed by a sudden desanskritization movement, which put an end to the ancient sanskritization process which had so far been at work among the Janajatis.[9]

Bearing in mind the linguistic and cultural diversity of Nepalese Janajatis, they succeeded in forming a unit by negation, mainly in withdrawing from caste society. This feature often qualifies the Indigenous Peoples or Janajatis in Nepal, with definitions such as: 'Indigenous groups are those that do not belong to the four *varna* [Hindu classes]',[10] or, more simply, 'Indigenous are the non-Hindu groups'.

The Janajatis, who mingled with the vast Hindu nebula for a long time, are primarily defined in an ideal or genealogical way, since 'Indigenous People refer to these communities ... which do not assert Hinduism as their traditional and original religion'.[11]

The present-day reality of a specific group's practices or values is thus not a determining factor: only their genesis is relevant,

---

[9] On desanskritization, see M. Lecomte-Tilouine, 2002.

[10] This self-definition is now also used by the Nepalese government, which contrasts with its attitude of incorporating the indigenous groups in Hindu society, made explicit in the Code of the country up until the 1960s.

[11] A definition quoted in *Himal*, vol. 7, no. 5, Sep/Oct 1994, p. 26.

hence the crucial role of history in self-determination and group identity.

Between Buddhism and Naturism

The simple negative definition 'non-Hindu' did not fit neatly into any religious box for the national census. One of the options adopted by the Janajatis and more so by those who decide for them (the ethnic associations' management committees), is to declare themselves Buddhists. Buddhism undoubtedly constitutes a convenient identity, which does not imply exclusion or degradation in contemporary Hindu society. By preaching peace and non-violence, it appears to be a particularly correct form of religiousness, which allows each individual to follow his path without harming anyone. It also fits in well with opposition to the Hindus since it was fought by the latter in the past. Last but not least, Prince Siddhartha was born in a region currently inhabited by Tharu and Magar Indigenous Peoples. The latter therefore consider Buddha as their ancestor and the religion he founded, as an indigenous creation. Foreshadowing the current ethnic revival, Buddha is sometimes even presented as the first indigenous martyr, victim of the Brahmans, as in Nar Bahadur Limbu's poem, 'The Murder of Buddha':

> You are Kirant, O Buddha, who acts for the beings' well-being ...,
> a Brahman killed you by giving you poison ...,
> nature had placed a stony heart in him.[12]

A good half of Nepalese Indigenous Peoples thus adopted Buddhism as their label, regardless of the link between their collective declaration and actual religious practices.[13]

[12]'Buddhako hatya', in N.B. Limbu, 2050 VS: 20–23.
[13]The percentage of those who declared themselves Buddhist in the census, which indicates individual adhesion even though collective instructions are circulated to reply to it correctly, actually increased, from 7.5 to 10.5 per cent of the total Nepalese population between 1991–2001.

However, this path to salvation was not unanimously endorsed. It should be said that it was brutally imposed in some cases, as among the Magars, who are strongly Hinduized, and currently comprise more than one and a half million individuals in Nepal. The Magar Association's national committee decided that all members of the group were to declare themselves Buddhists at the 2001 census, contrary to the opinion of a number of Magars who considered themselves Hindu.[14] This self-identification with Hinduism was hardly an obstacle for Magar activists, as it was easily attributed to ignorance: 'Today, except for some ignorant Magars who did not understand, all Magars agree on the fact that the Magars, like the other nationalities, are Non-Hindus.'[15]

On the other hand, the adoption of Buddhism meets another type of opposition which is much more difficult to circumvent. It is formulated by Keshar Jang Baral (2058 VS: 7) who protested against the Magar Association, which is trying to transform the 'Magars who venerate Nature, into Buddhists ... in the name of the fight against brahmanocracy and would thus erase their original basis'. Lok Bahadur Thapa (1995: 12) expresses a similar opinion: 'Some Magars say that Hindu religion should not be abandoned, others follow the Buddhist path, but Magars are worshippers of Nature.'[16] This idea is found among other Janajatis of Nepal, such as the Gurungs (or Tamus): 'They [the Hindu rulers] made a code of law which transformed into Hindus the Nature worshippers that are the Tamus' (Mekh Sim Kle Tamu, 2058 VS: 7).

Thus the alternative available to the Indigenous Peoples of Nepal in their self-determination was to promote a great religion influencing a number of them but with which many could never relate, or to promote a rather vague set of practices and values to the status of religion.[17] In their need to emphasize their autonomy,

---

[14]The campaign was partially successful, with 25 per cent of the Magars indicating Buddhism as their religion in 2001.
[15]Suresh Ale Magar (1992–93: 12).
[16]*Lapha*, 1995, vol. 3, no. 11.
[17]At the political level which is represented by the collective religious label of each Janajati group, this alternative appears in the fact that the other

the Nepalese Janajatis named their religious practices, which were considered up to that point 'nameless', as reminiscences, or as the popular part of Hinduism or Buddhism. They chose to call it 'natural religion'. However, this newly named religion does not yet figure in the national census, contrary to the Kirant religion, which officially appeared in 1991. The term Kirant (or Kirat) is used to designate the Limbus, Rais and Sunuwars, or the Janajatis of Eastern Nepal, yet today it tends to once again assume its original textual meaning of 'tribal' by including all the Nepalese Janajatis. In the 2001 census, 3.6 per cent of the Nepalese population declared that they profess a Kirant religion, which, according to Ch. Subba (2000: 107), is synonymous with 'religion of nature':

> Though their religion is known as Kirat religion, which is named after the Kirat nation, they are basically animists or nature worshippers.

In Nepal, 'natural religion' (*prakritik dharma*), 'religion of Nature' (*prakritiko dharma*) and 'naturism'[18] (*prakritivad*) are used synonymously. This form of religion is sometimes defined as equivalent to animism (*jivavad*), to shamanism (*jhankrivad*), or to Bon (viewed as a pre-Buddhist religion addressing the elements of nature), or as including them. The Janajatis' religious quest paralleled their movement of opposition to the dominant groups in Nepal, a fact which might explain why 'natural religion' is still not officially recognized. In India as well, where the Janajati movement is older than the one in Nepal, the label animism is used to designate 'tribal religion'. It has a negative connotation for Hindus and they claim that it was introduced by British missionaries to alienate the Janajatis from the 'national mainstream':

> Government is led by the assumption, insidiously set afloat by the foreign missionaries that since the janajatis worship trees,

---

half of the 61 indexed Janajati groups chose to present themselves as nature worshippers, not as Buddhists.

[18]This term differs from naturalism, a philosophy.

stones and serpents they are 'animists' and cannot be called Hindus. ... Do not the Hindus all over the country worship the trees?[19]

In Nepal, the Indigenous Peoples were barely influenced by foreign missionaries; instead, they developed a sense of autonomy along with the political liberalization of the 1990s.

To Be a Non-Hindu Naturist

The Janajatis preach a return to origins and intend to operate a *tabula rasa* of their alienation and domination by erasing 'foreign' Hindu influences. Their movement appears both as a kind of anti-clerical and rationalist trend as well as a manifestation of the crisis that Hinduism is facing, in particular its social morphology in hierarchical groups, now considered by many as incompatible with democracy and modernity.[20] To do away with a past seen as alienation supposes indigenous intellectuals capable of elaborating its reasoned criticism, of reconstructing its supposed stages and effects, within a context suitable for this exercise of distanciation. The role imparted to their relationship with nature in this process is twofold. The Nepalese Janajatis adopted an ecological ideology, which defines cultural and political domination as a corollary of a more global attitude of domination towards nature, and developed the idea that they are part of nature. The two ideas converge: once respect for nature is assimilated

---

[19] From 'Nailing the Lie of Animism', *www.hindubooks.org*. The quoted passage follows these words: 'The sense of alienation from the national mainstream that the janajatis (the "tribals") now feel is mainly due to the handiwork of the British. ... While the converts from janajati Hindus are designated in the census as Christians, the rest are enumerated as merely various "tribal" entities as distinct from Hindus.'
[20] In a declaration adopted at the First Asian Conference on the Rights of Indigenous/Tribal peoples of Asia, Chiang Mai, Thailand, May 18–23, 1993, the demand was made that 'casteism' would be recognized as a form of racism.

with respect for others, the Janajatis' self-determination as being an integral part of this nature to be respected and protected, results in a demand for specific rights. It places the Janajatis in an advantageous position in terms of legitimacy. This is especially true in a country where nature protection is a considerable source of income via international agencies, and where the sovereign was seen as the protector of the Mother kingdom.

Yet, despite its strength and its international legitimacy, the Janajati naturist movement faces certain difficulties in defining itself as autonomous and resistant in the Hindu context. Indeed, contrary to monotheist religions, with a limited corpus of sacred texts, or a single one, the endless Hindu polytheist universe renders the elaboration of a clear-cut opposition difficult. This opposition is rendered more difficult by ecological or naturist trends which also developed in many neo-Hindu movements and in modern Hinduism in general. Within these trends, ancient ritual practices are reinterpreted as old empirical scientific knowledge related to the environment and its protection. Thus, for S. R. Devkota:[21]

> The Vedas and the Upanishads mention that the Gods and Goddesses favor different biological resources. Knowledge of biodiversity, interrelation between living species and the environment, the need to maintain natural dynamics ... are mentioned ... Therefore, ecology was a sacred science for Vedic man.

In addition, the classical Hindu attitude towards nature is complex. The Hindu king's priority is to have his 'garden' well cultivated, but he should also protect wilderness, since his favourite sport is hunting, and furthermore, it is the abode of gods and ascetics, whose way of life represents the ideal for any Hindu. A stay in the forest brings merit to the Hindu householder and prepares him for the other life. He then breaks social

[21] 'Veda and Ecological Economics', in *www.environmentnepal.com*, 2003.

conventions and adopts a symbiotic attitude with the wild environment, with which he is literally intended to merge, by taking the form of an anthill or of a hillock covered by mushrooms, in the course of his meditation.[22]

This ideal is a commonly highlighted aspect of the Hindu relationship to nature, and one whereby Hindus commonly distinguish themselves from Westerners, by using the same arguments as the Janajatis with regard to themselves:

> An Indian's relation with nature differs from that of a Western man. In the West, man has separated himself from nature, mastered it, he believes, and used it to serve his own purpose. The Hindu unites himself with nature. From nature he came, to nature he returns as ashes. The relationship between a Hindu and nature is one of adaptation and coexistence rather than of mastery and subjection.[23]

However, for Hindus, the stay in the forest implies a radical break with the social group and its practices, whereas it is the reverse for the Janajatis, who claim that their original existence and only true culture, is to stay close to nature and to venerate it. For the former, the stay in the forest is individual[24] and beyond any social standards, even if it is normal to undertake it; for the latter, it is this distance from nature which produces anomie and even, in the long term, the complete disappearance of the group and its culture. In the Hindu imagination, the stay in the forest leads the ascetic to live in close contact with tribal people, who, along with trees and animals, constitute their perception of the woodland world. Shiva, the god who presides over this extra-mundane sphere, embodies a common figure between Hindus and the indigenous, in his wild shape of Kiranteshwar, 'the Lord of

---

[22] The Hindus normally leave for the forest alone to increase their merit, but their collective migration towards the wild Himalayas also presents a virtuous character in local mythology, as it would have been undertaken to safeguard the Hindu texts and customs from Muslim invaders.

[23] 'Nature Worship', *www.Atributetohinduism.com*.

[24] Leaving with one own's wife is only a transitory stage.

the Kirant'.[25] Yet, far from reconciling the two groups, Kiranteshwar is one Hindu figure that poses conceptual problems for the Janajatis in their anti-Hindu movement, and who provides them at the same time with proof that Hinduism is an incoherent religion born from muddled brains. They wonder today,

> 'How it may be that Brahmans venerate the lord of the Kirants whereas they do not let Kirants enter their house?'[26]

The same concerns emerge in a much more provocative expression under Gopal Gurung's pen (1998: 7):

> Shiva also was non-Aryan and non-Hindu; but he is venerated as Mahadev, greater than other Hindu gods. All Hindu devotees offer milk shower even to his linga (penis), they bow to it, worship it—a real piece of scene worth to see in their temples.

Following the same logic, Anabir Somei Magar draws the following conclusion from Shiva's Kirant nature (2053 VS: 3): 'Shiva was Kirant, and of Mangol origin. This means that Rais, Limbus and Kirants should be considered superior to Brahmans.'

For a long time however, the Kirants had developed an opposing perspective, by identifying their gods with great Hindu figures, as in the history of the Kirants by Imansim Chemjong (n.d.). In this account, Hindu gods reveal that they are one with the Kirant gods and the Kirant sacred text is sometimes called Rig Veda and sometimes by its Kirant name, Mundhun:

> When men thrived in the world, the ill deeds became numerous. A man named Yehang made austerities and obtained to speak

---

[25]This name used to designate tribal people in Hindu texts is employed by the Janajatis of Eastern Nepal (and more recently by all Nepalese Janajatis).

[26]Based on a conversation with Bhim Bahadur Gharti. Magars often reproach Brahmans for forbidding them entry to their houses, whereas they let their dogs enter. This idea is commonly expressed much more forcefully by: the Brahmans let their dogs that eat the Magars' excreta enter their houses, while they themselves are forbidden entry.

with the Supreme Being: ... 'humans are born and die such as animals. O Supreme Being, by which knowledge shall humans separate pure from impure, render pure the impure at birth and death?' The Supreme Being gave him the Rig Veda written on a skin as well as the knowledge to read it. Before the others, he taught the Kirants to read and write ... Later, this alphabet was lost because Kirants made war.

However, the holy alphabet was again given to the Kirants, this time by the Hindu goddess Saraswati, under the following circumstances:

In the 9th century, King Sri Janga restored peace and practised such austerities as it caused the appearance of Saraswati. The king asked for the gift of an alphabet and the goddess led him to the foot of mount Phoktang Lung. A door opened in the wall, leading to an enlightened cave whose walls were covered with inscriptions. From there, a second door opened, leading to another similar room ... The seventh door opened on the last room where the goddess indicated the last inscription and declared: 'Listen, O king, I am the wife of the Supreme Being who made the creation according to my instructions ... You Kirants, I wanted to make you wise, but you made war ... Thus, I left the Kirant country to go to Tibet. There, they listened to me ... Today I give you this last alphabet, learn how to read it, write it and diffuse it in your country.' ... The king read the inscription and copied it on a stone, then he returned with it and taught it to his people.

The story then relates a second disappearance of this knowledge following a two-sided acculturation, but stresses that some individuals secretly preserved it.

Later, Kirants became Hindu in the South and Tibetan in the North, using the Devanagari and Tibetan alphabets, but some people kept hidden the use of the old alphabet. In 1740, Kirants revolted against the Tibetan kings of Sikkim and a Kirant pandit, Sri Janga Devasimha, with eight disciples, started to propagate again King Sri Janga's alphabet. He was caught by Tibetans, and told them: 'I am King Sri Janga's avatar, I cannot be killed by a sabre or a spade'. Then they tied him to a tree and killed him with poisoned arrows.

The history of the Kirants seems to repeat itself over again, as:

In 1925, the Kirants of Kalimpong organised a meeting where Imansim Chemjong brought Kirant books, read them, and told the history of this alphabet and the martyr of Sri Janga Devasimha. The whole assembly then rose and shouted: 'we must learn the kirant alphabet'. So old books were sought in the villages, people learned how to read and write. The Mundhum, the text received from the Supreme Being, was written down in 1931. Then guru Phalgunanda and his 500 disciples went from village to village to spread the alphabet, to preach non-violence and to open kirant temples.

The Kirants' history depicts alternating contrasted phases, with the Kirants presented as oscillating between wilderness, orality, brutality and acculturation on the one hand, and erudition, asceticism and culture on the other. Yet, Kirant culture is supposed to have been safeguarded through the ages as a hidden treasure concentrated in its alphabet, which, ready-made and concealed in the heart of nature, was offered to them as a present by Hindu gods.

Another precursor of the ethnic movement, Santabir Lama, who published his work about the Tamangs around 1960, also saw a regressive evolution movement in the worship of nature by several Janajatis, and considered that it was a late development born from the impossibility of practising Buddhism due to a shortage of priests.[27]

The idea of the loss of an elaborate ancient civilization is still an important feature of the Janajati identity: thus, as we have

---

[27]He writes in *Syebu Syemu* (2016 VS: 14): 'It seems to me that the Magars, Sunuwars, Thamis and Hayus, as well as the Eastern Gurungs, because they couldn't find lama Buddhist priests, started to follow a savage religion (*jangali dharma*)'.

already seen, the Magars and Tharus claim to be the descendants of Buddha, and the Gurungs are now using 'secret genealogies' to reconstruct their past. If this idea persists, the most recent wave of Janajati revival since 1990 emphasizes the link to nature, which now forms its most distinctive feature. The Nepalese Janajati movement is thus neither simple nor monolithic: apart from the fact that different ideas coexist, sometimes in the same publication, the movement is heterogeneous for having been elaborated in different contexts depending on the groups and periods.[28] Although today all Janajatis profess unity, one can spot the Kirant groups of Eastern Nepal who started their revival as early as the 1920s during the authoritarian Rana regime, and whose rediscovered culture was disseminated by ascetics, leading to Kirant sectarism. The revival of the Tamangs of Central Nepal dates back to the 1960s, during the partyless panchayat regime, but it was less influential than among the Kirants, probably because of the high illiteracy rate among Tamangs and because of their strong Buddhization. Thus Singman Tamang (2004: 34–5) does not think it suitable to follow 'the path leading to the wild Age and the Stone Age' (*jangali ra dhungeyugtirakai marg*) in the twenty-first century. He considers that Tamang shamans (*jhankri*) are responsible for Christian conversions among Tamangs and deplores the fact that some Tamang authors attributed more importance to the shamans than to Buddhism and identified the Tamang culture in shamanic practices. As he notes: 'there are Jhankris among all the castes, and all the groups.' Finally a general move by all the Janajatis emerged with the 1990 People's Movement. Within this more recent wave, Magars probably form the most interesting case. Having been in contact historically with only Hindus, and therefore deeply Hinduized, the Magars were deprived of any cultural treasure around which they might have become federated, and their situation was particularly

---

[28]A good example of this type of work is that of H.B. Budha Magar (2049 VS), who presents several historical scenarios without choosing one alone or without trying to reconcile them.

favourable to the construction of a radical opposition. Their rediscovery of 'their' alphabet is as recent as 1992 with the publication of M.S. Thapa's book (2049 VS). Following a rather complicated history, this founding account leads the Magars to the Middle East and to the very origin of humanity, while the Kirants situate their culture at the heart of their local wild nature. Unlike the Kirant account, the Magar accounts ignore internal conflicts between indigenous groups or with Tibetans. This leaves room for a single form of antagonism between Janajatis and Hindus on which they founded the whole political history of Nepal. This movement of simplification led to a transformation of the long-standing Hindu neighbours into invaders and oppressors, though the latter also see Nepal as a land marked by their own culture, also for being the residence of their greatest gods and legendary figures. Moreover, until recently, the Magars perceived their high caste Hindu neighbours as close relatives and their distanciation implied a reversal of the strategies they had so far deployed. Indeed, deprived of any federation and means of communication, the Magars, like most Janajatis, had built their identity by slipping into the mould the Hindus made for them, thus describing themselves as the offspring of degraded individuals of royal caste who had found refuge in the forest, or as the wild descendants of Shiva. These pre-1990 myths of origin appear to derive already from contact between Hindus and Janajatis, and to reflect the latter's strong association with the wilderness, even when residing in the same village and sharing the same life-style as the Hindus.

The Janajatis were apparently never able to achieve self-determination, independently of the image projected on them by the dominant Hindus, and, as a matter of fact, any previous attempts to evade things natural were in vain. Thus, when Santabir Lama published the *Tamba kaiten*, the founding text of the Tamang group, around 1960, he introduced it in these terms:

> We were like a wild group. Thanks to the collection of the Tamba bards' oral texts, today Tamangs can say to the face of the world

what their old culture is: their songs, their language, their religious notions, ... because with the disappearance of the bards, the culture of the Tamang group had disappeared. (Lama 2022 VS: jha).

Yet, the rediscovered culture found by the Tamangs in this corpus, and which drives them away from wilderness, is precisely qualified as 'natural' by Surya Bikram Gyawali, the Brahman historian who wrote the Foreword to the book (at the request of the author, his friend). Gyawali comments:

These songs make only one body with nature. They explain to us how reality is understood by people who have a natural life (*prakritik jivan*). (Lama 2022 VS: jha)

This dialogue which fell on deaf ears suggests that the concepts of 'natural group', of 'natural culture' and 'religion' never ceased to be attributed to the Janajatis by the Hindus, before being appropriated and reified by the former to finally oppose the latter.

The reversal of perspective was made possible when the Janajatis accessed new concepts exceeding the local dominant Hindu culture, and in particular, when they participated in the forums organized by the UN in 1993 during the year of the Indigenous Peoples, and over the two subsequent decades, declared by the UN as the Indigenous Peoples Decades. In this broadened universe, Hindus no longer formed *the only* reference, but became assimilated, in the eyes of the Janajatis, into a vast human grouping of colonizers and dominators akin to Westerners. In the words of Mekh Sim Kle Tamu: 'Aryas acted in India like the English in America'.[29] With such an assessment, decolonization emerges as a possible issue, and attracted the Janajatis:

After three hundred years of reign, the British had to leave India and Africa. Now shall the Aryas leave Nepal? This is the great question which arises for the natives of Nepal. (Kle Tamu, 2058 VS: 7)

[29] Mekh Sim Kle Tamu, no date.

The Janajatis claim that they first suffered from the 'Arya' invasion, colonization and spoliation. But the form of colonization they were subsequently subjected to, in the name of nation building, inflicted far greater damage: though not a question of physical violence, forced assimilation and programmed acculturation had more dramatic consequences, it simply led to their total eradication.[30] An author such as Mekh Sim Kle Tamu (2058 VS: 7) asserts that the Hindu government erased the 'naturalness' (*prakritikatva*) of the country during the building of the Nepalese nation. By that, he does not mean a deterioration of the environment, or misuse of resources, but the eradication of 'natural' cultures. Today, as he continues to explain in what way Nepal lost its naturalness, 'even in Gurung villages, one does not hear Gurung spoken. And the Gurung stories are told by Brahmans, Gurung shows are performed by Brahmans' (*ibid.*).

Thus the Janajati naturist movement understands nature not only in its generally accepted meaning, but as also consisting of the human groups that partake in it and are threatened with extermination via acculturation. As a remedy, before it is too late, they ask for protection, through the creation of autonomous territories. This somehow calls to mind reserves for wild animals, where domestic species with which the former can reproduce, are forbidden in order to avoid debasing the race (such as the Wild Buffalo Reserve in Koshi Tapu).

But the Janajati request for protection against their acculturation is not based on the wild/domestic distinction, which in their eyes is not a definitive form; domestic buffaloes were commonly released in areas inhabited by wild buffaloes, which fertilized them, since their owners did not wish to breed males and females that did not provide any milk. The domestic and the wild species are distinguished by their environment alone: when the Magars of Northern Gulmi catch small wild animals such as partridges, pheasants or chickens, they raise them at home and immediately

[30] Contribution submitted by the Asian Indigenous Peoples Act, 3 June 1993 (A/CONF.157/PC/42/Add.12).

consider them domestic (*ghar paluva*). In a similar but counter move, in a number of rituals, they 'return' a chicken or a zebu to the forest so that it becomes wild. And in spite of their different environments, domestic species are still closely related to their wild counterparts as even the most domesticated of them, the dog, is said to never bark when a jackal comes to steal a chicken, because they are said to be like maternal uncle and nephew.

As the simple fact of being released into the wilderness transforms a domestic animal into a wild one and *vice versa*, the Janajatis express the idea that the natural purity of their groups can be restored by a return to their origins and the reconstruction of original indigenous territories. Acculturation, like domestication, is thus conceived as a reversible process, a fact that illustrates Haudricourt's thesis that there is a correlation between relation to nature and social practices.[31]

While domestication is not conceived as a definitive alteration of the species, by contrast, crossbreeding is very negatively perceived. Crossbreeds are designated in Nepali by the term *kachara*, which is used both for crossbreeds in the animal and human realms. In both cases, a *kachara* is defined as the offspring of two different *jati*. This term corresponds to species when speaking of animals, and to caste or ethnic group when speaking of humans. The worst form of acculturation for the Janajatis, because it is irreversible, is inter-group marriage.

An Undifferentiated World of Origins

'Religion of nature' is viewed as the original religion of Nepal, that of the Indigenous Peoples before immigration by the Aryas. This epoch is the Janajati Golden Age, which they forfeited, yet in which they never ceased to partake. This link to the past is understood in an evolutionary manner, using historical materialism. The Magars' strong preference for hunting, for example, or even their grouped dwelling is said to reveal the antiquity of their cultural

[31] See Haudricourt 1964.

development, contrary to the Hindus who build their homes far from others, a feature linked to the 'age of slavery'.[32] For Jagman K. Lam Tamu (2056 VS: 241), the practice of piercing an animal's body to offer it up in sacrifice, performed by some Tamus, indicates the age of their culture, estimated by the author to be 10–15,000 years old. In order to rediscover this religion of origins, current ritual practices, thought to result directly from this age and performed by individuals who have remained untouched by Hindu influences, should be adopted: 'the worships addressed to nature by Gurungs and Magars of the mountainous areas are "living history" (*jiudo itihas*)'. (Anonymous 2058 VS: 28)

The Janajati Golden Age presents two characteristics: there was no division between humans, no conflict, yet there existed a certain void in people's minds. Social division is foreign to the natural state of affairs for the Janajatis, who at the beginning, formed a vast single group. The original sin leading to the Janajati division is attributed to the Hindus, who classify and rank people hierarchically. They are held responsible for any division among the Indigenous people into various groups and even within these, into hierarchized clans. According to the Janajatis, the Hindus divide to assert their domination, but this also stems from an innate propensity:

> In order to hide their innate communal disposition, they cunningly pander the thoughtlessness of the indigenous people labelling them into different classes such as Bhotay, Newar, etc. And they impute communalism on those naive people. (Gopal Gurung, 1998: 2)

One sometimes finds confirmation of these views among Hindus: 'It is proper of the mental to divide, and to divide the divisions, ... [the *varna*] are natural divisions of men and women according to their natural tendencies.'[33]

---

[32]See Lok Bahadur Thapa Magar 2056 VS.
[33]Gaura Krishna, n.d.: 'L'interprétation de la caste', pages.intnet.mu/ramsurat/gaurakrishna.

The lack of determination and the void evoked by indigenous intellectuals to describe the original state of the groups they belong to, apply on many registers. First of all, it concerns religious ideas and practices:

> Naturists do not have any religious leaders (*dharmikneta*), in their teaching (*dharma sastra*), the most eminent people are their father and mother and those who helped them to grow. (Hitan Magar 1992–93: 6)

Those 'who helped them to grow' include the land and the natural resources on which the Janajatis rely. Another void is the lack of religious basis for the Janajatis' original political structures, which would have facilitated the imposition of Hindu rule:

> In the hills of the mountainous area, the autonomous natives' self-government had no socio-religious basis: this is why it was not difficult for the Hindus to fill this vacuum. In Tibet where Buddhism formed the basis of the government, it was difficult: this is why they could not thrive over there. (*ibid*: 5)

Guiding the individual in his relations with the surrounding world, natural religion is also characterized by an absence of specific ideas concerning the fate of man after death, another void which allowed Hindus to 'occupy' the Janajatis' spirits and their lands:

> It is the idea of paradise and hell elaborated by the Hindus, as well as their description of these places, which overall destroyed the Magar group. To go to paradise, to obtain happiness and a good rebirth, the frank and generous Magars made them gifts of gold, of land: it is thanks to this imaginary world that they obtained gold and land from them. (*ibid*: 6)

More generally speaking, the Magars formulate the idea that with Hinduism they 'started to make the difference between stone and divinity',[34] as if there was a time when the whole of their

---

[34] A frequently used expression, see for instance Giri Sirish (2050 VS: 7).

environment was held as sacred. They believe that Hindus chose to pervert their harmonious relation with nature by establishing their gods on the very sites selected by them to venerate stones and trees or 'what they find beautiful' in their environment, with no other notion of what is divine.

> First of all, the Magar priest, having sought a stone of beautiful appearance, brings it back, then he coats the ground at the foot of any tree, washes the stone and establishes it at this place. After having sprinkled vermilion powder and other ingredients on this stone, if he offers a sacrifice of chicken or goat, he also coats it with its blood. He encloses this space of branches. This is how Magars build their temples and they name them *than*, 'sacred places', and not 'temples', *mandir*. ... [T]he cunning Hindus, in order to subject these sanctuaries, acted in two manners:
>
> 1) By friendly alliance: after having approached Magars and made them Hindus, they placed statues of Hindu gods in the sanctuaries of the Magars. More than an ordinary stone, perhaps that appeared beautiful to the Magar and they thus accepted it.
>
> 2) By trick: Hindus plotters secretly went at night to deposit Hindu statues in Magar shrines which are not closed and where nobody resides. When the Magar priest comes back to his sanctuary and sees a new statue there he accepts it because he does not know opposition. (Ale Magar, 1992-93: 12).

In their depictions, the naive Janajatis are always fooled by the cunning Hindus. Since this type of explanation is deemed acceptable and often published, the basis on which the Hindus are portrayed as dominators and the reason they are not recognized as having a 'natural' past needs to be explored.

In Janajati literature, the most common explicit reason explaining these Hindu features is to present them as consequent to migratory practices. By their subsequent displacements, Aryas are thought to have accumulated a great diversity of knowledge, which rendered them cunning and led them to dominate and to enslave Indigenous Peoples.

> Peoples or groups who leave their place of residence to go far and migrate, become more progressive and cunning, while those who do not move are frank, straight, friendly and live according to their traditions ... They cannot lie and cheat the others. In Nepal, the frank groups are the Magars, Gurungs, Rais, Limbus, etc. ... As the natives do not have fraud in mind, they do not look badly on the people who come to settle on their premises. These immigrants influence the natives so that they divide, then they take their fertile lands and the natives find themselves in the situation of immigrants. (M. Ale Magar, 2050 VS: 6).

The effect of displacements is not only presented by the Janajatis as a long historical process affecting the groups at large, but also as determining behaviour among the various Hindu castes:

> More than men who remain in a place, those who move from one place to another, accumulate knowledge. Because they must face new problems and find solutions, they develop their experience, because they see new places and all kinds of people, they learn new things. This is why still nowadays, the Damai tailors who go from house to house to sew clothing are more skilful in the art of speech than the Kami craftsmen. (M.S. Thapa Magar, 1992: 4–5).

Migration and cultural borrowings thus confer superiority in terms of domination strategies, which in turn leads one to migrate farther to pursue one's domination over local populations by way of acculturation. However, it is not clear whether Janajatis believe that any form of acculturation has a mechanical effect of division and domination on them or if this is attributed to Hindu acculturation alone. Giri Thapa Magar (2050 VS: 47–8) metaphorically evokes the Janajatis' encounter with migrant Hindus in a fable where a sick monkey requests asylum in a village of wild boars. A compassionate boar takes care of the sick monkey. Once cured, the monkey asks for work and the boar suggests he pick fruit for him. But the avaricious monkey keeps more and more fruit and ends up bringing no fruit at all to the boar. When questioned by the boar, the monkey explains:

> – Brother boar, I have a big family and picking fruit is not an easy task; this is why we eat all the fruit we can, and sell the remainder.
> – But I planted the trees and watered them. Why would you take everything? ... Did you forget the history of your arrival in this village? ... Your race is fraudulent, come down the tree.
> – Not fraudulent, brother, but clever. We are not like you, strong and stupid, playing on the floor of the roots, and eating tubers or fallen fruits. We are the highest race of all living beings, we are clever, wise and beautiful.

This fable summarizes common stereotypes concerning the difference in nature and behaviour between Janajatis and Hindus: the former have strong links with the land, while the Brahmans, residing in higher spheres, are said to exploit the Janajatis' work.[35]

Indigenous Spirituality versus Hinduism

In their move towards an autonomous definition, several indigenous intellectuals emphasize their singularity *vis-à-vis* dominant Hindu society through the idea of mental provisions, in particular, with respect to the natural world, which would be specific to their groups. The Janajati mentality includes 'Indigenous spirituality' and 'Indigenous knowledge', both of which are founded on a relation of proximity to nature and would not employ dichotomous categories. According to Chaitanya Subba

---

[35] In a similar story told by a famous Brahman political leader, a young Brahman living in contact with Janajatis challenges the basis of his Brahmanical culture which imposes upon him: fasts, detachment from materialism, and intellectual torments, and praises the merits of the good savages enjoying all the pleasures in life. See M. Hutt, 2003.

(2057 VS), 'such spirituality serves the purpose of adaptation', and is based on proximity to nature, which in turn, he describes as proportional to the 'purity' of the indigenous culture:

> The more pristine or less contaminated their culture is, the more their spirituality is closely associated with nature. (Subba 2057 VS: 99)

Indigenous spirituality is thus inseparable from natural religion. In the same way that Indigenous Peoples define themselves in negative terms *vis-à-vis* Hindu society, so it is with their natural religion. The Janajatis view it as different from religions which 'regulate human relations', for it is thought to only take into account descent (in the worship of genitors such as parents, ancestors, the Earth) and sometimes seniority. These are presented as natural relations of indebtedness placing someone in the position of a worshipper. Deprived of bounds to any form of social or political organization, a religion of nature would find its first and most important definition in its opposition to 'communal religions', *jatiya dharma*, an expression applied to Hinduism and sometimes also to Buddhism. Hinduism, according to the Janajatis, was born when,

> to fix the rules of the society, some malignant people distinguished themselves. These men did not only consider what would be advantageous to the society, but also what would be personally beneficial for them and created many fallacious things in the society. (M. Ale Magar, 2050 VS: 6).

Hinduism is thus presented as having been created by a limited number of individuals, who fixed social rules for their own benefit. By contrast, natural religion is positively asserted as being the only truly universal path. It is inclusive by nature, contrary to Hinduism, and the Janajatis therefore contest the latter's presentation as a universal path to salvation: 'The vision of Pashupati offers liberation to all, but on the entry of his temple, it is written: "entrance for Hindus only"', notes Mohan Gurung (2050 VS: 33).

As we have seen, what is natural is conceived as older and better, and this perception is reflected in the Janajati evaluation of religion. For M.S. Thapa, the funerary practices of the Magars, who until recently buried their dead, are linked to a stage of cultural development related to the Stone Age, which the group has not completely put behind it. On the other hand, the Aryas' cremation indicates a posterior civilization stage, which is negatively connoted as related to slavery, and as being specific to 'communal religions'.[36] During their period of Hinduization, the practice of cremation spread among the Nepalese Indigenous Peoples and replaced the practice of burial, synonymous at the time with malevolent death and low status. Due to its 'non natural' character, the practice of cremation is currently being re-evaluated by the Janajatis who had adopted it in large numbers.

> The Kirants divided from a single group which followed natural traditions (*prakritik parampara*). Prior to the arrival of the Hindus, they followed the natural custom of burying their dead. Their priest, the *jhankri*, was also buried. Their natural religion was transformed into communal religion (*jatiya dharma*), such as Hinduism and Buddhism, in which the dead are cremated. Thus one calls the habit of burying the dead the Kirant tradition or the natural tradition (P.S. Lama, 2055 VS: 27).

Communal religions are also opposed to natural religion by the importance they are said to attach to the individual. For the Janajatis, the Hindus' *dharma* leads them on a personal quest for their own well-being, personal merit, and many other 'egoistic practices'. Indigenous spirituality, on the other hand, is said to aim at maintaining universal harmony by 'reciprocity between the hunter and the hunted, between humans, animals and plants' with 'human beings, animals and all objects of nature shar[ing] the same spiritual essence' (C. Subba 2057 VS: 102–03). In the Janajatis' opinion, the deities 'are like humans, having their own houses, families, societies, chiefs, shamans, territories, and songs,

[36]M.S. Thapa Magar, 2049 VS: 7.

dances and material possession. This is why humans propitiate the deities not to retaliate, rather to procreate and replenish their land with abundant supply.' (C. Subba 2057 VS: 102)

Presenting rites as a way of preventing the deities from retaliating, as Ch. Subba does, conveys the idea that human beings offend them. Harmony is preserved by compensation, in order to maintain good relations between the various categories of beings. It is this relationship, rather than the individuals who maintain it, that must be nurtured in order to preserve its ideal state. Based on the hunter-hunted relationship, or on a reciprocal and balanced relationship of predation, the Janajati 'harmony with nature' has nothing in common with its Hindu conception as non-predation and non-intervention.

The religion of nature is thus not simply viewed as a state of religiosity anterior to Hinduism and merely non-Hindu, but rather as anti-Hindu. This dimension is often expressed through opposed relationships with nature and is formulated in a violent or sacrilegious way by the Janajatis, using figures from the natural world that are objects of worship for Hindus but which they simply kill and eat. 'We Mongols are beef eaters not its worshippers', says Gopal Gurung (1998: 2), while Anabir Somei Magar (2053 VS: 14) states: 'Hindus venerate Baraha, Vishnu in his shape of pig, but the divinity whom they venerate is killed and eaten by Magars.'

This verbal and symbolic violence towards the Hindus comes quite naturally in response to the long period of Hindu institutional violence towards the Janajatis' dietary habits, including the death penalty for killing a cow.

Modernity of the Origins

Though considered by the Janajatis to be very ancient, natural religion is also opposed to Hinduism with regard to its scientificity. The latter now commonly claim that Hinduism is non-scientific, or even, 'anti-scientific'.[37] As proof of this, Mohan Gurung (2050

---

[37] Suresh Ale Magar (1995: 13) writes: 'Hindu *dharma* is anti-scientific (*avaigyanik*) and anti-democratic (*aprajatantrik*)'.

VS: 32) asserts that Hindu texts are not credible, when presenting several Hindu gods as born 'from non-natural sexual unions', from fire, or from fallen sperm.

To understand the significance of this type of criticism, one should bear in mind that until recently, Hindu depictions of the world were not taken metaphorically by the Janajatis. Take the case of an old Rai interviewed about the situation in his village around 1950, who recounts:

> We didn't know as much as today about the outside world. We heard from Purana about the Shree Langka, Ayodhya, Varanashi, and Badarinath. We believe that the Earth is flat and it is lying on water and held up by Shesh Nagha. (sic)[38]

The Janajati rationalism represents a 'natural reaction' in this context. It forms an important feature of the Janajati movement. The lack of logic prevalent in Hinduism is repeatedly demonstrated, in order to devalue and invalidate it:

> According to the Hindu religious tradition, animal sacrifices are offered to please the gods. Thus gods are carnivorous and like meat and fish. But it is said that the Brahmans who worship these gods should not eat meat. To eat meat is a sin, and this means that Brahmans are superior to gods. However, they worship gods. … In fact carnivorous gods are superior to the Brahmans. Why shouldn't the carnivorous people be too? The Hindu treatises cannot answer this. (Somei Magar, 2053 VS: 14).

By contrast, the Janajati movement aims at proving the scientific basis of natural religion. 'We are now in the scientific era'[39] recall many Indigenous thinkers, as if they were located at the two extremes of time: at the time of origin from which they have kept their natural religion and, in a simultaneous manner, in the ongoing scientific era. The Janajatis' dual inscription in

[38]Anonymous, 1993.
[39]Anonymous, 2058 VS.

time contrasts with their commonly alleged timelessness, even on official government websites, in which it is stated: 'time seems to have stopped in their sylvan hamlet'.[40] The Janajatis' participation in the current and future 'scientific era' stems from their professed exclusive knowledge concerning the environment.[41] They claim to be the depository of ancestral ultra-scientific knowledge, through which scientists have started to discover new curative substances. Here is another danger, since this knowledge is now likely to be diverted by foreign pharmaceutical firms and must therefore be protected. To this end, Nepalese Janajatis contributed to a text presented at the UN, in July 1999 by a group of Indigenous Peoples, stipulating that all forms of life or processes which create life are sacred for them and therefore cannot be the object of property.

Highly advanced compared to even the most developed sciences, yet keeping one foot firmly rooted in the origins of humanity, the Janajati movement is situated at the two extremes of time. This shift can quite simply be attributed to the fact that it emanates from urban and educated individuals, on behalf of groups seen as 'backward' and referring more particularly to their less 'contaminated' members. However, it seems to me, that this temporal bipolarity is fundamentally related to the actual

---

[40] *www.orissa.gov.in/people/tribe/tribehome.htm*; the full passage reads: 'According to their origin and habitat they are variously designated as Adimjati (primitive castes), Janajati (folk communities), Girijana (hill folk), Vanajati (forest dwellers), etc. However, these names do not bring out their essential characteristic of primal innocence and spontaneous living; they are the inheritors of immortality. Time seems to have stopped in their sylvan hamlets. Their ways of living with meagre needs of food, shelter and clothing and the vivre [sic] through music and dance seem to have remained unaltered through the ages of social evolution. The sacred God-nature-man relationship that works among them is an amazing experience to the fragmented and alienated mind of modern man.'

[41] In the field of botany, however, a preliminary ethno-botanic study which I carried out in 1986–87 in a multi-ethnic village of central Nepal revealed a striking uniformity in knowledge about plants, probably due to a long cohabitation of the different groups.

working of modern indigenous identity and to the possibility of its symbolic construction.

Indeed, this duality not only appears in the contents of the Janajati publications, but also in the form of their most common joint action, the meeting, whereby Janajatis show their true selves. On this occasion, a 'savage' is often invited with his typical bow and clothing, and plays the role of a mascot in the middle of a platform, surrounded by the leaders of the ethnic association, dressed in casual Western clothes.[42] Alternatively, some of these leaders, conspicuously sitting in the middle, who are disguised in 'traditional clothes', and in this case, with some distinct markers of their modernity, such as sports shoes, glasses or video cameras. The savage mascots apparently embody the group's lost past, and liven the ancestral fibre of those who left it for an urban life. The familiar but incongruous savage in the urban jungle is an object of curiosity for the public and readers of the indigenous press. After the speeches, this role is taken over by a dance troupe, through which each Janajati group displays its identity through a specific costume, choreography and music. The performance of folkloric dances displays the same *'décalage'*, since these 'natural' Janajati groups, when communicating an image of themselves, purposely cultivate a form of artificiality and unnatural appearance. They apply make up, revamp a typical village dress and present a show quite different from any seen in a village context. It is important to note that this folklorization differs somewhat from the situation prevalent in many regions of the world. Indeed, folkloric dance troupes often dress in costumes that are no longer worn or which were created to underline a distinct identity. In Nepal, on the other hand, many villagers still wear the traditional dress, but indigenous professional dancers stand out at once because of their brighter colours, brand new fabrics, shortened skirts, reduced belts, showy make up and accessories. Through this self-representation, the Janajatis voluntarily keep their distance from the real representatives of their groups, whether urban or

---

[42] For example, see Ujir Budhathoki Magar (2058 VS) about the behaviour of a Kusunda (hunter-gatherer) invited to the capital for an ethnic meeting.

rural. They gather around the artificial and constructed image of themselves, as if it were this very artificiality generated the symbolism needed for collective adhesion, by reconciling modernity, and the 'Stone Age'. This enables the Janajatis to merge the two centres of gravity around which their present-day identity revolves: the culture they partially lost, and nature, which takes the place of culture. By emphasizing two distant temporal references, they also manage to rid themselves of their historical past, one of subjection and alienation.

Being the guardians of ancestral knowledge about the environment, the Indigenous Peoples are also those who, through their practices, know how to preserve it in all its diversity. An international group of Indigenous Peoples claims:

> We are the first stewards of the forest. During all of history, we have nourished her biodiversity through our skills and practices, a wide variety of knowledge, and a holistic understanding of our environment. ... We are part of a wide system that unifies us with the forest through social, cultural, political, economic and ecological links, all expressed through our indigenous spirituality.[43]

By joining the worldwide indigenous movement, the Nepalese Janajatis have underlined that they are part of the biodiversity, and that they are the only ones capable of ensuring its protection. Consistent with this claim, their demand addressed to the government concerns the protection of nature. They denounce the fact that it is presently carried out to their detriment and that their existence is not taken into consideration in the decision-making processes regarding environmental issues. 'How could scientists forget the Bote dependent on natural resources by protecting savage animals?' asks Rashmi Thapa Magar (2000–01).

---

[43] A text signed by a group of Indigenous People's representatives (among whom Parshu Ram Tamang for Nepal) at the United Nations Framework Convention on Climate change Subsidiary Bodies, Lyon, September 2000.

In Nepal, 18 per cent of the territory is protected for its fauna and flora, and this area is likely to increase in the years to come. Indigenous Peoples obviously suffer in this situation since several parks have been created in areas where a relatively large number of them live, a good distance from intensive agriculture. But contrary to several regions of the world, the Janajatis are not the only groups affected by this problem, since there is a mixed population in most parts of Nepal. Nevertheless, they have made it their own concern, and consider it discriminating. Indeed, in addition to the groups merely facing economic problems because of nature conservation, the Janajatis also feel that their very existence is threatened by protection policies:[44]

> [T]he state is even now threatening the livelihoods of Indigenous Peoples in the name of protecting wildlife. Extensive reservation of parks and conservation areas for wild lives have been established in territories of Indigenous Peoples, disregarding Indigenous Peoples lives and cultures. Not only their traditional homelands have been taken over, but also their livelihood is at great stake since grave hindrances have been created for them in using forests, water and other resources. In Nepal, the government is concerned about the security of animals but not indigenous Peoples. (Lawoti 2001)

As close to nature as they may feel, the Janajatis hold that their fate is no less worthy of attention than that of animals and they

---

[44] Among the 40 common and special laws which are considered to be discriminating to the Janajatis by the Nepalese Federation of Indigenous Nationalities (NEFIN), a major part concerns nature protection, land and forest regulations, such as: Nationalization of Private Forest Act 2013, Local self-governance Act 2055, Land Act 2021, Nationalization of Pastures Act 2031, Land Taxation Act 2034, Forestry Act 2049, Protection of Water Animals Act 2017, National park and wildlife protection Act 2029, HM King Mahendra Nature Preservation Fund Act 2039, Plant Preservation Act 2039, Land and Water Resources Protection Act 2039, Water Resources Act 2049, Mine and Mineral Products Act 2042, (quoted in Lawoti 2001).

sometimes even describe themselves as an endangered species.[45] Here they raise a fundamental ethical question: should cultures in danger of extinction not benefit from the same attention and the same means as those given to environmental protection throughout the world?

> Biodiversity has been recognised and is protected everywhere in the world. The diversity of cultures, religions, social standards and values is just as important.[46]

The now fashionable issue regarding the Indigenous Peoples' responsibility for deforestation, for the disappearance of large mammals, and in particular of felines, is thus irrelevant to the Janajatis, who recall that they are threatened by extinction as well.

Interestingly, the opposition between Janajatis and Hindus which is currently on the rise in Nepal does not take into account the various groups' actual practices, the impact that each one might have had on the environment, but focuses mainly on a spiritual or symbolic level. Two different conceptions of man's ideal relationship with nature compete here. For the Janajatis, a group is natural not because it abstains from hunting or from taking anything from the forest, but because it takes part in it. This lifestyle is on the decline due to nature conservation. On the other hand, the ultimate Hindu ideal of non-intervention in nature truly corresponds to the modern protection policies implemented in Nepal. Spaces are 'separated', they were said to be 'set aside' by the king (until the abolition of the monarchy in May 2008), and they are set up as sanctuaries where human intervention is kept to a minimum. This modern government prerogative strongly recalls the Hindu king's traditional offering of land to gods, temples and priests in order to increase his personal merit. On the other

---

[45]Thus, in the presentation of the nationalities of Nepal published by the Rastriya Janajati Bikas Samiti, one can read about the Kusundas: 'Kusundas are probably the most *endangered species* of the aboriginal ethnic groups of Nepal.' Reproduced on www.nepaldemocracy.org/ethnicity.

[46]Anonymous, editorial of *Nagarik*, 3 (2–3), 2000–01.

hand, very few species are protected in the country, with a list of 38 protected animal species and only three plant species. The Nepalese government's way of protecting biodiversity is thus to place the wildest spaces away from the mundane world rather than to encourage the whole population to protect its most fragile components. This calls to mind the Hindu ideal of absence of intervention in nature, and in a certain manner, fits in well with the demand for autonomous territories expressed by the Nepalese Indigenous Peoples.

References

Ale Magar, Madan. 2050 VS (1993). 'Adibasibare kehi janakari' [Some information about the Indigenous Peoples]. *Soni* 2 (2): 6–7.

Ale Magar, Suresh. 1992–93. 'Hindu mandirma ahindu Magar pujari kina ra kasari?' [How and why non Hindu Magar priests in Hindu temples?]. *Lapha* 1 (2): 12–13.

____. 1995. No title. *Lapha* 3 (11): 13.

Anonymous. 1993. 'A study of Para village'. *Himalaya* 8 (2): 14–19.

Anonymous. 2058 VS (2001). 'Prakritivad ra Pye lhu sanghko sthapana' [Naturism and the establishment of the Pye lhu association]. *Janajati Manch* 6 (2): 28–9.

Baral, Keshar Jang. 2058 VS (2001). 'Magar samudayako vikas ra yasma dekhieka avrodhaharu' [The development of the Magar community and obstacles to it]. *Janajati Manch* 6 (2): 7–10.

Bhattachan, Krishna B. 'Traditional Local Governance in Nepal', Paper presented in a seminar on Strengthening Decentralization and Good Governance in Nepal organised by POLSAN and FES, Kathmandu, April 2002. (*nepaldemocracy.org*)

Budha Magar, H.B. 2049 VS (1992). *Kirat vams ra magarharu* [*The Kirat descent group and the Magars*]. Lalitpur, U. Bohora.

Budhathoki Magar, Ujir. 2058 VS (2001). 'Rajdhanima kusundasang arko jamkabhet' [Another meeting with a Kusunda in the capital]. *Janajati avaj* 8: 29–30.

Chemjong, Imansim, n.d. *Kirat sahitya ko itihas* [*History of Kirat literature*]. No place: Limbuvan Pratinidhi Mandal.

Dollfus, P. Lecomte-Tilouine, M, & Aubriot, O. 2001. 'Un araire dans la tête. Réflexions sur la répartition géographique de l'outil en Himalaya'. *Techniques et Cultures*, special issue: *L'araire en Himalaya*, 37: 3–50.

Gurung, Gopal. 1998. *Compile parts*. Kathmandu: author.

Gurung, Mohan. 2050 VS (1993). 'Dharmagrantha margadarshak ya pathabhrastak?' [Religious scriptures: guiding or misleading?]. *Gyavat*: 31–5.

Hitan Magar, Jaya Bahadur. 1992–93. 'Mangol janajatima hindu dharmako prabhava' [The influence of Hindu religion on the Mangol nationalities]. *Lapha* 1 (2): 5–7.

_____ 2056 VS (1999). 'Adibasi mangol janajati bhanne avaj' [The voice of those who are called the indigenous Mangol nationalities]. *Konja-Marum* 2 (5): 21–3.

Hutt, Michael. 2003. 'Reading Sumnima'. In M. Lecomte-Tilouine and P. Dollfus eds. *Ethnic Revival and Religious Turmoil. Identities and Representations in the Himalayas*. New Delhi: Oxford University Press. pp. 23–39.

Joshi, G. 2022 VS (1965). *Vir caritra* [*The adventures of a hero*]. Lalitpur: Jagadamba Prakashan.

Kle Tamu, Mekh Sim. n.d. 'Nepalma adibasiharuko samasya ra samadhanko upaya' [The problem of the Indigenous Peoples of Nepal and the mean of its resolution]. *Janajati Manch* 6 (1): 5.

_____ 2058 VS (2001). 'Tamu ekatako avashyakata' [The necessity of Tamu unity]. *Janajati yuva sandesh* 2 (7): 6–8.

Lam Tamu, Jagman K. 2049 VS (1992). 'Tamu samskriti: ek samiksa' [Tamu culture: a review]. *Tamu Sun*, reproduced in P. Onta, K. Yatru, B. Gautam eds. *Chapama janajati*. Kathmandu: Ekata Buks, 2058 VS. pp. 239–47.

Lama, Parman Simha. 2055 VS (1998). *Kirat jatiko utpati, vamsha ra antyeshti samskar parampara* [*The Kirant group: its creation, clans and traditions for the last rites*]. Kathmandu: Kokomhendo prakashan.

Lama, Santabir. 2016 VS (1959). *Syebu Syemu: Tamang jatiko bibahko riti, thiti ra git* [*Syebu Syemu. Wedding customs and songs of the Tamang group*]. Darjeeling: author.

_____ 2022 VS (1965). *Tamba kaiten. Tamangko purkhyauli riti, thiti ra git* [*Tamba kaiten. Customs and songs of the Tamang ancestors*]. Ilam: Shri Purna Bhandar. [First edition, 1959, Darjeeling].

Lawoti, Mahendra. 2001. 'Racial discrimination towards the indigenous

peoples in Nepal'. Report presented at the National Conference of the NPC, Kathmandu, 26 April 2001.
Lecomte-Tilouine, Marie. 1996. 'Le culte de la déesse Terre chez les Magar (Népal)'. *Diogène* 174: 24-39.
Lecomte-Tilouine, Marie and Catherine Michaud. 2000. 'From the Mine to the Fields. History of the Exploitation of the Slope in Darling (Gulmi)'. In P. Ramirez ed. *Resunga. The Mountain of the Horned Sage.* Kathmandu: Himal Publications. pp. 222-64.
Limbu, Nar Bahadur. 2050 VS (1993). *Kirati aitihasik savai* [*Historical account of the Kiratis*]. no place: M.H. Subba.
Rana Magar, Janak Bahadur. 2050 VS (1993). 'Mero binti' [My request]. *Gorak* 3 (2): 40-1.
Sagant, Philippe. 1976. *Le paysan limbu, sa maison et ses champs*. Paris: Mouton.
Sirish, Giri. 2050 VS (1993). 'Karmaka kura' [Matters of Karma]. *Gorak* 3 (2): 7-8.
Somei Magar, Anabir. 2053 VS (1996). *Goreto* [*Path*]. Butwal: Sahityak tatha Samajik Seva Manch.
Subba, Chaitanya. 2057 VS (2000). 'Nature and Indigenous Spirituality: the Context of Nepal'. *Janajati* 2 (2) [4]: 97-115.
Tamang, Singman. 2004. *Tamang jati: itihasdekhi vartamansamma* [*The Tamang group, from past to present*]. Kathmandu: Shyam Lekhak.
Thapa Magar, Giri. 2050 VS (1993). 'Svartha' [Selfishness]. *Gorak* 3 (2): 47-8.
Thapa Magar, Lok Bahadur. 1995. No title. *Lapha* 3 (11): 12.
____ 2056 VS (1999). *Magarant svayattata bare, ek adhyayan* [*A study about the autonomy of the Magar country*]. Pokhara: Magarant Rastriya Mukti Morcha.
Thapa Magar, M.S. 2049 VS (1992). *Pracin magar ra akkha lipi* [*Ancient Magars and the akkha alphabet*]. Kathmandu: D. Thapa Magar.
Thapa Magar, Rashmi. 2000-2001. 'Bot haraundai gairheka Bote jati' [The Bote group affected by forest protection]. *Nagarik* 3 (2-3): 11-15.

Subjectivity and Governance in the Himalayan Environment

BEN CAMPBELL

Sustainable timber for housebuilding, Langtang National Park
(Photo: Ben Campbell)

I want to thank the participants at the CNRS conference 2004, and those who discussed presentations of this paper at the Institute of Social and Cultural Anthropology, Oxford, 20 January 2006, especially David Gellner, Anne de Sales, and Nick Allen, and in March 2006 at Queens University Belfast, especially Kay Milton and Lisette Josephides.

A new cultural politics of environmentalism has emerged in debates over the relative claims to ecologically benign relationships between the various ethnic groups of Nepal. This in turn has consequences for claims to territorial autonomy. Marie Lecomte-Tilouine (in this volume) identifies the ethnic fault lines that are created by such claims, and notes in particular how a Hindu, non-interventionist, abstinent regard to the natural world finds a correspondence with the international ideology of environmental conservation, implemented through protected areas. The Janajati 'indigenous' groups' spokespersons argue for a greater natural connectedness of non-Hindu peoples and their religious practices, and for the legitimate recognition of relations to nature and supernature that celebrate reciprocal engagement with the non-human world, including the spiritual dimensions of hunting and sacrificial offerings to territorial beings. This raises several key issues about how to characterize 'animism' in Nepal, and how the idea of the environment as a singularized entity under threat from human activity, which lies behind projects to protect Himalayan biodiversity, can be problematized anthropologically, in order to understand Himalayan villagers' resistance to regimes of nature protection.

Using ethnographic material from fieldwork in Tamang-speaking communities of North-central Nepal, I argue that the Western concept of nature as a non-human domain cannot accommodate the villagers' territorially mobile practices of dwelling, their linguistic terms of understanding, or their subjectively encountered relations with plants, animals, and places. I will use the concept of 'environmental subjectivity' to explore aspects of human-environmental relatedness. By 'environmental subjectivity' I mean: one, people's personally situated ways of talking about non-human life-worlds, including their interface with them in daily practice and in narrative forms; and two, the ways that the environment is being made an explicit category for understanding and governance for managing change in rural society.

There are two key sets of writing this chapter works with. One is the recent batch of publications by Arun Agrawal (2003, 2005a, 2005b) that discuss subjectivity as a factor in the operation of devolved forest administrations by villagers in Kumaon in North India. In these, he argues, the central objectives of environmental governance in protecting forests have been effectively appropriated and internally rationalized by villagers in a process he calls 'environmentality'. His book is a major contribution to theorizing environmental protection that inserts questions of subject positions into otherwise over-formalized literatures dealing with political ecology and common property resources. But it has significant flaws in its restricted treatment of 'subjectivity' to formal contexts of resource management. The second approach I want to consider, in relation to the Tamang material, is the 'perspectivism' that Eduardo Viveiros de Castro has developed in Amazonian anthropology. His argument that Amazonian lived worlds invert the Western metaphysics of (single) nature and (multiple) cultures, can provide valuable insights for analysing Himalayan ethnography, and the phenomenon of 'animism'.[1] My intention is to discuss the relational nexus in which ecological social practice is constituted, and to consider the extent to which subjectively lived worlds in the Himalayas can be seen as many natures participating in a single culture, rather than many cultures relating to a single nature. In particular, many useful alternatives

[1] De Castro's work marks a major departure from the notion that has driven much of the anthropology of the environment, which assumes that non-human nature exists 'out there', and every culture has a particular set of categories and meanings to impose on it. The point is that this assumption makes a scientific virtue out of the culturally specific practice developed in western modernity of treating the non-human as material, mute, and manageable. By contrast Amerindian perspectivism makes humans and non-humans participants in a continuous society of interaction. Humans and other creatures are seen as all having common ontological desires, and intentions for the making of homes in the world, and as sharing common concerns for foods and drinks appropriate to their bodily differences. This contrasts radically with the human exceptionalism of the European enlightenment, that attributes people with unique powers of intentional agency. Descola's (2005) inspired attempt to put de Castro's perspectivist theory in a comparative anthropological framework, which creates a somewhat unsatisfactory default category for of 'analogism' for the part of the world this collection covers, concerning traditional agrarian societies, has provoked an anti-typological response from Latour (2009).

are offered for considering struggles over contested natures by Viveiros de Castro's (2004a) suggestion that the fundamental terms for our understandings of ourselves as biologically integral persons, and of our interactions with the material world as mediated through the utility and value of commodities, provides a radically different way of being in the world from one enfolded in ideas of giving and predation, enacted between differently embodied but mutually attentive animate subjects.

The Janajati people's claims for greater closeness to nature combine mythological points of reference with migration histories, elements of evolutionary models of society, and contemporary global environmental discourse favouring indigenous inclusion. This is all very fascinating as a politics of 'the indigenous', and a study of transformations in 'the environment' as a vehicle for discussions about modernity, but this is a different task from an ethnographic focus on bringing new, critical understandings to lived human-environmental relations in the Himalayas. How, then, can animistic subjectivities be characterized, and distinguished from modernist perceptions of the environment that make forests an object of rational resource management?

Realizing Environmental Responsibilities

Agrawal's environmental subjectivities typify an inner adoption of general conservation principles by people reflecting on their chosen actions to improve their living conditions. The light-bulb-illuminating moment at the beginning of his account is his follow-up conversation with a man who had previously expressed scepticism about forest protection, but four years later, was saying that the forests were too important to leave to government officials for whom this task was but a job. For him and his fellow villagers, by contrast, 'it is life' (Agrawal 2005a: 2), and that beyond any local impact of forest council participation, such work mattered 'for the country' (ibid: 2).

Agrawal's analysis of local communities' motivations for organizing themselves to manage forests as common property resources in the *van panchayats* in Kumaon is an extremely sophisticated intervention in debate about how conservation principles can be devolved and appropriated in local communities' mindsets and institutional capacities. Agrawal argues that after incendiarist resistance to the Forest Department in the 1920s, Kumaon's village communities have adopted reformed, non-coercive colonial models for the devolution of forest responsibility in autonomously regulating their own civil forest protection schemes. They have thereby willingly enacted central policy 'at a distance', in terms of a rationally modern project of statehood that minimizes uncertainty in the conditions affecting people's lives. The clarity of Agrawal's argument that integrates analyses of common property, political ecology and subjectivity is admirable, and the insight it gives as to how power can be seen to operate in populations of citizens, as contrasted to the subjects of sovereign princes, is most valuable. However, there are issues that need to be interrogated in the conceptual underpinnings of Agrawal's premise, its handling of power and subjectivity, and its applicability to contexts other than Kumaon.

His argument that people engage with forest protection the more they perceive both scarcity and need, and that this furthers state objectives, does not easily tally with the evidence that in many cases, not just in Kumaon, target-driven councils promoted by government have supplanted already existing local initiatives. Such cases have not always resulted in greater local participation, but the reverse. Sarin et al. (2003: 54–55) provide examples that show how some villages of Uttaranchal have refused having their civil forests incorporated into the Forest Department's sphere of influence, and wherever incorporation has taken place, people's motivation level to participate has dipped. The subjectivities involved appear to be far more unpredictable and recalcitrant than the thesis of rational perception of scarcity and organizational compliance for conservation would suggest.

Furthermore, the notion of subjectivity in Agrawal's analysis has little meat apart from membership of forest committees. To speak of environmental subjectivities, as ethnographers might want to, would require a fuller contextualization of subject formation in people's whole experience and their relationship to forests and places. Beyond the collective organizational level where the politics of forest use are explicitly worked out, more informal contexts for practices of the self in everyday life and activity should be included.[2] How forests figure in people's lives and enable their possibilities of agency in social interaction need to be considered. In this respect, for instance, ethnographic work such as Linkenbach's on the neighbouring area of Western Garhwal is illustrative. She mentions how women 'enjoy working in the forest, because by going there they can withdraw from social control for at least some hours' (Linkenbach 2000: 258), and that 'besides the heavy work females have to carry out in the jungle, the forest is a space of secrecy, joy and relaxation, where for a limited time-span one can disappear from the sight of other village people and behave more freely' (ibid: 258). This is an important dimension to understanding human-environmental relationships in terms of gender, complementing the critique of women's general lack of access to decision making in forest committees, already eloquently demonstrated by Bina Agarwal (2001).

Arun Agrawal's treatment of power is in terms of how hegemony cannot operate as a vertical imposition of central authority, and needs participation from below, that in this case, requires the environment to be perceived as a non-human domain capable of rational management. He clearly identifies the cognitive specificity of his terminology in saying 'Environmental subjects are those for whom the environment constitutes a critical domain of thought

[2] Raffles mentions in his comments to Agrawal's *Current Anthropology* article (Agrawal 2005b) 'the complex and deeply biographical practices through which environmental subjects 'make themselves' and equally 'are made' (Agrawal 2005: 184). Narotzky writes in her contribution to the same attached commentaries 'we are not enlightened as to what sorts of social relations within the village communities enhance or inhibit participation in forest councils' (Agrawal 2005: 183).

and action' (Agrawal 2005a: 16), and that 'environmentality is about the simultaneous redefinition of the environment and the subject as such redefinition is accomplished through the means of political economy' (ibid: 24). He does not interrogate ethnographically the ubiquity of this position in relation to forest environments, something that a less managerially oriented notion of subjectivity might reveal.

There is a noticeable silence in Agrawal's book about the late-modern, reflexive history of state-directed projects towards the environment and the wholesale re-evaluation of development and conservation policies in the Himalayas, since Ives and Messerli's (1989), and Thompson et al.'s (1986) critique of the science behind planned interventions in this region. This is missing from Agrawal's discussion of 'the strategies of knowledge and power that created forested environments as a domain fit for modern government' (Agrawal 2005a: 6), and as a result, important debates over the contentious use of 'scientific' knowledge about environmental knowledge and conservation policy are left out of the picture.

However, the key area of concern with Agrawal's work, from which I want to make a departure into an alternative analysis of environmental subjectivity, regards the translatability of Himalayan people's multiple interactions with forests, and mountain ecology into 'environmental' concerns. Agrawal deduces rather than demonstrates that there has been a cultural shift in the transformation from 'fire-wielding, state-defying, rebellious hill men' (Agrawal 2005a: 11) into compliant participants of governmentalized communities, and that this depends on a 'discursive belief' that 'nature is an entity discrete from humans and endangered by reckless human actions' (ibid: 201). Following Viveiros de Castro's arguments over treatments of nature in Amazonia, I want to insert an 'equivocation' into this process of translation that would recognize salient differences in how humans and non-human others are both thought about and lived with. Or, to put it in J. Pottier's (2003) terminology, significant locally complex realities of development are misrepresented in the reporting of them to central offices of accountability.

Obscure Environments

Environmental relations and subjectivity vary cross-culturally with reference to relationships with land, productive activity, and conceptions of exchange with natural and supernatural powers. There are substantial differences in how comparative ecological citizenship and subjectivity can be seen from the inside (Milton 1996, Descola 1996, and Ingold 2000). In talking of a citizenry my purpose is to focus on qualities of negotiated subject positions where certain registers and life-practices of personhood, intentionality and mutuality are actively worked out. There is another 'identity politics' of the environment of a very different order than that of the Janajati movement, which would simply see 'the Tamang' as historical victims of environmental injustice. It is the area of identity where relationships of kinship, gender and community are lived out in habitual practices of everyday interactions, and constant processing of elements in exchanges between people, places, and the various species of animals and plants subjectively engaged with in these environments.

With national parks and other protected areas attempting to change communities' environmental use patterns, the question arises how such interventions interact with people's sense of self? If social relationships are linked in presumably significant ways to the environments in which they are lived out, and the relationships of access and control to these environments are then radically altered, some crisis of identities can be expected.

One of the key arguments for participatory conservation is that local or indigenous peoples have traditional concepts of oneness with nature, and these could be complementary to the goals of conservation (Ramble and Chapagain 1990, Müller-Böker 1995). I argue that such statements need to be far more equivocal about the natures being brought into commensurability. Tamang notions of human selfhood are not radically separated from those of other species in nature, and instead of a 'oneness' with the environment, subjectivities are constituted through perceptions of intrinsic differences. Clan membership provides the Tamang with a core sense of identity and being, that is an idea of natural human type transmitted in the bones of the body. Someone without a clan identity is quite simply not a 'someone'. Though the term for clan is *jat*, the same as used to designate natural species, this is not a naturalness confined to species in the western scientific sense. It is not 'weird biology' as Viveiros de Castro puts it. The idea of 'kinds' depends on erotic and often conflictual relationships with others for the reproduction of these kinds, similar to the characterization of the 'potential affine' in Amazonia (Gow 2001: 306). The fertility of marriage between clans extends a general notion of erotic alliance between clans, as naturalized entities, to potential fertile exchange among other non-human kinds. The Tamang understanding of encounter and conflict between life-kinds gives an ontological framework to human social life within inherently gendered engagements of relational difference. This is sustained through the bi-partite 'Dravidian' opposition of parallel kin groups as against affines and cross-cousins. This context of encountering the qualities and challenges of living-with-otherness presents to the actor a reciprocally affected world through which matters, such as livelihood activities, are channelled. Against this context of being alive to the world in its difference, the environmental regulation generated by projects of nature conservation are problematically confronted. Park officials are not just affecting villagers' access to resources, but impose regulatory barriers across existential territories of being human in context.

In the prism of modernist nature protection, human presence is perceived as inherently destructive of ecological integrity. Other terms than 'integrity' and 'interference' are needed to understand the pragmatic and ontological problems the Tamang villagers face when nature is made into a designated entity outside their bounds. Describing and analysing human-environmental relationships in these circumstances needs to interrogate rather than simply depend on the nature-culture opposition.

In my first ethnographic work with the Tamang, I had naively imagined people would produce relatively consistent narratives about the landscape, explain their 'Indigenous Environmental Knowledge', and discuss plants, animals, soil and seasons with some reflexive facility. Instead, I found people's environmental knowledge and relationships to be discursively fragmented and not at all like a textualized body of knowledge. Their environmental practices and the contexts in which environmental factors became meaningful did not easily translate into linked strands of verbalized discourse, accessible in a straightforward fashion to the ethnographer.

Many villagers only knew specific names for a basic range of the most useful plants. They seemed too individually diverse and contradictory in their interests, activities and interpretations to justify the quest for a core cultural disposition toward the environment, beyond the commonality of their dispersed agro-pastoral production in mobile animal shelters (*godi*).

It was only with time that I realized a fuller 'environmental' packaging was possible with the various kinds of data I had. Unlike 'kinship', which is a far more explicit and symbolically coherent language of relational identity, and social practice for the Tamang, the 'environment' needed to be constructed as a synthetic analytical composite of various aspects of practice and perception in the world. There was no 'indigenously' recognized entity of nature or environment, nor was there a coherent and explicit, singular cultural response to it, which classificatory 'models of nature' would imply.

Putting together fragments of myth, healing chants, and narratives of migration and place, I eventually saw an indigenous eco-relational sensibility that was expressed in stories of an animated landscape of interacting, diverse beings. Men, women, kings, lamas, shamans, gods, spirits, creatures, vegetation and geology took part in accounts of life process, and cosmic connection. The characteristics of their relations were manifested in wilful intentionality, erotic attraction, species conflict, bio-type mutation, treacherous deceit, and personal fate. Issues of power were a constant theme in these narratives. They were very different kinds of power than that exercised by the national park authorities in claiming territorial dominion over the forest as a domain to be protected from human intervention. It was rather an ecology of power, recognition and contest, in which acting subjects confronted the otherness of life kinds, inhabiting distinctive 'own worlds' of being, and entered relationships of coercion, alliance and trickery with them.

I cannot but recognize similarities with how Viveiros de Castro (2004a) talks of 'trans-specific kinship relatedness', and of affinity as a 'socially fecund' ontological condition that rather than following after natural difference, 'is one of the primordial givens from which the relational matrix ensues. It belongs as such to the fabric of the universe'. This is not to suggest a precise equivalence of the Amazonian and Tamang or Tibeto-Burman schemes of life, but the key principle common to ideas of affinity and bodily difference that cut across humans and animals bears something of a shared animistic, perspectival disposition.

Among the narratives I came across in Rasuwa District, one version of the Tamang origins of humanity tells of a breakdown in people's co-operative hunting relationships with brother-in-law forest spirits (*tsen*). Such stories are spoken of as belonging to a time 'when people spoke with gods', after which relations with, and the perspectives of, other beings can only be accessed through shamanic ritual. The *nyalmo* yeti-like creatures entrap hunters and solitary animal herders by playing on these people's self-projection into other creatures' worlds (see Willerslev, 2007 on mimesis and seduction among Siberian hunters), and then have children with their captives. Another tale has a disobedient yak ignoring her older sister's entreaty to return to high mountain pastures, and as a result, remains in the lowlands, becoming a water buffalo to be eaten by people down there. And, to emphasize the comparisons, Viveiros de Castro (2004a) states,

> The great Amerindian origin myths of culture always have their central *dramatis personae* related by trans-specific affinity... Human kinship 'originates' from these transnatural alliances, but must never let itself be sucked back into them.

This evokes immediately the title of Brigitte Steinmann's book on the eastern Tamang of Khabre District: *The Children of the Monkey and the Demoness*.

Affinity in the Making

An effect of ethnic activism in Nepal has been to generate talk of proper, authentic and distinct ethnic groups, but this is not always appealing to villagers, whose demography, location, and economic relations may stress diversity over coherence. Introducing an early paper of mine, David Gellner once described the distribution of the Tamang populations as being like a doughnut around the outer Kathmandu valley. In Rasuwa District, the north-south geographical alignment extending into Tibet resembles more a baguette with a mixed filling, in terms of imagery for people's ethnic sociality. Tamang is the predominant language in the district, but within this community are groups who distinguish themselves as not being 'Tamang' clans. For the most part, these consist of Ghale clans, who claim former royal status, but there are also Gurung (pronounced *Krung*), and occasional Newars, known as *Bei*. The main distinguishing feature of these clans is that they do not eat beef, but they do inter-marry with Tamang clans, and share a common Dravidian kinship structure premised on bilateral cross-cousin marriage. Intermarriage does not then corrupt the notion of a clan's distinct humanity for those clans that maintain a prohibition on beef-eating. The generational passage of male bone is kept unaffected by admixture of beef-eaters' female flesh, as the logic of affinity perpetuates a radical distinctness to bodily transmitted gender. The multiple natures of humans, and of others, are thus held distinct (as 'givens' in Viveiros de Castro's terms) despite the flux of conflict, alliance, carnal desire and mutual attentiveness. In this way, even if repeated cross-cousin marriages are enacted with Tamang clans, the clans such as Ghale, Krung, and Bei will logically insist they are not Tamang, and retain their bodily distinctiveness through inheritance of bone, name, house god (*tim ki lha*), and dietary prohibitions.

In terms of ecological practice, there is nothing to distinguish these clan groups. All depend on mobile agro-pastoralism, and hold fields, mostly unirrigated, in a range between 1,000 and 2,200 metres altitude. Indeed, it is most often through the practice of living initially as hired livestock herders, that new clans have been established as village residents, rewarded after years of work with a daughter from the village, so becoming affines, and thus finding classificatory locatedness in the moiety relations of cross and parallel kin. The impact of national park regulations since the mid-1970s has profoundly restricted the sorts of subsistence practice known to previous generations, representing a situation similar to the 'unprecedented intrusion' (Agrawal 2005a: 4) experienced by the Kumaonis of the early twentieth century (Campbell 2005b).

During my research on human-environmental relations in this area in 1997–8, I had asked villagers to tell me any stories and myths concerning plants and animals, as well as their personal agro-pastoral biographies. The main shaman, a Ghale, had been the principal source. His account of being captured by the forest-dwelling *longai* (Nep. *ban manche*), being looked upon as food by the *longai* children, and seeing them eat soil and worms as their food and sauce, is one of the closest parallels to Amazonian perspectivist ontology from my research material.[3] The head lama, also a Ghale, had not only recited for me songs of cosmo-genesis, but had accompanied me in the monsoon up to the sheep pastures over 4,000 metres, and spoke of the former village headman's defence of these pastures against neighbouring herdsmen. Personal biographies often entered how relations with the non-human were given narrative shape.

The head of the *Bei* (Newar) family told me he also had a story to tell. He had arrived in the village aged about ten, and was fostered by the former headman. His birth-place was said to be Asan Tol in the centre of the Kathmandu bazaar. Why he came to live with the headman's household was never made clear to me. One might assume that scandal or poverty was a factor. The headman who took the boy to the village had many contacts and ritual friends between Tibet and Kathmandu, and was a significant trader of sheep and goats, taking them from the edge of the Tibetan plateau down to sell at Tundikhel in Kathmandu. The

---

[3] The shaman can be seen explaining this part of his life story in my film, *Shamanic Pilgrimage to Gosainkund*.

villagized Newar narrator claimed that the following story was told to him by the old people of Kathmandu. As a narrative offered by someone who moved in to another ethnic and ecological world, it might be possible to reflect on the transformations of meaning that can be attached to myth, or to see mythic narrative as having an ability to travel across specific social contexts. Its subject matter is intriguing from the point of view of someone who moved into a remote forested mountain side, and married there.

Affinity Lost and Found

The story went like this:[4]

> In olden times there was a couple with five sons. Each son had a wife. The youngest daughter-in-law stayed with her own parents. The family was rich.
> Then the four daughters-in-law decided to live separately.
> The old couple would not allow this. In time, nobody bothered to work any more. Such rich people turned poor.
> The old couple spoke together in a room. The man said he had heard there was a fortune-telling Jainsi (Brahmin) in a far off place. He went off with a pint of rice and a coin to give the Jainsi. The man put down the pint of rice and coin, and the Jainsi said 'Before you were rich?'
> 'Yes,' he replied.
> 'You and your wife have five sons, and the five sons have five wives, yes or no?'
> 'Yes.'
> 'Of the five daughters-in-law, the youngest stays with her parents, is it true?' he asked.
> 'That's indeed true,' said the old man.
> 'Bring in your daughter-in-law, and you will be as rich as before.'
> The old man returned and told his wife what happened. The two of them decided they should go and retrieve their daughter-

[4]This is a slightly abbreviated version.

in-law. They arrived at their daughter-in-law's father's house, and said 'Daughter-in-law let's go home!' The daughter-in-law said nothing. The morning of the next day they returned home with the daughter-in-law.

She did not enter the house. She did not eat in the house. She picked nettles for her food. The next day again she was given nettles.

In the months of Pus and Magh, no-one looked for the daughter-in-law. The whole family went off to work in other people's fields. They ate food in the house. All the food wages they brought back, they put in a store. From the month of Phagun they worked their own fields, and things improved, like before.

Later the family fell out again. The youngest daughter-in-law did not accept her position, and the other daughters-in-law said it was not their fault.

Again the mother and father deliberated. They said it would not do now to take the daughter-in-law back to her family. 'It won't do to take her back, it won't do not to. It has not worked out having her here. Call our youngest son to come and talk.'

'Youngest son, we cannot take [her] back to your father-in-law and brother-in-law. Here she does not get on with the other daughters-in-law. Will you obey my words or not?'

'I will obey father.'

'If you obey my words, take your wife who has a gift of silk cloth, and wears a golden ring. If you hear my words, both of you go off. Take her into the big forest.'

The couple left and after walking a long way, reached the big jungle. Both were tired by now. Having reached the forest they stopped to look for lice in each other's hair. The wife was exhausted and sleepy. She lay her head down on her husband's thigh, making a pillow of her silk cloth. She got comfortable. And then the husband left her there.

The husband made his way back home. 'Where did you leave daughter-in-law?' his father asked.

'In the big jungle, on a flat piece of ground.'

The youngest daughter-in-law awoke. Wherever she looked was jungle. Though she had come with her husband, she realized he had abandoned her. She was hungry. She wandered off, and eventually came to the cattle herd of a bear. There were many, many cows. The woman was afraid. 'I'm afraid,' she said. She climbed up into the top of a tree. She thought, 'I will look and see what the bear brings back home.'

While looking from the tree top, she saw the bear make a ball of milk skin from the pan. The bear then let the cattle loose and took them off to pasture. The woman was hungry by now, and watched frightened, as the cattle reached a hill ridge some distance off. The woman dropped down from the tree, and stole the piece of milk skin. She then climbed back into the tree. When the cattle were brought back the bear tethered them.

'I look for my piece of milk, it's not here! Oho! My old milk that has never gone missing, what has happened today? It's lost!'

The next day, the bear made two pieces of milk. 'If the thief takes one piece, there will be another piece for me.' The bear again let the cattle loose, left for pasture, and reached the hill ridge.

Still much afraid, the woman came down from the tree. She took both milk pieces, and climbed back up the tree. 'There are no people here who eat food, and I have found instead milk [khorauni].'

The bear returned with the cattle, and tied them up. It looked for the milk [khorauni].

'The thief has taken both! For two days now, my stuff that has never been lost has gone.'

The next day, the bear made three pieces, thinking 'if the thief takes two, one piece will remain for me.'

The bear sent the cattle off again to pasture and crossed the ridge. Once again the woman came down from the tree. She took all three pieces. The woman ate till she was full.

When the cattle returned, the bear figured if the thief had taken two pieces, one would be left. 'There! All three have been taken. Oho! Now it is three days my stuff I have never lost has gone.'

The next day, the bear was angry. After milking the cows and the water buffaloes, it heated the milk in a pan on the fire place. The fire got crackling. The milk boiled. 'Was it this hand that ate the khorauni?' It plunged its right hand in the milk. 'Ouch Ouch, it's burning!' It then plunged in its left hand. 'That's not done it!' it said. The fire kept on burning, and the bear plunged its mouth into the boiling milk. The bear died.

The woman was watching from above. When it was time for the cattle to pasture, they called out 'gaa-gaã gu-gū'. With the cattle bellowing with hunger, the woman said 'Just as I was hungry, so are the cattle!' She came down, not sure if the bear was dead or not. The cattle made even more noise.

'Oh Permessere Lachmi, you are hungry, I have come down.' She took them off into the forest. 'There's no-one here, no-one, only me!'

She came to a place of humans. The land had been abandoned. She stayed there keeping the cattle.

Eventually, in this place where people had once been, other people came. The woman became the land-owner. They made swiddens. They made fields, they made a house. In time they became wealthy.

The old man and woman [the parents-in-law] deliberated at home. 'At a certain place there are wealthy people. Maybe they will give a little food. It's worth seeing!' The youngest son and his father made plans. The next day they left. The daughter-in-law recognized her husband. She recognized her father-in-law. They did not recognize her; the man did not recognize his own wife. The woman made them a place to eat and fed them till they were full. She gave them each a load of food to carry away.

Reaching their house [they said] 'At that place there is a rich woman. Food and sauce, alcohol, it really is a place they will give you anything.'

After staying five, six days, the son and his father went again. When they got there, they were given hides and rugs to sit on. Alcohol, food, and sauces were given them.

When they had finished eating, [the woman said]:

'Before, were you two from the rich family of Tengen? Is it true?'

'Yes,' they said.

'The mother and father had five sons, is that true?' The daughter-in-law asked.

'It's true,' they said.

'The youngest daughter-in-law was abandoned in the forest, is it true?'

'Did your daughter-in-law have a silk cloth?' She asked.
'Did your daughter-in-law have a gold ring?' She asked.
'She did have them!' they said.

They whispered together. She brought out the silk cloth, and the gold ring, placing them down in front of her father-in-law. With this they were taken by surprise. They cried. They did not speak.

She tried to give them alcohol. They would not drink. They did not eat food.

The woman said she had not taken another husband. 'Father-in-law, my husband from before is here. Take this food away with you, though when I was with you I just ate nettles. If you want to live here, bring all the family.'

They came back all together.

Let me be explicit that my interest in presenting this myth here is to bring together concerns of social relations within the affinally articulated, internal diversity of Tamang-speaking communities in Rasuwa, on one hand, and the symbolic potency of affinity in structuring the personal relationships for reproducing the circumstances of domestic livelihood, which is a negotiated or coerced sharing of another's world. This myth was told by an in-marrying man, for whom this narrative, along with his name and his body, was all he brought from a world apart in Kathmandu. It confronts dilemmas of affinal subsumption and resolves in favour of neo-locality.

The myth's first half is driven by attempts to resist affinity on both sides, and only at the end is domestic unity painfully arrived at. Dynamics of food and property carry the events along. The myth gives a special, almost magical efficacy to the matrimonial gifts of the cloth and gold ring, but has a profoundly unsettling vision of property and the fortunes of good livelihood. Wealth comes and goes as an effect of interpersonal relations, and even the apparently solitary bear has its whole world disoriented by the unprecedented loss of its dairy produce. The daughter-in-law appropriates the herd of the bear, though with a nod to the sacred in the form of acknowledging the divine qualities of cattle (an endowment by chance that could be interpreted as standing for the ideal dowry gift). The daughter-in-law's initial resistance to affinal domestic food and her consumption of nettles, contrasts to the family's income of food from labour in kind, and the later elaborate offerings of food to the father and son demonstrate a belated action of reverse hospitality to the relations of culinary hierarchy, that were rejected by the young wife at her earlier involuntary stage of affinal residence.

The forest is where the unresolvable social relation of affinity is discarded, by the crime of the men. The young woman, realizing her abandonment, wanders through its dense reaches, only to find a productive settlement occupied by a bear, and she herself climbs a tree, like a bear. She then steals from the bear, just as wildlife scavenges on human subsistence, and can be seen as culpable for its demise (her own criminal act). In several ways then, the forest is a mirror of society, but the daughter-in-law finds a place of previous human settlement, and initiates a forest colony of agricultural activity and habitation, becoming herself the landowner when other people join her. The forest is used in the narrative as a site of concealment and refuge, also as a source of wealth and autonomy, in contrast to the dysfunctional model of family life as patriarchally headed and neglectful of in-laws. This myth posits a moral critique of virilocal residence and property, from which perspective the forest appears as remote, dangerous and fearful. At the same time, the myth sets the forest as a place for abandoning social constraints and for making possibilities of living well.

In the narrator's own life story, affinity has been the means of this man's social incorporation, some might say 'tribalizing' him, in the process. The affinal pathways of Tamang kinship provide a basis for effectively making communities that are not restrictively bound around domestic social enclosure, and the protection of name, status and women's honour. His personhood and biography demonstrate a locally unique position of extension to the world outside, attributed to him by his affines and classificatory kin, and in his person these qualities were perceived as valuable to the community.

He frequently occupied a position as mediator between villagers and outsiders. He was the only man to have taken seriously the promotion of apple tree orchards by the state agricultural office. He was the contractor of village labour for road repairs. He was a skilled timber worker, directing the felling and cutting up of trees when licences had been obtained from the national park. He was selected by the shaman as the ritual path-maker for the bombo's procession to the pilgrimage lake. He was an embodied point of contact to the ethnically outside society, a professional public face as the village's own inside outsider (in some ways comparable to Amazonian communities' naturalized white people), and with the name (Ganesh Man Shrestha) to go with it. Flowing from this distinct clan identity, his daughter was seen as knowing practices of caste-coded hygiene alien to most Tamang villagers, and was given village extension roles by district health officials. His oldest son joined the army (enrolling with the surname Ghale!), and his youngest son, unusually tall and strong for the village population, is the knife-wielder of choice at the buffalo sacrifice of Dasain.

Affinity, as played out in Tamang kinship subjectivity, gave this man a distinct perspective for who he could become: not simply someone with a different family name that other clans could marry with, but presenting a different kind of human person among the kinds of people that live in the village. This, I would suggest, provides biographical substance to the man's interest in the myth, which he claims is what he carried with him from his childhood in Kathmandu far away. In his fields way below the village in a clearing he made in the lower forest, perched above the Trisuli River, he undoubtedly identified with the imagery of creating productive lands out of the jungle. There were indeed plenty of bears in this area too!

What will this myth mean to the grandchildren of Ganesh Man? The narrator's telling transforms through his own personal biography, what it is that matters in this myth. We need not expect that his version as narrated to me corresponds closely to myths told in his birthplace of Asan Tol: 'the life-course process of mythopoesis, while experienced as closer and closer fidelity to an ancient source, is in fact the ongoing genesis of new myth versions' (Gow 2001: 87).

Certainly this myth was not recognized as a distinctively Newar story by a Tamang friend in the UK I have discussed it with. It reminded him of great-grandfathers' stories *'bedam'*, that are 'heard by ear' (*nabing tse teebala*), and in this valley of historical trans-Himalayan traffic, narratives of this sort would have moved along the pathways of goods, people and social exchange between Kyirong and Kathmandu. With the state of Nepal in its recent crisis of insurgency, indeed the Tibetan Autonomous Region of China to the north increasingly beckons (Shneiderman 2005), and relocation, temporary or permanent, in new environments offers people new opportunity.

My interest in this myth is, therefore, in it being the narrative property of a man who moved, and became part of a village society and language community he was not born to, but among whom telling tales is an act of identity communication, and among whom the act of conjugal residence builds a network of classificatory relationships and livelihood possibilities. However, ethnographers of the Nepal Himalayas will want to ask a key question about the qualities of affinity in the myth and the narrator's experience. In anthropological terms there is a massive gulf in the gendered differentiation of respect hierarchies between Tibeto-Burman groups and Hindus. Men on the Tibeto-Burman side of the gulf owe respect and service to the wife's family. The respect asymmetry is reversed in the Hindu social logic. However, unlike funeral practices, and certain food and drink habits, different perspectives on affinal asymmetry are not recognized by each side as the fundamental misperception (Lecomte-Tilouine 1993), that they are in sociological terms. This constitutes a silence which demonstrates a perplexing quality of misrecognition, and possibly, a refusal to explicitly relativize human practice in a realm that is not seen as constructed, but consonant with 'the fabric of the universe'.

This presents us with a logical problem with how human differentiation as *jat* does get explicitly worked into *emic* theories of inequality, in terms of cross-cousin marriage, diet and religion, as if of a natural kind (for a Ghale to eat beef would be to denature his/her intrinsic being), and yet the different social conventions of respect hierarchy are not explicitly perceived. The myth of the reluctant bride who, rejected by her affines, appropriates a domestic livelihood from a bear in the woods, and is then sought out by her former affines, who do not recognize her, is perhaps a singularly apt narrative for a man who has crossed over this gulf of misrecognition.[5]

Animism and Allegory

Janajati activists claim a grand scale of ethnic differentiation made in terms of a positively valued closeness to nature, but by looking at myths such as this one, it could be argued that pathways leading across lifeworlds (whether social or natural) are made visible. One might consider how the myth would be responded to by someone approaching it as a fabulous allegory, or when viewed from an animist perspective. In his discussion of 'institutional' and 'brute' registers of knowledge, Viveiros de Castro strongly pushes against metaphorical interpretation, and argues against the standard anthropological device of metaphysically demoting 'the indigenous distribution of the world to the condition of metaphor' (2004b: 12).

For Nepali villagers, who spend most of their lives toiling away to raise livestock and crops off a hectare or so of unirrigated terraced fields that they defend at night against bears, boars and porcupines, and tell their grandchildren stories of humans entering worlds where bears also keep livestock, the contiguity of domains is perhaps too close to simply assume a metaphorical intent. Indeed, if greater attention, if not credence, were to be given to animistic and other narratives of extra-human sociality, the characteristics of people's environmental subjectivities in the sense of kinds of relatedness that transcend human/non-human

[5]To be ethnographically correct, it is important to point out the literature in which gender contrasts between the Tibeto-Burman and high-caste Hindu social practice can be seen to be mediated by historical Newar institutions (Gellner 1991).

divisions could be more accessible. In an article on the insufficiency of 'cultural' understandings in community forestry projects (that aim to hand over control to communities, just as in Kumaon), Ram Chhetri commented,

> Natural habitats are like human population[s]: they too have a culture and social structure if [we] are willing to see it. In many ways the 'forest societies' (consisting of vegetation and wildlife of various species...) are like human societies—full of variations in culture and structure across places. Some are mono-cultural and others are not. In Nepali language we talk of the *Jaat* of trees and animals. Some forests have few *jaat*s and others have many. Just as human societies which vary by ecological or geographical belt. Maintaining or enhancing the multicultural nature would be tantamount to conservation of [the] ecosystem while eliminating one or the other could be considered an equivalent of 'ethnic cleansing'. (Chhetri 1998: 92).

This is not perspectivism as defined by Viveiros de Castro where different species are said to understand themselves *as human* in their own terms, but nor is it simply an allegorical way of 'thinking through nature' as Graham Clarke (1995) put it, that gives commentary on or illustrates social phenomena by means of non-human metaphoric reference. I would suggest that the human/non-human divide is not a satisfactory or solid framework for operations of metaphor to work as they do in a modern world of biologically natural force and social 'form' (Viveiros de Castro 2004a).

The Tamangs' preoccupation with coercive affinity, sociality and oppositional struggle (that in myth is not confined to inter-human relations) in effect means the relational is a problem for the villagers, rather than an idea of mutually stable positions between which flows of goods, rights and services can be expected to move, as if in mechanical circulation. In realizing particular moments of relational interaction the actors are aware of degrees of provisionality at work. Relations need to be constantly made and remade. Deliberate and conscious practices of relational selfhood and anticipation of the other's response are required to bring into being the possibility of interaction. When the Tamang ask the question *'rang-ta ta daba?'* which in simplest translation is 'what relation are you [to an other]', this evokes simultaneously the meanings of: 'what are the precise kinship terms exchanged in a relationship with someone', 'what are the possible ethical implications of these terms' and 'what does this person mean to you in a history of interaction with him or her'. Strategies for making relationship draw creatively on multiple registers of relational possibility (not just clan solidarity and affinal asymmetries, but histories of residence, friendship and activity). The effects of frequent village in-marriage and complementary matriline reckonings (*ama gyam tse*) produce room for manoeuvre in how people can actively slant the character and tone of moral inflections to kin relatedness, particularly in circumstances where ambiguity or overlapping connections exist. This can be especially important environmentally, in interactions between people of different villages when negotiations for cooperative activity in herding, forest product gathering, crop guarding and so on, are invariably conducted through cultivated rhetorics of clan solidarity and affinal respect.[6]

This applies to relations with the state as much as among extensive kin rhetorics. Indeed, rather than accept them at face value (as Agrawal does) a relatively seamless interface between central policy objectives and environmental responsibilities devolved to local actors, that presumes espousal of shared intent, many

---

[6]Bamford (1998) discusses the plasticity and fluidity of social relations of the Kamea in New Guinea in terms more of a *becoming* than a *fait accompli* and contrasts this to sociality in Africa or Asia. It could be argued that where Tamang interactions are not directly concerned with landed property her observations on the emergent sociality of environmental activity do bear comparison:

'The resources that the Kamea depend on for a living, land and species are not simply appropriated via pre-existing social ties, but instead furnish an important venue through which social distinctions are created in the first place. Gender and different categories of social relationships *sediment out* of the different uses to which the non-human environment is put' (Bamford 1998: 29). She emphasizes it is not a case of separate orders of society and nature that then need to be brought into relationship.

studies of participatory development outcomes have been shown to mask processes of 'disambiguation', and 'negotiated translation' (Pottier 2003), in the circulation of knowledge about the effects of interventions on local realities. Strategies for making perspectives and subject positions commensurable can exist in villagers' representation of their motivations to adopt government schemes (and they do not have to be seen as inauthentic in doing so).[7]

In a comment made on Agrawal's 'environmentality' article, Ajay Skaria questions its approach to power. This turns on the notion of the impossibility of a 'governmentalised totality', and Skaria argues that though Kumaoni councils may achieve environmental outcomes consonant with the state's goals, this need not be read as a 'governmental intimacy' in Agrawal's terms. As the forest councils were instituted precisely because the state could not directly control the forests, they can instead be seen as belonging to a 'politics beyond governmental power' (Skaria in Agrawal 2005b: 184). Skaria questions whether the category 'environment' that constitutes the object of the state's intentions is the same as, or is translatable as, that with which the Kumaonis operate. For Skaria, the environment as object of government 'is displaced by other techniques of the self, other histories' (in Agrawal 2005b: 185). Here we see a space opened up for thinking about the politics of environmental engagement, (Campbell 2005a), which would take the idea of an environmental subjectivity beyond the extent to which people might contribute to funds for village forest protection, and into the different sorts of understandings and relationships (at variance with those propounded by village decision makers), that people may have with forests, what kinds of trees and wildlife they should preferably contain, and the intimate pleasures, fears, and solidarities for the future they give rise to.

[7]An example of this process is, for example, shown in Nightingale's account of a Nepalese village elite's participation in community forestry. The District Forest Officer asked the village's literate men if they wanted to take over their forest. A village leader said 'OK, we do not understand, but we are ready to try it' (Nightingale 2005: 596).

In contrast to seeing the state as a looming block or a governmentalized totality, traces of power are revealed in multiple forms.[8] The interrelation of these different forms, and the persistence of attempts to singularize power in rationalizing environmental control are areas for further attention in the evolution of participatory conservation. The awkward relationships of neo-liberal frameworks for conservation further complicate the picture. Such development agency projects are explicitly about rolling back the state, and releasing entrepreneurial activity and civil society into environmental service provision. Participatory approaches are seen as both conceptually preferable and cost-effective, but both the communities and forests that emerge from such interventions carry the imprint of generic incentives that instrumentalize relationships to forest environments.[9] These come in the form of credentials for territorialized group membership and exclusion, and the requirement for management plans through which entitlements are negotiated, and preferred types of forest regeneration are defined. In the making of formal village bodies for forest protection, relations of power congealed in committees that reflect gender, caste, or class inequalities of agrarian landholding, may be projected onto differential access rights to forest produce, and the designed composition of forest plots. This can subvert the role of forests as a fallback reserve (or refuge) of subsistence options to people, who are otherwise marginalized through unequal landholdings. Agrawal's analysis leaves on one side how power becomes mobilized in people's contestations, bargainings, transgression of others' boundary definitions, and in acts of non-compliance, that Bina Agarwal, by contrast draws attention to in her work (Agarwal 2001: 1642).

[8]In his lucid response to comments made on his environmentality article, Agrawal (2005b) quotes from Borges on the lonely contemplation of the multiform exactness of the world.
[9]An understanding of how 'universalistic' the language of community conservation is, comes from learning about other cases in completely different environments, such as van Helden's (2001) account of sustainable forestry in New Guinea.

The insistence in contemporary participatory conservation projects to demonstrate tangible benefits to the poor, furthermore converts all subject positions to an economic scale, and risks neglecting the qualitative differences in which non-commodity logics operate among people like the Tamang. This is another area where Viveiros de Castro's work can be valuable. His discussion of the need for anthropologists to point out where realities and perspectives do not simply translate is of importance, especially in regard to the idea that nature is something unproblematically 'out there', which happens to be seen differently by different cultures. This separates notions of social form and natural force, that cannot be presumed to operate outside of modernist world views. And in particular, his arguments that the framing of people as having 'rights' to resources that enable them to exchange objects, imposes a univocal understanding of people's relationships to things, whereas relations that are rather characterized by gift and debt, deserve to be recognized as entailing different kinds of intentionality for which things have purpose.

> In a regime where things and people assume the form of objects, relations are exteriorised, detached from persons in the form of rights. All relations must be converted into rights in order to be recognised, just as commodities must have prices to be exchanged; rights and duties define the relative value of persons, just as prices define the exchange rate of things. (Viveiros de Castro 2004a)

This passage can be juxtaposed to good effect alongside Nightingale's (2005) arguments that neo-liberal characteristics can be seen in community forestry projects in Nepal. She analyses how these community-oriented projects foster rule-governed subjectivities responding in appropriate ways to advantages presented by professional expertise in the better management of forest resources. Communities in this model are assumed to have a shared culture which is the source of collective values that individuals then apply in practical choice behaviour. An alternative view would be that the rules of the game and the determination of values are located in the arena of practice, where differentiations of people and things are publicly negotiated. Nightingale points out there are apparently different kinds of power that adhere to textual knowledge and maps (where women and manual labourers are mostly illiterate), in contrast to the arena of committee decisions, where the authority of precedent offers room for challenging the letter of the forest group operational plan's code. In other words, the conversion of people's forest relationships into formally accountable rights gives rise to a certain kind of subjectivity, consonant with institutional and use privileges, which individuals acquire by virtue of group membership. Nightingale shows how the surface appearance of equality as individual members of the forest group is not simply confused by the contradictions of text-based and meeting-based authority, but also in the tolerances of behaviours (such as service castes' continued illicit selling of fuelwood) that presuppose ongoing, intrinsic inequalities between categories of people.

Conclusion

In reflecting on the differences between animistic and neo-liberal environmental subjectivities, a whole set of contrasts can be drawn out that are routinely ignored in environmental policy literature, and possibly, in indigenous empowerment discourse, which often wants to hold to primal connections *and* to contemporary eco-legitimacy at the same time. Whereas modern conservation requires the environment to be recognized as a scientifically knowable entity out there (separate from the seeing subject), the animistic perspective places the subject in deliberate interaction and co-substantiality with it (especially for shamans). The modern environment is manageable by forward-looking, local democratic decision processes, whereas the animistic environment is characterized by a constant inter-mixing of intentions, desires and cross-purposes between different beings, with whom peaceable relations may only be maintained by ongoing gifts and offerings to achieve cooperative alliance (whether with humans or non-humans).

In contrast to institutional studies, I have found it important to understand environmental subjectivities by talking about kinship. The story of the daughter-in-law and the bear told by a Newar living among Tamangs, with its affinal encounters that stretch credibility into human and non-human extremes, belongs in an extant tradition of folk discourse (*ukhan, katha*) which speaks of the world of deep rural peasantry, in which material outcomes of household decision making are critical, but are not contained in a dualistic split of the natural and the social, or of the material and symbolic. The pressing environmental questions now facing Himalayan people can no longer be mystified by ancient stories, but nor can these be simply replaced by modern myths of rational choice over resources, devoid of relational complexity.

It is the purchase of both old and new myths that seems to characterize late capitalist environmental discourse, in the desire to privilege non-modern locality in terms of cultural and biological diversity, and to apply a coherent framing for local action in global responsibilities. Down at the village-forest interface, I would argue that the ethnographic ground remains largely misrecognized, and misunderstood. A host of studies has shown how problematic has been the introduction of environmental protection in Nepal (Campbell 2005b), and to move this task from a default 'ethno' focus, and the privileging of assumed shared cultural constructions of the environment, the concept of 'environmental subjectivity' may be very fruitful. It does need to be made of relevance beyond the political-economy mechanism that Agrawal places it in, and given flesh and rootedness in practices of daily life.

In the myth at the centre of this chapter is the tale of a young woman's career through dysfunctional domestic relations, affinal rejection, and abandonment in the forest, only to eventually experience a reversal of fortunes after she supplants a bear from its herding enterprise. She takes up a position in a tree to observe the bear going about the everyday duties of cattle camp management, and here takes up the ontological perspective of another being. Rather than a Nepalese version of 'Goldilocks and the Three Bears', I interpret this account as opening a perspectival window, because in its separation, encounter with otherness, and resolution, it follows a similar narrative form as encounters with the quasi-human *longai* or *nyalmo* (Campbell 1998), which are about dangerous crossings over into other worlds, of a distinctly perspectival variety. This is not to say that a non-animist reading *à la* Goldilocks could be made by certain Nepalis, who might be more familiar with the actual Goldilocks story than the ontology of Tamang village shamanism. This is an important point to elaborate on as regards the borrowing of certain ideas from analyses of Amazonian perspectivism. If there are perspectival moments that I have picked up from Tamang discourse on non-human worlds, as Caroline Humphrey points out for attempts to apply perspectivist interpretations on Inner Asian contexts, a key difference with the Amazonian situation is that there is nothing like the 'integrated mythical cosmological system' as appears in the Amazonian case. 'With various diverse inputs into Mongolian culture, especially from Buddhism, such a single system could hardly have existed in historical times' (Humphrey 2007:174).

Precisely because of the varieties of belief in Nepal, and the asymmetries and dissonances between groups of people with differential power over symbolic hegemonies and their playing out on the ground of local environments, the traces of perspectivist ontology are temporary occurrences. Yet the fact that subjectivities are granted to non-humans (and not only in myth), and that the subjectivity focus can illuminate how actual people's lives are conducted in relations of environmental intimacy and experiences of power, makes the case for including perspectival-animist among other possible modalities for examining human-environmental relations in the Himalayan region. Environmental subjectivity needs further nuancing in the sorts of exchange and reciprocity nexuses that people take up in multiple subject positions. Indeed, unlike the stark gift/economy contrasts of Melanesia or Amazonia, the Himalayan ethnographic context could prove a remarkable comparative field in showing the range of reciprocal positions and modes of exchange simultaneously, and strategically, deployable in representing human-environmental relationships. Arguably, one of the principal causes of objections to nature protection in Nepal is the specious distinctions it imposes not only between the human and non-human, but also between the supposed opposition of valuing the environment as either commercial or protected.

Contemporary villages are sites where problems are experienced by the people themselves in relating and mixing the different kinds of knowledge available to them. Animistic, shamanic understandings can be abruptly dismissed by people who in other circumstance might entertain them (Steinmann 2001: 376ff). An example of a rhetorical practice to reject perspectival, animistic thought, is a frequently-heard Tamang phrase that embodied an absurdist characterization of human/non-human indifferentiation: *'Ra ta mam, kli ta bap'* translated as 'calling a goat "grandmother", calling shit "beer"'. It serves to bring the person addressed down to earth, to 'get real', and not to confuse categories, but pay attention to the distinctiveness in which all things deserve to be seen. The contexts of experience where such kinds of human/non-human connective logics are given value, indeed reached for with urgency (bouts of sickness, sudden misfortune, lightning strikes etc), need to be set against those where scepticism of old tales can be confidently advanced.

If some examples show that ideas of environmental protection are making headway in certain places (see Campbell 2005b), it is questionable that these are instances of the sorts of quasi-evangelical environmental subjectivity which Agrawal writes about in Kumaon. 'The environment as a resource' provides a modern metadiscourse beneath which social meanings and relationships are battling out the problems of livelihood and forest health in domestically situated frameworks, encountering pragmatic household reproduction and community (village, ethnic, class) dynamics. But 'resource' does not offer the same kind of possibility for diplomacy as shamanism does between 'different ontological worlds' (Viveiros de Castro 2004b: 3), rather it constitutes a language that vacates alternative relational logics of territoriality and environmental practice, while at the same time offering a vehicle for pathways of patronage and state extension. 'The environment as a scene of tributary relations' is another mode that is still practised, if less visibly so, and which deserves to be seen as a connecting model of subjectivity, providing frameworks of motivation that feed into modernist protection stances.[10] The modern governmentalized community, the tributary (including sacrifical), and the perspectival-animist are perhaps three modalities of environmental subjectivity, all of which have their own kinds of relationship to powers of place and kind, and between which dialogues of self and otherness are articulated from very different standpoints of knowing translatability.

References

Agarwal, B. 2001. 'Participatory Exclusions, Community Forestry, and Gender: An Analysis for South Asia and a Conceptual Framework'. *World Development* 29 (10): 1623-48.

Agrawal, A. 2003. 'Sustainable Governance of Common-Pool Resources: Context, Methods, and Politics'. *Annual Review of Anthropology* 32: 243-62.

_____ 2005a. *Environmentality: Technologies of Government and the Making of Subjects*. Durham: Duke University Press.

_____ 2005b. 'Environmentality: Community, Intimate Government, and the Making of Environmental Subjects in Kumaon, India'. *Current Anthropology* 46 (2): 161-90.

Bamford, S. 1998. 'Humanized Landscapes, Embodied Worlds: Land and the Construction of Intergenerational Continuity among the Kamea of Papua New Guinea'. *Social Analysis* 42 (3): 28-54.

Bhatt, N. 2003. 'Kings as Wardens and Wardens as Kings: Post-Rana ties between Nepali Royalty and National Park Staff'. *Conservation and Society* 1 (2): 247-68.

Campbell, B. 2005a. 'Introduction: Anthropological Encounters with Environmental Protection'. In B. Campbell ed. *Re-Placing Nature* Special issue, *Conservation and Society* 3 (2): 280-322.

_____ 2005b. 'Nature's Discontents in Nepal'. In B. Campbell ed. *Re-Placing Nature*. Special issue, *Conservation and Society* 3(2): 323-53.

---

[10] See Nina Bhatt (2003) for a historical study of the royal hunting visits to national parks.

_____ 1998a. 'Conversing with Nature: Ecological Symbolism in Central Nepal'. *Worldviews.* 2(2): 123-37.

Chhetri, R. 1998. 'Cultural and Socio-Economic Perspective on Biodiversity Conservation: The Case of Community Forestry Program'. In R. Chhetri and P. Yonzon eds. *Conserving Biodiversity in Nepal's Community Forests.* National Biodiversity Action Plan Project. Resources Nepal.

Clarke, G. 1995. 'Thinking Through Nature in Highland Nepal'. In O. Bruun and A. Kalland eds. *Asian Perceptions of Nature: A Critical Approach.* Nordic Institute of Asian Studies. London: Routledge. pp. 88-102.

Descola, P. 1996. 'Constructing Natures: Symbolic Ecology and Social Practice'. In P. Descola and G. Pálsson eds. *Nature and Society: Anthropological Perspectives.* London: Routledge. pp. 82-102.

Descola, P. 2005 *Par Delà Nature et Culture.* Paris: Editions Gallimard.

Gellner, D. 1991. 'Hinduism, Tribalism and the Position of Women: The Problem of Newar Identity'. *Man* 26 (1): 105-25.

Gow, P. 2001. *An Amazonian Myth and its History.* Oxford: Blackwell.

Humphrey, C. 'Inside and Outside the Mirror: Mongolian Shamans' Mirrors as Instruments of Perspectivism' *Inner Asia* 9(2):173-96.

Ingold, T. 2000. *The Perception of the Environment.* London: Routledge.

Ives, J. and B. Messerli. 1989. *The Himalaya Dilemma: Reconciling Development and Conservation.* London: Routledge.

Latour, B. 2009. 'Perspectivism : 'Type' or 'bomb' ? *Anthropology Today* 25(2) :1-2.

Lecomte-Tilouine, M. 1993. *Les Dieux du Pouvoir: Les Magar et l'hindouisme au Népal central.* Paris: CNRS Editions.

_____ This volume. 'To be more Natural than Others: Indigenous Self-determination and Hinduism in the Himalayas'.

Linkenbach, A. 2000. 'Appropriating the Himalayan Forests: Ecology and Resistance in Garhwal (North India)'. Habilitation thesis. University of Heidelberg.

Milton, K. 1996. *Environment and Cultural Theory.* London: Routledge.

Müller-Böker, U. 1995. *Die Tharu in Chitawan: Kenntnis, Bewertung und Nutzung der natürlichen Umwelt im südlichen Nepal.* Franz Steiner Verlag: Stuttgart. Translated as *The Chitawan Tharus in Southern Nepal: An ethnoecological approach.* Stuttgart: Franz Steiner Verlag, 1999.

Nightingale, A. 2005. '"The Experts Taught Us All We Know":

Professionalisation and Knowledge in Nepalese Community Forestry'. *Antipode* 34 (3): 581–604.

Pottier, J. 2003. 'Negotiating Local Knowledge: An Introduction'. In J. Pottier, A. Bicker, and P. Sillitoe eds. *Negotiating Local Knowledge: Power and Identity in Development*. London: Pluto Press. pp. 1–29.

Ramble, C. and C.P. Chapagain. 1990. *Preliminary Notes on the Cultural Dimension of Conservation*. Report no.10. Makalu-Barun Conservation Project Working Paper Publication Series. Kathmandu: DNPWC/WMI.

Sarin, M., Singh, N., Sundar, N. and R. Bhogal. 2003. *Devolution as a Threat to Democratic Decision-Making in Forestry? Findings from Three States in India*. Working Paper No. 197. Overseas Development Institute, London.

Shneiderman, S. 2005. 'Swapping Identities: Borderland exchanges along the Nepal-TAR frontier'. *Himal*. November-December, 18 (3): 32–3.

Steinmann. B. 2001. *Les Enfants du Singe et de la Démone: Mémoires des Tamang, Récits Himalayens*. Nanterre: Société d'ethnologie.

Thompson, M., Warburton, M. and T. Hately. 1986. *Uncertainty on a Himalayan Scale*. London: Ethnographica.

Van Helden, F. n.d. '"The report was written for money to come": Constructing the case for conservation on mainland Papua New Guinea. Paper given to "People Protecting Nature" Conference'. Oxford Brookes University. October 2005.

_____ 2001. 'Through the Thicket: Disentangling the Social Dynamics of an Integrated Conservation and Development Project on Mainland Papua New Guinea'. PhD thesis. Wageningen Universiteit: The Netherlands.

Viveiros de Castro, E. 2004a. 'Le don et le donné: trois nano-essais sur la parenté et la magie', *ethnographiques.org*, N° 6, Nov. 2004 (online edition).

_____ 2004b. 'Perspectival Anthropology and the Method of Controlled Equivocation'. *Tipití, Journal of the Association for the Anthropology of Lowland South America* 2 (2): 3–22.

Willerslev, R. 2007. '"To Have the World at a Distance": Reconsidering the Significance of Vision for Social Anthropology'. In C. Grasseni ed. *Skilled Visions and the Ecology of Practice*. Oxford: Berghahn Books. pp. 23–46.

Political Aspects of the Territorial Cult among the Mewahang Rai

MARTIN GAENSZLE

Territorial cult in Bala: ca:wa pujā (Photo: Martin Gaenszle)

Fieldwork for this article was carried out between 1984–91. Since then there have been considerable changes, nevertheless I have retained the 'ethnographic present'. I am grateful to C.N.A.S. for being granted affiliation in 1984–85 when the major part of my fieldwork, on which this study is based, was conducted. I also would like to thank Franz-Karl Ehrhard, András Höfer, Joanna Pfaff-Czarnecka and Prayag Raj Sharma for their stimulating comments on an earlier draft, and Philip Pierce and Bernadette Sellers for revising my English. Nepali terms are transliterated according to Turner's system (1980); for the system for transcribing Mewahang terms see Gaenszle 1991: 357 (in addition /ɛ/ has phonemic status and is written as 'ä').

Rituals focussing on 'divinities of the soil' can be read as indicative of a group's traditional concepts about the forces of 'nature' and the ways these can be legitimately used and controlled through the 'civilizing force' of ritual action. Such rituals are found among most ethnic groups in Nepal. Though they have a place in the Hindu tradition, it is among the Tibeto-Burman groups that these divinities have special prominence: they are usually represented by an aniconic rock formation at which offerings of blood are given (mostly in spring), and are often associated with a specific village territory. In Nepali they are generally referred to by the term *bhume* (< Sk. *bhumiya* 'belonging to the soil'), but this Indo-European background cannot be taken as an indicator of their origin. Whereas among the Magars and some Rai groups such as the Thulungs, there seem to be no indigenous terms (Lecomte-Tilouine 1993a, b; Allen 1981), among the Tamangs, they are known as *syibda-nè:da* (Höfer 1981: 12f., 163f.), and among the Gurungs as *sildo naldo* (Pignède 1966: 307ff.), or *shyolto-nolto* (Strickland 1982: 54), terms apparently cognate with Tibetan *gzhi-bdag gnas-bdag* 'master of the territory', lit. 'owner of the ground'. Among the Kulung Rais, the territorial spirit is known as *tos* (McDougal 1979: 37f., Schlemmer 2004: 350ff.), and among the Mewahang Rais, as *ca:ri* and *ca:wa* (Gaenszle 2000: 122ff.).[1]

Clearly what gives these divinities vital importance is the strong link with the forces of 'nature' in general, and fertility and prosperity in particular. Often they are associated with the coming of the monsoon rains which greatly dominates the agricultural cycle and take on a cosmological dimension: without the heavenly waters, the earth remains barren.[2] In Rai mythology,

[1] In a narrow sense, *ca:ri* refers to the village territory and *ca:wa* to the village waters, but both terms also signify inherent divine power, though the latter is not conceived of as anthropomorphous (see below).

[2] In his article on Tibetan megaliths, Macdonald pointed to an ancient cosmological concept of fertility which is widespread in Asia: 'It is the fertility value of the megaliths which seems to be the principal concern of the peoples that put them up. (...) In monsoon Asia, this fertility is, to some extent, considered everywhere, and with sound reason, as the result

the primal ancestress Sumnima, who lives solitarily on the earth, almost dies of thirst because Paruhang, who resides in the sky and was rejected by her, brings about a severe drought. But after she is forced to consume the only 'water' available, Paruhang's semen, the variety of species (namely tiger, bear, monkey and the first man, as well as plants, like bamboo, and the thorny creeper) is born. This important myth shows that for the Rai there is no fundamental distinction between 'nature' and 'humanity': both are derived from the same ancestral source and thus mankind is linked through kinship with the natural world (Gaenszle 2000: 235ff.). With the annual monsoon rains, this story of primal creation is re-enacted; supported by the commemorative and foundational soil rituals, the fertility of the land and the jungle is reinvigorated, and thus prosperity cannot be achieved without paying ritual tribute to the ancestors and their deeds. It is the imposition of a ritual order—or 'culture'—which enables the Rai to control the primal forces. This is also a recurrent theme in mythology, where the orphaned 'culture hero' establishes various institutions and traditions after vanquishing certain 'savage' powers (Gaenszle 2000: 248-69). Considering its existential significance for the community, it comes as no surprise that this annual cult, which makes reference to the divine creator ancestors, as well as to the less remote village founders, also has a strong social and political dimension.[3]

This political dimension of the territorial cult is the topic of this chapter. The Mewahang Rais of the Western Arun valley have

---

of the interaction between the rain and the earth, that is to say, of a harmonious relationship between the sky, the earth, and the subterranean world, between the living and the dead, between the celestial and earthy waters' (Macdonald 1984a: 20).

[3]In his comparative article on deities of the soil and demons in the Himalayan religions Toffin (1987: 86), though only in passing, draws attention to '...the close relationship which the deities of the soil (or of the territory) have with the local power and the monopoly exercised by the village chief over their cult. This trait is particularly perceptible among the Tibeto-Burmans for whom command over men comes with command over the divinities of the soil—which is the reason for the generally collective dimension of their territorial cults, be it at village or at clan level.' (my translation)

an important festival for the divinity of the territory, which is called *ca:ri pujā*, or *dhuli pujā* or also *bhumi pujā*. This is not simply a religious festival but at the time of research, it relied on the traditional kinship-based political system of the village. I will first describe the mythological and historical context of the festival and then its ritual performance in the case of one particular village, and will end by drawing comparisons with data from neighbouring villages. If it is true that there is something typically Tibeto-Burman (or tribal?) in the celebration, some interesting conclusions may come out of comparing it with the Hindu festival of *Dasaī*, which is also celebrated by the Mewahang and contains certain homologies with it. I will then try to show that the two festivals can be interpreted as expressions of two different concepts of sovereignty.

Myth

To clarify how the concept of *ca:ri* is understood by the Mewahang Rai, a good starting point is to look into its mythological background.

In the village of Bala, which is the main focus of this study, a myth is recounted in which the forefathers of the present residents are depicted as the first legitimate settlers on the territory. The following is a summary of the myth (presented in Gaenszle 2000: 288, 302f.)

> Before the Mewahangs there were Sampange Rai settlers on the territory of Bala. However, the *ca:ri* kept troubling these settlers and even killed some of them.
> Eventually the forefathers of the present-day Balalis, Yungthu *rājā* and his three sons, came and took possession of the land. Though the Sampanges had set up the *sakhewaluŋ* stone in an attempt to pacify the *ca:ri*, they were not able to perform the necessary rituals. Only the Mewahangs had proper knowledge of the *muddum* to pay reverence to the territorial spirit, and therefore they chased the Sampanges away and established

themselves as legitimate settlers. From then on the Mewahangs performed the offering for the *ca:ri* every year, giving a blood sacrifice and offerings of beer.

Today no Sampange settlers inhabit the territory of Bala. With few exceptions, all Mewahangs in Bala claim descent from Yungthu: in fact, the three sons of Yungthu are said to be the clan-founders of three clans bearing the three brothers' names. Two of these clans (A, B) are the biggest clans in Bala today, whereas the third clan (C) has, according to the second part of the myth, been driven out (see second part of the myth, quoted below) The seniormost clan (A), i.e., those who claim descent from the eldest son of Yungthu, may be regarded as the dominant clan: it is in the senior line of this clan that has traditionally inherited the post of *jimmāwāl* (tax-collecting headman). Other Mewahang clans in Bala are either immigrants from other villages (three clans) or an offshoot resulting from the fission (one clan). Besides the 50 Mewahang households in Bala (in 1985), however, there are also around 35 Kulunge households in the village, mostly in the upper part. These Kulunges immigrated from the Mahakulung area in the Hongu Valley about seven generations ago, and because they mainly occupy the higher regions above the Mewahangs where they rely primarily on dry field crops (millet, maize, barley), they are in fact today a majority on the traditional Bala territory.

The remaining part of the myth is also pertinent to our topic as it recounts the subsequent fission of the original territory.

> The three brothers eventually decided to divide their inheritance into three parts. But after some time, the descendants of the younger brother started to fight those of the elder brothers using black magic. The latter fought back in the same way and finally drove the surviving members of the youngest brother's clan out of the village.
>
> After having lived in a different village with affinal relatives for several years, the descendants of this clan came back and occupied wasteland (Makruk) on the Bala territory which had

not yet been claimed by anyone. They made an attempt to recover their share of the property in Bala village, but were turned back a second time. Eventually they decided to remain in Makruk. They later asked for user rights of the highland pastures and the post of a *jimmāwāl* of their own. Both were finally granted to them.

There are good reasons to regard this story as containing a kernel of historical truth. Clan C is in fact dominant in Makruk even today, and the post of *jimmāwāl* is passed down through the seniormost line of this clan. (There is even documentary evidence about a lawsuit following this expulsion). Moreover, as we shall see, there are indications that the *ca:ri* on one level is conceived as still being one, while on another level, has divided in two. Let us therefore turn to the historical background of the story.

History

The term *ca:ri* is closely linked to the term *kipaṭ*, and both are often used synonymously in the sense of 'ancestral land'. Under the *kipaṭ*-system, ownership of land resided with the community and could not be transferred to outsiders by individuals. This system, which may be regarded as a modified continuation of customary rights sanctioned by the newly-established Nepalese state (Regmi 1972: 49), was conceded by the Shah kings to the Kiranti groups in eastern Nepal as a form of partial autonomy: the task of tax collection and certain judicial functions were delegated to traditional local chiefs.

These chiefs, given the official title of *rāi* (or *jimmāwāl, subbā, dewān* etc.), were thus confirmed in their political position. They not only had considerable powers but also enjoyed certain privileges. Foremost among these were the rights to services and gifts (presentations) from their 'subjects' (*raiti*), known as *ṭheki beṭhi*.

The term *ṭheki* refers to the gifts which had to be rendered to the chief as a token acknowledgement of his control over the land. Immigrants like the Kulunges gained access to land only through the good will of the *kipaṭiyās*, after presenting them with a gift called *cārdām*. Twice a year, parts of the harvest had to be presented as a kind of tribute (*walak*). And on *Dasaī*, those immigrants who made use of the pastures within the territory had to contribute a sacrificial animal (sheep), while all the *raiti*, including the Mewahangs, had to give one container of alcohol to the chief as a sign of their allegiance.

Besides these gifts, the *raiti* were obliged to supply the chief with free labour (*beṭhi*), usually five 'daily labourers' (*khetālā*) annually per household. In the case of immigrants, however, the chief could actually demand more than the customary five days of labour. As they were dependants, they were forced to comply with the chief's will.

There were also other ways in which the chiefs benefited from their powers, but as it is not of import for our study and I have written in greater detail about this elsewhere (Gaenszle 2000: 55ff., 62f., 67f.), it suffices to say that there were good reasons why the post was attractive, not only in terms of prestige and status, but also with regard to economic benefits.

In the following sections I will concentrate on the changes in the position of the headman (here called *jimmāwāl* or *tālukdār*) in the village of Bala, because these changes have affected the organization of the territorial cult as celebrated in that village.

The first documentary evidence about the existence of a *rāi* in Bala is dated V.S. 1910 (AD 1853), but the title was conveyed probably well before that. He belonged to the 'senior' clan (A), and his descendant in the senior line, now in the fifth generation, is the current *jimmāwāl* of Bala. Until the end of the nineteenth century, the chief's post in Bala was solely assigned to this line. I have no evidence about when the post in Makruk was established, but there is some indication that it was around the middle of the nineteenth century.

As Bala, situated west of the Sankhuwa Khola, belongs to the *Mājh Kirāt* division, the abolishment of the *kipaṭ*-system started in 1907, when irrigated rice-lands in that region were converted to *raikar*, i.e., individually held property formally owned by the state and taxable according to size. Under the *kipaṭ*-system the object of taxation was not the land but the household: the tax was called *sermā* and was Rs 4 per household in 1853—not a small amount if one considers that a *tolā* of gold was Rs 42 around that time! Though the *kipaṭ*-system survived for *pākho*-land (dry fields) until the early 1940s and for pastures until the land reform in the 1960s, partial abolishment at the beginning of the century complicated the tax collection procedure, as the size of fields had to be calculated, and the registration of holdings became more extensive.

It seems at least partly related to this fact that after 1900, the number of authorized *rāi* increased from one to four within about twenty years.[4] Through the payment of a specified amount of money (Rs 25, I was told), other individuals could acquire the title of *rāi*, and with it the accompanying privileges mentioned above. This was called *raiti kinnu* ('buying subjects') because the *rāi* thus obtained control over 'his own' subjects within a specific area of authority (*jimmā*). These new functionaries, however, only collected house tax and taxes for *pākho* fields (after their abolishment as *kipaṭ*), whereas the collection of *khet*-taxes remained the 'privilege' of the original line of *jimmāwāl*. The newly appointed *rāi* were usually called *tālukdār* (a general term for 'tax functionary'), while the term *jimmāwāl*, signifying here a somewhat higher status, was reserved for the older line of chiefs. Today, however, the term *jimmāwāl* is often used indiscriminately (like the more neutral term *pagari*), while the term *jhuṭṭāwāl* has come to take the place of *jimmāwāl* in the older sense.

It is significant that two of the three new posts went to other lineages of the A clan, whereas only one was acquired by a member of clan B. However, one of the A clan *jimmā*s (A') later further subdivided into three, one of which came under the authority of a Kulunge line (= K, the other was obtained by a member of a clan which had split off from A, = A*). Evidently political power was slowly dispersing into all sections of local groups, though still in unequal portions (see Figure 7.1).

[4]Unfortunately no documentary evidence on the establishment of these posts has been available.

1.	Yungthu						
2.	A						C
3.	A	A'		A"		B	
4.	A	A'	A*	K	A"	B	

Figure 7.1: Division of the ca:ri

The crucial point for this study of the territorial cult is that the organization of the *ca:ri pujā* examined here is based on these political divisions: in principle, all the *jimmā*s celebrate their own festival, hosted by the *jimmāwāl* and *tālukdār*. This is true for the four *jimmā*s of the first division (considering the major rite for the soil), but the second (sub)division is only partly reflected at cult level, as the rites are occasionally celebrated jointly. For example, in 1991—after the death of the A'-*pagari*—*jimmā*s A' and K joined to hold the festival together.

Thus the political division of the original ancestral land, the *ca:ri*, first into two halves, one half of which further divided into four, and later into six *jimmā*s (see Figure 7.1), is reflected at the level of ritual activity. With this in mind, let us have a closer look at the cult as it is celebrated in Bala.

The Rite

The sacrifice to the *ca:ri* as laid down in the myth is celebrated in the month of *māgh* (January/February). As the offerings are presented at the ancestral stone, *sakhewaluŋ*, the rite is also known as *sakhewa pujā*. The senior lineage of clan A finances the offerings of a pig and a clay container (*ghyampā*) of millet-beer (*jāṛ*). No priest is required for the rite, but according to one myth, it was previously celebrated with a drum (*ḍhol*), which is nowadays only used by knowledgeable shamans (*selemi*) (Gaenszle 2000: 288). Today (at the time of my research) the ritual address to the *ca:ri* in the form of the ancestral stone is delivered by the Mewahang elders. The *kipaṭiyā* villagers assemble and receive parts of the offerings as *prasād*. The non-*kipaṭiyās*, however, i.e., the Kulunge settlers, are excluded from the rite and do not receive *prasād*.

Though this 'original' *ca:ri pujā* is still celebrated in Bala, its importance seems to be on the decline. It is no longer performed annually but at a three-year interval. Instead focus has shifted to another rite which is also called *ca:ri pujā* (or *bhumi pujā*) but is meant more generally for the prosperity of the community. It is held every year in the first week of *cait* (March/April) when the first rains moisten the dusty soil, and, in fact, it is expected to rain on the day of the ritual. The celebrations actually consist of a sacrifice for the communal spring or water tap (*ca:wa* M., *panero* N.) and another for the territory (*ca:ri*). Because of the dusty state of the soil, the latter celebration is also called *dhuli pujā* N., this expression also being used metonymously for the whole festival. It is this double ritual focussing on the elements of water and earth which brings the political organiztion outlined above into play—and is the object of this study.

Raising the Head-Soul of the Priest: phäkhaŋ/nakchoŋ-mi saya po:kma

The first ritual activity on the day of *dhuli pujā* is for the benefit of the priest who is to hold the sacrifices. As his task is considered to be particularly difficult and dangerous—due to the power of the *ca:ri*—his head-soul (*saya*) has to be raised with the help of the members of the *pagari*'s lineage by whom he is 'hired'. All of them have to bring a *mānā* of alcohol or beer and provide the two chickens necessary for the rite. The latter is then held at the priest's house by a village elder who is accompanied in his chanting by the sponsors. The beer, alcohol and chickens are consumed afterwards by all the participants.

Traditionally the priest here is called *phäkhaŋ* or *nakchoŋ*, depending on which clan the priest belongs to: if he is from clan A (in Bala) he is *phäkhaŋ*, if from clan B then he is *nakchoŋ*. This distinction is explained in terms of patrilineally inherited priestly 'competence': originally—it is said—priests of clan A— the 'owners of the *ca:ri*'—performed the rite by drumming on a wooden container (*āri* N.) placed upside-down on water, while the priests of clan B did this with the two-sided drum (*ḍhol*). Actually, I was told, a *phākhaṇ* should perform the rite, but as no one is currently able to do this, the rites are all held by *nakchoṇ*. This latter term has a complicated semantic background and raises some general issues concerning the classification of priests. Apart from the above-mentioned distinction, the term also denotes the priestly role of the elder who sends the dead person on his way (M. *lam ti:ʔma*, N. *bāto lāune*) during the funeral rites, irrespective of his clan. It is interesting in this context that in Yaphu and Mangtewa the priest who is specifically in charge of the local territorial cult there, is also called *nakchoṇ*, whereas the common term for the tribal priest is *yatakpa*, though the term *ṇo:pa* is also used (as in Bala). These latter terms distinguish the tribal priest from the *makpa*, the Jhankri-like shaman. The evidence is not quite clear but it seems to indicate that the *nakchoṇ* (plus the *phākhaṇ* in Bala) is a kind of subclass of the *ṇo:pa* closely associated with territoriality. There are certain parallels among the Kulunges which corroborate this conjecture.

Pouring Beer on the Hearthstones: situluṇ tukma

Immediately after the *saya po:kma*, a small rite is held for the priest at his hearth which is called *situluṇ tukma*, lit. 'wetting the hearthstones'. This is a common domestic rite performed by elders in the context of more complex ancestral rituals, such as the *nāgi*, *Saraṅdew*, or the *nuwāgi* (first rice offering). The three hearthstones are considered to be the 'seat' of the ancestors: they are called *ma:khaluṇ*, *pa:khaluṇ* and *tapteluṇ*, referring to 'mother', 'father' and a protective force warding off evil influences.[5] By the act of pouring beer on the three symbolic stones, the ancestral forces are satisfied, and thus their benevolence, thereby ensuring the household's prosperity.

[5] The etymology is explained as follows: *ma:khaluṇ* < M. *a:ma* 'mother' + M. *khaṇma* 'to see' + *luṇ 'stone'; *pa:khaluṇ* < M. *pa:pa* 'father'; *tapteluṇ* < M *taptemma* 'to ward off'.

After the *saya po:kma* at the priest's house, participants proceed to the *pagari*'s house, where the same rite is held at his hearth. From there they go to the house of the *pagari*'s closest agnate, and continue the beer offering at the other main households of the lineage in an order of increasing genealogical distance from the senior line. This is exemplified in Figure 7.2.

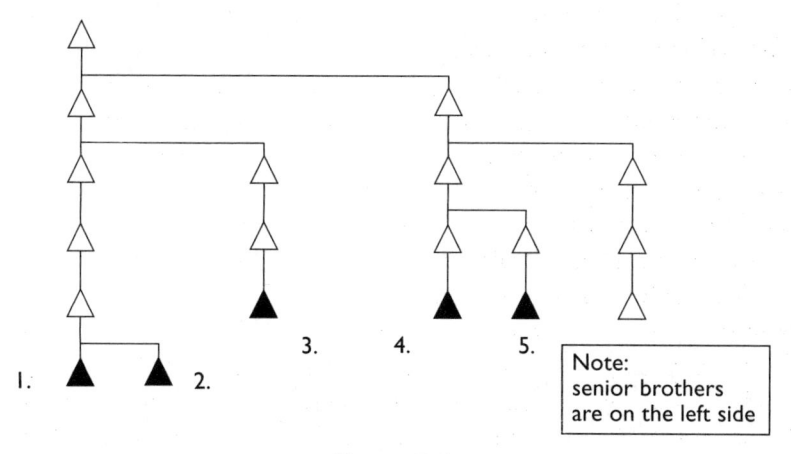

Figure 7.2

Note: senior brothers are on the left side

How may this be explained? The villagers themselves could give no specific reason apart from it being a time-honoured tradition. However, this communal focus on the hearth, not occurring in any other context in such a 'linking' manner, recalls another ritual practice which is found among the neighbouring—and closely related—Lohorung Rais. There, I was told, in the context of the annual rites for the *ca:wa* (water tap), villagers go to the 'senior house', that of the *jimmāwāl*, where the hearth fire is extinguished. The same is then done in all the other households, and for one night, no fire is allowed to burn in the domestic hearth. The next day, a new fire is started at the *jimmāwāl*'s house by rubbing a *bhakimlo* twig, and this fire is then passed to all the households. This ritual practice, again, is very similar to the renewal of the hearth fire among the Tharus, which is performed during the foundation of a new village shrine, a rite which has the features of a 'village cloistering' (Krauskopff 1987: 143).

Thus, the beer sacrifice consecutive to the ancestral hearth in the main households may be seen as a ritual expression of intracommunal cohesion.[6] Though there is no symbolic isolation (no taboos on communication, etc.) this practice is comparable to the rituals of 'village cloistering' in South-East Asia to which Macdonald has drawn attention (1984b). Considering that most rituals among the Rais are entirely domestic, this 'linking' of an otherwise domestic rite carries special significance.

Offering to the Territorial Water: ca:wa si:ʔma

Afterwards, in the late morning, the various *jimmā*-s perform their respective *ca:wa* sacrifices, some at the main water tap called *maca:wa* (A, A*, A″), one (A′ + K) at the water tap in the lower, and one (B) at the one in the upper village. In principle, the offerings are made separately for each *jimmā*, even when they occur at the same *ca:wa*. But it is also possible for two to join together for this rite, as was done by A and A* in 1991 despite the fact that the remaining part of the festival was celebrated separately. It is significant that the Kulunge *pagari*, though he can hold his own rite, may not partake of the *prasād* of the *ca:wa* sacrifice which he hosts. The reason given is that the *ca:wa* is of particular sanctity and purity.

The water taps are decorated in the early morning with two branches of the *kaṭuj*-tree (*Castanopsis tribuloides*) and two sticks of a thin kind of bamboo, *nīgalo* (*Arundinaria hookeriana*), each being 'curled' at four places with a knife. A banana leaf is placed on the spout of the tap, to serve as the 'altar' for the offerings: rice grains and ginger, which have all been washed beforehand. The outlet of the basin below the spout, through which the water

---

[6]It seems significant in this context that in Mangtewa, the *nakchoŋ*, after having performed the communal sacrifice for the *ca:ri*, is carried to the house of the *jimmāwāl* in charge where he makes an offering for his hearth. This could be interpreted as being a 'focal' offering for the whole community.

runs, is blocked for the rite, as it is necessary for water to collect to form a little pool.

The priest stands in the water with a gourd (*ciṇḍo*) in his hand, sprinkling beer on the offerings while he chants. Two assistants stand at his side, one holding the sacrificial cock, which has been donated by the household in charge of cleaning the water tap (in exchange it is exempted from other communal duties). The cock is sprinkled with beer until it shakes (*parchāune*) as a sign of the deity's acceptance. It is then beheaded, its blood is sprinkled on the rice offering, and the body is then thrown into the water of the pool where it continues to jump around for a while. The head is put on the banana leaf.

After this the priest proceeds with a ginger divination: he cuts pieces of ginger with a *khukuri* knife in such a way that they fall on the banana leaf 'altar'. If the piece falls with the cut side downwards or misses altogether, it is inauspicious, but if the cut side is turned upwards, it is a good sign for the following harvest and overall prosperity. The villagers watch with great interest and cheer after each auspicious fall. Eventually, the water barriers are removed, so that the water starts flowing out again. The priest and his assistants distribute *ṭikā* in the form of the wet rice grains to everybody else. Others may help them, or people can pick some grains for themselves. Then the households using the water tap have to present a *mānā* of alcohol, which is then redistributed. The priest is given beer from the gourd, and alcohol is exchanged among all the participants (the cock is prepared as a special dish and consumed by the leading elders). The water tap is now open again for public use.

Offering to the Territorial Soil: *ca:ri si:ʔma*

In the late afternoon, the *raiti*s gather at a field close to the *pagari*'s house. They are expected to bring a gift called *peruṅgo*, a term which refers to the small wicker basket that contains the contribution: traditionally some game (forest birds, fish, deer) worth five rupees. However, it is also possible to contribute a *mānā* of rice, some chilies, ginger, salt, or—more recently—cash, with which meat is bought (the amount was raised to ten rupees in 1991). These compulsory contributions are later cooked and distributed to the participants at the joint evening meal.

The line of the *pagari* has special obligations: its major households contribute the six chickens for the sacrifice instead of the *peruŋgo*. Moreover, each of these households contributes a *mānā* of rice for the *pahunā bhāt* (*ridamdu*), the rice kept for guests who happen to be present during the feast. This underlines the role of 'host' assumed by the *pagari* and his agnates. They 'receive' the gifts by the 'subjects' resident on the *ca:ri* and in return 'feed' them (*raiti khuwāunu*). Though the *raiti*s themselves supply the items for the meal, and in fact each participating household brings its own pot of cooked rice which is presented at the altar and later shared among them, the *pagari* is in charge of organizing the feast that takes place on his land. He acts like a donor or distributor of the territory's produce—and in this sense he is similar to the *ca:ri* itself.

The structure of exchange becomes clearer when we consider another contribution to the sacrifice: the *ṭhek māsu* N. Twice a year a trip to the upper Sankhuwa valley is undertaken to harvest wild honey on the cliffs there. Three men from Bala and three from Makruk/Cirkhuwa gain the right to do this and share the profits by presenting one *dhārni* of pork to each of the eight main *jimmā*s (four in Bala and four in Makruk/Cirkhuwa) during the *dhuli pujā*.[7] This practice is interesting in that it reveals a continuing conceptual unity of the original *ca:ri*. Moreover, the fact that this *ṭhek māsu* is put on the altar as an offering to the *ca:ri* shows the fundamental idea of reciprocity, which implies that to consume the produce of the *ca:ri* (here: honey) one has to give something in return. The recipient is the deity which later returns it as *prasād* to all the participants. But on another level, one might argue, the *pagari* is also a recipient as he is responsible for 'collecting' the gifts and organizing the rite. In this interpretation, the contribution of the 'subjects' could be seen as a kind of tribute

---

[7] The four main *jimmā*s in the two villages take turns to organize the trips, so that the people from one *jimmā* get the chance to go every four years.

which is symbolically given to the chief—representing the *ca:ri*'s secular aspect—as acknowledgment of his status, but which is later directly consumed by the collectivity.

The altar for the *ca:ri pujā*, called *taguʔ* M., resembles that of the *dewā* sacrifice held twice a year for each household:[8] central to it is a construction of *kaṭuj* branches which are stuck in the ground (and to which the *thek māsu* is attached), and in front of this, the offerings are placed on a banana leaf. They consist of (usually four) heaps of cooked rice garnished with various meats, fish and ginger. To the right, on a separate leaf is an offering of rice grains as well as fish and ginger—this is for the Hunting Spirit (Molu Śikāri). Offerings of beer and pots of cooked rice are placed around the *kaṭuj* construction, and the six sacrificial chickens are tied to pegs forming a semicircle. The priest sits in front of all these offerings facing the hillside.

Now the question arises: to what deity is this rite addressed? To clarify this point, it is of interest to have a look at the words of the ritual chant. This is not a fixed text, but like all ritual texts among the Mewahang Rais, a ritual speech which, while following certain traditional patterns and idioms, is put together by each priest according to his own inspirational knowledge. In the text which I recorded in 1985 the deity is addressed as *'kharukhom taŋma wuʔmakhom taŋma'* ('Owner of the Crops') or *'ca:riku taŋma'* ('Owner of the *ca:ri*'). This figure was identified by my interpreters as *Khartok*, a female deity said to roam the fields carrying a basket (N. *thunse*).[9]

It seems that the *ca:ri* is not addressed directly but in a personified form—as *Khartok*. In fact, the same address is used in the *ca:wa pujā*, which indicates that the two rites are directed to two different aspects of the same deity. However, most informants explained that the four heaps of cooked rice presented at the

[8]During this rite, blood offerings are presented mainly to the *buṛhenis* (N.), 'old women', i.e. female ancestors who are regarded as controlling the wealth and prosperity of the house.
[9]This deity has similarities with Tāmpuṅmā, the Limbus' forest deity, who is also seen as an old woman wandering around the edges of the village with a basket (Sagant 1969: 112).

ca:ri pujā proper are for the *buṛheni*s (ancestral 'Old Women'), the recipients of the *dewā* sacrifice, as the altar is structured alike. What is most probably taking place here is an assimilation to the more common *dewā* rite: some older men attested that in previous times only one heap of rice was given—for *Khartok* (cf. Gaenszle 1992).

The execution of the rite is also similar to the *dewā*, if one disregards the textual differences: the chickens are sprinkled with beer until their bodies shake, the assistant kills the chickens (but here with a blow on the neck), and after an interlude, during which the chickens are cut up, the chants resume and the meat is added to the offerings. After this, however, other than during the *dewā*, a ginger divination is performed, as in the morning at the water tap. The altar is eventually dismantled and *prasād* is given to the gathering, while parts of the offering are reserved for the priest and some for the village elders, *purkhā*s.

After the communal meal, in which all participants are 'fed', a small rite is held during which the *pagari* and his agnates thank the priest for taking on the difficult task and present him with his share of the offering. He, in return, blesses and wishes them prosperity etc. At the end of this ritual dialogue, the priest is carried on the back of one *pagari*-agnate to the headman's house. There a gourd of beer which had previously been placed on the domestic house-altar (*khamaŋ*) is ritually 'taken out' (accompanied by chanting) and shared among the participants. Later the same is done in all the households where an offering for the hearth took place in the morning—thus finally ending up in the house of the priest.

Local Comparisons

The other Mewahang villages have territorial cults similar to the one described. Considering that the villages are only a few hours' walking distance apart, it is astonishing for an outsider that they all celebrate the cult in strongly localized versions. This, however, is typical for autochthonous groups like the Rai who have developed

Political Aspects of the Territorial Cult among the Mewahang Rai 207

a multitude of ritual traditions. Here I would like to roughly outline major traits of the cults in three neighbouring villages. As I did not witness their performance, my data has to rely on interviews in the respective localities. However, I think that it will become evident in this short survey that there are basic common ideas underlying the variant practices.

In Tamku, the *ca:ri pujā* (also *bhumi pujā* or *dhuli pujā*) is held on the day of *Śrī pañcami* (in the month of *māgh*). As in Bala, first a sacrifice is held for the water, though here it is divided into two parts: as the water tap does not coincide with the water's source, the cock sacrifice takes place at the spring, whereas the divination with the ginger root is held at the central tap below (which is nowadays no longer used for drinking water because there are modern concrete taps with better water from a tank). Though an ancestral stone called *sakhewaluŋ* exists, there is no sacrifice for it. Instead the *ca:ri pujā* is also referred to as *sakhewa pujā*. In the past the *raiti*s brought the *peruṅgo* gift, and this pork was consumed at the common meal, after the *dewā*-like sacrifice, on a field close to the water tap. However, nowadays the 'subjects' no longer feel obliged to come and the cult is mainly an internal affair among the *jimmāwāl*'s relatives (this is also an overall tendency in the other villages). The three *jimmāwāl* of Tamku join together to hold the rites at the traditional site, and they also act as hosts who contribute the sacrificial chickens and give rice to 'feed' the *raiti*s. There is no particular class of priests to deliver the ritual addresses. This is presently done by a *purkhā* (village elder) who is not from the *jimmāwāl*'s line.

In the village of Mangtewa, the cult is still of great importance. On the Wednesday around the fifteenth of the month of *phāgun*, three different sacrifices are performed: first that for the *ca:wa* (water), then one for the *sakhewaluŋ* (ancestral stone), and then the *dhuli pujā* proper, which in this case, is held at a central shrine. Though these rites are all held on the same day, there is a curious distinction involved at a social level. The *sakhewa pujā* is associated with one particular clan (A), which in earlier days seems to have been dominant: the members of this clan are sometimes referred to as '*rājā*'. The rite was previously performed by a man from this clan only, but as there is now no knowledgeable person from this group, it is currently performed by a man from another clan. It is interesting that at this rite, during which chickens are offered to the ancestral stone, there are no 'immigrants' (mainly Kulunges, Kamis) as participants (cf. similar practice in Bala). At the *ca:wa* and *dhuli pujā*, on the other hand, everybody participates, contributing to the feast in various ways: the Mewahang raise money to buy a pig and a chicken and bring cooked rice (N. *cokho bhāt*) and beer, the Kulunges bring 'birds' (e.g. N. *kālij* 'pheasant', N. *muṣṭe* ?, N. *bhyakuro* ?) which constitute the so-called *choŋwadam* (M. *choŋwa* 'bird' + M. *dam* 'offering'). It is said that the Mewahangs' expenditure is actually much higher than that of the Kulunge 'immigrants' who are 'fed' by the former. Thus the traditional owners of the *kipaṭ* land, the Mewahangs (also called *'jimi'*), act as hosts for the non-*kipaṭiyas*. The seven *jimmāwāl* of Mangtewa, however, do not seem to play a major role. Nevertheless the significance of the political division becomes evident in the way the festival is organized: every year one of the seven *jimmās* is in charge of preparing it, and the priest (a man from clan B) who holds the *ca:wa* and *dhuli pujā*, and who is also called *nakchoŋ*, is carried to the house of his respective *jimmāwāl*, where he holds a ceremony for the hearth. Thus another solution to dividing the cult has been found in expressing the political division of authority while preserving the ritual unity of the village.

As a last example of local diversity, let us consider the village of Yaphu. Here the two rituals of the territorial cult take place on two different days: the sacrifice to the *ca:wa* is held in the month of *cait* on the first Friday (a similar festival is repeated in *bhadau*), and the one to the *ca:ri*, called *damyuŋ* (M. < *dam* 'offering', + *yuŋma* 'to place'), is held one week later (i.e., on the Friday of the second week in *cait*). Whereas during the latter, a pig and nine cocks are sacrificed, at the former, the blood offering consists only of two cocks; the major contribution by the villagers is millet beer (one *pāṭhi* per household). As in Bala and Mangtewa, the *ca:ri pujā* seems to be the politically more important one. All villagers have to contribute an amount of cash with which the sacrificial animals are bought. The priest performing both rites is called *nakchoŋ*, and here this is clearly a category exclusively used in the context of the territorial cult: he is the only person in the village eligible to hold these rites and thus he is 'the' *nakchoŋ*. It is significant that in this role he cannot become a shaman (*makpa*), even though the present office-holder told me that he had already had prescient dreams before he was asked by the community to assume the task of *nakchoŋ*. The *damyuŋ* rites start in the house of the *nakchoŋ* who makes offerings to the hearth and to the house deity (*khamaŋ*). Accompanied by villagers, the beating of cymbals and a drum, carried by attendants he then proceeds to the sacrificial place above the village. The *jimmāwāl*s do not seem to have any important role, but still the division of *jimmā*s comes into play: the sacrificial pig, after being offered to the deity, is divided into small pieces (*cokto*), and these are handed out to all the villagers. This meat, a *prasād* from the deity, is known as *dhuri māsu* ('house meat') and is seen as a form of compensation for the house tax—called *dhuri*—which under the *kipaṭ* system had to be paid to the *jimmāwāl*. Thus in Yaphu, the village chiefs also—at least indirectly—'feed' their 'subjects', and in this respect resemble the territorial deity.

Territory, Redistribution and the Legitimation of Power

When one looks at the variants of the territorial cult among the Mewahang Rais, it becomes evident that despite the obvious differences there are several basic features common to them all.

All the cults are concerned with the duality of *ca:ri* and *ca:wa*, the deities of the soil and water, which are the crucial elements for agricultural prosperity. This duality of soil and water is also common among the Gurungs (see Strickland 1982: 88ff., 205), and reappears in a modified way among the Magars in the twofold deity *sime bhume* (de Sales 1991: 195, Oppitz 1986: 116, Lecomte-Tilouine 1993b: 129). Moreover, if one considers the fact that *ca:wa* water relies on rainfall and that the timing of the cult is related to the beginning of the agricultural cycle and is—at least in Bala—associated with the first rains, the duality may be taken as a variation on the well-known dichotomy of earth and sky (Macdonald 1984a).

Closely linked to this twofold deity is the sacrifice to the ancestral stone (*sakhewaluŋ*). Only in Mangtewa are all the rites held on the same day—while in other villages the cult seems to have disappeared—and the territorial deity is clearly manifested in this rock. Wherever it is held, the sacrifice to this megalith is the more exclusive social event: it appears to be the privilege of the 'first'—or dominant—settlers, excluding the later non-*kipaṭiyā* 'immigrants'.[10] I write 'first' in quotation marks, as they were not necessarily the first to clear the land. As can be seen from the myth summarized at the beginning, it is a well-remembered fact in Bala that before the coming of their ancestors, the land was inhabited by other people. But it was their ability to perform the proper sacrifice which gave them the status of first *legitimate* settlers. The situation seems to be less clear in Mangtewa, where I was told that the '*rājā*'-clan A controlling the *sakhewa pujā* (at least originally) was actually a latecomer among the Mewahang clans. Thus ritual and political dominance is less related to historical fact than to mythically justified claims to power.

With the increase of acknowledged *pagari*s or *jimmāwāl*s[11] during the Rana period, which increasingly diluted the authority of the former lines of chiefs, the onus appears to have shifted away from the *sakhewa pujā* towards the *ca:ri/ca:wa* cult, which, because of its independence from an ancestral shrine and associated claims, was more suitable for the purpose of

---

[10]Such a link of the soil deities with 'first settlers' or 'village founders' is fairly widespread among ethnic groups of Nepal (see Strickland 1982: 61, Krauskopff 1989: 83, Lecomte-Tilouine 1993a: 132; 1996). It is also common in the tribal cultures of India, e.g. in Bastar (Sundar 1997: 25ff.).

[11]From here on, I use the word *jimmāwāl* in the wider sense (including the *tālukdār*), as in Eastern Rai villages the distinction between the two terms (referring to authority over dry field vs. wet fields) which is found in Bala, does not exist.

integrating the newly-empowered lines of headmen. Whichever form these changes may in fact have taken, the headman's close link with the soil under his authority prevailed. The *jimmāwāl*, the man in charge of the land within his *jimmā*, retained the functions of organizing the territorial cult, hosting it for his subjects, and 'feeding' them. Even though the *kipaṯ*-system was abolished in 1964, these social practices still existed in 1985—with the exception of Yaphu, where one can only recognize traces of the older system.

While the *jimmāwāl* is the political representative of *ca:ri* territory, the ritual interaction with the deity (or deities) is the task of the *nakchoŋ*, the specialist in this rite. However, it must be emphasized that the two roles may coincide (in at least one case that has been witnessed). The obscure category of *phäkhaŋ* in Bala, which is only used in connection with the territorial cult and parallels that of the *nakchoŋ* in respect to the chief's clan, may be taken as an indication that the headman was also originally the officiant of the cult and that the disjunct role of *nakchoŋ* was a later development. Though this assumption cannot be corroborated further by evidence, similar links between the headman and the officiant of the soil cult are documented for other neighbouring groups (Höfer 1981: 26; Krauskopff 1989).

One of the most striking features of the territorial cult is the practice of collective contributions which appear as gifts to the headman. When I first witnessed the cult I had the impression this was a kind of archaic tax: the force of the obligation, though already clearly weakening, became evident when a quarrel erupted between a *jimmāwāl* and a *raiti* who did not bring enough. But the more I started looking into the actual distribution of the acquired gifts, the more I became aware that nobody accumulates any wealth: the food is instantly consumed by the very community that contributed it. Though the situation may have been different when all *raitis* still came and respected their obligations, the general impression is that the *jimmāwāl*, by hosting the feast and 'giving' the food, bears some of the expense rather than draws any actual benefit. Any redistribution is entirely symbolic.

Excursus: The Festival of Dasaī

At this point it is worthwhile comparing the territorial cult with another important festival, which takes place in autumn and can be regarded as typically Hindu in character—*Dasaī*.[12] This festival, as it is celebrated among the Mewahang Rai, has many striking parallels with the *ca:ri pujā*. The festivities on *nawamī*, the day of the blood sacrifice for Durga (*mār*), are also hosted by the *jimmāwāl* or *tālukdār* and celebrated in his courtyard. The *raitis* of the respective *jimmās* assemble to witness the decapitation of a sheep (or if not affordable, a cock) in front of an assortment of old weapons—symbols of war—which are the focus of the offering. After the blow is struck the *pagari* distributes *ṭikā* to the participants, aided by his close agnates. Alcohol and most of the meat is later distributed as *prasād* to those present. Before the abolishment of the *kipaṭ*-system the *raiti* were obliged to come with gifts (usually a *mānā* of alcohol, or beer). The contribution of the 'immigrants' was generally larger: in Tamku, for example, they had to give cash (*āṭh ānā*) in addition to the other gifts, and in Bala, as mentioned above, the Kulunges who made use of the pastures contributed the sacrificial sheep. Today, however, only some loyal households bring gifts of alcohol, and the *pagari* have to provide the sacrificial animal at their own expense. In any case, it becomes clear that, as in the territorial cult, the headman traditionally acts as host during these festivals, receiving gifts which he redistributes to his subjects.

The similarities between the two festivals may help to explain why the celebration of *Dasaī* quite easily became integrated into the ritual cycle of the Mewahang Rais. As there was already a territorial cult with a similar structure, the Hindu festival—for the Rais—was only a variation on the same theme, allowing the headman at the same time to participate in a transregional

---

[12]On the political dimension of this festival at local level in central Nepal, see Gaborieau 1978 and especially Krauskopff & Lecomte-Tilouine 1996.

symbolism which linked him directly to the royal power and thus legitimized his own position.[13]

But there are also significant differences between the two traditions. First of all, the rituals are concerned with entirely different deities; whereas the territorial cult is directed to the deity (or deities) of the soil and water for the fertility of the cultivated land and general prosperity of the territory, the *Dasaī* festival centres on the goddess *Durgā*, the deity of war who is victorious over the buffalo demon *Mahiśāsura*. This military aspect of the festival is manifested in the display of weapons, and though the modest assemblage of rusty knives, swords and *khukuri*s in the Mewahang villages can hardly stand comparison with the army's parades, during *Dasaī* celebrations in the capital of Kathmandu, it is clear that both are symbols of power and demonstrations of strength. Unbescheid in his study of the *Dasaī* festival in Gorkha stresses:

> The function of the king is further the protection of his kingdom and his subjects. For this protection it is indispensable, that he makes war and this could happen best—for practical reasons— after the rainy season, that means at or after Durgāpūjā. The ritual is therefore interspersed with military accents. (Unbescheid n.d.: 39-40)

The Rai headmen, as representatives of royal power at the village level, tried to replicate the rites held in the capital in a

---

[13] While I agree with J. Pfaff-Czarnecka (1993) that *Dasaī* is an important Hindu symbol as a ritual of political power, I have no evidence—in the case of the Mewahang Rais—that the festival was 'instrumental' in the competitive power struggle among the local elite. It is probably true that the headmen were the ones who had the maximum interest in establishing the cult, but, as we have seen, some basic features of the festival were already there; so rather than adopting anything entirely new, the Mewahangs have only interpreted a transregional symbolism, which they came to be acquainted with through various contacts (including ascetics, Brahmans, calendars etc.), in terms of their own tradition—in order to be part of the wider cultural framework.

local setting. It is significant that while the timing of the territorial cults differs considerably between Mewahang villages, *Dasaī* is one of the few older festivals which are 'national' in character, held at the same time almost all over Nepal. The ideal of the sychronization of ritual activity became apparent when a *jimmāwāl* on *nawami* listened to Radio Nepal to follow the time schedule of the sacrifice in Kathmandu.

Finally let us consider the differences in the system of exchange. We have seen that the gifts brought by the *raiti* during the *ca:ri* sacrifice contribute to a communal meal which is hosted by the *jimmāwāl/tālukdār* and for which the latter—and his line—provide a special share of cooked rice. It is the headman who 'gives', and even though he himself only gives little in addition to the things that had just been 'given' to him before, he is the one who 'feeds' his subjects. Therefore, though the festival is not simply a self-financed community banquet, it clearly implies and expresses a hierarchical reciprocity: the headman, to whom reverence is paid, reciprocates with cooked food (and drink) in a gesture of generosity. This is precisely the kind of reciprocity implied in the sacrifice: the villagers pay reverence to incite the *ca:ri* to be nourishing and bountiful.

At first sight, the system of exchange during the *Dasaī* festival is very similar. During the latter the *raiti* also pay reverence to the headman with gifts, and the latter redistributes the alcohol and meat of the sacrificial animal, thus 'giving' as *prasād* at least part of what had previously been given to him. However, there is no communal meal, and this may be taken as the expression of a different kind of social hierarchy, where the gulf between chief and subjects is more pronounced. Rather than on 'feeding', the emphasis is on protection: the focal symbol is the *ṭikā*, the blessing given by the headman to his subjects. Even though *ṭikā* is also given during the *ca:wa pujā* it is not such a focal symbol, but just one among others.[14]

---

[14]Though it is methodologically not unproblematic to compare contexts of contrasting social complexity, the difference between the two traditions becomes more obvious if one considers the *Dasaī* festival as it

Conclusion

The rituals discussed here may all be described as rituals of power, or more exactly, rituals which in one way or another, express, and reconstitute political authority through a complex, partly symbolic performance that legitimizes the existing political hierarchy. However, the tribal cult and the Hindu cult differ in their conception of territory, nature and sovereignty.

Our major focus has been on the traditional territorial cult as it is celebrated among the Mewahang Rais of one particular village, including a comparison with other variants in neighbouring villages. Central to these cults is the notion of *ca:ri*, which refers to the local divinity of the soil as well as to the territory controlled by it. Legitimate ownership of the land on this clearly circumscribed territory is seen as deriving from the ritual capability to appease this divinity, and thereby the territorial forces of nature and wilderness. Political power, in short, derives from the subjugating power of the 'civilizing' process. It may be recalled that the Mewahangs in Bala, according to their myths, established the cult

was celebrated in its 'original' form, as the royal cult of the ruling dynasty. In Gorkha, the festival for Kālikā set in action a complex system of distribution which linked the various castes in the social hierarchy, as well the various localities of the realm, into a whole of which the deity— and the king—were the centre (Unbescheid n.d.: 35ff., 1986: 232–40). Even today, on the seventh day (*phulpāti*), fishermen (*Mājhi*) bring fish and potters (*Kumāl*) bring earthenware pots for the deity (Unbescheid n.d.: 18). On the eighth day, 33 buffaloes are sacrificed which—according to a document from B.S. 1963—had to be provided by 32 well-specified surrounding districts (*thum*) (Unbescheid n.d.: 23). Unbescheid concludes: 'The environs from which the gifts come let assume that they may be considered as tribute which was intended for the king as well as for the goddess.' (Unbescheid n.d.: 37)

This tributary nature of the *Dasāī* gifts is also documented for other areas (e.g. Nuwakot, see Pfaff-Czarnecka 1989: 154ff.). Though the sacrificial gifts are usually redistributed, the tributaries do not always benefit in proportion to their contribution. The Tamangs in Nuwakot, for example, are mere spectators in the rites, though they have to present animals to their absentee landlord in Kathmandu (*op. cit.*). What they always get in return, however, is the protective *ṭikā*.

not because they were the first to settle on the *ca:ri*, but because they were the first to establish an effective ritual link to it with the help of their *muddum* and thus became the first *legitimate* settlers who were able to control the land by virtue of their ancestral knowledge. It is the knowledge of ancestral creations and origins, knowledge of the genealogical link all the way back to the times of Sumnima and Paruhang, and knowledge of the ancestral migrations and village foundations which are crucial for legitimate access to the natural resources, as these ultimately derive from the first divine ancestors. As stressed in the myth, this knowledge is only adequately expressed in the use of the distinct ritual language during ritual performance. This unique traditional concept of ownership through ritual control seems to explain the ongoing importance of the cult. On a human plane it is the headman who has authority over the land: like the divinity which represents the *ca:ri*, he is referred to as 'owner of the *ca:ri*', and like the *ca:ri* he receives gifts and in return 'feeds' the people. The judicial authority of the headman seems to derive from his territorial authority; for example, illegitimate sexual unions 'pollute' the *ca:ri*, and for this reason the headman has to be 'compensated' by payment of a fine. Thus the form of sovereignty implied here may be described as truly territorial.[15] The prosperity of the territory's natural resources and the power of the chief (which presupposes his proper knowledge of the ancestral past) are intrinsically linked.

[15] It would be a challenging task to compare these notions systematically with related ones from the Tibetan religion, but this would exceed the scope of this chapter. One would have to look more closely at the Tibetan local gods, or 'mountain divinities', such as the *yul lha*, the *sa-bdag*, or the *gzhi-bdag* ('masters of the soil'). These latter, as Tucci writes, 'are bound to that particular piece of soil over which they preside', and no work there can be undertaken without their consent, as 'man is ... their subject' (1980: 722); also cf. Mumford 1989: 110–11. As is well being known, with the establishment of Buddhism these local forces had to be 'bound', subjugated or tamed (Samuel 1993: 219ff.), converting wilderness into a part of civilized society. Moreover, we would need to look into the political rituals of Tibetan kingdoms. An interesting study of a ritual of political unity in Baragaon is presented by Ramble (1992/93).

On the other hand we have seen that the Hindu festival of *Dasaī*, as celebrated at village level, is in many ways structurally similar to this Rai cult: it also focusses on the figure of the headman, who acts as host, recipient of gifts and distributor of *prasād*. But at the same time, the adopted festival exhibits important differences: rather than dealing with a particular link with the soil, the *Dasaī* festival emphasizes the protective power of the warrior goddess Durgā, of whom Kālikā is one form, the patron deity of the Gorkha kings and focus of the royal *Dasaī*.[16] Here the headman acts only as an intermediary or representative of the king in whom sovereign powers traditionally resided. Thus the kind of legitimate rule to which expression is given here, extends not so much over the soil and its inherent force as over the subjects inhabiting it, who have to pay tribute in order to gain the blessing of royal protection.[17] Therefore this kind of sovereignty could be called 'protective'. As the two notions of sovereignty have a different emphasis, it is usually not seen as a contradiction but rather as a form of complementarity that both rituals are celebrated by the same headmen: They have to assert their authority not only in traditional terms, as controllers of the soil, but also in 'national' terms, as royal representatives.

Yet the festival of *Dasaī*, though it may appear from the local perspective as basically just another cult focussing on the headman, in point of fact acknowledges a fundamental shift in

---

[16]It is significant that according to oral traditions, the goddess Kālikā was brought to Gorkha from Lamjung by Drabya Shah as his *kuldewatā* when he came to conquer the place in the middle of the sixteenth century (Unbescheid n.d.: 35). This shows that while the divinity of the soil is stationary the patron deity travels along with its kin group (also see Sundar 1997: 26). The importance the deity had for the rulers can be seen from the architectural structure of the royal palace in Gorkha: it consists of the *rājā darbār* and the *Kālikā darbār* (temple), the latter being just about the same size as the former. Like Taleju, for the Newar kings in Kathmandu, Kalika was the goddess protecting the king and his realm in Gorkha.

[17]Strictly speaking, the state was not the proprietor of *kipaṭ*-land, and so only the household, not the land could be taxed. Thus royal control of the territory was only indirect (Burghart 1984: 108f.).

the source of power that has taken place: it now resides in the capital Kathmandu.[18] In continuing their own tradition of offering to the soil, however, the Mewahangs express their longstanding and intimate link to the land, whose divine powers, fertility and prosperity they alone are able to control through their rituals.[19] This is a clear political claim, which has gained particular force since the establishment of the Makalu-Barun National Park on the territory of the Mewahang in 1992. There is a certain—non-coincidental—irony in the fact that while this state project aims at wildlife conservation (as well as the development of tourism) on the western side of the upper Arun valley, at the same time plans are being made for a large hydroelectric-project (Arun III) on the eastern side, where an access road from the south is currently under construction.

References

Allen, Nicholas J. 1981. 'The Thulung Myth of the Bhume Sites and Some Indo-Tibetan Comparisons'. In C. von Fürer-Haimendorf ed. *Asian Highland Societies in Anthropological Perspective*. New Delhi: Sterling. pp. 168-82.
Burghart, Richard. 1984. 'Formation of the Concept of Nation State in Nepal'. *Journal of Asian Studies* 44 (1): 101-25.
Gaborieau, Marc. 1978. 'Le partage du pouvoir entre les lignages dans une localité du Népal Central'. *L'Homme* 18 (1-2): pp. 37-67.

[18] It is significant that after 1990 it has become a political issue whether the Rais should celebrate *Dasaī* at all.

[19] Lecomte-Tilouine, who compares the political significance of the Magar *bhume* cult with the Parbatiyā *bhume* rituals, comes to similar conclusions regarding the Magars' strong territorial attachment. It involved an intercultural misunderstanding when the Magars, in spite of retaining ritual control over the soil deity, nevertheless lost control over their territorial property, because the Parbatiya notion of *bhume* has different implications than that of the Magars (Lecomte-Tilouine 1993a: 133). So here too, differing concepts of legitimate rule confronted each other.

Gaenszle, Martin. 1991. *Verwandtschaft und Mythologie bei den Mewahang Rai in Ostnepal. Eine ethnographische Studie zum Problem der 'ethnischen Identität'*. Wiesbaden: Franz Steiner Verlag.
_____ 1992. 'Ancestral Types. The Classification of "Deities" among the Mewahang Rai of East Nepal'. In V. Bouillier and G. Toffin eds., *Puruṣārtha* 15. pp. 197–218.
_____ 2000. *Origins and Migrations: Kinship, Mythology and Ethnic Identity among the Mewahang Rai of East Nepal*. Kathmandu: Mandala Bookpoint. (English Translation of Gaenszle 1991).
Höfer, András. 1981. *Tamang Ritual Texts I. Preliminary Studies in the Folk Religion of an Ethnic Minority in Nepal*. Wiesbaden: Franz Steiner Verlag.
Krauskopff, Gisèle. 1987. 'Naissance d'un village tharu'. *L'Ethnographie* LXXXIII: 131–58.
_____ 1989. 'Prêtres du terroir et maîtres de la forêt. La centralisation politique et le système de prêtrise Tharu à Dang et Déokhuri'. In V. Bouillier and G. Toffin eds. *Prêtrise, pouvoirs et autorité en Himalaya*. Paris: EHESS. Collection *Puruṣārtha* 12, pp. 79–100.
Krauskopff, Gisèle and Marie Lecomte-Tilouine, eds. 1996. *Célébrer le pouvoir: Dasaī, une fête royale au Népal*. Paris: Editions du CNRS.
Lecomte-Tilouine, Marie, 1993a. 'About Bhume, a Misunderstanding in the Himalayas'. In G. Toffin ed., *Nepal: Past and Present*. New Delhi: Sterling Publishers, pp. 127–33.
_____ 1993b. *Les dieux du pouvoir. Les Magar et l'hindouisme au Népal central*. Paris: CNRS Editions.
_____ 1996. 'Le culte de la déesse terre chez les Magar (Népal)'. *Diogène* 174: pp. 24–39.
Macdonald, Alexander. 1984a [1953]. 'A Note on Tibetan Megaliths'. In A. Macdonald, *Essays on the Ethnology of Nepal and South Asia, vol I*. Kathmandu: Ratna Pustak Bhandar. pp. 15–27.
_____ 1984b [1957]. 'Notes on the Cloistering of Villages in South-East Asia'. In A. Macdonald, *Essays on the Ethnology of Nepal and South Asia, vol I*. Kathmandu: Ratna Pustak Bhandar. pp. 81–101.
McDougal, Charles. 1979. *The Kulunge Rai. A Study in Kinship and Marriage Exchange*. Kathmandu: Ratna Pustak Bhandar.
Mumford, Stan Royal. 1989. *Himalayan Dialogue. Tibetan Lamas and Gurung Shamans in Nepal*. Madison: The University of Wisconsin Press.

Oppitz, Michael. 1986. 'Die Trommel und das Buch. Eine kleine und die grosse Tradition'. In Bernhard Kölver ed., *Formen kulturellen Wandels und andere Beiträge zur Erforschung des Himalaya*. Sankt Augustin: VGH Wissenschaftverlag. pp. 53-125.

Pfaff-Czarnecka, Joanna. 1989. *Macht und rituelle Reinheit. Hinduistisches Kastenwesen und ethnische Beziehungen im Entwicklungsprozess Nepals*. Grüsch: Verlag Rüegger.

―――― 1993. 'The Nepalese Durga-Puja Festival Or Displaying Military Supremacy On Ritual Occasions.' In C. Ramble & M. Brauen eds. *Anthropology of Tibet and the Himalaya*. Zürich: Völkerkundemuseum der Universität Zürich. pp. 270-86.

Pignède, Bernard. 1966. *Les Gurung, une population himalayenne du Népal*. Paris, La Haye: Mouton.

Ramble, Charles. 1992/93. 'A Ritual of Political Unity in an Old Nepalese Kingdom'. *Ancient Nepal* 130-133, pp. 49-58.

Regmi, Mahesh Chandra. 1972. *A Study in Nepali Economic History 1768-1846*. New Delhi: Manjusri Publishing House.

Sagant, Philippe. 1969. 'Tâmpungmâ, divinité limbu de la forêt'. *Objets et Mondes* 9: 107-27.

Sales, Anne de. 1991. *Je suis né de vos jeux de tambours. La religion chamanique des Magar du Nord*. Nanterre: Société d'Ethnologie.

Samuel, Geoffrey. 1993. *Civilized Shamans: Buddhism in Tibetan Societies*. Washington and London: Smithsonian Institution Press.

Schlemmer, Grégoire. 2004. 'Vues d'esprits. La conception des esprits et ses implications chez les Kulung Rai du Népal'. Ph.D. thesis. Nanterre: Université Paris X.

Strickland, Simon S.,1982. 'Belief, Practices, and Legends: A Study in the Narrative Poetry of the Gurungs of Nepal'. Ph.D. thesis. Cambridge: Jesus College.

Sundar, Nandini. 1997. *Subalterns and Sovereigns: An Anthropological History of Bastar 1854-1996*. New Delhi: Oxford University Press.

Toffin, Gérard. 1987. 'Dieux du sol et démons dans les religions himalayennes'. *Études Rurales* 107-108: 85-106.

Tucci, Giuseppe. 1980 [First edition 1949]. *Tibetan Painted Scrolls*. Kyoto: Rinsen Book.

Turner, Ralph L., 1980 [First edition 1931]. *A Comparative and Etymological Dictionary of the Nepali Language*. New Delhi: Allied Publishers.

Unbescheid, Günter, 1986. 'Göttliche Könige und königliche Götter. Entwurf zur Organisation von Kulten in Gorkha und Jumla.' In B. Kölver ed., *Formen kulturellen Wandels und andere Beiträge zur Erforschung des Himalaya*. Sankt Augustin: VGH Wissenschaftsverlag. pp. 225-47.

──── n.d. 'Between Mythological Dependence and Ritual Freedom: The Celebration of the Festival of Dasai at the Kālikā-temple in Gorkhā.' Mss. (Published in French in: Krauskopff, G. & M. Lecomte-Tilouine, 1996).

'Wilderness of the Civilization'
Knowledge and Perception of the Jad Pastoral Community

SUBHADRA MITRA CHANNA

Pine forest in Uttarakhand (Photo: Marie Lecomte-Tilouine)

'Wilderness of the Civilization'   223

Western cultures see a dichotomy between themselves and the so-called 'Other Cultures', a dichotomy which when translated in terms of nature and culture, would mean that while Judeo-Christian religions make a distinction between nature and culture, non-Western cultures need to be examined in the light of the existence or non-existence of such a distinction, yet taking the 'dichotomy for granted' (Descola and Pálsson 1996: 3).

Anthropologists of Western origin routinely look upon non-Western cultures in opposition to their own Judeo-Christian roots; moreover having definite and clear-cut classifications is a Western system of thinking. Thus to scholars like Durkheim, 'religion' is characterized by a definite boundary. This may not however always be how people elsewhere see the world.

I found it very difficult to make such a distinction with respect to a community that I am studying in the Himalayas, one that has had long-standing associations with civilizations harbouring two recognized universal religions of the world, namely Hinduism and Buddhism. The tiny group of Himalayan pastoralists is situated in a remote village tucked away behind a tiny town of a few hundred people in a place called Harsil. Harsil is on the way to Gangotri as one climbs up from the foot hills at Rishikesh and goes through the pilgrim town of Uttarkashi, and the group, the Jads, formed an object of study that was just as varied as it was small.

First of all, this small group of about 600 persons were bound to each other by the fact that they lived together and had common resources and lifestyle, rather than by any common origin or cultural history. In fact, many of them came from different places through marriage and became integrated in the local community. What was common to them was that most were part of communities inhabiting the various river valleys in Garhwal, having a pastoral economy and trade as the basis of their livelihood and sharing common pastures in winter in the foothills. In summer, they would graze in the fields that were their exclusive domain and in winter, they would go to lower altitudes where they shared their world with the local Hindus and other pastoral communities. The identity of being a Jad, is a product of and reproduced by belonging to a pastoral landscape that includes the grazing routes and pastures, the settlements and sacred objects and concepts that are seen as specific to only those who occupy this landscape and who get the right to move along the routes that are recognized as the symbolic property of the Jads (Channa 1998).

The Garhwal Himalayas are the site of some of the holiest shrines of the Hindus and since ancient times, pilgrims from the plains have been coming to these mountains. The Jads are part of a larger generic category called Bhotiya (Fürer-Haimendorf 1975, 1981) that encompasses the small traders and sheep-breeding communities dotted along the Himalayan borders of countries such as India, Nepal and the autonomous province of Tibet; they have provided local transport to pilgrims, travellers and local cultivators. Thus their familiarity with Hinduism is not new and they recognize the sacred nature of the geographical region occupied by them. As traders, they have had long-standing trading relations across the Tibetan borders with the Huniyas that practise a kind of popular Buddhism. An important problem here is that today's widely accepted religions such as Hinduism and Buddhism were influenced by Westerners during the colonial period. As Tambiah (1990: 5) writes 'by the beginning of this century, Western scholars had already labeled the great religions as isms, such as Hinduism, Buddhism, Confucianism, etc. In this labeling and delineation of the so-called doctrinal texts, the beliefs and tenets, of the religious virtuosi and intellectuals were given prominence as the core of the ism under study.' Thus what was recognized as Hindu or Buddhist beliefs and supernatural beings was integrated into the beliefs of local villagers, although they were quite different.

The concept of 'having a religion' is itself not familiar to those people to whom the world exists in the form of a truth for which there can be no doubt or debate. In fact it is only recently that they have been introduced to the concept that a religion is something that one must possess. It has become linked to their identity and relationship with other cultures, as part of the process of 'subjectification'. The recognition of a separation of various kinds of beliefs linked to social power is something acquired by the intervention of a holder of superior power, namely the modern

Indian state that is mostly a representative of the religious and social elite. As my friend Kaushalya told me (Channa 2002), in her childhood their only link with Hindus was to sit by the wayside and watch the pilgrims go up to the sacred site of Gangotri. 'We are *junglee* people, we would sit by the wayside and ask the pilgrims for small gifts.'

For the Jads, the world is peopled by humans and sacred beings and the various parts of the landscape are distinguished as ordinary or sacred. Thus the river Ganga is sacred and that is a matter of fact; it is not specific to anyone's interpretation of the world. The belief in purity and sacredness of the Himalayas is shared with the Hindus, who view the high peaks of the Himalayas as Mount Kailash, the abode of the gods. It is also believed in Hindu mythology, that the way to the heavens is from the mountain peaks. The five Pandava brothers, along with their common wife Draupadi, are said to have passed along these mountain routes to ascend to heaven. But the myth relates how one by one, beginning with Draupadi, they fell by the wayside. As each fell, they asked Yudhistir, the eldest brother, why they could not climb further. And Yudhistir, who is also the son of the god of Dharma and the lord of death, Yama, explained to each, their individual sins. Ultimately only Yudhistir entered the gates of heaven along with his dog, who was none else than the god of death himself. The myth thus upholds the extreme sanctity of the highest mountain peaks. The Jads told me several times that they considered themselves extremely fortunate to be living close to the source of the river Ganga and have the sacred river flowing through their village. Many parts of the landscape are associated with the journey of the Pandavas. But unlike the majority of Hindus, for the Jads, the Pandavas still live with them in their land as lineage gods, *kuldevtas*. The world for the communities inhabiting the mountains, including the Jads, is 'cosmotheistic' (Carmichael *et al.* 1994: 6). It is a living nature with a will and a mind of its own. Humans have to interact by cajoling, pleasing and manipulating, but they cannot dominate or dictate terms to their environment. They must live according to the terms defined by it of which they are an integral part. In fact, this manner of thinking is shared with the Hindus and the local form of Buddhism. The Western view of man's superiority over nature or a dichotomy between man and nature is unknown since revivalist Hinduism knocking at their door is also drawn from a unity of all living and non-living beings.

This does not mean that the world is undifferentiated: it contains various categories of beings, and things are considered as *sangma* (pure) or as dirty or ordinary. One can, without much difficulty, understand *sangma* as the 'sacred' in a Durkheimian sense. What is *sangma* is set apart and circumscribed with taboos. The natural things are imbued with properties of various kinds that can be either beneficial or harmful to human beings. The supernatural carries various categories of power, usually of malevolence, and the higher sacred beings or gods and goddesses that are to be propitiated also come in many forms.

Superior powers can be propitiated through various rites and rituals, kept happy by the observance of taboos and if things get out of control, one can ask for the help of some sacred specialists. These are the Buddhist lamas, the Hindu *pandits* and *tantriks* and the local healers and also the gods who manifest themselves in human bodies during rituals such as *panoh*. All specialists are marked by special powers and it does not matter to which system they belong.

The Jads thus hold a world view that recognizes the existence of the sacred as a matter of undisputed truth and the recognition that people belong to different religions is a recent introduction. To the local pastoralists, who are called either Jads or Rongpas, having 'a religion' is now a sign of being superior and it is for this reason that some of them, especially those with a higher social standing or standard of education, have begun to call themselves either Hindus or Buddhists or even both. With regard to the pastoral communities who are regarded as tribal by the local Hindu communities, 'being Hindu' was a mark of superior social status. Therefore, for a low status group like the Bhotiyas to be Hindu or to have a religion was a sign of social promotion.

On the other hand, to become Hindu or Buddhist, the Jad need not change their world view. The sacred character of nature is not alien to Hinduism and very few persons of the Jad community were aware of what Buddhism was all about. The local lamas practise rituals and read horoscopes and deal with the supernatural dangers in their own ways that are perfectly compatible with the local understanding of the world. Thus the lamas are responsible for tying protective amulets on the caps of small babies and for putting up the Buddhist prayer flags or *tarchok* on roofs at the Buddhist New Year, Losar. Hindu priests also perform rituals of various kinds, including healing ones.

For the Jads, the Hindus believe in the sacred nature of the river Ganga, a belief to which they wholeheartedly subscribe. They have also begun to recognize some of the Hindu deities, such as Bhagwati. But Hinduism is not a uniform or fixed religion. Every one knows its regional character and the local variant called the *pahari* version is based on the enactment of the Mahabharata (Sax: 1995). The Mahabharata performance reflects an interesting change in this region, a simultaneous movement towards a Hindu as well as a *pahari* identity (Channa: 2005).[1] At the same time, the Hindu identity of the Jad is only acceptable as a local *pahari* one, not as a pan-Indian Hindu identity.

Thus to pass off as Hindu is more to do with a change in identity and political consciousness than with any religious transformation.

Indeed, for the Jads, there can be no change in that there is no 'belief'; there is only knowledge, which is based upon substantive interaction with the environment. And the Jads consider themselves uniquely privileged to be in possession of such knowledge. For example, when I asked a young girl what she would like to become when she grows up, she said she wanted to become a doctor. But she also added that she wanted to come back to the mountains to practise, for the following reasons: 'The people of the plains do not understand us. They do not know about the cause of diseases and about the supernatural world. When I become a doctor I will be able to treat the local people because I will understand them better.'

[1] On the 'pahari' identity, see Berreman (1972, 1983).

The Jads's conception of the world is not quite independent of the beliefs of the local Hindus or the Tibetan peasants' version of Buddhism. There exists in this region a local set of ideas drawing historically upon multiple sources spanning long periods of contact between various populations. But what is most important is not the content of the beliefs but the fact that they are not representational; here knowledge is not linked to a theory but to the very fact of being. This recalls Rabinow's remark that epistemology is a product of seventeenth century Europe, while 'For the Greeks there was no sharp division between external reality and internal representations' (Rabinow 1990: 235).

In the region studied, there is no scope for alternate representations and the fact that there are different religions can only mean that different people pay allegiance to different gods or tap alternate sources of power, not that the world or its nature differs.[2] In a way this view comes closer to the philosophy of modern science that recognizes no scope for variation as long as there is no alternative experience. Thus for the Jad, to say that forests are the spirits' abode and that each Deodar tree is a god is the same as for a scientist to say that hydrogen and oxygen molecules combine to form water. For the people who inhabit the mountains the world around them exists as given truths, they never say 'we believe'; they always say 'It is'.

Hinduism itself has evolved and crystallized over a period spanning the colonial and present times, where it has assumed an identity that is at once, monolithic and politico-historical. Changes in the world view of local communities such as the Jads reflect these transformations especially as they too are drawn into these politics of identity. Thus the people of Bhagori have been trying to forge an identity for themselves, like taking the name Jad, to assert to outsiders, that they are a community, masking

---

[2]For people having polytheistic religion it is not difficult to simultaneously subscribe to different systems of beliefs. Deliège (1997: 264) says regarding the Paraiyars of South India: 'The reality of the Hindu pantheon is not questioned by the Christians, but for them it is made up of malevolent beings who control the evil spirits, the *pesu–pisasus*. For the Hindus, on the contrary, the "Christian gods" have to be sure, a positive value.'

their internal fragmentations and also to develop a religious identity: either Hindu or Buddhist. In addition, the positive discrimination policies of the Government of India brought the notion of tribal identity, to the extent that some, like Narayan Singh, the local big-wig, was keen to tell me that they were 'mongoloid' and Bhotiya. Such self-consciousness was not visible in older men and women, who were not even particularly familiar with the name Jad, or Bhotiya. To them they were just people who occupy a specific village and had some gods in common, especially the village god Meparang. The younger generation, like Manoj Jhagpangi and some young women, opted to break away from the Hindus for a Buddhist identity. I observed Manoj sitting at the local tea stall trying to master a Buddhist chant from a friend. Two girls were thinking of becoming Buddhist nuns. All this was happening as a backdrop to the separatist movement of the mountainous region of Uttar Pradesh that culminated in the formation of a new hill state, Uttaranchal, in the year 2001. There was a definite tussle between the older and the younger generations, as the latter was more radical in its separatist identity and therefore more ready to take on an identity other than the mainstream plain-dwelling Hindu one.

Another aspect that one has to consider is the concept of rationality, which in the postmodern idiom, has a dynamic and transient character. It is a product of a social milieu and not a given truth, a 'world historic process', as Weber stated. To understand the world in a particular way may be an outcome of what Ingold (1992) would say is an 'engagement' with the world. People think according to their relationship with the world which surrounds them.

The Jads worship the sun as 'mother sun' (āmā Nyāmā) and they rationalize this in terms of their identity as pastorals that separates them from the tillers of the soil, the *zamindars* (farmers) and also emphasizes their cultural dependence on animals. As my friend told me 'the animals will perish without the sun and the sun also sets in motion the cycle that ensures rain. The heat from the sun evaporates water that forms clouds that brings snow. When the snow melts on the higher reaches, the grass grows for our animals to graze.' However this attempt at a rational explanation may itself have been borrowed or learned behaviour, one more attempt at upgrading oneself in the eyes of the 'outsider', the elite woman from the plains.

Her explanation was akin to that of Narayan Singh when he told me with regard to the possession rituals: 'the people here have no other entertainment, so these things are like their entertainment.' On the other hand with regard to the same performances, Kamli, a low caste woman told me: 'there are the gods' entertainment. When they want to play, they descend to the earth and perform.' In fact, Narayan Singh also believed that the gods descend: 'Only a god and can lick a hot iron and not get burned, or put a stake through his cheek and not bleed. The gods do descend into the bodies of the persons getting possessed, for no human can do what they do.'

Nature, Culture and Gender

Gender has occupied a prime place in the nature-culture debate among Western scholars and for a long time there has been a trend to equate woman with nature and man with culture. This dichotomy parallels the ones between rationality and intuition, and mind and body. The Jads too recognize some kind of differences between men and women and these are also related to the difference between work, space and the nature of being, the last being associated with concepts of purity and impurity. The most important of these for day-to-day life is the spatial association of gender that can be translated in their terms as a continuous expansion from the inner to the outer domain. Women belong to the inner spaces of the home, the rooms, the village and the forests near the village. Men are not to be seen inside the house, they are appropriately located in the outer domains of the village public spaces, in the forests away from habitation, on the grazing lands and in far away places for trade. To the Jads, men belong to the wild (*jungal*) and women to the village (*ūl*). But forests are not opposed to the village: they stretch out from the *rega*, those forests adjoining the village to the *danda*, pastures where shepherds graze the animals, up to the *taak*, the remote mountains tops that are inaccessible to humans. The sacredness of the forests increases as one moves away from the village, that is the least sacred of spaces. The *rega* contain sacred supernatural beings, the *matriyāl*, who are jealous and dangerous. Both men and women who go to the forest must not wear red or orange clothes, and should not appear too beautiful. Indeed, the forest spirits do not like humans to wear their colours, the red and orange of the Deodar pollens. They are particularly jealous of beautiful women and make them ill.

In the forest, one must talk in whispers, not drop rubbish and never have sex. Women can move around there to collect shrubs and branches for fuel and fodder for their animals. They also collect various other forest produce such as *shukwa* (a kind of incense), *pili pithai* (the pollen from deodar trees) and various berries and medicinal herbs, mushrooms etc. But women must never spend a night in the forest. Therefore they should only go so far as to be able to return before sunset.

Men can go further, into the *danda*, the pastures that are forbidden to women. In fact, they spend months wandering in these forests, grazing their animals. Men are sacred beings in themselves and thus remain safe in the forest and perform rituals to ward off evil spirits and to placate the forest deities. Their sheep protect them too, for they are like 'Lakshmi' (the Hindu goddess of wealth), because their eyes shine like fire in the night. Additional protection is provided by the dogs that are expert hunters and adept at chasing away bears and tigers.

Men go to distant lands to trade and stay away from the village for long periods of time. To the Jads, men have nothing to do with village social life, they simply do not fully belong it, for it is run by the women. At first sight then, men are associated with nature and women with culture. But these remote spaces form the domain of spirits and gods. Women occupy the village but this space is less sacred than the realm of men. The more one moves away from habitation and man-made things the more *sangma* (pure) is the world. Thus men are more *sangma* than women;

they are also in control of the part of the world that defines them as a community. It is the use of pastures and grazing routes, access to mountain passes and trade partners that define the Jads as a people, as Jad. Men thus define identity and its transmission. Women conserve and reproduce this identity.

The Jads associate men with the blood that runs through their lineages, which is also associated with the *kuldevta* (lineage gods). Blood signifies biological ties of descent. Women are associated with milk that denotes kinship and the ties of sociability.[3] Their role in the latter is obvious in the fact that women, while moving from one household to another, create alliance ties and their co-operative work groups in the village are sustained by and reproduce ties of kinship and friendship. Thus on a fine morning I met a young girl going to the fields, 'I am going to help my elder sister (*didi*) with her fields today.' But the so-called sister was the daughter of her father's previous wife, whom he had divorced and then married her mother. Even the 'sister' was the child of a previous husband of the previous wife, and not of her own father. Yet she was a close enough person who needed help. The wider and more close-knit the circle of kin, the more help one can get while doing horticultural work that is mainly the domain of women. If a woman cannot mobilize enough 'relatives' she has to fall back on hired help. These are poor young men who spend four months (*chaumasa*) in the village, picking up jobs as hired labour. Some of them are hired by men too to shepherd the animals. Thus women have to achieve their goals by maintaining and reproducing social relationships while men work separately, on their own and need less help in what they do.

Men and women also separate their economic spheres. Women keep domesticated animals like horses, cows and mules in the village that they hire out as pack animals and for the transport of pilgrims. Sometimes a goat may be kept to provide

---

[3] Unlike anthropologists, the Jads consider kinship from the point of view of a female Ego. Thus to them cross-cousin marriage means a woman marrying her mother's brother's son and not the MBD marriages typical of textbooks in anthropology.

milk for a child or a sick person. They do not otherwise drink milk. Women take all the decisions regarding the disposal of money they earn by selling the shawls they weave and the clothes they knit. The prices are fixed by the person who has made the article and it is she who keeps the money. Girls begin to work at a young age, and by the time they are twelve or so, girls start earning money according to their skills and talent. No-one, not even a mother will take a decision on the price of an item that her daughter has made. Young girls are often seen at the local market driving bargains with local customers entirely on their own. A girl and a boy are considered grown up as soon as they are capable of earning money and doing productive tasks. On this register men and women are equal. Initially I had the habit of asking a man in the village about the price of a shawl or piece of woollen cloth and the reply was always 'I will have to ask my sister, mother or sister-in-law' about it. I soon learnt to ask the name of the person who had made it and then talk to her directly. I often found myself negotiating with a twelve-year-old girl with an acute business sense who would explain the amount of raw material put in, the labour cost and time taken and so on about all the rational considerations that she had taken to price something.

Men rarely have any tasks to do around the village and most of them spend their time either playing cards or dice under trees or sitting at eating places. Women on their part are almost always seen working, in groups or sometimes alone. A woman who is weaving a carpet works alone only because she has to concentrate on counting the knots. But those who are knitting or spinning wool or working in the fields work in groups. They make beer (*chang*), cook and wash utensils. They fetch water and fire wood, take care of domestic animals and get fodder for them from the forests. No woman seems too old to work. While interviewing the oldest man in the village who was then about ninety and lying in the sun doing nothing, I was taken aback when he told me that his wife had gone to 'work in the fields'.

Men are occupied with tasks that take them away from the village. They go grazing sheep that takes almost all year, spending four months each at high and low altitude pastures, the highest of which are at around 10,000 feet and the lowest around the Himalayan foothills. Several months of the year are spent travelling along the waterways taking the sheep up and down. The sheep are sheared by the men, near the village settlements and the wool handed over to the women to be processed. Men also engage in trading, and that was in fact their major activity until recently. The backbone of the Bhotiya identity is based on the salt trade with Tibet, and in colonial times they were discovered by the British as potent trade links to get borax and shawl wool (Brown 1994).

As they grow old, men take on more womanly tasks like spinning wool and carrying children slung on their backs. There is little gender difference between old men and women, who both do the same tasks except that women remain active to an older age. Once men are incapable of travelling and grazing sheep, they spend their time spinning wool and looking after children. Since they have now stopped earning money they rarely gamble or play dice.

Men are associated with the right side, the pure side and women with the left. More importantly, men are associated with open spaces, the mountains and forest, and the women with enclosed spaces, the house and the village. The Jads build their village appropriately in a depression or enclosed space, a *gurgur*. Open spaces are dangerous for domestic life and especially for the vulnerable bodies of women. All sexual activities must be carried out in closed spaces. The Jad rooms have no windows and they keep out both the cold winds and evil spirits. The newly-born child and the new mother are kept in confinement and not taken out into the sun till the baby is one month old. Then a lama comes and exposes the baby to the sun with appropriate ritual protections.

The fear of open spaces is a result of actual daily experiences of involving oneself in the environment. The mountainsides are full of deep gorges and rapid streams. Many people get lost in the mountains and lose their lives falling off cliffs. Men are associated with blood that also stands for danger and death as much as it stands for lineage and descent. While in the pastures, men sometimes have to make offerings of sheep to local deities; the sheep may die of natural causes like falling off cliffs and these are skinned and eaten by them. Men may also lose their lives in conflict. To the Jad, a man's life is always in danger but that is how it should be. Women need to be protected because the entire reproduction of society depends on them. The saying goes *'Ladka aur bakra hi katta hai'* (Only boys and male goats are slaughtered). This refers to the practice of sacrificing only male animals in rituals.

Women are not supposed to take part in any violent activity including the breaking of a coconut. Women are like milk that nurtures, gives life and creates relationships. Women create and protect, they do not destroy.

A very important dimension of Jad social organization is the *kuldevta*, the lineage god. The *kuldevta* is inherited in the male line but is almost always taken care of by women. The reason is that the *kuldevta* resides in the house, within the domestic domain ruled by women. Some women, like Kamla Devi, take care of both the *kuldevta* of her husband, who came from a village outside, and of her father, who had been part of the same village. She is the natural caretaker of her husband's *kuldevta* but is also in charge of the *kuldevta* rightfully belonging to her brother, as the latter was in the army and stayed away from the mountains.

This brings us to the very important notion of the sacred and its relationship with geography. For the Jads, the mountains alone can be the abode of sacred beings as any place below Rishikesh is viewed as polluted and cannot be *sangma*. The *kuldevta* only live on the *pahar*, not on the plains. For the people of this region, the term *pahar* is meaningful in terms of not only a geographical space, but it is also an identity. It refers to the historical relationship between the dominant majority of the plains and the marginal communities of the mountains, regarded by the former as culturally and socially inferior. The mountain people reciprocate this sentiment by regarding their plains as 'impure' and dangerous.

The Jad notion of wild and dangerous on one hand and familiar and orderly on the other hand is parallel to what Knight (1996) says about the Japanese ideas regarding man-made forests and natural forests. It is nature that is seen as orderly and the sacred character of nature is also linked to its aesthetic and functional properties. To the Jad, the tops of the mountains, where the snow is unspoilt by human presence is the most beautiful, the most *sangma* and also the most conducive to health and well-being. The shepherds consider the higher reaches of the mountains where they have the high altitude pastures, as the best for grazing, safest and economically most productive. The wool that is sheared after the sheep have grazed on the higher pastures is longer, finer, and fetches a much higher price than the wool that is sheared after the sheep have grazed on lower-altitude pastures that are dirty, full of thorns and where the water is polluted. Here the sheep get sick, their hair falls off and their coat gets dirty and thorny.

The plains are dangerous places to be in, not for a lack of civilization but because of it (civilization being equated with urban centres and their inhabitants). When the Jads refer to themselves as *junglee*, or wild, they are not using a self-derogatory term. To them it means that they are purer, cleaner and more harmonious than the *desi*. As soon as they reach the plains they get fearful and suspicious. Stories abound of people being robbed and cheated. In the lower reaches, even their identity is lost. They are no longer the unique groups of Rongpas who alone can access the pastures at Purumsumdu, near the Indo-Tibetan border. They share the lower-altitude pastures with people who are their affines, the Bhotiyas from Niti, Mana and Kinnaur. So, there they conform to an identity bestowed on them by the people of the plains, namely a generic category of Bhotiya but not the unique identity of being Rongpa, the people of the villages of Neilang and Bhagori.

The Jads intermarry with the people with whom they share lower altitude pastures. Some of the men from these groups upon marriage to Jad women acquire rights of access to higher-altitude pastures as well as to the Jads' grazing routes. In that case, their identity changes to that of Jad and similarly, those Jads who leave their community to marry women in these places, become a part of them. Such marriages are however preferential and not rigidly prescriptive. The Jads have no strict rules of marriage within any category and the repetition of marriages is more based on familiarity, the actual scope of interaction and the sharing of similar world-views. But the merging of identities is never total.

Another kind of interaction takes place for trade. The Jads carry out trade with the plains people not from the pastures, but from their camp at Chor-Pani situated in a dense forest near Rishikesh. This camp consists of families including women and children and replicates a village, though temporary. For this reason, it needs to be situated in a safe place which for the Jads means deep into the forest, away from so-called civilization. Only the men go out from the safety of the camps to the nearby town for trade and for getting in supplies.

Women need safety and safety means enclosure, but not of an urban kind: rather it must be an enclosure in nature, within the purity of natural beings and spirits. To the Jads, the forest is a sacred space, inhabited by spirits who can be malevolent, but they know how to deal with them. By contrast, the world beyond contains human beings who do not belong to the same world as the Jads, they do not know how to deal with them. They are dangerous and the women and children need to be protected against them. Only the men must face the danger if need be. Safety lies in knowledge of the familiar, in aesthetic purity and in being hidden from the 'outsider's' gaze. Thus, from the road, one cannot suspect the presence of the Jad village at Bhagori. It is situated about sixty feet below road level, shielded by a thick patch of forest and a fast-flowing stream.

The Jads maintained another kind of trade relation with their traditional trade partners on the Tibet side of the border. This was based on the *mitra* system where the relationship was intense and the partners in trade would come and stay at each other's house for several months while they were trading. Such relationships were inherited, for the Tibetans, by both son and daughter and, for the Jads, only by men. The relations were of fictive consanguinity and thus no marriage could take place between the partners' families. The relationship with Tibetans was a much warmer one than with the Hindu traders on the plains. It was based on equality and sharing. The Tibetans lived at higher altitudes that made them less dangerous and closer to the Jads. High and pure, down and impure are closely interlinked in the local cosmology and therefore, it is 'civilization' that is wild and dangerous.

Hinduism and the Jads

As is now well recognized, the monolithic character of Hinduism is a product of the nineteenth century and a large part of this process was a backward projection to a glorious past from where a monolinear sequence was constructed (Dalmia: 1999). We will now examine the manner in which the Jad identity has been constructed with respect to the changing faces of Hinduism.

The ancient textual doctrine of *sanatana dharma* did not oppose the forest to civilization. In fact in the *varnashrama*, almost three out of four *ashramas* are appropriately spent in the forest. Thus while studying, a *brahmachari* normally lives with his guru, and most ancient sages made the forest their dwelling place. Again, at the end of the period of domestic life (*grihasthashrama*), a person may go for *vanaprastha*, that is to live the life of a hermit in the forest and then if he or she lives long enough, he can take *sanyas* and wander around as ascetics. Though there are no rules for the last stage, a *sanyasi* may choose to live deeper in the forest.

From the time of the ancient texts there were people recognized as belonging to the forests but the important difference between them and the followers of the *sanatana dharma* was that these forest-dwellers, pastorals and hunter-gatherers were not part of the *varnasharama*. They did not in fact belong to any of the recognized *varna* (the four classes forming Hindu society) and most importantly did not follow vedic rituals or make use of the services of the Brahmins. When Hinduism consolidated its identity, such people were usually called tribes, *vanya jatis*, and recognized as not belonging to the *varna* categories. From the point of view of mainstream Hindus, the Jads are certainly not Hindu or part of any caste system. The sentiment expressed by the Brahmin *pandit* from Mukhpa who had come to the village for a marriage ritual was that 'these people are *junglee* and have no sense of ritual or religion'. He candidly admitted that he comes to them only because of the gifts of shawls and wool that they give him. The local Hindus, both Garhwalis and others, think likewise.

Until quite recently the Jad were content to live as *junglee*. But formal education and political consciousness has made a difference in the outlook of the boys and girls who have now become aware that the concept of *junglee* looked as seen from the other side is derogatory. At the time of my fieldwork, the younger generation was already showing signs of frustration and discontent with the identity imposed on them by outsiders. They had recognized that their way of life was stigmatized and looked down upon.

Although the *pahari* upper castes had never considered the Bhotiya as their equal or as caste Hindus, in the political struggle for a separate Uttarakhand, they did solicit their support and also recognized the superior economic power and by now high educational status of many of them. The Jad, both men and women, literate or uneducated, were politically conscious and ready to assert their identity as equal to that of the Gahrwali Hindus.

For the past few decades they have been systematically pressing for a *kshatriya* or upper caste Hindu identity. To this end, they have changed their lineage names to adopt Gahrwali Hindu *kshatriya* names such as Negi, Bhandari, Rawat etc. Those opting for a more pan-Indian identity have chosen names like Kapoor. Original names like Jhangpangi have been almost abandoned. But some of the young people who have come into close contact with the plains people now realize that a mere change of name is not going to give them their desired status. Some young men and women have now been looking for a separate identity from mainstream Hindus, such as Buddhism. The merging of a Hindu identity with Hindu revivalism and right-wing status has also put off some young people.

However all these changes are only superficial. They have not transformed the manner in which the Jads look at the world, their concept of rationality and their understanding of what is knowledge. What the more 'exposed' among them have understood is that 'outsiders' do not understand the world as they do and that this difference is a hierarchy. There is very little difference between the Jads and their Hindu hill neighbours, the local Garhwalis, in terms of cosmology and rationality, and until recently, the Jads never had any major difficulty with their identity and self-esteem.

Their social world used to contain people of an equal or slightly higher or lower status, like the local Gahrwalis and Tibetan *mitras*, the Koli weavers and the untouchable cobblers. The rest were too distant to matter, such as the Hindu pilgrims from the plains who simply passed by. But now the nature of interaction is completely changing. The students who go to school or college are suddenly told that their way of thinking is superstitious; their rituals are 'exotic' or 'strange'. Their beliefs are not rational and knowledge is untrue. Educated young men and occasionally women have to take up jobs in alien environments where they are subjected to more feelings of inadequacy. The impact of media is also quite strong. But all this certainly does not mean that they too have started to believe that their beliefs are wrong or that they are forming a self-depreciating identity. On the contrary, the Jads have a very healthy self-image. They have not yet reached a state where they would start disbelieving their rationality or the 'facts' of their environment.

The Changing Scene

There is very little transformation at a cognitive level in the way in which these people in a mountain village look at and understand the world around them. Every child in the mountains is firmly entrenched in his /her belief in the sacredness of nature, in the spirits and gods who are part of their social and ritual life. The plains people often speak disparagingly about the 'superstitious' *pahari*. They look down upon beliefs in ghosts and spirits although most of them make pious pilgrimages to the holy shrines situated in the mountains. Local people have less use for the textual sacredness of these spots but they believe in the living gods who constantly interact with them. I was frankly taken aback during my initial period of fieldwork in the mountains by the manner in which people constantly referred to their conversations with the supernatural beings, their sighting of the spirits and living world of nature which was part of their social world. Every natural object was animate, conversational and interactive.

The closer interaction with a changing middle class of reformed Hindus, especially through trade and education has brought about a transformation in which they have realized that 'outsiders' do not believe in what they *know to be true*. But rather than a transformation in the way people relate to the world and in their cognition of nature and the sacred, it led to concealing this. Quite often in the village I would find that young people were reluctant to talk about their beliefs and looked at me with suspicion, fearing another condescending reaction, the kind they have become used to from their peers in urban colleges and colleagues at work. The projection of themselves as Hindus or as Buddhists is to me still like a superficial mantle, taken on to cover what they feel as their vulnerable selves. What people here fear most is ridicule and the superior gaze of 'outsiders'.

During the later part of the last century, the Hindutva or radical right-wing Hindu movement has been projecting a Hinduism that finds little response in the mountain people, although some of them do subscribe politically to the ideology of the right-wing parties. People have learnt to build compartments paying lip service to majority or dominant value systems while safeguarding their original beliefs. I will take one example. Some time in the nineties, just before I began my fieldwork, some of the Jad community had advocated vegetarianism as part of becoming Hindu, but this was soon abandoned because the *kuldevta* of most households expressed anger at being forced to follow a vegetarian diet that none of them liked.

Through their gods, they express a divine objection to assimilation. In their mountain village shielded from the outside world by dense vegetation, the Jads prefer to carry on their conversation with their *glah* and their *kuldevtas*. They still tread softly in the forest and make offerings to their spirits and to the ghosts of the sixty passengers who died when their bus fell from the highway into the village below. Each deodar tree in the forest is a *devta* and the Jads look up at the white snow-capped mountains from their village and believe that they actually live with the gods on the high altitudes away from the pollution of civilization in the plains below.

As Clifford (1990: 113) has pointed out quoting Raymond Williams (1973) the 'fundamental contrast between city and country, aligns itself with other pervasive oppositions, civilized and primitive, West and "non-West", future and past'. Such oppositions play a definite political role for a particular purpose, namely to identify and justify hierarchies. The Jads, situated far from the need to establish hierarchies, have never thought in terms of oppositions. However, such oppositions are pervasive in the thoughts of mainstream Hindus from the plains in which the Jads are situated at the 'other' end of a hierarchy, looked down upon as *junglee* in a derogatory sense. The Jads have also responded to this by moving from a position of not recognizing any separation between nature and culture to one where they have now started to equate 'culture' or civilization as negative and nature as positive. The 'civilization' down there (in the plains) is negative both in terms of traditional concepts of *sangma*, as well as politically in the backdrop of the hill separatist movements. The plains are a wilderness full of dangers contrasted to the pristine purity of unspoilt nature symbolized by the high peaks of the Himalayas.

References

Berreman, Gerald. 1972. *Hindus of the Himalayas*. Berkeley: University of California Press.

───── 1983. 'The U.P. Himalayas: Culture, Cultures and Regionalism'. In O.P. Singh ed. *The Himalaya: Nature, Man and Culture*. New Delhi: Rajesh Publications. pp. 227–66.

Brown, C.W., 1994. 'What we call 'Bhotiyas' are in reality not Bhotiyas'. In M.P. Joshi *et al.* eds. *Himalaya: Past and Present*. Vol. II, Almora: Shree Almora Book Depot. pp. 147–72.

Carmichael, David L., Jane Hubert, Brian Reeves and Audhild Schenche. 1994. 'Introduction'. In D. Carmichael *et al* eds. *Sacred Sites, Sacred Places*. London: Routledge. pp. 1–8.

Channa, Subhadra. 1998. 'Rethinking Anthropological Concept of "Tribe"'. *Eastern Anthropologist* 51 (2): 121–37.
____ 2002. 'The Life History of a Jad Woman'. *European Bulletin of Himalayan Research* 22: 61–81.
____ 2005. 'The Descent of the Pandavas: Ritual and Cosmology of the Jad of Garhwal'. *European Bulletin of Himalayan Research* 28: 67–87.
Clifford, James. 1990. 'On Ethnographic Allegory'. In J. Clifford and G. Marcus eds. *Writing Cultures: The Poetics and Politics of Ethnography*. New Delhi: Oxford University Press. pp. 98–122.
Dalmia, Vasudha. 1999. *The Nationalization of Hindu Traditions: Bharatendu Harischandra and Nineteenth Century Banaras*. New Delhi: Oxford University Paperbacks.
Deliege, Robert, 1997. *The World of the 'Untouchables': Paraiyars of Tamil Nadu*. New Delhi: Oxford University Press.
Descola, Philippe and Gisli Pálsson. 1996. 'Introduction'. In P. Descola and G. Pálsson eds. *Nature and Society: Anthropological Perspectives*. London and New York: Routledge. pp. 1–21
Fürer-Haimendorf, Christoph von. 1975. *Himalayan Traders: Life in Highland Nepal*. Great Britain: John Murray.
____ 1981. 'Introduction'. In C. von Fürer-Haimendorf ed. *Asian Highland Societies in Anthropological Perspective*. New Delhi: Sterling. pp. i–xii.
Ingold, Tim. 1992. 'Culture and the perception of the environment'. In E. Croll and D. Parkin eds. *Bush Base: Forest Farm: Culture, Environment and Development*. London: Routledge. pp. 39–56.
Knight, John. 1996. 'When Timber Grows Wild: The Desocialisation of Japanese Mountain Forests'. In P. Descola and G. Pálsson eds. *Nature and Society: Anthropological Perspectives*, New York: Routledge. pp. 221–40.
Rabinow, Paul. 1990. 'Representations are Social Facts: Modernity and Post-Modernity in Anthropology'. In J. Clifford and G. Marcus eds. *Writing Cultures*. New Delhi: Oxford University Press. pp. 234–61.
Rao, Aparna. 1998. *Autonomy: Life Cycle, Gender and Status among Himalayan Pastoralists*. New York: Berghahn Books.
Sax, William. 1995. *The Gods at Play: Lila in South Asia*. New York: Oxford University Press.
Tambiah, Stanley. 1990. *Magic, Science, Religion and the Scope of Rationality*. Cambridge: Cambridge University Press.
Williams, Raymond. 1973. *The Country and the City*. New York: Oxford University Press.

Love and Vengeance in Indus Kohistan

CLAUS PETER ZOLLER

Gold washers near the Indus (Photo: Claus Peter Zoller)

The high mountains of Indus Kohistan are part of Kohistan District in the North-West Frontier Province of Pakistan on the western side of the river Indus. The author conducted field research in the area between 1997–2001 on Indus Kohistani, the major language of this area, and on the regional folk traditions. Indus Kohistani belongs to the small but archaic and therefore very interesting Dardic branch of Indo-Aryan. The majority of the people of Kohistan depends largely on livestock and agriculture, and still follows seasonal migrations to the alpine pastures (transhumance). The whole population follows the Sunni creed of Islam. Still, various pre-Islamic elements have survived to this day, notably the belief in fairies, giants and supernatural snakes. However, for the past few decades the area has come under the influence of Pashtun culture and way of life. Among the many consequences of this has been a ban on the worship of local saints (all shrines or *dargāh* have been destroyed) and the suppression of regional performance traditions.

Another feature permeating the Kohistani way of life is the never-ending blood feuds, frequently caused for the pettiest of reasons (see Muhammad Manzar Zarin and Ruth Laila Schmidt 1984). These feuds seem to be closely connected to the egalitarian and acephalous character of Kohistani society (Arne Knudsen 2001). I do not suggest that the institution of blood feuds has been adopted from the Pashtuns. Most likely it is an old practice, the spirit and the details of which closely resemble those described for the so-called Kafirs, more than a hundred years ago by George S. Robertson. In this chapter, I show that there also exists a most intimate relationship between romantic love affairs and deadly shooting sprees, a relationship which can be aptly framed within the complementary notions of culture and nature. The delineations are based on my fieldwork observations, talks and interviews, and on the analysis of Kohistani oral traditions as I have recorded.

The postulation of an opposition between nature and culture as constituting a central element in the Kohistani life-world is a hermeneutic strategy rather than something that is obviously reflected in the Kohistani symbolic culture. In other words, the opposition is never overtly expressed in a particular cultural activity but is a possible way of reading this society. I can say that I describe both explicit and implicit or tacit knowledge (on these notions see William Sax 1990: 505), with the implicit knowledge having been collected and ordered systematically by me from stray observations, casual remarks, and pieces from oral traditions. However, I further insist that there are particular features of the *physical landscape* of Kohistan which provide the template for my elaborations.

Love is inherent in all human cultures and may be defined as acting intentionally, in sympathetic response to another person. However, Kohistan is a part of Pakistan where public displays of affection, even by married couples, is a strict cultural taboo. Women here are hardly ever visible in public spaces, and only men, frequently armed with Kalashnikovs, rule the market. Yet all—at least all men—talk about love. In Kohistan, love is a liminal experience; it is not found between legally married spouses, but only between men and women pursuing an illegal relationship; it forces lovers to swing between human society and nature in order to protect themselves in a deadly serious sport—a sport that is, however, pursued by the great majority of Kohistanis.

Let me begin by illustrating this with an excerpt from an interview carried out by my colleague, the social anthropologist Wiegand Jahn, in 1999, in Indus Kohistan.[1] He was interviewing the then 55-year-old Fazl-ur Rahman.[2]

> Fazl: In Kohistan we say: silver has two colours: it contains something dark and something shining yellow. But in the face of my beloved I can see seven different colours. The outer edge of the eyes is black, the eyelids are pink, the eyeball is white, the pupils glimmer in their own colours, the lips are dark red, the teeth bright white, and the cheeks have their own pink colour.
>
> Wiegand: Did you ever have a lover?
>
> Fazl: I had a lover for 25 years. And that was true love.
>
> Wiegand: What do you mean by 'true love'?
>
> Fazl: It means we never did anything indecent.

---

[1] I am grateful to Wiegand Jahn that he gave me permission to use this interview here. This interview was conducted in Urdu.
[2] This is a fictitious name.

Wiegand: What do you mean by 'indecent'?

Fazl: We had no sex.

Wiegand: Never?

Fazl: No! That was love! We touched hands; that was all we did.

Wiegand: When you met her, what happened then?

Fazl: We exchanged presents, and listened to each other's worries, and we tried to help solve each other's problems. At our rendezvous spot, I fixed a recognizable sign: I laid a stone in the branch of a tree and wrapped a colored ribbon around it. I had fixed such signs all along the way. They are still there, and when she comes back and walks along there, she remembers me.

Wiegand: Do many Kohistanis have a lover?

Fazl: All. There is no Kohistani without a lover.

Wiegand: Imagine once you get to know that your daughter has a lover. What will you do then, will you kill her?

Fazl: At once! I will shoot both her and her lover. We do not ask, we do not think, it is inevitable.

Wiegand: But wouldn't you feel terribly sad? Doesn't it hurt very much when one shoots one's own daughter?

Fazl: She has made a very big mistake. There is no sadness there, only the weak are sad, the brave ones are never sad. But you cannot kill your own mother. She bore you in her womb before you were born. That would be a great sin.

Wiegand: We really have difficulty understanding this. You men, you have your affairs, you enjoy them, but you would kill your own daughter or sister for something similar. Don't you think this is strange?

Fazl: Yes, it is strange. But it is our duty.

Further on, I discuss some of the more culture-specific elements found in this interview, but let me point out here that a typical Kohistani love affair seems to include all three components described by Robert Sternberg (1986) in his triangular theory of love: intimacy, passion, commitment; with the important qualification, however, that sexual consummation remains explicitly excluded.

Here we may discern three spheres of Kohistani society: the

public open sphere which is absolutely male-dominated, the *private* hidden sphere of the households, and the *secret* 'virtual' sphere of the lovers. Public and private spheres are both characterized, among other things, by notions such as honour, shame and duty, and concealment of one's love-related emotions. They contrast with the secret virtual sphere of the lovers which is characterized by the expression and living out of love-related emotions. Later in the chapter, I discuss the different violent ways of penetration and conquest that regularly take place between these spheres.

The above interview makes it clear that there must also be secret discourses associated with the lovers' secret virtual sphere. But there are also rather 'public discourses' on this topic, namely those camouflaged, as it were, in the oral traditions. Thus, the theme of love also appears in Kohistani oral literature. In fact, it is the most important theme, and I tend to believe that oral poetry is an important means for the Kohistanis to express their love-related feelings and dreams, feelings for which there is otherwise little space for expression within the public and private spheres. But first, I would like to say something about who performs what kind of oral art in this area.

In Kohistani society, three groups of people are engaged in oral art. First, there is the general population singing songs and recounting tales. Of course, not everyone does this, but people point out some person or other with the reputation of being an excellent singer or story-teller. The second group comprises the old caste of professional musicians, called Ḍom. It is their traditional task to perform at all kinds of festive occasions. However, many, or perhaps most of them, were expelled from Kohistan in the 1970s, because their artistic activities were declared incompatible with Islamic tenets. I will take up this point again and suggest an interpretation of the recent hostility towards traditional art forms. The third group of performing artists is called by the Arabic word *Šā'ir*. They do not comprise a caste, but all of them have found their vocation in the wake of an unsuccessful love affair, that is, when their love for a certain person was not reciprocated.

When I started working in Indus Kohistan I was well aware of the precarious social situation of the Ḍom. While there is no problem in organizing an evening recounting fairytales, and while *Śā'irs* and their performances are still tolerated, open hostility greets the *Ḍoms'* traditional performances. I therefore waited a full year before I slowly started establishing contacts with those *Ḍoms* who had not been forced to quit their homeland. In order to record their performances I had, however, to bring them either down to Islamabad or up to the city of Gilgit. In the course of my work with the *Ḍoms*, I organized two public performances in Islamabad. The very positive reactions of the *Ḍoms* and other Kohistanis to my efforts clearly demonstrated how strongly their tradition has come under pressure from dominant cultural forces in the area.

There are at least two reasons for the marked hostility of 'official Kohistan' against traditional oral art. The first is that everything related to love is tolerated only in the form of a shadowy and secret existence, and has to be segregated from all public space. The second point relates to the fact that poetry all over South Asia is, to a very large extent, an *expressive* oral art. In other words, it is *inspirational*. Although Kohistani artistes are quite reticent on this point, there is no doubt that at least some of them understand their vocation as a calling originating somewhere 'outside' themselves, e.g., coming from God. And this was recognized as a challenge by those who do not want to tolerate the presence of any higher authority besides the orthodox religious authority they themselves represent.

On the other hand, the fairytales are said to be inherited from the fairies and the giants, thus they have a kind of 'historical' dimension, and they deal with a world outside human society. Consequently, power agency is not the issue here, and fairytales can be related everywhere in Kohistan.

The religious functionaries, who represent *haq* 'law', have not only marginalized the *Ḍoms* and the lovers, but also the shamans. Both shamans and *Ḍoms* traditionally used a drum, and in many places between Karakoram and the Central Himalayas one comes up against the idea that the drums are animated during performance as it were by fairies. Consequently, the drum has also been outlawed. When shamans and *Ḍoms* hold performances—either secretly within Kohistan or more openly outside the district—

they use a jerry can instead of a drum, nowadays. A wooden drum can be animated by a fairy, because there is a close link between fairies and trees, but it is not the same with a steel jerry can.

Ignoring, for the sake of argument, the manifold differences between the various regional cultures of Northern Pakistan, I will reconstruct the following general historical scenario for that area. Prior to Islamization (which seems to have taken place in Indus Kohistan just a few generations ago, see Alberto M. Cacopardo and Augusto S. Cacopardo 2001: 35), or at least prior to the rise of strict forms of Islam, ideas must have existed about a difference between culture and nature, where nature was associated with otherworldliness, purity and numinosity (Jettmar 1975: 216–17). The border between the two spheres was not an absolute one in that numinous entities could temporarily or permanently live in the human world, while humans could temporarily or permanently stay in the other world. The official Islam of Kohistan never seriously questioned the reality of fairies, giants, subterranean snakes etc., but it has tried to perpetuate the divide between the two worlds—can we already understand Fazl a little bit better?

The consequence of this rigidification process was not only a shift in the status of lovers, musicians and shamans into illegality, but it apparently also led to an impoverishment of oral traditions. The modern artistic productions of Northern Pakistan—even though many of them are indeed good—do not have the same artistic rank and quality as comparable productions of the Central and Western Himalayas to which they are closely related. Moreover, one clearly observes among the epics of Kohistan—which once recorded, as it were, the historical past of the community—a transformation of the literary features typical of epics into those typical of fairy tales. A central process here is the decontextualization of the plot away from a 'historical' framework and a recontextualization into a context that is (almost) segregated from Kohistan's time and space.

The religious authorities of the area have been quite successful—all *dargāh*s have been destroyed and the dangerous drums have been replaced by harmless jerry cans—but lovers, musicians and shamans have not given up completely. The latter two—musicians and shamans—are still active underground or outside the area, and for the lovers—who can only meet in the wilderness—it is clear that their relationship is, in a way, 'legal'. In several love songs I recorded, there are lines like the following: 'I feel like being fatally ill; that experience of love is *halāl* ('legitimate').'

Or: 'I feel as though I am fatally ill; to look into your eyes is *halāl*.'

Or: 'A man has been killed without committing a sin; someone hit him with the bullet of a gun.'

This last quote refers to a lover who got shot by a relative. Obviously a love affair, which is definitely *harām* ('forbidden') from the general viewpoint of Kohistani society, is nevertheless 'legal' from a viewpoint outside society. It is 'legal' in the wilderness, the home of the fairies, giants and supernatural snakes.

The idea of the two spheres of culture and nature or society and wilderness has a concrete equivalent in Kohistani landscape and settlement patterns, and can be seen in a horizontal and a vertical dimension (see Figure 9.1).

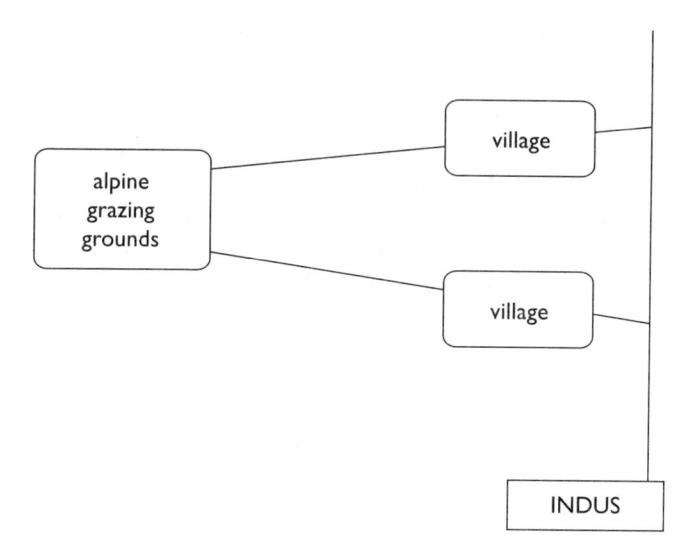

Figure 9.1

a) The horizontal dimension

Traditionally, communication between settlement areas during the winter months was extremely limited because moving from the mouth of a side valley to the next along the Indus was almost impossible due to the rugged and steep mountains flanking the Indus. Thus families from different valleys typically met during the summer months high up on the alpine grazing grounds. I was told that this was also the time when love affairs were reactivated or new affairs began, and when blood feuds were carried out. Karl Jettmar (1983) is of the opinion that the new communication facilities also led to changes in the patterns of blood feuds.

b) The vertical dimension of the mountains

Table 9.1: Activities in Various Areas

Area	Activity	Types of beings	Purity degree[3]
high mountains	hunting	men and fairies	+
alpine pastures	herding	men and women	±
permanent settlements	agriculture	men and women	±
settlements in plains	business	men and women	−

So it is clear that the *proper* place for love affairs are the meadows and forests up in the high mountains. Lovers have no business inside permanent settlements and if they are identified there they have to be eliminated as intruders. The wilderness is, by definition, a society-free sphere. As a result, equality predominates between the actors in the wilderness, and the theme of communication is 'love' in its two states of union and separation. Within society the theme of communication is 'respect' with its two manifestations of honour and shame. And it is worthwhile adding here that both Wiegand Jahn and I have consistently been told that in

---

[3] In many areas of the mountains of North Pakistan, the landscape is traditionally divided vertically into sections associated with different degrees of sacredness. The highest alpine areas are the most sacred ones whereas the bottoms of the valleys are regarded as impure.

Kohistan, husband and wife never love each other (apart from some rare exceptions), but that their relationship is characterized by mutual respect.

We have seen Fazl pointing out that he would, at any time, be ready to kill his own daughter if she would be shown to have an illicit relationship, with the words, 'We do not ask, we do not think, that is inevitable.' During conversations I had with Kohistanis on this topic, it was said time and time again that such actions—killing 'unlawful' lovers, carrying out a vendetta (*qatliām*) or a nocturnal cattle raid together with the rape of women (*dhāṛ*)—are always executed in a state of extreme emotional excitation. It is as if the Kohistanis wanted to tell us: 'Look what happens when lovers show up amongst us: affection tips over into hate, and pure love turns into brutal sexual abuse. All this is the negative inversion of a loving relationship when it enters the confines of society.'

In such moments, wilderness lays claim to some space within society. After having worked on some cultures in the Indian Himalayas, which were traditionally dominated by warrior codes and ethics (see Zoller 2007), I was always surprised to hear in Kohistan that in order to carry out a killing or a vendetta, every means is permitted: a culture of vendetta with no rules or ethics. On the basis of my metaphor of the wilderness within society this seems to make some sense: as in such moments there is absolutely no restraint on emotions, there is equally no control over the actions performed by the persons involved.

The picture of the two spheres and the proper and improper movements between them is, however, not yet accurate enough. In order to show the typical movements of actors between these spheres, I have to expand the geographical and historical angle beyond northern Pakistan.

From the medieval ages until modern times, one finds throughout the northern part of South Asia the literary genre of ballads (Hindi *lok-gāthā*) or folk romances. These include *Māluśāhī* from Kumaon, *Ḍholā-Mārū* from Rajasthan, *Hīr-Rānjhā* from the Punjab, *Sassī-Punnū* from Sindh/Balochistan; the older ones are *Padmāvat* and *Mṛgāvatī* in classical Hindi.

They all describe a love affair between a hero and a heroine, the many obstacles they have to overcome, and their final happy union or tragic separation. In order to search for and win his beloved, who lives in a far-away 'otherworldly' Elysium, the hero has to become an anchorite, i.e., a 'liminal' figure. He does this because he has to leave his normal world and enter a kind of otherworld. Many fairytales of Indus Kohistan follow exactly the same pattern. A typical tale may have the following structure (at first glance this will look very simple, but many tales have complicated plots, sometimes with stories within stories):

A fairy enters the human world in the form of a hare/rabbit. The prince sees her and thinks, 'I must have her' and starts to chase her. While searching for his unknown beloved fairy, at a certain place the prince orders all his companions to stay back and wait for his return ('If I do not return within twelve years, understand that I am dead'). He is now going to enter a kind of 'otherworld' where the fairy lives. Assisted by all kinds of magic helpers, he finally wins her and returns home. End of the story.

The worlds through which these actors move are of an extremely abstract nature, very far from the here and now: after every few sentences it is said, 'At one time or other...', 'at one place or other...' This corresponds to some extent to the fact that beyond the inhabited and cultivated areas, very few place names are found in Kohistan.

The main difference between these Kohistani fairytales and the above-mentioned romances is that fairytales lack a spatiotemporal link with reality, whereas romances are traditionally understood to have occurred in the historical past. The latter are, in a sense, 'historical' stories with an ahistorical plot. Both genres share the feature of a dual-dimensionality of 'this world' and an 'otherworld'. If the hero is able to act successfully, then the plot consists of a movement from 'this world' to the 'otherworld' and back into 'this world'. In the case of the fairytales, the hero is always successful. However, if the movement remains incomplete, as it does in some of the folk romances, the hero and heroine are doomed to die. In some cases, such incomplete movement seems to be an indispensable prerequisite for the heroine to become deified.[4]

In the case of our human lovers from Kohistan, the problem is not that they might not find their way back home; their problem is that they are *not allowed* to return home. If they were, i.e., if their relationship became public knowledge, then they would *naturally* have to be killed. But as long as this does not happen, they live, albeit with a split identity, as demonstrated by Fazl.

Kohistani love songs are clearly embedded in this greater South Asian tradition. The songs are usually structured as dialogues: the boy says something, the girl answers etc. And in some songs I recorded the boy says, 'I am an anchorite (i.e. a Faqir or Malang)' or 'I have become mad (i.e. he is like a Malāvat Sufi)'. In other songs, the boy and girl are equated with the *totā* (parrot) and the *mainā* (starling) or with Laila and Majnun (legendary lovers in the Indian subcontinent whose story ended with the death of both). There is an interesting verse in a song where the girl says to the boy: 'Don't let me be killed by someone, because then you will resent it, and you'll be aggrieved, and you'll be driven to despair. But I will walk (in the shape of a fairy) over the alpine meadows, and I will be the most beautiful one among all my girl friends.' So the girl indicates here that if she is killed by her own or her friend's relatives, she will not become a goddess like the famous Hindu heroines from the folk romances, but at least she will become a fairy.

The image of the hero as an anchorite and the heroine as a fairy—both in the folk songs and the tales—clearly expresses that their relationship is 'pure' and not desecrated by sex. In the love songs and, as I guess, also in reality, the same concept is realized by promoting the idea of separation (*judāī*). In the love songs, the girl bemoans her fate that her lover lives in a distant country,

---

[4]There still exist the ruins of an abandoned temple formerly devoted to Sassī not far from the Pakistani town of Talagang, and there is the mausoleum of Hīr in the Pakistani town of Jhang, which is a pilgrimage centre for lovers.

and for Fazl, it is important that his beloved can see the signs he has placed along the way, so that she may remember him.

The actors of the songs are, as far as I know, always 'I' and 'you'. 'I' am dying of love for 'you', but 'you' are far away, 'you' have a cruel heart, etc. The singers can say this, because the situation of every oral performance has an ambivalent aspect: the things expressed are, at the same time, both true and untrue. When the singer sings of his love, he enacts the heroic lover but at the same time he does not forget that he is also the tea seller from the bazaar. So this is, in a way, different from the actual rendezvous pursued in Kohistan under utmost secrecy and danger.

But there is also a link connecting the two realms. We have seen that real love adventures are tolerated as long as they remain secret. The same thing put into other words is: they are tolerated as long as they are without consequence. The love songs never describe marriage, and they never describe the birth of a child. This means, that both the real love stories as well as those found in the songs, as well as (as I show further on) those told in the Kohistani tales, engender, as it were, a form of love which is almost completely segregated from the dimensions of society, history, and real time and space. I think this is just one step away from mystical love poetry.[5]

It does not appear to be a matter of luck that love songs usually describe a state of suspense with no 'solution' at hand. Somehow similar is again the situation in the fairytales: they end when the prince has successfully brought home his fairy. The unequal relationship between a human man and a superhuman fairy is regarded by local people as being without potency with regard to the creation of offspring. Thus they too are based on that principle of pure and timeless love.

So we have seen that there is a close correspondence between the oppositional notions of culture and nature on the one hand,

---

[5] I thus also think that it is not by accident that the Punjabi romance *Hīr-Rānjhā* has had such a great influence upon medieval Punjabi Sufi poetry. I cannot, however, pursue this point here.

and the Kohistani practices of secret love affairs and vendettas on the other. They are embedded in the particular characteristics of the landscape of the area and reflected in their oral literatures. Moreover, Are Knudsen, following Mary Douglas, proposes (2001: 1) to designate the society of the Palas valley in District Kohistan as an 'egalitarian enclave', and he points out (ibid.) that 'In egalitarian enclaves belonging holds a special meaning because of the tendency of the enclave to shed its member.' Those who are mostly at a risk of falling out of such 'egalitarian enclaves' (I have called them 'settlement areas') and who are thus mostly concerned with the issue of belongingness, are 'the poor, the belligerent, the weak and the wronged' (Knudsen, ibid.) and, Knudsen should have added—the lovers. Knudsen continues (2001: 2-3), 'Thus, belonging has an affective dimension... The affective element is communicated in song and poetry and acted out in illicit love affairs and clandestine romances. Being party to an illicit love affair is an essential expression of belongingness but at the same time, the strongest repudiation of it. Loving and longing are eulogized in vernacular song and poetry, but the slightest hints of illicit romances lead to obliteration of unfaithful women who, unable to flee, are killed by their brothers, fathers or husbands. The antithesis of belonging is therefore not defection and migration but obliteration and death.'

This is not the place to deal with the other conclusions of Knudsen's highly readable monograph. But the above quotes demonstrate Knudsen's rather similar views to mine on 'culture and nature', and on love and death in District Kohistan. Nevertheless, I doubt whether entertaining a secret love affair, which is a subversive and desperate enterprise, is a straightforward expression of one's desire and right for belonging. After all, it has to remain a secret and can only signal belongingness in the most general way, namely that all Kohistanis know that everyone else has a lover.

Love implies intersubjective acceptance, and takes place in a system of intimacy that is sharply separated from the family system. A family serves for reproduction and socialization, but in a Kohistani love affair, the lovers refuse to care for reproduction and they despise social norms. The latter attitude might be the reason why many Kohistani words for 'lovers' just mean 'thieves'.

Love became the reason for celebrating a marriage in Western societies from the nineteenth century onwards (see Niklas Luhmann 1982). Wedlock and love are thus frequently not interconnected. In Kohistan, they remain instead in opposition to each other in the sense that it is almost inconceivable to be married to one's lover. Seen from the perspective of the sociologist Luhmann's theoretical system, wedlock and love are two independent systems that have nothing in common with each other. However, secret love affairs are apparently interwoven with the system of hereditary law: a love affair is not so much immoral as it is illegal. Consequently, legal action has to be taken when a secret love affair has been uncovered. But then why does almost every man in Kohistan entertain a secret love affair? I suggest applying here Luhmann's concept of social binary codes, realized within the communication system of love as the central difference between what he terms 'plaisir' and 'amour' (Luhmann 1982: 108 ff. *et passim*). Whatever forms love takes in each individual case, it is always a pleasurable enterprise for those partaking in it. The participants can take pleasure from the developments, successes and failures of their affair, and they can take pleasure from their clever strategies by which they try to conceal their affair from the eyes of others. This pleasure is certainly intensified by the fact that the love affair is lived out in a field demarcated by the poles of legality and illegality: it is a pleasure to try to deny one's love affair any control by law. However, going beyond the sense of a defiant 'you can't catch me', love affairs in Kohistan are indeed also disguised ways of signalling 'you might kill me, but you won't succeed in chasing me out of Kohistan.'

References

Cacopardo, Alberto M. and Augusto S. Cacopardo. 2001. *Gates of Peristan: History, Religion and Society in the Hindukush*. Reports and Memoirs, series minor vol. 5. Roma: Istituto italiano per l'Africa e l'Oriente, centro scavi e ricerche archeologiche.

Jettmar, Karl. 1975. *Die Religionen des Hindukusch. Mit Beiträgen von Schuyler Jones und Max Klimburg*. Stuttgart etc.: Kohlhammer Verlag.

Jettmar, Karl. 1983. 'Indus-Kohistan: Entwurf einer historischen Ethnographie'. *Anthropos* 78: 501–18.

Knudsen, Are. 2001. *Boundaries of Belongingness in the Palas Valley, Pakistan*. Dr. Polit. Dissertation, Faculty of Social Science, University of Bergen.

Luhmann, Niklas. 1982. *Liebe als Passion: Zur Codierung von Intimität*. Frankfurt: Suhrkamp.

Robertson, George S. 1987 [First edition 1896]. *The Kafirs of the Hindu-Kush*. Karachi: Oxford University Press.

Sax, William S. 1990. 'Village Daughter, Village Goddess: Residence, Gender and Politics in a Himalayan Pilgrimage'. *American Ethnologist* 17 (3): 491–512.

Sternberg, Robert J. 1986. 'A Triangular Theory of Love'. *Psychological Review* 93: 119–35.

Zarin, Muhammad Manzar and Ruth Laila Schmidt. 1984. 'Discussions with Hariq: Land Tenure and Transhumance in Indus Kohistan'. In *Working Papers*, Berkeley: University of California Center for South Asia Studies.

Zoller, Claus Peter. 2007. 'Himalayan Heroes'. In Brückner, H., H. van Skyhawk and C.P. Zoller (eds.) *The Concept of Hero in Indian Culture*. New Delhi: Manohar. pp. 237–74.

Conceptions on Tibetan Relics

Rachel Guidoni

Pearl-relics from Mount Kailash, Tibet (Photo: Rachel Guidoni)

This work is part of my Ph. D. thesis in Anthropology, completed in 2006 at the University Paris X-Nanterre. I am indebted to M. Lecomte-Tilouine who has invited me to publish this article. The first draft of this chapter was corrected by F. Meyer, and E. Ary improved the first English version.

Relics and the cult surrounding them constitute an important part of religious life among Tibetan populations. Indeed, they are essential to both the Buddhist and the Bon traditions. However, they have only been sparsely studied until now, and the few works dedicated to them have considered them mainly as the object of very elaborate classifications.[1] Personally, I have tried to account for their place and function mainly among contemporary Tibetan communities established in exile. It has revealed that they occupy an essential position, enjoy a rich terminology, and enter a wide range of conceptions and uses. Unfortunately, many of these functions have not been given proper attention, probably because they are hardly mentioned in Tibetan literature. However, closer scrutiny reveals that they are of great value in the eyes of devotees.

In this chapter, I analyse specific properties of two of the most common Tibetan relics. I will particularly consider the nature and the circumstances of their emission, as these features seem rather prodigious, compared to Catholic and ancient Buddhist models. Indeed, religions in Tibet have developed their own systems of concepts and practices centred around relics, quite independently of those used in ancient Buddhism.

Christian and Buddhist Classifications

Before going into these topics in more detail, it may be useful to briefly remember Western conceptions of relics. In the Catholic tradition, the word 'relic' derives from the Latin *reliquiae*, 'remains'; it designates material goods belonging to Christ and to the community of saints who were recognized as such by the Roman Catholic Church. Relics can be divided into two categories:
- Corporeal relics: these are the remains of a living body or a corpse, and can designate everything from the full body to very small parts of it.

[1] See, for example, Yael Bentor, 1994:16–30; Dan Martin, 1994: 273–324, and 1992: 183–91.

– Relics of contact: This includes clothes that touched the body of a saint and objects used by him. This contact may have happened during the saint's life or after his death.[2]

Originally, Christians from the East paid homage to the tombs of martyrs who gave their life as a token of faith. This cult became so popular that devotees started to open some graves to distribute parts of the body to those who, partly because they lived far away, could not venerate the martyr directly at his tomb. From the fourth century onwards, this cult grew significantly as pontifical authorities no longer limited it to martyrs and their bodily relics: the cult was opened to venerable men (especially bishops), the cult of personal belongings (objects and clothes) was authorized, and the veneration of objects of Christ's Passion was also allowed.

After the twelfth century, another change took place as some monks and nuns revealed their sanctity during their own lifetime, usually by accomplishing miracles: it was therefore possible to venerate their relics before they died. But even then, the relics discovered at their death held a very special value. The same can be said about Jesus Christ, with the relics of Christ's Passion and of his death being more valuable than those left from his lifetime. Any Christian is much more eager to pay homage to the fragments of the Holy Cross or to the Holy Shroud than to be shown, for example, the teeth He lost in youth. Actually, a relic in Roman Catholic thought appears to have a very special relation with death. Furthermore, it is always connected with the body of the saint. This relation to the body is the one condition for it to be considered a relic.

In the Buddhist tradition, it is hard to estimate the first occurrence of relics, as written sources claim that Buddhas from the past had already left some. These relics were venerated during the time period between the death of one Buddha and the coming on earth of the next one. Some texts such as the *Mahāvaṃsa* (the Sri Lankan historical chronicle, fifth century AD) or a commentary of the *Abhidhamma Vibhaṅga* by Buddhaghosa (an Indian scholar from the same period) affirm that the relics of each Buddha from

---

[2]*Dictionnaire de droit canonique*, t. 7: 569.

the past have to disappear entirely before the coming of the next one, yet Tibetan texts, without mentioning present-day informants, very commonly refer to relics of the previous Buddhas.

In ancient Indian Buddhism, two generic terms could be used to designate relics: *śarīra*, 'body', and *dhātu*, 'element'. Early texts make it clear that those of the historical Buddha Śākyamuni (fourth-fifth century BC) were the most famous. Theravāda Buddhist documents dated before the fifth century AD contain classifications ranking relics into three subdivisions:[3]

śarīradhātu or 'corporeal relics'

This category refers to the full body or one of its parts. Ancient texts do not give details of the nature or the physical appearance of this kind of relic, yet in later texts, they are sometimes described as small crystalline fragments, usually in the shape of beads, found inside the crematory ashes of saints. Some explain that finding these pearls is proof that the late practitioner had reached the highest possible spiritual level.

pāribhogikadhātu or 'relics of contact'

This group includes garments and objects that were used by holy men, and more generally, all objects with which they came into physical contact. The monastic robe and the alms bowl were particularly esteemed, although many other objects were also included in this category.

uddesikadhātu

This last group gathers together all the objects and monuments intended to recall the events of a saint's life. This category includes stupas built on places they visited, images or statues commemorating a special event, texts they wrote, etc. These relics need not have been in contact with the body, but they can still be considered as relics since these places or artefacts evoke the memory of an important religious person. Buddhist experts refer to this group as 'commemorative relics'.

So, from an Indian point of view, a relic is a material object which evokes a saint's life: it includes their body or an effigy of

[3]See John S. Strong, 2004: 19, and Kevin Trainor, 1997: 89.

them, the objects they touched, the places they visited. More generally, everything associated with a holy figure is likely to be considered his relic, *dhātu*.

Tibetan Relics

In Tibetan literature, two generic terms are used to designate relics. The first one is *ringsel* (*ring bsrel*), 'long lasting'.[4] It can be applied to the three classical subdivisions of: bodily relics, relics of contact, and commemorative relics. In addition, it can designate any sacred object such as texts (especially *dhāraṇī*), effigies of deities or religious masters, sacred pills, and sometimes small clay figurines moulded in the shape of stupas or deities and called *tsha tsha* (therefore containing relics of a holy man).

The second term is *dung* (*gdung*), the honorific word for bone. It is mainly mentioned in Tantric literature, where it refers to pearl-like relics which are classified according to their colour (white, blue, green, red or yellow), size, and the different parts of the human body they come from. Sources are not homogeneous as almost every text provides different names for the subdivisions of *gdung*, but this type of relic is always divided into five parts. For example, the *Sparkling Body Tantra* (*sKu gdung 'bar ba'i rgyud*) details a list of five *gdung* called *sha ri ram*, *ba ri ram*, *chu ri ram*, *nya ri ram*, and *bse ri ram*.

However, in the common language used nowadays, *ring bsrel* and *gdung* have both very different and much more restricted meanings: *ring bsrel* designates a relic in the shape of a pearl, and *gdung* is only used to qualify bone fragments. Furthermore, when contemporary Tibetans are asked about what they conceive of as a relic, they mostly describe small hard shiny pearls, called *ring bsrel* or *'phel gdung*, 'increasing bone', or organic parts likely to be shed by the body: bones, teeth, fingernails or hair. So there is an important difference between written and oral sources.

---

[4] A discussion on the ancient meaning of *ring* and its evolution has been lead by Michael Walter, 1998: 63–8.

The study of relic classifications draws the same conclusion. Tibetan literature carries a great number of different classifications but when we look at their contents, it becomes clear that the word 'relic' is understood in its widest meaning. *Ring bsrel* is most often used and classified into four categories, even if typologies ranging from two to six are also well known. These classifications are usually based on criteria relating to the nature of relics: products of corporeal origin are gathered in one group, those of textual origin figure in another one, and so on. Sometimes, they are classified according to their physical appearance. For example, ancient Buddhists conceived a group formed of 'pearl-like relics similar to mustard seeds', a model which is very popular in Tibet. Other times, relics are ranked hierarchically, in which case texts always occupy the highest rank. In written sources, the notion of relic is then understood as any sacred material object, and forms a category much wider than what is meant by it in English since it includes objects which not necessarily derive from the body of saints.

Among contemporary Tibetan communities, the situation is quite different. For example, people do not admit the idea that a text may belong to the category of *ring bsrel*, even if the fact is largely developed in scholarly works. They also protest if you call *gdung* a pearl-like relic, even if Tantras largely confirm such a usage. I could enumerate many more examples. In reality, present-day Tibetans share a common knowledge about relics' terminology and classification which has few echoes in textual data. For them, a relic is necessarily something extracted from a holy body or a holy place. It is well conceived of as an object that has emerged from a sacred source, but does not include all sacred objects. Moreover, when evaluating a relic, an important criterion they consider is the circumstances in which it has appeared, especially from whom or where it comes, the place where it was collected, and if emission occurred spontaneously or not. Finally, all these questions reveal their interest in knowing if it dropped naturally or if it was, in a way, requested.

This enquiry is quite important in estimating the value of a relic, and it seems that the more unexpected its origin, the more valuable it is. Any artificial procedure or any intentional happening is less valued.

When Tibetans are asked how they identify relics, they respond by making a reference to their physical properties: a *ring bsrel* is a pearl-like relic, a *rang byung* is an object on which a sacred image has naturally formed, a *gdung* is a fragment of bone, a *na bza'* is a cloth worn by a deceased high-status practitioner, etc.[5] They also provide information about the saint to whom it belonged and sometimes add details on the way it was collected. For example, when they describe the content of a reliquary, they may say that such and such a relic was collected from the funeral pyre of a certain saint, while another was offered by a disciple on a certain occasion. These circumstances establish the relic's history and constitute its identity. These are quite interesting and on some occasions, even remarkable. For example, after Geshe Lama Konchok passed away in 2001 in his monastery in Nepal, his body was cremated, and the remains found in the pyre revealed a huge number of relics. Among them, his tongue was found with a self-appeared image (*rang byung*) of the goddess Tārā, his heart had not burnt at all, and whitish pearls were still coming out of his bones many weeks after his cremation. All these relics, presented as a sign of his high spiritual level, were carefully preserved, and later, enshrined in different stupas.

From a Tibetan point of view, both the Catholic and the primitive Buddhist definitions of relics can be seen as restrictive, because relics neither emanate necessarily from the body of saints nor, considering the last Buddhist subdivision, refer to locations and objects associated only with a saint's life. The Tibetans have developed a wide category of relics which go far beyond the limit of holy men's personal history.

I will illustrate this fact by focusing on two topics: the first will concern their nature and clarify where Tibetan relics can

---

[5] All through this chapter, I refer to men but this does not mean that only men produce relics. The fact is also attested with women, even if they are comparatively fewer in number.

come from. The next will consider the circumstances of their emission and under what conditions relics can be produced.

The Nature of Relics

It is commonly admitted among present-day Tibetans that the body of a saint is not the only potential source for relics to appear. This specific trend, which seems foreign to early Buddhist traditions, is often mentioned. Relics can, for example, spontaneously emerge from holy places: a mountain, a cave or a river, and they can also be emitted from sacred receptacles: a stupa, statue of a deity, a portrait of a religious master. In this case, these relics have the shape of small beads and are referred to as *ring bsrel*, 'long lasting', or *'phel gdung*, 'increasing bone'. Another kind of relic consists of sacred images that appear spontaneously, *rang byung*. But contrary to pearl-like relics, they are likely to appear only on human bodies or natural locations. Yet, whatever their place of origin, they all bear the same name, and are venerated and used in the same way as relics from the body.

Though human bodies, natural locations, and manufactured objects are prone to produce relics, in reality, this miracle is only possible for those sources that are recognized as granting blessings (*byin rlabs*), i.e., it is necessary for them to be sacred. So, according to Tibetan principles, any source of sacredness may theoretically produce relics as a form of blessing. The only exception for which I have found no mention is the Holy Scriptures, although they are included in textual traditions. However, written sources consider them as part of the category of *ring bsrel*, yet none ever described such books as having shed pearl-like relics or as having shown self-appearing images.

If we follow Tibetan conceptions and consider relics as an object or a figure extracted not only from human bodies but from any 'sacred receptacle' (*byin rten*), it is possible to observe two main types of relics, depending on their physical appearance: some are pearls that appear naturally, others are spontaneously appearing images.

'Natural' Pearls

The most common type of relic is what is commonly called the pearl-relic. This has the shape of a small round bead, and is hard and shiny, mostly white but can also be of different colours.

These pearls, included in the category of corporeal relics, are supposed to drop from the body of a saint during their lifetime. However, they may also drop from their body at the time of death, during the funeral, and even for a long time afterwards. Data are not homogeneous on where exactly they form inside the body: some people mention the bones, others indicate the blood, the brain, etc. But all agree that this is the result of the spiritual virtues of the person in question. The most famous characteristic of such relics is their power to multiply, and this is essential, as it enables new ones to appear regularly, even after the passing away of a saint, when the pearls come out of their bodily relics. Tibetans declare that these *'post mortem* beads' mostly originate from hard parts of the body (teeth, bones and pearl-relics), but rare mentions indicate that some are emitted from unburnt organs (heart, tongue and eyes) or from the salts that are used to mummify religious masters.

It is widely believed that these pearls can also be emitted spontaneously from holy places. When they originate from a saint's body, they are impregnated with the sacredness of the source they come from, and therefore, when one is found, it is kept carefully and worshipped for the blessing it continues to grant. For example, Mount Kailash is famous since some of these pearls can be found near stones and rivers. Pilgrims always keep a careful watch in case such a bead drops in their path: it is a very auspicious sign for the one who finds it.

Some beads may also drop from sacred monuments. The stupas of Svayambhūnāth and Bodnāth in the Kathmandu Valley were particularly famous until recently for having provided such pearl-relics, though the miracle is about to die out. (at least, this is a belief which was shared by most of the informants I met there). Stupas containing mummified lamas may also emit relics, and devotees explain that it is the body that operates this miracle.

Various testimonies indicate that such beads would sometimes emerge from the stupa containing the body of Tsong kha pa (fifteenth century), founder of the dGe lugs order, which stands within the complex of the lGa' ldan Monastery, in Central Tibet. Whenever devotees could find one, it was carefully preserved because it was supposed to multiply on the condition that it was kept carefully and properly venerated.

Spontaneous Images

This category designates physical supports on which an extraordinary sign has emerged spontaneously. This kind of relic is held in high esteem as it is believed that such images occur without being influenced by any external factor. They can depict any kind of sacred picture: a deity, a sacred letter or a full *mantra*, all of them appearing in relief or as a hollowed-out image. Such images can form themselves on stones, tree leaves, and even bodily relics. This type of relic is called *rang byung* or *rang byon*, 'appeared from itself'.

It sometimes happens that after the cremation of a lama (*bla ma*), one finds fragments of his bones showing sacred images. It is particularly mentioned regarding the skull and bones of the upper part of the body, mainly the arms and the hands. I was shown such a relic attributed to the great yogi Thang stong rgyal po (fifteenth century), the phalanx of whose hand bore a relief image of the full body of Avalokiteśvara. In Bhutan, the royal family owns a vertebra of gTsang pa rgya ras (twelfth century), which bears a representation of the deity Karsapani; this relic is known as Rangjung Karsapani, 'the self-appeared Karsapani'. Sometimes, written sources, especially *dkar chag* texts enumerating the sacred deposits inserted within stupas for their consecration, mention relics which none of my informants ever talked about; that of sacred images formed in the sperm or in the nasal blood of religious masters. Nothing is said of how they were collected or preserved. But according to the texts I went through, figures of deities are the only certified ones, and these relics are kept similarly in stupas with the greatest care.

The expression *rang byon* can also apply to sacred images formed on the surface of natural elements. One of the most famous spontaneous images is a picture of Goddess Tārā coming out of a rock in Pharping, Nepal. People visiting it regularly explain that the image comes out more and more clearly and that its details constantly become more vivid. They also say that since the main goddess is now easily recognizable, the twenty-one other aspects of her are appearing all around her on the same stone.

These two different types of relic, the small beads and the images 'formed by themselves', share two characteristics. The first one is their place of origin. Beyond their actual diversity, all locations—whether a human body, a natural place or an artefact—are viewed as being impregnated with blessings (*byin rlabs can*), so it is possible to see relics as the 'emanation and materialization of the sacred'. Indeed, devotees quite naturally evoke this link between a relic and the concept of sacredness. One Tibetan ascetic explained to me that common people may also have pearl-like relics in their crematory ashes, yet as these are devoid of any blessing, they are not worthy of being kept and venerated. So it is the property of being imbued with blessing that partly gives a relic its value. But it must be borne in mind that if all relics are impregnated with blessing, the reverse is not valid: not every blessed support can be considered as a relic.

The second characteristic is their way of materializing. Strangely, all these relics appear in a way we may call 'natural', meaning that there is neither external agent, nor technical intervention. Their being born of a sacred location does not surprise devotees who note that the source is sacred, as if this quality were enough to explain this kind of creation. However, this natural property is not systematic, and Tibetans readily admit that although any sacred place is capable of emitting relics, not all do. Here, another criterion has to be taken into consideration: both the source and the devotee can influence the production of relics. The relic thus establishes a link between a faithful devotee and a sacred receptacle. It highlights the virtues of both its emittor and its receptor.

Circumstances of Emission

It almost never happens that relics emerge continually from a particular source. They usually come out in an irregular way. Two factors can determine their production: one concerns the source, the other the devotee likely to be present. Schematically, one may sum up these circumstances into three statements, ranked according to the degree of external intervention:
- the production of relics is totally unpredicted, they come out themselves;
- the production is partly stimulated by an external agent, be it the source, the devotee, or both together by different means;
- the production is triggered intentionally. Either the source can show this power or the devotee can employ certain techniques, especially funeral practices, to obtain this result.

Spontaneous Production

It sometimes happens that a holy man has pearls dropping from his body. This production is not always mastered as some great men can even lose some while walking or resting. Some informants insist on the involuntary character of this production, which is explained as the result of meditational practices and spiritual accomplishments. These whitish pearls are said to form on the surface of the skin, then they fall when they have reached a certain size. The process has sometimes been compared to drops of sweat forming on the skin.

Similarly, some pearl-relics can emerge naturally from holy places, regardless of the presence of devotees worshipping at the location. This event can happen anytime, but it is often observed and testified on an auspicious day or occasion, a detail which is never mentioned in the case of saintly men. Some holy places are indeed famous for shedding pearls on the fifteenth day of the month, or on other auspicious days in connection with the site. For example, relics may drop in larger quantities in mTsho padma (Rewalsar, India) on the first month of the Tibetan calendar, as Padmasambhava (eighth century AD), to whom the place is dedicated, is supposed to be born in this month. A stupa can also emit relics early in the morning, before people's arrival, and the first person to arrive will just see beads lying on the ground.

A source able to emit relics by itself is seen as particularly holy, so the relics found by chance are highly valued as they indicate the profound sacredness of the source. These by-products are held in high esteem as devotees believe they are saturated with the blessings of the source and contain virtues equivalent to that of the source. These relics function as a kind of substitute, concentrating all the blessings in a small and easily transportable object, and in this way, they make it possible to worship the support somewhere other than where it actually lies.

Assisted Production

When relics are needed but are unavailable, it is possible to seek some. However, the disciple's behaviour and devotion seem to be taken into consideration by the emittor, as many testimonies agree that the source 'evaluates' one's faith before dropping a relic.

A devotee may come and request some relics, for example, if he needs some to consecrate a new stupa, or if he plans to provide a few to a dying relative, as the ingestion of a relic is reputed to avoid rebirth in the lower realms. The request for relics particularly concerns renowned religious masters. But I have not heard of Tibetans going to a sacred place and praying for relics to emerge. They feel satisfied at being infused with the blessing from the holy place, and those eager to 'capture' more blessings may ingest earth or suck stones. It is also common to take home whatever can be collected on the spot: earth, stones, water, etc., as every element of a sacred place contains its virtues.

Leaving aside the devotee's request, the sacred source may actually be unable or unwilling to provide relics. For religious masters, the question of their willingness is essential, and they may estimate the sincerity of the devotee before honouring them. For holy places or sacred artefacts, the situation is different: they may be unable to emit relics if the place has been affected by certain kinds of pollution (*grib*). The same is presumably true if the devotee is responsible for bad deeds in the past. This confirms the idea that although a sacred source is naturally disposed to provide relics, external agents such as impurity or insincerity, may hinder the process.

The custom of visiting a religious master and asking him for one of his personal belongings is quite popular. A particularly well-known case is that of the Buddha Śākyamuni giving some of his hair to his two first lay disciples, Trapaṣu and Bhallika, who had asked for an object they might worship during his absence.[6] I would not affirm that this story is very popular in Tibet, yet the tradition still strongly persists, of devotees asking a great practitioner for a relic, be it for personal use or community benefit. Those who honour the request may give some bodily relics (hair or finger-clippings, pearls dropped from their body) or religious objects of theirs: rosary, monastic cloth, consecrated pills or protective threads, etc.

It is not uncommon to hear stories where the nature of the gift, or the quantity offered, is explicitly said to be conditioned by the faith of the devotee making the request. Similarly, production of relics may be facilitated if his motivation is considered pure. To put it in other words, it is considered that a strong and sincere faith may help the extraction of a relic; whereas a devotee whose motivation is not that pure may disturb the process and even cancel it.

On the other hand, the production of relics may be conditioned by the state of the sacred source. If a holy man is willing to provide a relic, then the devotee is almost sure to see his or her request satisfied. However, if he is not well disposed, then the devotee has little chance of obtaining anything at all. For sacred places, this ability is expressed in terms of interrelations with the environment, as it is a reaction to external factors that may restrict production. A sacred location unable to provide relics is explained in terms of pollution; a pollution produced by insincere visitors or impure elements around the location. This argument is particularly relevant to the stupas of Bodnāth and Svayambhūnāth

[6]This legend is analysed in John S. Strong, 1998: 79–107.

which now fail to emit relics since visitors are often described as being ill-behaved, and the activities organized there as inappropriate. The locations have not lost their sanctity but external factors have had an impact on their faculty to diffuse virtues: their blessings are thus confined within them.[7]

The assisted production of relics can therefore be summarized as an 'exchange of good will' between a devotee and a sacred receptacle. It constitutes the potential result of an interrelation based on purity. A religious master can choose to give a relic, in the same way that the disciple can influence the production according to the extent of his faith. If both the source and the faith of the devotee are pure, all conditions for the emission of relics are present. However, if there is either insufficient purity or a lack of willingness, then the miracle may not happen.

Intentional Production

This kind of production involves any technical means directed toward the production of relics, even if this aim is not the only or the main one. Among various techniques, the disposal of the dead body constitutes an important part. Of course, this concerns only the corpse of holy men because when ordinary people die, the impurity of their corpse involves the necessity of getting rid of the body as quickly as possible.

When religious masters die, impurity does not affect their body. In fact, they have studied, practised and meditated all their life in order to purify their conscience and reach spiritual fulfilment. This practice of virtuousness, which they had already followed in their previous lives, saturates their body. In other words, the spiritual accomplishment they achieved during their lifetime impregnates their physical body. At the end of their life, both their conscience and their body are imbued with this purity. This is why their dead bodies are not viewed as being impure or dangerous. Moreover, the veneration of religious masters is seen

---

[7]This situation is also explained by some Tibetans as a consequence of the Kaliyuga: the period of degeneration that we undergo inevitably affects all sources of salutary blessings.

as a virtuous deed since they are considered to be a 'field of merit' and whoever worships them can accumulate good deeds. This belief remains valid forever after their death. That is why devotees are eager to collect their bodily remains which can be used as eternal substitutes for the deceased saint.

Tibetans have many funeral practices; for holy men, the two most common methods of disposal are cremation and mummification. Between these, cremation is accorded first preference, and it is probably linked to two prestigious antecedents: India and the Buddha. Mummification, on the other hand, reminds us of the techniques used in Central Asia. Mummification was once adopted for Tibetan emperors, who were mummified before being buried (at least from the seventh to the tenth centuries). This practice was gradually adopted by the religious domain, and came to be used mostly for high lamas.

The cremation of religious personalities consists of a fire-ritual (*sbyin sreg*) where the corpse is offered to the fire deities (*me lha*). The body burns inside a sacred space as the pyre has the shape of the stupa whose bottom is covered with the drawing of a *maṅḍala*. When the pyre is opened, the ashes are collected carefully by monks and dignitaries, and each relic discovered is listed. The most common relics are: bones (*gdung*), teeth (*tshems*), hair (*dbu skra*), whitish or coloured beads (*ring bsrel, 'phel gdung*), sometimes organs (tongue, heart, eyes) and pieces of garments. Ashes and bone powders are also kept, they are mixed with clay to mould *tsha tsha* or used for medicinal preparations. So all the remains are recovered and either distributed to devotees, or deposited in important and sacred places.

The mummification of Tibetan high practitioners is done by using salt. The body is seated in the lotus position, then totally dried up by placing it in a wooden chest filled with salt for many months. Mercury is sometimes introduced through the mouth to empty out the entrails. The wooden chest is regularly opened, the body taken out and the salt changed. Special care is taken to withdraw the fat rising to the surface of the body, as mummification by using salt releases oil in substantial quantity. Monks remove it by pressing hot roasted barley dough onto the skin. After the corpse is completely dry, the original form of the body is built up with wet paper and glue, then covered in gold, dressed in ceremonial clothes and kept in a special stupa after a consecration ritual (*rab gnas*) has been performed.[8] Embalming or the use of lacquer is not attested to in Tibet. The most common mummification process requires a huge quantity of salt which itself becomes an esteemed relic. It is particularly effective in treating diseases. The dough used to absorb the fat from the skin during mummification is rolled into small pills which are distributed to devotees. All these products are very much appreciated as they are saturated with the corporeal fluids from the holy body: a sick person can ingest some in order to improve his condition. And for those about to die, absorbing such a relic can contribute to a better rebirth.

Before concluding this chapter, it may be relevant to add a few words about 'other' pearl-relics. Not only great beings, but also holy places and sacred receptacles could shed some. However, certain animals sometimes also have the power to produce such relics. At least, they bear the same name, *ring bsrel*, and share the same appearance. Yet they cannot be mistaken for those previously described because these animals' *ring bsrel* are black.[9] The fact has especially been attested to with pigs, fish, poultry and eggs. Beads are said to be hidden in the animals' flesh or inside the egg, and they are very small, so people may ingest them without realizing it simply by eating this kind of food. But their ingestion is considered to be very risky as these 'relics' are situated at the opposite end of the spectrum to sacred relics. While sacred relics help a person to achieve liberation, ingestion of animal-produced beads invariably leads to hell.[10] Besides, their name is very clear: they are called 'malevolent pearl-relics' (*sdig pa'i ring bsrel*).

[8] For a description of a recent mummification combining Tibetan traditional methods and Western techniques, see Guidoni, 2005, 'Entre relique et reliquaire. L'exceptionnelle momie de Gling Rinpoche (1903–1983)'.

[9] However, the colour is not an infallible criterion as there are non-animal's black relics. But I will not enter into any detail here.

[10] Many informants reminded me of this danger to explain why reincarnated lamas and oracles should refrain from eating this kind of food.

This counter-example is interesting as it indicates that the contemporary category of *ring bsrel* is a group of objects showing opposite values. Those emitted from sacred sources, the most numerous, are kept for their blessings, but those that are invisible and hidden in animals' flesh are harmful. Interestingly, the only dangerous ones can be those that are absorbed involuntarily, as the 'good relics' must always be first collected, and then used as one pleases.

Relics and their Position in Nature and Culture

These ideas on two of the most famous Tibetan relics lead me to emphasize two ideas. First of all, all kinds of relics are invested with what I temporarily call a 'vital power'. We have seen that not only bodily relics, but holy places and sacred receptacles may also emit pearl-like relics. These pearls themselves have an autonomous life as they can multiply after having been produced. On the other hand, sacred figures may also appear on any support. Moreover, these relics perpetuate the presence of the saint as they continue, even after death, to bestow his blessings and thus maintain his 'presence' among devotees. In some cases, relics are even able to move and diffuse light. These properties are exactly those of living beings who can grow, move and reproduce themselves. Their possibility of dying is also attested to in Indian Buddhist texts, though I have not heard of this conception among Tibetans.[11] For them, the vital property seems linked to a kind of eternity, as if a relic were the permanent part of a sacred source, on condition that no external factor (pollution, lack of faith) threatens it.

This vitality becomes particularly obvious when informants describe 'mother pearl-relics' (*ring bsrel a ma*) and 'children pearl-relics' (*ring bsrel phru gu*). According to many informants, the

---

[11] Schopen developed this idea from a text included in the Vinaya of the Mūlasarvāstivādin Order. After a monk had torn down a stupa containing the mortal remains of a monk and thrown the bones away, the nuns in charge of the building declared: 'Our brother is from today truly dead!' (Schopen, 1998: 260).

phenomenon is likely to occur with any *ring bsrel*. Mother-relics, quite big, may produce small beads, the so-called children, provided that they are kept properly in a dark and clean place, and they are venerated accordingly. It is said that mothers do not like to be moved from one place to another, otherwise they may no longer be fecund; it is also said that children are usually not able to produce descendants. This idea strongly recalls the way gold production is conceived of. Indeed in the Tibetan world, gold nuggets are considered as living entities based in subterranian realms and being able to generate children, i.e. gold sand or dust, if they are not disturbed too much.[12] In this way, pearl-relics and mineral products share exactly the same process of generation, and are sensitive to the same external factors.

The second important thematic is that relics, especially bodily ones, do not necessarily come after the time of death: it is possible to obtain some even during one's lifetime. In the case of a reincarnated lama, they may even be available from the time he is recognized as such. This point again underlines the connection between relics and life, which is, from my point of view, one of the most relevant specificities of relics in the Tibetan world.

Now that we have clarified all these concepts, it might be pertinent to confront them with the categories of nature and culture as they are generally understood in Western thought. In our specific context, a 'natural relic' would be one extracted by itself, sans any technical or external influence except the course of time and the process of nature. On the other hand, a 'cultural relic' would be one resulting from a certain technical process. But, is this distinction relevant in our case, and is this distinction validated by Tibetan discourses or written sources?

For the first question, I am tempted to say that the distinction is pertinent. Indeed, upon reflection, this distinction provides an interesting way of creating new associations of relics, putting

---

[12]This belief was one of the reasons Tibetans were reluctant to exploit their subsoil. On beliefs concerning gold nuggets, see Lucette Boulnois, 1983: 88-90. I also addressed this subject in my M.A. thesis in Anthropology, *Les pierres précieuses dans la tradition tibétaine*, University of Paris X-Nanterre: p. 25.

together objects that usually do not share features and separating others that used to be linked in the Tibetan way of thinking. As a matter of fact, we could clearly identify some relics emerging spontaneously, and others produced after a more or less technical process. Yet some relics fit in with both specificities; they are those I call 'relics produced with assistance'. Thus, from a theoretical *etic* point of view, these two categories show some coherence.

As for the second question, which considers the *emic* perspective, none of the texts I have read, and none of my informants ever categorized relics in this way. If a pearl is emitted from a cave or if a deity appears on a bone, a Tibetan will consider all these emanations as being spontaneous (*rang bzhin nas byung ba red*, 'they have appeared naturally'), and resulting from the sacredness of the source. Even relics discovered after funerals are thought to be natural; it is believed that they would have come out anyway, and human intervention alone cannot explain their appearance. So I hardly believe that a Tibetan would accept this new categorization between 'natural' (*rang bzhin*) relics and 'cultural' ones (which I would translate as *rang bzhin med pa*, or *bzos pa red*, as it implies an external intervention); he would rather see all of this as an artificial distinction.

And it is quite easy to note that Tibetan people express some disinterest for artificially made relics. Although I do not have a lot of information on this subject, false relics constitute a well-known phenomenon, associated either with materialistic or spiritual values. On the one hand, relics bear a high economic value, and there is an important, but surreptitious trade of these goods. Those interested in making a profit do not miss the opportunity of introducing false relics into this network.[13] On the other hand, some people have appropriated relics for their personal fame, convinced that showing such goods will arouse veneration among their disciples. Such a purpose is admirably described by Padma gling pa (1450–1521) in a brief treatise called

[13]These exchanges are kept very secret and during my fieldwork in India and Nepal, I could not collect as much data as I had hoped. Yet, the little information collected has revealed a very dynamic trade.

Realization of ring bsrel *according to Garap dorje's method.*[14] He is one of the rare authors to have written on this topic.

Appropriating a relic is a complex process. First of all, one has to acquire the *ring bsrel* of a Buddha or a yogi. Once such a pearl is in one's possession, it is put in a ritual skull cup (*thod pa*, skt. *kapāla*) and covered with medicinal plants. Mantras must be recited for one week (the author gives no explanation concerning this period of time) and thereafter, the relic is removed from the skull cup and hidden in one's armpit. The author further elaborates that when the time of death is near, one just pops the *ring bsrel* in one's mouth. Thus after cremation, people will find pearl-like relics in the ashes, and this sign will convince them of the perfect fulfilment of the deceased.[15] It is noteworthy that our author concludes his text by asking readers not to disclose the process: he reveals it to only a few high-status practitioners 'so as to contribute to the propagation of the Buddhist doctrine'.

This text is remarkable as it does not suggest a way of making relics *ex nihilo*. More simply, it indicates a trick for appropriating others' relics for the sake of the deceased's *post mortem* glory. So it is not so much concerned with a 'realization' requiring relics as with a 'rehabilitation', and this description strengthens the 'natural' production as there is no artificial process at work. Indeed, the author does not reveal a method of 'creating' *ring bsrel*, he just explains how to recover some. Yet the fact that the method must be kept secret shows that it is not entirely 'natural' and could be prejudicial to the person who resorts to it.

Even if Tibetans are fond of spontaneous relics emitted from sacred sources, the natural process is much more valued than any artificial one. Instead of considering the categories of nature and culture in this particular context, I would suggest considering

[14]The full title of the text is 'Kun bzang dgongs pa kun 'dus las / gSang khrid kyi rgyab skor ring bsrel gyi sgrub pa dga' rab rdo rjes mdzad pa', in *The Rediscovered Texts of the great gTer ston Padma gling pa*, New Delhi, 1976, vol. Ba, f. 433–6.

[15]Padma gling pa adds that this process is exactly the same if one wants to leave spontaneous images (*rang byon sku*): one simply has to put them in one's throat before dying.

spontaneous and non-spontaneous relics. They set up a difference which is relevant from an *emic* point of view, at least in the context of relics and their cult within both Buddhist and Bon traditions.

It must be clear that the distinction between spontaneous and non-spontaneous relics does not affect the question of their authenticity. A relic found after a technical process is no less true than another one that appeared naturally. The way they come to be there can sometimes justify their value and instil a certain hierarchy, which is not standardized. However, any risk of there being false relics is avoided by a wide range of methods. As soon as a relic is proved to be authentic, it can enter a whole range of uses, all of them governed by the blessings it is infused with. It can consecrate a place, provide well-being, protect or cure its carrier, and most of all, it can avoid rebirth in the lower realms. In a way, the profusion of uses justifies the necessity for multiplying potential places of production.

References

Bentor, Yael, 1994. 'Tibetan relic classifications'. In Per Kvaerne ed. *Tibetan Studies. Proceedings of the 6th Seminar of the IATS*. Oslo: Institute of Comparative Research in Human Culture. pp. 16–30.

Boulnois, Lucette. 1983. *Poudre d'or et monnaies d'argent au Tibet*. Paris: CNRS.

Guidoni, Rachel. 1996. 'Les pierres précieuses dans la tradition tibétaine'. Master Thesis, Université Paris X-Nanterre.

―――― 2005. 'Entre relique et reliquaire. L'exceptionnelle momie de Gling Rinpoche (1903–1983)'. In Philippe Borgeaud & Youri Volokhine eds. *Les objets de la mémoire*. Annuaire 2004/05 *Studia Religiosa Helvetica*, X–XI. Berne: Peter Lang. pp. 193–218.

Martin, Dan. 1992. 'Crystals and Images from Bodies, Hearts and Tongues from Fire: Points of Relic Controversy from Tibetan History'. In *Tibetan Studies. Proceedings of the 5th Seminar of the IATS*, Narita: Naritasan Shinshoji, pp. 183–91.

―――― 1994. 'Pearls from Bones: Relics, Chortens, Tertons and the Signs of Saintly Death in Tibet'. *Numen* 41: 273–324.

Naz, R. dir. 1965. *Dictionnaire de droit canonique*. Paris: Letouzey et Ané.
Schopen, Gregory. 1998. 'Relic'. In Mark C. Taylor ed. *Critical Terms for Religious Studies*. Chicago: University of Chicago Press. p. 260.
Strong, John S. 1998. 'Les reliques des cheveux du Bouddha au Shwe Dagon de Rangoon'. *Aséanie* 2: 79–107.
—— 2004. *Relics of the Buddha*. Princeton: Princeton University Press.
Trainor, Kevin. 1997. *Relics, Ritual and Representation in Buddhism. Rematerializing the Sri Lankan Theravādā tradition*. Cambridge: Cambridge University Press.
Walter, Michael. 1998. 'From old Tibetan *Ring* to classical Tibetan *Ring bsrel*. Notes on the terminology for the eminent deceased in early Tibet'. *Acta Orientalia (Hung.)* LI (1–2): 63–8.
'Kun bzang dgongs pa kun 'dus las / gSang khrid kyi rgyab skor ring bsrel gyi sgrub pa dga' rab rdo rjes mdzad pa'. In *The Rediscovered Texts of the great gTer ston Padma gling pa*. New Delhi. 1976, vol. Ba, f. 433–6.

Plant Growth Processes and Animal Health in Northwest Yunnan

ANDREAS WILKES

Yak-cattle hybrid grazing on a mid-mountain pasture above the Doyon Valley (Photo: Andreas Wilkes)

The research is part of a Ph.D. dissertation which has been funded by the Economic and Social Research Council of the United Kingdom. All names of individuals are pseudonyms except where explicit permission to use real names was given.

This chapter is based on research in Doyon, a transhumant agro-pastoral community in Northwest Yunnan, China, which lies at the southeastern limit of the Himalayan mountain range. Much of the literature on transhumant agro-pastoralism in the Himalayan region has been concerned with the interaction of spatial resource use and time, illustrating that spatial mobility over the annual cycle not only enables farmer-herders to make good use of a variety of fodder resources but also limits potential conflicts between agricultural production and livestock management (e.g. Fricke 1989; Casimir and Rao 1985; Ehlers and Kreutzmann 2000; Stevens 1993). Rather than providing a detailed account of herders' spatial use of forage resources, the main focus of the chapter is on how villagers understand the process of plant growth and its implications for animal and human health. It is seen that the forces that drive the annual cycle of plant growth enabling the growth of crops for feeding people and grass for feeding livestock, also adversely affect both humans and cattle. In order to maintain the health of their cattle, most villagers feed them meat. The chapter describes two cultural models through which villagers explain the interactions between plant growth processes, and human and livestock health. It also describes some incidents which occurred in interactions between villagers and the staff of a Chinese non-governmental organization (NGO) which has been working on problems in animal husbandry in the village. These interactions show that cultural models concerning plant growth and animal health underlay the ways in which villagers 'indigenized' the exotic fodder technologies introduced by the NGO.

The remainder of this section describes the research setting and the role of cattle in household livelihoods. The following section describes how the growth of plants is explained by villagers, and describes the impact of these processes on animal health. The practices which villagers employ to maintain cattle productivity throughout the year, and the cultural models used to explain these practices are then described. The same cultural models also apply to notions of human health. The analysis of technology extension processes as described here shows that these cultural models underlay the villagers' evaluation of exotic fodder technologies and the way they planned to tackle new problems arising in livestock raising. The concluding section summarizes the implications of the cultural models described for the ways in which nature, society and domestication are conceptualized, and stresses that attention to local knowledge is essential if development projects are to better meet the needs of agro-pastoralists in the Himalayan region.

The Doyon Valley

My research has been conducted in the Doyon valley, which lies in the Nujiang (Salween) watershed in Yunnan, adjoining Tibet. Doyon is composed of twelve hamlets, mostly of 30–40 households, but the largest hamlet, Bahang, has more than 70 households. The majority of the two thousand or so inhabitants of Doyon are of the Nu ethnic group, speakers of a Tibeto-Burman language (Gros n.d., Barnard 1934). Approximately one third of inhabitants are ethnically Tibetan, although some of these recognize that they have Han Chinese ancestry. The settlement of Tibetans in Doyon is intimately related to the establishment of a French Catholic mission in the valley in the last years of the nineteenth century (Gros 1996 and Espinasse 1990: 127–8), in which Tibetan was the language of instruction and prayer. Intermarriage between Nu and Tibetans has been common, and some individuals adopt either Nu or Tibetan identities in different situations, and most are bilingual. One hamlet is inhabited almost entirely by Lisu, speakers of a language in the central branch of Loloish, a language of the Lolo-Burmese subgroup of Tibeto-Burman (Dessaint 1980). These people migrated to Doyon in the first two decades of the twentieth century to escape severe taxation in their former home in the Yangzi River valley, more than one hundred kilometres to the east. A large number of the inhabitants of Doyon are Catholic, but Tibetan Buddhism is also common in many hamlets. About 45 Lisu have recently converted to Protestantism.

As in other agro-pastoral communities throughout the Himalayan region, seasonal movement of livestock is important both for animal health and for minimizing the potential conflicts between animal husbandry and agriculture. For those villagers who are 'serious' about raising animals, fodder procurement strategies have their animals' health and well-being at heart.[1] Fodder resources in Doyon are scattered over different altitudes and in different habitats, with different growing seasons and access conditions. The herder must consider the needs of his/her livestock and the availability of nutritious fodder in different locations at different times of the year. In early-mid May, just before the corn (*Zea mays*, or maize) fields are planted, livestock are moved from the villages (at altitudes of 1900–2500 m) to mid-mountain pastures (at altitudes of 2600–2800 m), moving on a month or so later to the higher alpine pastures (2900–3400 m). In autumn, when high-altitude pastures are covered with snow or grass production declines, the livestock must seek fodder sources at lower altitudes, and the herds return to the villages after the corn harvest in mid-October. Households with few livestock or insufficient labour may entrust the herding of their cattle to other households during the summer period.

In the vicinity of the villages, there is little green fodder in the winter and spring months and agricultural crops are important sources of dried and supplementary fodder. The main fodder for most households is dried corn stalks and leaves which are stored after harvest. Some also store dried grasses (Tb: *puma*) collected in the summer months, to be fed in the winter and spring. While most households have a vegetable patch where they grow cabbages, garlic, chilli and other food items, some households also plant turnips (*Raphanus sp.* and *Brassica sp.*) in the autumn. The leaves of these root crops can be cut several times during the winter months, before the roots are dug out to be chopped, boiled, and fed as fodder. These vegetable gardens are always

---

[1]Some villagers, observing other villagers' livestock management practices, conclude that not all villagers care in the same ways about their animals.

fenced in order to prevent predation by livestock. All the year round, pigs and cattle are fed twice a day, a meal of corn flour cooked in water, sometimes supplemented by other fodder plants or leftovers. The work of fodder preparation and feeding is most commonly done by women, but men may also undertake the task when their mothers, wives or daughters are unavailable.

Functions of Cattle in Livelihoods

In Doyon, the household is the basic unit for organizing the making of a livelihood. While occupied with short-term needs for much of the time, in the local conception, a livelihood is not *made* in any one year or even over a short period. A livelihood is the accumulation of assets and potentials which enables a household to maintain and hopefully enhance its standard of living over a longer period.

The term for villager (Tb: *miseŋ*) means 'one who labours'. Its opposites are either officials (who earn a salary) or 'good-for-nothings' (Tb: *qiomba*) who do not labour as they should. In the local Tibetan dialect, the labour activities engaged in by household members are generally divided into two categories: 'qinora' and 'necha'. Qinora (lit: 'at home') is a category including activities done at home, such as fetching firewood and water, cooking, feeding pigs and chickens, spinning wool—in short, what are considered typically female activities. It also includes raising cattle and ruminants, even though these activities do not take place solely at the house, and may also be done by men. 'Necha' means 'to go and find money', and includes activities such as looking for and selling medicinal plants, wage labour in or outside the village, and in general, short-term activities which are aimed at earning a cash income. It is stereotypically a male sphere of labour, though women also take part. Both qinora ('home-based') and necha ('cash-income generating') activities contribute to the household's livelihood, but in different ways.

The underlying goal of a household's various livelihood activities is to establish and increase the household's 'basis' or 'wealth'. Tibetan and Nu speakers in Doyon talk about this in terms of 'jiadeng'.[2] 'Jiadeng' literally refers to the cornerstone of a house,[3] and metaphorically refers the 'base' or 'basis' of a household's economy.[4] Some explained to me that 'jiadeng' refers to 'what is originally there', i.e. fixed assets, while others stressed that it refers to 'what is normally there throughout the year', i.e. resources which the household can regularly draw on. Still others stressed that 'jiadeng' refers to the assets which can be handed down to the next generation (again, a notion of fixed assets, but viewed in a longer time-frame). These meanings are easily reconcilable. In addition to physical assets such as permanent arable land and the house itself, 'jiadeng' consists mainly of livestock. This is why cattle raising is included in 'home-based' labour even though it also involves herding on the alpine meadows for several months of the year: raising cattle keeps the household's wealth basis going, irrespective of the physical location of the activity. A household's sustainability in its long-term upward trajectory is conceived of in terms of a gradual accumulation of assets that in the shorter-term can be transformed into other forms of wealth or streams of income (e.g. by selling cattle) without excessively eroding the 'base', or that in the longer-term will become inheritable assets.

Most of the types of work in which villagers are engaged are actually 'cash-income generating' (*necha*). For example, soon after corn has been planted in May, whole hamlets suddenly become deserted as the majority of villagers go off to seek *Cordyceps sinensis* and other wild medicinal plants. But the contribution made by 'cash-income generating' activities to the household is not seen

[2] The Lisu equivalent is 'dizi' (possibly a loanword from Chinese). It is constituted by jiqieŋguo, 'that which is normally at home' (e.g. livestock), while *duduhuagə* (lit: 'to find for oneself') or *puhuagə* (lit: 'to find money') refer to gaining cash income which also 'goes freely' from the household and is not incorporated into the 'dizi'.

[3] Or more precisely, the stones put under the main pillars of the house to support and stabilize them.

[4] Cf. the similar use of 'base' as a key metaphor by members of mixed farming communities in Colombia (Gudeman and Rivera 1990, especially Chapter 4).

as being the same as the contribution of 'home-based activities'. 'Cash-income generating' activities bring in cash income but, as villagers often say, cash can easily be 'eaten up' or frittered away. A comparison between different types of medicinal plants illustrates the contrast between the two categories of labour. In the 1960s and again in the early 1980s, many households planted *muxiang* [La: *Radix aucklandiae*] on the mid-mountain slopes above the hamlets. In those days the procurement price for *muxiang* root was high and its sale was guaranteed by the government. After reform of the procurement system, prices dropped, there was no longer any guarantee that the county trade company would purchase *muxiang* root, and so the *muxiang* plots were left to waste. In 2003, *muxiang* was once again in demand by businessmen who came to Doyon to purchase medicinal plants, and many households returned to their former plots to dig the roots for sale. One man explained the difference between *muxiang* and the other medicinal plants thus: '*Muxiang* is normally there throughout the year, so it is part of the "jiadeng". Others like *Rhizoma gastrodiae* [a wild plant] are only collected in May to June, so they are not part of the "jiadeng". [Collecting] *Rhizoma gastrodiae* is "necha" and after bringing in the cash, the income is eaten up, so it does not contribute to the "jiadeng".' If we were to speak of 'domestication of medicinal plants' like *muxiang*, they are domesticated not just in that they are cultivated by people—after planting, *muxiang* in fact requires practically no management—but in that, through cultivation they are brought into the sphere of permanent household resources. Their cultivation becomes 'qinora' and a base for development, income which can be invested in cattle and other items that constitute the 'household base'. Land and livestock are the most important components of the 'household base', and among all types of livestock, cattle are culturally the most salient.[5] For many Doyonees, raising cattle is what keeps a household going in the long term.

[5]Calculation of salience (Smith 1993) from the results of freelisting of livestock terms by 78 people in three hamlets showed that in all hamlets and for most individuals, cattle were the most salient type of livestock.

Functions of Cattle

Cattle, yak-cattle hybrids, goats, sheep and chickens are the commonest animals raised in Doyon. Most cattle raised are ordinary cattle (*Bos taurus*) of Tibetan stock,[6] with a few yak-cattle hybrids (see Bishop 1998: 30-4). A small number of yaks are raised, mainly for breeding, and a few households raise ducks, rabbits or guinea pigs. As this chapter will focus on bovine management, Table 11.1 summarizes the main functions of bovines in household livelihoods. In addition to the main functions noted, all bovines also serve as a valuable reserve and may be sold when necessary, and all except yaks—which are never raised in stalls—provide manure.

Table 11.1: Functions of Bovines in Doyon

Livestock type	Functions
Cattle (Female)	milk production butter production (for consumption, sometimes for sale) reproduction
Cattle (Male)	ploughing from ca. 3 years old breeding sale (when old)
Yak-cattle hybrids (Male)	Ploughing
Yak-cattle hybrids (Female)	milk production butter production (for consumption, sometimes for sale) reproduction (rarely, as subsequent generations degenerate)
Yaks (Male)	Breeding
Yaks (Female)	breeding (rarely)

As part of my investigations into the factors contributing to and inhibiting growth in bovine herds in Doyon, in addition to general discussions on raising livestock, I undertook a survey of

---

[6] Some individuals have part 'Dutch dairy cow' or 'Soviet cow' ancestry resulting from breed-improvement efforts in the past.

90 households distributed over three hamlets, and asked them about all the changes (increases and decreases) in livestock holdings that had occurred over the past year (February 2002–March 2003), and the causes for each. The survey found that the vast majority of increase events were due to cattle being born. Most calvings occurred in March-April, which most villagers say is the preferred time for calving for two reasons. Firstly, calves born in these months will be able to feed on grass on their own by the time they reach the alpine meadows in late May. Secondly, several months of milk yields can be expected before both grass and the lactating cow dries up in September-October. Only one household reported buying a cow. Figure 11.1 shows the main factors causing decreases in bovine herds in Bahang hamlet. Disease was the commonest cause of decrease and could occur throughout the year. The next most significant categories of decrease event were 'falling down mountainsides' (occurring most frequently in April) and wolf attacks (mostly in the summer, when herds are on the alpine pastures). From Figure 11.1 it is clear that

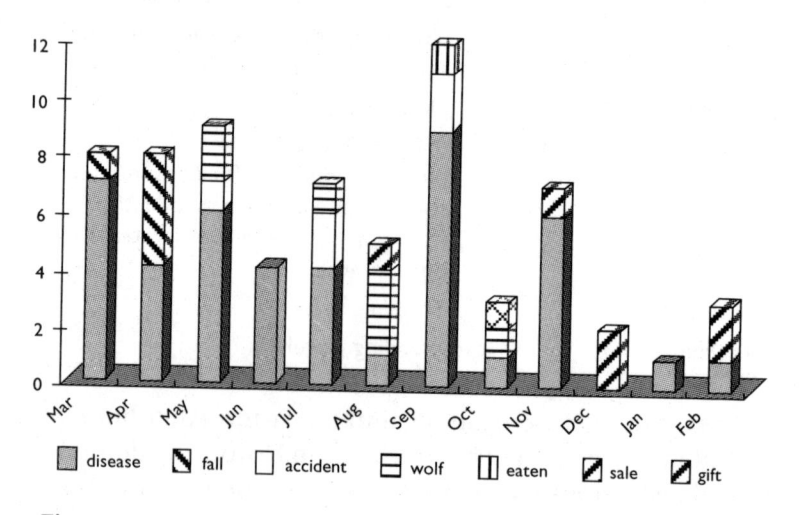

Figure 11.1: Causes of Decrease in Bovine Herds in Bahang Hamlet, March 2002–February 2003

cattle are rarely sold or given away. Those that are sold are old and unproductive, and are sold to the agents of beef restaurants in the nearby county town. Beef is rarely available for consumption in the village and is therefore rarely eaten by villagers.[7]

These survey findings concur with the statements of most villagers that they are currently aiming to maintain and increase their herds, and that sales are always incidental—for other reasons, never planned. With households seeking to maintain and increase cattle herd numbers, cows are highly prized (bulls being used for ploughing and reproduction), and the aspects of cattle productivity with which villagers are most concerned are: maximizing the survival of current stocks, calving rates and yields of butter. It is notable that these objectives even run counter to the objective of state support for animal husbandry, which is to increase output of animal products for sale. Most technicians assume that the lack of sales is a sign of the poor management of livestock by herders and due to their mal-adaptation to the market.

It is the pursuit of productivity in terms of these functions that motivates the practices which I will describe in the remainder of this chapter. The focus will be on cattle, the practices employed to maintain cattle productivity and beliefs underlying those practices. Instead of focusing on how cattle and herdsmen utilize the spatial features of their landscape and vegetation to maximize productivity throughout the course of the year, I will focus on another aspect of temporal processes: the process of plant growth and its impact on cattle (and human) health. Given the importance of the seasonality of plant growth to bovine health and productivity, it is surprising that there has been little reported research on how processes of plant growth are understood by herders.

Understanding these practices and beliefs took me to several of the twelve hamlets in the Doyon valley. Much of the data used

[7] However, a small number of households slaughter F3 yak-cattle hybrids after one month or so as they are known for being prone to illness. The meat of these calves may be consumed at home, but such events are rare.

here focuses on Bahang hamlet, where mixed Nu-Tibetan descent is most common, but where Tibetan is the lingua franca. Following general discussions with villagers over several months on issues related to cattle productivity and management, in March 2004, I conducted a questionnaire on the topics with 14 individuals (13 of whom were of mixed descent, and one fully Nu). The questionnaire covered plant growth processes, cattle and human health and cattle management practices.[8] Most interviews were conducted in the local dialect of Tibetan, but some were in Nu or Lisu. For this chapter, I have chosen to present the practices and concepts in Tibetan, but they are fully translatable into Nu and Lisu also, and terms in these languages are given where appropriate.

Temporal Processes in Plant and Animal Domains

Plant Growth

One starting point for the exploration of cattle management practices and related knowledge is provided by the answer to the question: how do plants grow? For the villagers of Doyon, the answer to this question focuses on an annual cycle of a 'gaseous essence' associated with water and soil, mostly called 'qiabo' (literally: 'water gas'), sometimes known as 'sebo' (literally: 'soil gas').[9] In the local dialect of Tibetan, 'bo' means gas (and is also used to refer, for example, to butane gas used for cooking in urban areas). 'Qiabo' is a gas associated with water (Tb: *qia*), which rises from the ground beginning in the second half of December. It is also sometimes referred to as 'soil gas' (Tb: *se* = soil), as it is seen to rise from the soil, and its presence can be

[8]This was analyzed using Cultural Consensus Analysis (Romney *et al.* 1986). The results of the CCA are not presented in detail here, but are reflected in the qualifiers 'many' or 'most' etc. which appear throughout the account here.

[9]In explicating this knowledge, I will follow the Doyon villagers' custom of interspersing statements of knowledge with observations which provide evidence in support of that knowledge.

seen both in changes in soil moisture in early spring and in the mist that rises from the ground in March-April. The mist is said to be due to the heat of 'qiabo', which raises soil temperature gradually through these months. Without sufficient heat in the soil, crops cannot grow properly.[10]

A sign, pointed out by several villagers, that 'qiabo' begins to rise in mid-late December is that one variety of white rhododendron blooms on the slopes above the villages at this time. Grass and other plants begin to sprout between February and March. As 'qiabo' rises from the ground, 'beneficial' (Tb: *pintu, pingba*) properties[11] are brought up by the 'qiabo' from the soil to the plant. The plants then grow to their mature state, as the 'beneficial' elements flow into the extremities of the plant, forming flowers and seeds, where these 'beneficial' elements are concentrated, before flowering or seeding. Thus, if the 'qiabo' was not rising in the rhododendron tree in the second half of December, it would not be possible for it to flower. The seeding of most grasses and flowering of many other trees and plants in August-September is a sign that 'qiabo' has reached a climax and will soon begin to recede, a process that continues through the autumn. By early December 'qiabo' is at its lowest ebb in the annual cycle. During this period, 'qiaobo' is said to be in the ground, but to remain there until the next annual cycle begins.

The main sign that 'qiabo' is receding, that it remains in the ground, is that in the winter months (Tb: 'geŋse', roughly October to March) the grass which grows on the slopes surrounding the villages turns dry and yellow. The recession of 'qiabo' into the ground *causes* the drying out of these and other plants.

The Nu term for 'bo' is 'ungsa', whose polyvalence is more noticeable than that of 'bo'. Like the Tibetan term 'bo', 'ungsa'

---

[10]Ruminant faeces is said to be a better fertilizer than bovine faeces, because the former is said to be 'hot' when placed in the soil, while the latter is 'cold'.

[11]Even when speaking in Tibetan, the Chinese term for nutrition (Ch: *yingyang*) is often used to refer to what it is that is brought up, although there is no direct Tibetan equivalent of the word 'nutrition', which is glossed in Tibetan as 'beneficial things' (Tb: *pintu*).

also refers to a 'gaseous essence', but also refers to 'breath'. One of the commonest usages of 'ungsa' can be heard when climbing the steep mountain slopes with villagers who may say: 'ungsa m'al' (literally: 'breath is not there', or 'I'm out of breath'). In this sense, 'ungsa' can also be said to refer to strength. Even villagers whose mother tongue is Tibetan will sometimes use the Nu expression in this way.

Impacts on Animal Health

Clearly, if grasses are dried and yellow for five or more months of the year—which is also most of the period during which cattle are grazed in or near the villages—this cannot but impact on the health of cattle. Dry grass is perceived to have no nutrition, and apart from 'filling their stomach' is thought to have 'no benefit' (Tb: *pingba ni lo*) for cattle. The winter period is in general associated with cattle becoming increasingly thin, and drying up if they were previously lactating. While a bull or cow in poor health may have strength (Tb: *sho*) to perform arduous tasks, they are said to have no stamina, and thus 'no strength' (Tb: *sho ni no*). By contrast, grass is said to be the most nutritious when it is seeding in August: the 'beneficial elements' are all concentrated in the seed. This is evidenced by increased milk yield and butter content in August, and the change in the colour of the butter from a whitish yellow commonly seen in the spring and early summer, to a deeper shade of yellow, and also in the larger amount of butter that can be produced from the same volume of milk.

Thus, in winter, grass is dry and not nutritious, so the cattle are in poor health. It does make sense in the local conceptual framework to say that 'in the winter cattle have no strength because they cannot eat nutritious grass'. Yet this does not tell the whole story. As the 'qiabo' rises, especially in March and April, it also rises into the bones of cattle (and as we shall see further, people). As it rises, the oil content of the marrow decreases, and the marrow is said to 'dry up' (Tb: *goŋ geŋ*). The hole in the bone is filled with water and the meat of the cattle becomes increasingly watery. This is evidenced by the fact that if you slaughter cattle (or pigs for which the same process occurs) in the spring or summer, the meat will be full of water, so that when fried, the portion will shrink substantially.[12] With the marrow of the cattle having dried up, the cattle have no strength. 'It is not possible for cattle to have strength if they have no marrow.'

We are now in a position to understand why so many cattle die in spring falling down mountainsides. Most of the grass on the steep slopes is dry and unattractive to cattle. At the same time the cattle are weak, having shrunken marrow in their bones, and especially weak if they have just calved. It is thus easy for cattle to simply lose their footing, and this often occurs as they try to reach out to a newly sprouted leaf on a high branch.

Some villagers put the increase in water in bone marrow down to the effects of a lack of nutrition due to dried winter grass. For many others, however, the impact of 'qiabo' occurs in addition to the lack of nutrition: they maintain that feeding green grass or vegetables to cattle in the winter-spring months would not prevent the cattle's marrow from drying up. Thus, the annual cycle of 'qiabo' is an important temporal process affecting animal health in its own right.

Maintaining Cattle Health and Productivity

For the people of Doyon, the productivity of their cattle is seen largely in terms of calving rates and butter yields. Given that every year, the annual cycle of plant growth provides the fodder for higher milk yields and butter content in the summer months, but places the cattle under severe nutritional stress in the winter, it is interesting to ask whether there are any ways in which villagers seek to maintain the health and productivity of their cattle.

The key practice which can promote both of these goals (higher calving rates, and higher milk yields with higher butter content) is feeding meat (Tb: *xiajiu*, lit: 'feed meat') to the cattle,[13] and it

---

[12]This is the reason why no cattle sales take place in the spring months, as shown in Figure 11.1.

[13]The practice of feeding meat of dead livestock to cattle is reported for Qinghai in Gesangben and Duozang Caidang (2000: 58) where it is

was by making investigations to explain this practice that led to the research findings reported in this and the preceding section. In 2003–04, 23 out of 29 households owning cattle in Bahang hamlet fed meat one or more times during the year. In general, meat may be fed at any time.[14] Most villagers will feed meat to a cow which has just calved, especially if calving occurs before May when fresh grass becomes plentiful. Cattle which have thinned and weakened over the winter are often fed meat before making the arduous walk to the alpine meadows in May. Many individuals perceive that—unless a cow calves—there is no need to feed meat during the summer months when fresh grass is plentiful. The preferred time for calving is generally before May, which means that each year, the herders hope their cows are pregnant by August.[15] If a cow shows no signs of becoming pregnant, she will sometimes be fed meat in the hope that this will hasten conception.[16] Bulls may be fed meat before ploughing (which is done in mid-May). Some households feed meat to all cattle in their herd, while others will give meat to only lactating cows or particularly weak cattle.

The commonest meats fed are chicken, goat and pork. Lard and eggs are also fed, and although not meats, the act of feeding lard or eggs is recognized as 'xiajiu' because it has the same objectives. Chicken is prepared by killing, plucking the feathers and then mincing the meat and blood of a chicken, and forcing

---

mentioned as one way of overcoming the lack of grass during a severe snowstorm. Some villagers take feeding meat to cattle as a marker of typically 'Tibetan' practices. In Zhongdian—a Tibetan area of Yunnan—I have heard of cattle being fed meat for similar reasons as those described here, but was unable to find herders to knew of 'qiabo'. So it cannot be concluded that the practices and beliefs reported in this paper are 'typically Tibetan' rather than 'Nu' or 'Lisu'.

[14]Cattle which have eaten meat are not to drink cold water. This is to ensure that they do not get diarrhea, so meat is rarely fed on rainy days in the summer. Cows in advanced pregnancy are rarely fed meat for fear of inducing a premature birth.

[15]Cattle in Doyon are almost always left to mate freely.

[16]The practice of feeding increased amounts of nutritious fodder to hasten conception is known in many areas of Europe, and in English, is called 'flushing'.

the mince down the cow's throat. When goat meat is fed to cattle, it is common for a leg or other portion of the dead animal to be first stewed, and the meat then minced and force-fed, with the soup being fed in a trough. The pig-head is sometimes taken from the smoked pig which each household prepares for its annual meat and lard supplies. The head is stewed, minced and then force-fed. Lard and eggs (without shells) are also force-fed, often to calves which are sometimes unable to digest meat. Feeding lard and eggs also saves on the use of meat, which is not in abundance even for human consumption. Beef is not fed. Apart from a lack of availability, this is thought to be improper. Feeding meat to cattle may be done by either men or women, depending on who is available when the task is to be performed.

There are common reasons for feeding meat which all villagers agree upon: it can help a cow recover strength after calving, increase the yield of milk and butter content of the milk, and improve its chances of falling pregnant again that year. In the case of bulls, it increases their strength for ploughing. For all cattle, when fed in April-May, it improves their strength making it more likely that they will survive the tough walk to the alpine pastures. However, the benefits of feeding meat are not immediate. Whether a cow's health or strength has been replenished cannot be observed immediately, but only by observing its performance later in the year or during the following winter. For example, if meat is fed in April to a cow that has just calved, its strength can be seen to have been replenished in August from the colour of its butter and the butter content of its milk. Also, if the cow's health has not been replenished, then come October when the grass begins to dry, the cow will grow thin rapidly, whereas a replenished cow would only grow thin gradually, leaving it in a better state of health by the following March-April.

Although most villagers agree on these potential benefits of feeding meat, community members have different explanations as to why these benefits should accrue.[17] These explanations,

---

[17] Analysis of the social distribution of knowledge of the two cultural models (Wilkes 2005) shows that this knowledge is learned through the

which I shall call the 'pragmatic' explanation and the 'vital energy' explanation are discussed here. The application of these models to practices in managing the health, fertility and productivity of cows is one of their main significances. So in explaining these beliefs I will use the example of a cow (as opposed to bull), but the same principles apply to both.

The 'pragmatic' explanation

Cows are in increasingly poor health / thin (Tb: *nyexian*) as the winter progresses, and after calving. Remember also that for many villagers, the preferential time for calving is March, when there is a shortage of fresh grass. So in order to improve the health of cows, they must 'convalesce' (Tb: *lesu*, lit: 'preserve life'; Nu: *gongwaxi*). Whereas for people 'preserving life' means both to rest and to eat well, for cattle the main method of 'preserving life' is to eat meat (Tb: *xiajiu*). In extreme cases, if a cow in poor health does not 'preserve life', it may die. Feeding meat is beneficial (Tb: *pingba*) for a cattle's body, because there is something beneficial or useful (Tb: *pingba*) in the meat, sometimes glossed using the Chinese term for 'nutrition' (Ch: *yingyang*), and sometimes using the Chinese term for 'replenishing' (Ch: *bu*).[18] When a cow has been properly fed meat, its body will become 'strong and healthy' (Tb: *nyejia*) or 'strong' (Tb: *sho*). Only when a cow's body is strong

---

practice of raising cattle together with other individuals, and is not determined by individuals' characteristics such as gender, age or ethnicity. Because social relationships involved in cattle raising are complex, the degree of shared knowledge is also not determined by the degree of kinship relations.

[18] The term 'bu' is associated in Chinese with replenishment of 'qi' or 'vital energy'. This association is not necessarily carried over into its usage here by the villagers. Some villagers explained that they learned the Chinese terms 'nutrition' (Ch: *yingyang*) and 'replenishing' (Ch: *bu*) during mass meetings in the 1960s and 1970s where they were taught the basics of household management and nutrition. Other villagers were unsure whether 'bu' was a Chinese loanword or a Tibetan term. The best translation in Tibetan I was given is 'pingba' (literally, 'beneficial').

and healthy will it be easy for it to fall pregnant again in the summer (and thus calf the following spring). If a cow's body is strong and healthy it will have a higher milk yield, with a higher butter content in the milk. Conversely, if after a cow calves in spring it is not fed meat, it will be not as strong and healthy later in the year and thus less able to get pregnant, or will get pregnant only towards the end of the year, resulting in a later calving the following year and thus a shorter period of lactation.

Thus we can see that the feeding of meat to cows is a way of improving the health of the cow's body, increasing milk and butter production in that year, and also of ensuring fertility and ensuring a continued supply of calves, milk and butter in the following year.

The 'vital energy' explanation

While almost all villagers would agree on the workings of the model described above, some villagers explain the process in terms of 'vital energy' (Tb: *bo*; Nu: *ungsa*; Ch: *yuanqi*).[19] The term used for 'vital energy' (Tb: *bo*) is the same as the term for the 'gaseous essence' we encountered above. When a cow is thin and its body in a poor state (Tb: *nyexian*), this is taken as a sign that there is insufficient 'vital energy' inside the cow's body. After a cow calves, it loses a lot of vital energy and is often therefore in a poor state. Feeding meat is 'replenishing' (*bu*, using the Chinese loanword) and will induce more 'vital energy' in the cow's body. When vital energy has been replenished sufficiently, the cow's body will be 'healthy and strong' (Tb: *nyejia*) or 'strong' (Tb: *sho*), and it will be easier for it to get pregnant, and will produce more milk with a higher butter content.

In this model, if the meat fed does not replenish the cow with vital energy (for example many do not perceive pork to be replenishing), then it will not be possible to improve the

---

[19] 'Vital energy' is also a key concept in traditional Chinese veterinary medicine. A belief in what appears to be a similar phenomenon has also been reported among the Aymara in the Andes (Hiroyasu 1996).

condition of the cow's body. If there is insufficient vital energy in the cow's body, it will be difficult for it to get pregnant. Thus, feeding replenishing meat enhances vital energy and leads to the benefits just described.

Human Health

People and animals are in some ways considered to be the same. Certainly the villagers of Doyon see both as subject to the same natural processes, though I do not take literally the often-expressed view that 'the only difference is that cows cannot speak'.

'Qiabo', as it rises from the ground, is also seen by many to impact on human health. However, many villagers also expressed doubt about sayings which they were aware of, referring to their own lack of personal experience and awareness of these effects. Many villagers feel that starting in January, but most noticeably from March when 'qiabo' rises at a greater rate from the ground, it also rises into the bones of people, and their marrow begins to become watery, losing its oil content. Individuals prone to arthritic pains were often the most direct in making the link between the annual cycle of 'qiabo' and their health. Many maintain that in the early summer, people's marrow is full of water so they have no stamina for arduous labour. (A few individuals, however, said they had noticed the lack of strength over this period, but never having heard of marrow drying up put it down to the heat of the season.) People's state of health begins to recover from August-September, as the 'qiabo' ceases to rise and begins to recede.

When people are physically exhausted or chronically plagued by illness or lack of strength, this is often referred to as a sign of or caused by a lack of 'vital energy' (Tb: 'bo ni no'; Nu: 'ungsa m'al'). In the spring, when 'qiabo' has risen into the bones of people, this also causes a lack of stamina for arduous tasks. To counter the effects of 'qiabo', and to maintain health when tired or ill, people need to 'convalesce' (Tb: *lesu*). 'Convalescing' requires both taking time to rest and eating well (or 'eating better to be healthy'). The latter consists of eating pork, pork fat and butter tea. Most butter produced is self-consumed rather than sold. Another important food is smoked pork. Again, pigs are almost never sold, but each household will slaughter and smoke one or two pigs each winter. This is made by slitting the dead pig's stomach, gutting it and smearing inside and out with salt and pepper or other spices, before sewing it up and leaving it to smoke over the hearth for months. Many households' annual supply of meat and lard comes from pigs preserved in this way. Fermented corn beer (Tb: *qioŋ*) fried in butter is said to be a 'replenishing' (Tb/Ch: *bu*) drink in March-April especially. During work parties organized to share labour when corn planting in May, meat and fermented corn beer is a compulsory offering by the host. Elder villagers who remember the annual grain shortages in the summer months (Tb: *xia gugu la*, lit: 'the period when even chickens' bellies rumble') particularly stressed the need to eat well during this period. In any case, all villagers stress that eating oil or fatty foods and paying attention to what one eats is an important part of 'lesu', the way in which people keep themselves healthy through a mixture of diet and resting. Most agree that in order for people to have 'vital energy' in their bodies (or good health in general) it is necessary to eat meat. Drinking distilled corn spirit (Tb: *a'ra*), sometimes with chicken or other meat boiled in it (a specialty called Tb: *xia'ra* or Nu: *xiala*) is also said to aid in driving water from the bones and thus helping to prevent arthritic pains.

While many villagers do not speak of 'vital energy' for cattle, they are more likely to do so when referring to human health. Apart from general exhaustion, which is sometimes spoken of as a lack of 'vital energy', childbirth is the most obvious time when the loss of 'vital energy' and the need to 'convalesce' (Tb: *lesu*) is spoken of. Child birth is seen to entail a great loss of 'vital energy'. So, after childbirth, women are expected (or required by their parents and in-laws) to 'convalesce' for a period of at least one month. This involves eating 'replenishing' meats such as goat and most often chicken which are in greater supply, as well as eggs and fermented corn beer.[20] Most villagers prescribe eating young cocks which have not yet crowed and hens. Most explained this in terms of the meat of these being more replenishing, but one explained that young cocks in particular are more energetic, so—in a fashion of metonymic association—the energy associated with the young cocks will be taken on by the convalescing mother. If women do not convalesce in this way, their 'vital energy' will not be restored, and illnesses later in life—especially arthritis—will be common.

Local Knowledge and Technology Development

In spring 2003, the Center for Biodiversity and Indigenous Knowledge, a Chinese NGO based in the provincial capital, began discussions with villagers in Doyon on starting a project which would aim to support their livelihoods.[21] It was agreed with village committee members and influential individuals in the community, that a two-week rapid assessment would take place. The assessment began with a meeting with the aforementioned people. Another meeting was held a week later to provide feedback and confirm the problems and issues elicited, and another week later a planning meeting was held. The assessment team included six people from the provincial capital (including one who spoke Dulong, a language similar to the local dialect of Nu), one county animal husbandry technician (who spoke fluent Lisu) and one villager, who later became the project's local coordinator. As advisor to the project, I facilitated the assessment activities, taking part as a team member in these and many subsequent activities.

The assessment took place initially in two hamlets at the bottom of the valley near the village office and market place, and then subsequently split into two groups, one working on the west side

[20] Pork is not fed as it is said to cause swelling which may be fatal.
[21] For more details on the project and its goals, see *www.cbik.ac.cn* or *www.cbik.org*.

of the valley, and the other on the east. The assessment began by employing a variety of rapid appraisal tools (such as household resource flow charts and resource mapping) as well as informal discussions to understand how different resources contributed to making a livelihood in Doyon. The findings from these activities were summarized by the assessment team and then problems or issues identified for further investigation. Of relevance here are two such issues: the spread of a weed (*Rumex nepalensis*) on the alpine meadows and winter fodder shortage.

Rumex Nepalensis

One component of CBIK's project with the villagers involved developing measures to control the spread of *Rumex nepalensis*, an endemic species of dock which has spread extensively—and in some places densely—on some of the alpine meadows in Doyon (see Shen *et al.* 2004). Initial interest was expressed by several herders in finding effective ways to control the plants, and during the rapid assessment in April 2003, several of them volunteered to do experiments on the impact of digging out Rumex by the roots, on the impact of slashing it down at the base of the stalk, as well as slashing accompanied by planting clover in the hope that the latter would out-compete the regeneration of Rumex. By the end of the year it was clear that, although digging roots could be made to work, none of these methods would be realistic options given the scale of infestation on the rangelands. Thus the earnest search for an alternative began, and herbicides became the focus of villagers' hopes (one of them had suggested using hydrochloric acid) and NGO staff's searches for available means. Given the absence of an already-existing Rumex—or dock-specific product, it was eventually decided to start trials with standard herbicides for broadleafs, such as Roundup. I took part in one discussion with Shen Shicai, the NGO project staff, and Paul, the villager who had been employed as the local project coordinator. The discussion took place in Chinese, in which 'qiabo' was referred to as [Ch:] 'shuiqi' (lit: 'water gas') or 'shuifen' (water content).

> Shen: So when should we start spraying the test areas [with herbicide]?
> Paul: It's best to wait until the 'shuiqi' starts to rise and the leaves have started to sprout...
> Shen: Nutrition comes through the leaves, via photosynthesis, so if you don't let its leaves grow it won't be able to photosynthesize, so it won't be able to get a lot of the nutritional components it needs...
> Andreas [to Paul]: And *your* meaning is that at this time the 'shuiqi' is rising and the nutrition is going *outwards*... ...
> Paul: [nods] Into the leaves.
> Andreas: So you are saying if you get rid of the leaves...
> Paul: If the leaves die, the 'shuifen' [in the Rumex] is... basically has nothing to soak it up. All the 'shuifen' is inside, nothing to suck it up...it will burn it out [or 'explode'] inside, and leak out, and then the inside will not be able to contain very much 'qi' ['vital energy', or 'gaseous essence']. In the second year, it will basically be unable to sprout...
> Shen: Because, from the situation [we observed] last year, the growth of Rumex happened all year round, right? It doesn't matter when it started to sprout [Ch: fengen], because others have already sprouted, right? So it would be unable to sprout.[22] This [death of the leaves] would definitely have a certain amount of a controlling effect. But because the timing is different you have to take different measures...and then the one we sprayed the year before, if it grows again this year, we could spray it again...
> Andreas: So when should you start spraying herbicide at Sewalongba pasture?
> Paul: May.[23]

[22] Shen is 'talking across' Paul here. What he means is that once the Rumex sprayed with herbicide has failed to sprout at the same time as Rumex nearby, that means it will not sprout in that year.

[23] Paul is thinking of May because by May the newly sprouted Rumex leaves will be a few centimeters high.

Shen: Is April no good?[24]
Paul: Not before April 20th.
Shen: That's about right.
… …
[A few minutes later, after discussing potato growth, and a lapse in the conversation]
Paul: I've never heard of this for people, but animals and plants will hibernate. People don't need to hibernate…
Shen [expressing not comprehending]: People don't need to hibernate?
Paul: Rumex is mature in August, so after August the 'shuiqi' starts to get less and less…many plants and animals, in the summer they get what they need for the winter ready, and then in the winter they have what they need to stop them rotting. Then in the spring, they…once it is spring…how to express this?…For example, imagine I am Rumex: 'Ah! Spring has come, I don't need to preserve any anymore, I can be wasteful!' But once they run into any trouble, they will have no more reserves left…The most important thing in plants is the 'shuifen'.

I cannot claim that this is how most villagers in Doyon would reason about the way in which herbicide acts together with 'qiabo' to kill a plant. Indeed, given the novelty of the situation—the use of chemical herbicides on Rumex—Paul's reasoning here may be tentative and possibly idiosyncratic. However, this example shows that Paul's reasoning about the links between seasonality and plant growth drew on the understanding of the annual cycle of 'qiabo' as presented earlier in this chapter. In this sense, Paul found this knowledge relevant to and thus useful in his considerations of the problem currently faced. For Shen, however, a lack of previous acquaintance with this knowledge was a potential hindrance in his discussions (and larger collaboration) with Paul. Given that the decision over when to spray the herbicide would ultimately rest with Shen (as the herbicide would have to

[24] Shen is thinking of late April because that is just before the Rumex leaves sprout.

be brought by him from the provincial capital), this small vignette illustrates how local knowledge can so easily be sidelined, even in supposedly 'participatory' development projects. The following section gives other examples of situations in which local knowledge of the impacts of fodder on animal health are communicated with project staff, but in these cases, the power to make decisions relating to this knowledge lies with the villagers concerned.

Winter Fodder

Almost all individuals with whom the assessment team spoke emphasized that the lack of fodder in winter is a major problem. For the members of the assessment team, one way in which the significance of this issue was made apparent to them was by looking at the household resource flow diagrams produced in joint discussions between the assessment team members and villagers. These visually communicated the fact that a large proportion of corn produced by the villagers was used as fodder and that many households had to purchase corn in order to meet their annual fodder needs. In subsequent discussions, other impacts of the lack of winter fodder became apparent: poor cattle health, and the frequent morbidity and mortality of cattle.

Based on the almost unanimous statement that lack of winter fodder was a problem, the project started a number of farmer-managed trials with exotic grass species (e.g. *Lolium perenne, Trifolium repens, Medicago sativa*) and fodder storage technologies (e.g. silage fodder). Concrete tanks were to be used for producing silage fodder from corn stalks and leaves, while plastic barrels were to be used for the other fodder sources which are available in smaller amounts at different times of the year. Project staff visited the experimenting farmers every month or so, asking about grass growth, factors farmers perceived as impacting on grass growth and their ideas for the potential of the grass and silage fodder. By December 2003 the grass was being cut and fed, and in March-April 2004, the silage fodder was being fed to the experimenters' livestock. The project staff continued to interview experimenters and their neighbours in order learn about farmers' criteria for evaluating these technologies.

Here, I present two situations in which it appears that the understandings of plant growth and animal health are relevant to villagers' considerations of the fodder technologies: the evaluation of the technologies, and considerations regarding how to make successful silage fodder at different times of year.

Situation 1: Evaluation of benefits of fodder technologies
David is considered one of the most experienced herders in Bahang, and serves as the local vet using traditional curative practices. Considering the high respect with which he is viewed in the hamlet as well as his own commitment to cattle raising, Paul arranged that he was allocated a plastic barrel for making silage fodder. He also saw the clover planted by some other experimenters in Bahang and heard about how the pigs liked to eat this new fodder grass. Interviewed by NGO staff in February 2004 about the impact of the technologies he suggested: 'These barrels and concrete tanks, and your grass, are all very good, but I think they are still not as good as a mu [1/15th of a hectare] of *manjing* [*Raphanus sp.*], *luobu* [*Brassica sp.*] or barley.'[25] When asked why, he opined: 'It seems that the livestock eat all of these fodders, but we *know* that *manjing* or barley is replenishing [Tb/Ch: *bu*]. All we need is to get some fencing up and we can have unlimited amounts of *manjing* and *luobu*.' Not only are these plants known to be replenishing to cows, but the leaves of *manjing* and *luobu* can be cut several times in the winter, regrowing to be cut again, thus ensuring a supply of replenishing fodder. Further discussion with David and other villagers resulted in a small fencing experiment in Bahang which began in March 2004. If David's reasoning had not been picked up on, it is most likely that the project would just have continued its efforts to get villagers to

---

[25] David had in fact voiced the same opinion during the needs assessment, but this was not picked up on by the NGO staff involved.

grow exotic grass species, and the question of why some villagers are not interested would most likely have been the sole focus of the project's explanatory investigations.

Heavy snowfall occurred on 15 April 2004 which took the lives of about 50 cattle in the village.[26] Cattle, horses and other livestock had to be kept in their stalls for several days. Many villagers who had not taken part in the experiments were only able to feed the last remains of corn stalks harvested the previous October, or [Tb:] *puma* (dried grass collected and stored the previous year). The previous year Joseph had planted a small plot of *Lolium perenne* (black barley grass). He had begun cutting and feeding Lolium in January, and was still able to feed it during the snowfall. Joseph was enthusiastic about the grass:

> Look! This is the first time I have been able to make butter in winter. In the past, all we had at this time was a bit of dried corn stalks. The cows would be really thin, with little milk, so we would just leave the milk for the calf to eat. But this year I have been able to make butter in winter. After eating the grass, the cows have more milk so we can milk them. It's really replenishing (Ch: *bu*). Next year I want to plant this grass in my vegetable patch.

Situation 2: Planning to make silage fodder
After the first year's success with silage fodder experiments in Doyon, Paul was given a digital video camera with which to make a video (to be narrated in the local languages) of how to make silage fodder at various times of year. Among the most common winter fodder crops grown in Doyon are *luobu* (*Raphanus sp.*) and *manjing* (*Brassica sp.*). Both are root crops, whose leaves can be cut several times during the growing season before digging out the root to feed as fodder. In the preparation of silage fodder, a key factor determining whether the silage will rot and become unpalatable is the water content of the material used. Given what we now know about the seasonal changes in 'qiabo' in Doyon,

---

[26]This was the figure reported by the village committee to the Civil Affairs Bureau, responsible for providing disaster relief and compensation.

we should not be surprised that even when the same crop is used for making silage fodder, its treatment must vary at different times of year:

> We plant *manjing* in August, and its leaves start to grow in October. In November its root starts to grow, while its leaves are still growing but slower than before. And then the leaves start to turn yellow and from December there is no water content in the leaves. From December to January it will not sprout any more leaves until February when the 'qiabo' starts to rise again. We use its leaves for fodder in October and November, and start to dig out the roots in November, leaving some aside for seed. How you treat the *manjing* [for silage fodder] depends on the time of year. In November the *manjing* has a lower water content. In March it has grown lots of leaves and has a thick root and more water content. So in March we will need to use some method to reduce the water content— like drying it in the sun—before making silage. If it rains in March when we want to make it, if the household has prepared some *puma* [dried grass collected in August and stored over the following winter] then it will be best to mix it with that. Mixing it with corn flour would be good, but most households won't have much left by March.

Conclusion

This chapter has described how members of a transhumant agropastoralist community in northwest Yunnan understand the process of plant growth, how this impacts on animal and human health and the measures they employ to maintain cattle health and productivity. The knowledge (or cultural model) which underlies the practice of feeding meat to cattle, with which my investigations began, is useful in explaining a variety of observed behaviours, also including:
- The phenomenon of cattle falling down mountainside, and its timing;

- The timing of cattle sales;
- The provision of meat and corn beer for work parties in the corn planting season;
- The diet of chicken and eggs prescribed for new mothers.

The knowledge elicited through my investigations also invites a reexamination from the perspective of the light it sheds on local conceptions of nature and society, and its implications for the role of local knowledge in development.

Nature and Society

One of the key causes of the practice of feeding meat to cattle is the perception that the health of cattle is adversely affected by the annual cycle of 'qiabo', a gaseous substance that emerges from the ground, and that can weaken the bones and thus reduce the strength of cattle. This annual cycle is also widely perceived by villagers to affect human health. Stated thus, these processes are perceived to be caused by 'nature' as a category that is perceived of as distinct from a 'cultural' or 'man-made' sphere. However, the impacts of these processes on human health also illustrate that people are seen as related to nature in intimate ways not perceived elsewhere. In this sense, a strict dichotomy or opposition between 'nature' and 'society' no longer appears to apply.

Cattle, as conceptualized by the people of Doyon are to some extent paradoxical animals. On the one hand, they are a token of bestiality, the less-than-human. To call someone 'livestock' [Tb: *sejian*] or 'cow' [Tb: *beloŋ*] is a great insult to their intellect and the subtlety with which they conduct social affairs. On the other hand, cattle are the very basis of human sociality, being seen by all as one of the main assets that constitute the (metaphorical) 'foundation' of the household. In this respect, the inclusion of cattle within the social sphere is emphasized. Indeed, ideally no household should be without them. We have also seen that in many ways cattle are seen as similar to humans in the way in which their health is affected by natural processes. Most households which raise cattle attempt to maintain the health and strength of their cattle by feeding meat. For the Doyonees, this practice is seen as perfectly natural (i.e. 'in keeping with laws of nature') because cattle are to *some* extent 'the same as people', who also need to eat meat to maintain their health and strength.

Since the mid-1990s, challenges to Western conceptual dualisms have become increasingly common in anthropology (see Descola and Pálsson 1996, Ellen and Fukui 1996). To some extent debates such as those over 'monist' as against 'dualist' views of the relations between nature and society, and between nature and culture, may be misguided. As Ellen (1996: 15) notes, 'whether some *thing* is natural or cultural may depend on the level of abstraction in our arguments, our methodology, or on the time phase or context, not on any intrinsic qualities' [emphasis in original]. The research reported in this chapter suggests that the same ambiguity in these distinctions applies to any attempt to characterize the nature-society dichotomy in Doyon. At times, cattle are seen as quintessential of the social, and are fed meat just as people are. Yet, it is also obvious to villagers that cattle are not people, but animals that survive by being fed by people. For them, this is what makes the difference between 'livestock' [Tb: *sejian*] and 'wild animals' [Tb: *rda*].

Local Knowledge and Development

This chapter also showed that the same cultural understandings are used by villagers in the 'indigenization' (Phillips-Howard 1999) of exotic technologies, such as herbicides, fodder grass and silage fodder techniques. The examples given showed how easy it might be for the significance of local knowledge for development cooperation to go unnoticed. However, when the power to make decisions lies with villagers—e.g. when they are choosing whether to adopt or not adopt an exotic technology—understanding the basis of villagers' decisions is crucial. Without an understanding of local notions of what constitutes a 'nutritious' fodder, a choice not to adopt exotic grasses or silage fodder would, to many development workers, seem irrational or simply wrong. This shows one way, then, in which the interactions between development workers and villagers can lead to consolidation of mutual disrespect and mutual accusations of ignorance, which has often been noted to characterize such interactions (Long and Long 1992).

Although the examples given here may seem to the reader either prosaic or trivial, they are, in my experience, the stuff of which interaction between development project staff and villagers are made, and drive to the heart of the issue of the 'interaction of knowledge systems' with which much of the literature on 'indigenous' or 'local knowledge' is concerned (see e.g. Warren et al. 1992, Purcell and Onjoro 2002). These examples also show how easy it is for what might appear to be 'unimportant comments' (i.e. local knowledge) to get sidelined in development interactions. For anthropologists interested in documenting what happens in development processes, the case presented here suggests that a focus on the specific situations in which indigenous knowledge is applied would be a useful strategy for examining the factors which make local knowledge more or less useful in development. For practitioners of development (including anthropologists) for whom local knowledge is of interest, the research reported here suggests that a focus on *practices*—whether feeding meat or expressing a lack of interest in exotic fodders—as opposed to knowledge itself, is an appropriate way to begin research. It may be, as in the case described here, that local knowledge exists that can explain those practices, but this should not be presumed (Vayda *et al.* 2004). Neither should it be presumed that such knowledge as is elicited is 'correct' (ibid.). However, even if that knowledge cannot be validated through Western scientific methods, this case does suggest that one should take seriously the possibility that local knowledge matters for the outcome of development interventions. Whether correct or not, where it does exist, local knowledge is an important basis for decision-making by those whose development we seek to promote. Where knowledge that can explain people's practices can be shown to exist, I concur fully with the opinion of Carmen Hess (1997: 50) in her study of development initiatives among agro-pastoralists in Ecuador, that:

> ...speaking across distinct knowledge systems is only possible if developers accept the people's worldview as the basis for proper communication. If developers ignore the local views prevalent among the indigenous people they deal with, they destroy the only basis for legitimate cross-cultural communication and, consequently, for active co-operation...

References

Barnard, J.T.O. 1934. *A Handbook of the Rawang Dialect of the Nung Language.* Rangoon: Superintendent of Government Printing and Stationery.

Bishop, N.H. 1998. *Himalayan herders.* Fort Worth and London: Harcourt Brace.

Casimir, M.J. and A. Rao. 1985. 'Vertical Control in the Western Himalaya: Some Notes on the Pastoral Ecology of the Nomadic Bakrwal of Jammu and Kashmir'. *Mountain Research and Development* 5 (3): 221–32.

Dessaint, A.Y. 1980. *Minorities of Southwest China: An Introduction to the Yi (Lolo) and Related Peoples and an Annotated Bibliography.* New Haven: HRAF Press.

Descola, P. and G. Pálsson. 1996. *Nature and Society: Anthropological Perspectives.* London: Routledge.

Ehlers, E. and H. Kreutzmann eds. 2000. *High Mountain Pastoralism in Northern Pakistan.* Stuttgart: Franz Steiner Verlag.

Ellen, R. 1996. 'Introduction'. In R. Ellen and K. Fukui eds. *Redefining Nature: Ecology, Culture and Domestication.* Oxford: Berg. pp. 1–36.

Ellen, R., and K. Fukui eds. 1996. *Redefining Nature: Ecology, Culture and Domestication.* Oxford: Berg.

Espinasse, J. ed. 1990. *Tibet 'Mission Impossible': Lettres du Père Etienne-Jules Dubernard (1864–1905),* Paris: Librairie Arthème Fayard.

Fricke, T. 1989. 'Introduction: human ecology in the Himalaya'. *Human Ecology* 17 (2): 131–145.

Gesangben and Duozang Caidan. 2000. *Qingzang Gaoyuan Youmu Wenhua* [Nomadic Culture on the Qinghai-Tibet Plateau]. Lanzhou: Gansu Nationalities Press.

Gros, S. 1996. 'Terres de confins, terres de colonisation. Essai sur les Marches sino-tibétaines du Yunnan à travers l'implantation de la Mission du Tibet'. *Péninsule* 33 (2): 147–211.

____ n.d. 'Ethnological Introduction', http://victoria.linguistlist.org

Gudeman, S. and A. Rivera. 1990. *Conversations in Colombia*. Cambridge: Cambridge University Press.

Hess, C. 1997. *Hungry for Hope: On the Cultural and Communicative Dimensions of Development in Highland Ecuador*. London: ITDG publishing.

Hiroyashu, T., 1996. 'The Concept of Vital Energy among Andean Pastoralists'. In R. Ellen and K. Fukui eds. *Ecology, Culture and Domestication*, Oxford: Berg, pp.187–212.

Long, N. and A. Long eds. 1992. *Battlefields of Knowledge*, London: Routledge.

Phillips-Howard, K.D. 1999. 'The indigenization of exotic inputs by small scale farmers on the Jos Plateau, Nigeria'. In G. Prain, S. Fujisaka and M.D. Warren eds. *Biological and Cultural Diversity: The Role of Indigenous Agricultural Experimentation in Development*. London: ITDG publishing. pp. 80–91.

Purcell, T. and E.A. Onjoro. 2002. 'Indigenous knowledge, power and parity: models of knowledge integration'. In P. Sillitoe, A. Bicker and J. Pottier eds. *Participating in Development: Approaches to Indigenous Knowledge* (ASA Monographs 39). London: Routledge. pp.162–88.

Romney, A.K., Weller, S.C. and W.H. Batchelder. 1986. 'Culture as Consensus: A Theory of Culture and Informant Accuracy'. *American Anthropologist* 88: 313–38.

Shen, S.C., Willson, A. and D. Melick. 2004. 'The Spatial Distribution of Rumex nepalensis in a Sub-alpine Rangeland in NW Yunnan'. CBIK Community Livelihoods Program Working Paper No. 8.

Smith, J.J. 1993. 'Using ANTHROPAC 3.5 and a Spreadsheet to compute a Freelist Salience Index'. *Cultural Anthropology Methodology Newsletter* 5(3): 1–3.

Stevens, S.F. 1993. *Claiming the High Ground: Sherpas, Subsistence and Environmental Change in the Highest Himalaya*. Berkeley: University of California Press.

Vayda, A.P., Walters, B.B. and I. Setyawati. 2004. 'Doing and Knowing: Questions about Studies of Local Knowledge'. In A.J. Bicker, P. Sillitoe and J. Pottier eds. *Investigating Local Knowledge: New Directions, New Approaches*. London: Ashgate Publishing.

Warren, M.D., Brokensha, D. and L.J. Slikkerveer eds. 1992. *The Cultural Dimension of Development: Indigenous Knowledge Systems*. London: ITDG publishing.

Wilkes, A.J. 2005. 'Ethnic minorities, Environment and Development in Yunnan: The Institutional Contexts of Biocultural Knowledge Production in Southwest China'. PhD. thesis, University of Kent.

Terrace Cultivation and Mental Landscapes in Southern Yunnan

PASCAL BOUCHERY

Terraced landscape in Yuanyang district (Photo: Pascal Bouchery)

It is generally acknowledged that the way societies give shape to their environments by transforming them materially is, to a large extent, the product of cultural preconceptions. Reconsidering this particular aspect of the dichotomy between 'material culture' and 'symbolism', the purpose of this article is to examine the validity of the converse proposition, i.e., the process by which a specific shaping of the environment impacts on the way this environment is culturally constructed. I argue that, in the particular case of the Hani society in Yunnan, the cosmological conceptualization of the local environment is grounded in a practical experience of wet rice agriculture and irrigation management. The principles on which the irrigation system is based provide a conceptual framework facilitating various analogical transfers from which each village community constructs a religious interpretation of the surrounding landscape.

The Hanis, who number about a million and a half, are mountain-dwellers speaking languages of the Tibeto-Burman family. They are scattered over a wide mountainous area along the south-western frontier of China stretching from Southern Yunnan as far as the foothills bordering the upper Chaophraya basin in Thailand, and from Kengtung State in Myanmar to Lai Chau Province in Vietnam. Groups living in the Ailao Range flanking the southern bank of the Red River (called *Honghe* in Chinese) in Yunnan have carved an impressive landscape of staggered rice-terraces along the slopes of their mountains, on a scale that can be compared to other elaborate systems of waterworks and farming devices in Nepal, the Central Cordillera of Luzon in the Philippines, or the island of Bali. Ancient Chinese sources such as the *Book of Southern Barbarians* (*Manshu*), a geographical report written at the end of the Tang era, suggest that rice-terrace agriculture in this area may date as far back as the eighth century.[1] That possibly makes the rice cropping system,

---

[1] More detailed information appears in written chronicles of the Ming era, with a description of irrigation channel construction and the method of opening new terraced fields.

which the ethnic minorities of central Yunnan practise, one of the oldest forms of terraced agriculture in the world.[2]

A few empirical studies have been carried out on the Hanis' rice-cropping technology (Bouchery, 1996; Huang 2000; Li 2000; Li and Chen 2000; Mao 1991; Wang 1999), the most recent one being Adachi Shimpei's interesting presentation of the agro-ecological aspects (2007). However, few studies have yet attempted to establish a link between terraced-rice cultivation and the Hani system of beliefs, although in the case of the neighbouring Yis of Yuanyang, who also rely on the same mode of subsistence, Formoso (2006) has shown that the terrace and the terraced landscape are significant symbols used as traditional motifs on the women costumes.

A brief presentation of the traditional rice-cropping system is necessary here in order to provide the basis for understanding the nature of its relationship with the religious interpretation of landscape. The Hani terms appearing in the text pertain to the

[2]It is still unclear whether the Hanis brought their terracing system along with them when they first moved into the area coming from the northern bank of the Red River, or whether it was later developed *in situ*. Representatives of the Halo group in central Yuanyang, whose ancestors certainly were among the first settlers to rely on terraced cultivation in the Ailao range, say that their ancestors only grew dry crops at the time of their arrival in the region, and that terraces were absent. Interestingly enough, no mention is made of rice in the first part of their epic poem *Aphö tsopo-po* recounting their ancestral migrations. In *Numa-ame*, the original mythical settlement, they are said to have cultivated maïze (*tsedu*), millet (*tseçi*), sorghum (*sulo*) and buckwheat (*hwale*), all species which are more specific of Northern Yunnan and Western Sichuan where most probably the Hani originated. Millet in particular (*Panicum* ssp.) was of great importance in central Yuanyang prior to the introduction of maïze. According to the same oral tradition, rice was grown by the Hanis before they settled in the Ailao range, and rice-terraces were first introduced in an unidentified site called *Rero*. Halo informants estimate that terracing first took place in their region at the time of their ancestor *Sumodzo*, from whom they can count 44 generations. Ancient bronzeware has also been discovered which depicts the ploughing techniques and folk customs of the local inhabitants. Whatever credit can be accorded to the oral tradition, it is likely that the Hanis' terracing system is at least a thousand years old.

language spoken by the Halo subgroup which is spoken around the Yuanyang township of the Honghe Autonomous Prefecture; they differ significantly from those reported by Shimpei (2007) from Shalatuo Township area which are of unidentified origin.

The Rice-cropping System

The Hanis' agricultural system is one of mixed farming including management of pond-field cultivation of rice, swidden cultivation of rice and maize, multiple cropping of domesticated plants and raising of livestock. Despite the number of cultivated species,[3] as well as the fact that wet and dry farming is closely associated everywhere, primary economic and cultural focus is on paddy. On the slopes of the Ailao range, wet rice is almost exclusively cultivated in terraced pond-fields, and similarly, all terraced irrigated parcels are primarily devoted to paddy cultivation. Save for rice, the Hanis of Honghe never grow in their pond-fields anything other than Taro (*Colocasia esculenta*), Arrowhead (*Sagittaria sagitifolia*) and Water dropwort (*Oenanthe javanica*), never in pure stands, but always associated with paddy. The lack of sources of water as well as poor soils locally account for the absence of terraced cultivation in some areas of the Ailao range, as for instance, in the Laomeng Circle of Yuanyang District. But wherever clayey soils are available in large quantities and the area is rather densely populated—as in the mountain range bordering the southern bank of the Red River in Honghe, Yuanyang and Jinping districts—most of the space is devoted to terraced paddy-fields and farmers attention primarily focuses on inundated terraced parcels and the various waterworks involved. There

[3] A rapid survey of cultivated plants in Yuanyang in areas ranging from 800 to 1,500 m in altitude indicates that as many as 150 different species (most of them traditional) are locally cultivated in terraced irrigated parcels, dry fields (terraced or not), swiddens, gardens or surrounding forests. In addition, several cultural varieties have been developed for the major plant species.

may be as many as 200 graduated levels and 3,000 terraces on a single slope.[4]

Rice (*Oryza sativa*) is by far the most important of all cultigens, followed by soya and maize. Paddy is cultivated in pond-fields up to 2,000 metres. Double-cropping is possible below 800 m, but the location of the vast majority of Hani terraced fields between 1,200 and 1,600 m makes the entire region a single cropping area. Among the ten varieties of rice annually grown in terraced-pond-fields of one village of Shencun administrative circle, eight are traditional and belong to the temperate race of *O. sativa* L. var. *Japonica* (*keng* in chinese) characterized by round grain, while about one third of the varieties are glutinous (*honyao*).[5]

The Terrace

The terraced field (*shade, desha*) is the basic element of cultivated landscapes in the Ailao Mountains. The Hani irrigated terrace consists of a portion of soil (*habe*) comprising a flat inundated enclosure (*çlaodao*), a low retaining dike or bund (*sha-gogae*), two dike walls simply called 'walls' (*dabosï*) uphill and downhill, sometimes reinforced by stones, a shallow cut (*öhae, hetü*) into a dike to allow the inflow of water, another cut (*çlokhae*) into the retaining dike to remove the excess water and a drainage conduit

[4]At first sight the impressive size of the terraced landscapes in the Ailao Mountains may give a casual observer the impression that the Hani farmer possesses vast surfaces of land and that rice is abundant everywhere. This is not the case, for in Central Yuanyang a household of five people manages an average joint holding of 0,25 ha of cultivated land (5 to 8 parcels), out of which 75 or 80 per cent are specifically devoted to paddy cultivation. Yields most often ranging from 2 to 5 t./ha, combined with the fact that a single annual cropping is only possible in most areas, often permit the members of one household to be self-sufficient in rice for only nine months of the year. For the three remaining months, selling vegetables and eggs at the markets of Yuanyang township or off-season employment outside the village had become a necessity in 1995, as well as the only way for supplying farmers with a little cash.

[5]All the traditional non glutinous varieties grown in Central Yuanyang District produce grains with a red pedicarp.

used to dry up the field if necessary or to prevent an overfilling of spillways after storms. The level enclosure, the dike and the adjacent dike wall altogether form a unit in terms of ownership.

Repairs and new constructions of terraces usually take place in winter during the dry season. Slope terracing may proceed either upward or downward, depending on the natural inclination of the slope and soil quality. The most common soils found in the Ailao Mountains are yellow or brown clayey soils originating from metamorphic rock formed in the Paleozoic Era.[6] The steeper the slope, the more multiple cuts are needed in its surface. Ideally a new terraced field should be built up only over an old one— i.e. one in which the soil has already become hard and compact. For this reason and also in order to enrich the soil with nitrogen, the Hanis of Yuanyang cultivate dry crops in their new terraces for the first three or five years before filling them with water, mainly maize (*tsedu*) and soya (*nüçi*), either associated or alternated. Yields are very low during this period compared to the sum of work involved for the construction itself. In the past, in order to strengthen the stability of terraces, wooden logs were sometimes planted horizontally into the ground at each extremity of one parcel and later covered in earth. This practice has now died out as a result of both deforestation and government restrictions.

At the time of the construction of a new terrace, no rough gravel fill is laid at the bottom of the parcel to provide for drainage. In most areas, once inundated the parcel should ideally remain under water permanently, otherwise soil hardness is said to limit the growth of plant roots. On the other hand, a soil constantly kept under water becomes silty and unadapted to ploughing or harrowing by water buffalo. The problem is solved either by a periodical removal of all water from the pond-field or by filling the bottom layer every year at the time the field is made, with a mixture of tree branches and sand.

Traditionally, the soil is enriched only by using animal (*dzekhü*) and green manure. In Yuanyang, chemical fertilizers are

---

[6]*Yuanyang Xianchi Bianxe Weiyuanhui*, 1990: 44. See also Adachi Shimpei, 2007: 174.

still hardly used, partly because of their cost and partly because natural manure once spread in the field is said to benefit the soil longer, usually for two or three years. Green manure consists mostly of paddy stalks and soya grown in and around the pond-field, left in place after the harvest and later buried in the ground. For this reason, a long and narrow parcel is highly valued, for the soya plants cultivated on the enclosure dike supplies more natural fertilizers than a large round shaped pond-field. Animal manure is mixed with water and then carried and distributed over the inundated terraces, not directly but through an irrigation channel from a place located above the first field to be enriched.

Agricultural Equipment

The tools used by Hanis for centuries for 'carving' their slopes and farming their mountainous territory are remarkably simple: hoes, ploughs without wheels, harrow, levelling rakes, sickles and metal wedges. Tools specifically linked with wet-field terraced agriculture chiefly include the hoe (*tsae, tsö*), the plough (*nyuchae*) and the wooden harrow (*nyuka*), the last two being pulled by a water buffalo. Each parcel is ploughed and harrowed three to five times every year. The hoe (*tsu*, as in Yunnanese) is the universal basic tool for building and repairing terraces. The Hanis of Yuanyang use two main types of steel or iron flat-bladed hoes, one in paddy-fields with a concave edge and another with a straight edge in dry fields. Hoes serve for all types of work: digging, earth packing and smoothing, cutting clods, ploughing the corners of fields, water sluicing as well as weeding. Levelling down and smoothing the surface layer are done with a large wooden flat rake. Stones are extracted from the paddy-field with a pick axe (*yankhan*), while boulders are dug out with metal wedges used as levers (*sodu*), then split and broken into pieces with a hammer (*djipu*) and later used to consolidate the dike walls. Two types of long-bladed sickles (*ye*) are used, one (*yehu*) for weeding and paddy reaping, another smooth edge type (*yema*) is for everyday

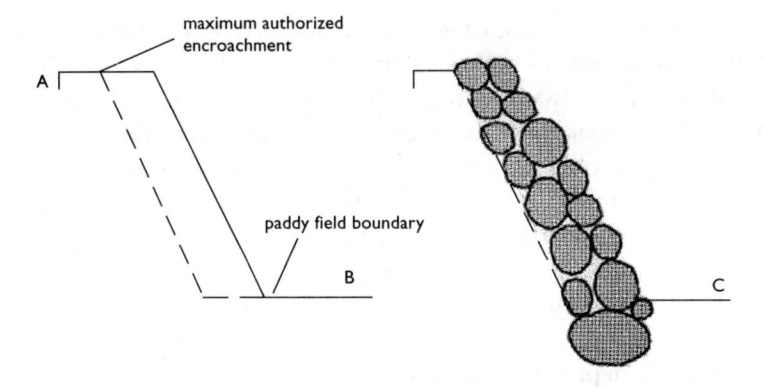

Figure 12.1: Method used for Stone Walling

use to cut vegetables in gardens and at home. All-purpose billhooks are also widely used.

Irrigation and Drainage System

Hani irrigation is based mostly on the principle of continuous flow and fixed proportional water division. The irrigation system consists of diverting water from the numerous mountain streams and springs and channelling it to the fields through a series of bifurcations of the main flow. Irrigation segments are of two types: major irrigation channels (*laoga-gama*) and secondary channels (*laoga-gaza*). The first ones, carrying water from the main sources at the head of channels supply it to the highest paddy-fields in such a way to encompass the entire irrigated area of one village. Therefore a *laoga-gama* is often several kilometres long and requires constant maintenance. Main channels are frequently paved with stones, especially in the section which passes through the village (Figure 12.1). Whenever a point is reached above a cluster of fields receiving water from a main channel, a piece of wood with most often two or three notched cuts (*adzo doma laoga*) is placed across the channel and used as a weir to divide the flow into several parts. Most dividers found in the Ailao Mountains are made of logs, though a few have been carved out of stone and may be as old as five centuries. The water then either goes to a first pond-field and flows from higher to lower plots by means of inter-plot spillways, or goes to a secondary irrigation channel passing through terraced areas and following the natural inclination of the slope, before it is deviated to a first parcel further down. At lower levels of the irrigation network, simple earth weirs are used as flow dividers. At the end of it, excess water is transferred from one of the lowest pond-fields into a drainage channel. All combinations of these three basic irrigation and drainage types are possible depending on the shape of the slope and accessibility to water. The flow can first be diverted from a main channel to higher fields, then be transferred by means of a spillway into a drainage channel, and again reach another cluster of parcels downhill until it is finally poured into the lowest drainage channel.

Ideally the uppermost layer of terrace soil is maintained in a wet muddy condition through all seasons, so terraced pond-fields require meticulous care in the regulation of water throughout the year. The irrigation system (Figure 12.2) is used to carry water

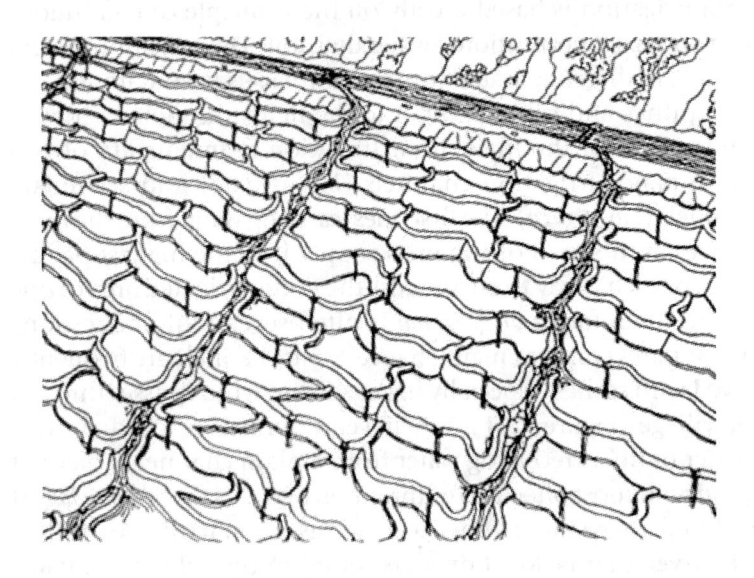

Figure 12.2: The Irrigation Network

and also some fertilizing elements. Animal or green manure is not deposited directly in the fields as elsewhere in China, but mixed with water in a place located above the first field to be enriched and then distributed over the terraces.

Springs, irrigation and drainage channels are all collectively managed in the village and are never owned or appropriated privately, even when they occur in, or cross, pond-field property. Fields are owned and managed on a household basis. In Yuanyang, farmers are not allowed to manipulate the flow, as fixed proportional flow division structures are set up to guarantee an equitable share of water for everyone. The maintenance of the irrigation network is entrusted to a specialist called *laoga-laepha* (literally 'guardian of channels'), who is selected by the village representatives. His first duty is to act on behalf of the whole community by daily checking and maintaining the main channel (*laoga-gama*), mostly by taking out fallen leaves, mud or stones that have accumulated there and that may disrupt the general distribution of the flow. In coordination with the village administrative head and the traditional council (*tsomo-dama*) he also organizes and is in charge of the collective repairing of the main channel (*phulao-laoga-do*) that usually takes place every year after the harvest. In addition, the *laoga-laepha* is responsible for keeping the markers which testify to the amount of water allotted to the main channels. Once initially fixed by the village council, all measures of various weirs are identified by a series of woodcut marks of corresponding lengths that are kept safe in the *laoga-laepha*'s house. From then on, any modification to the irrigation network and the subsequent allocation of water can only be collectively decided by the village assembly and the village headman. Should a dispute arise regarding access to water, the *laoga-laepha* would immediately be able to check whether someone has attempted to modify the cut of a wooden board by comparing with his own set of woodcut marks (Figure 12.3). The water allocation, and the width of the open cut, is calculated according to crop water requirements, not the surface of the fields to be irrigated, hence the key-variable for re-allocation is the amount of grain usually harvested in one given area.

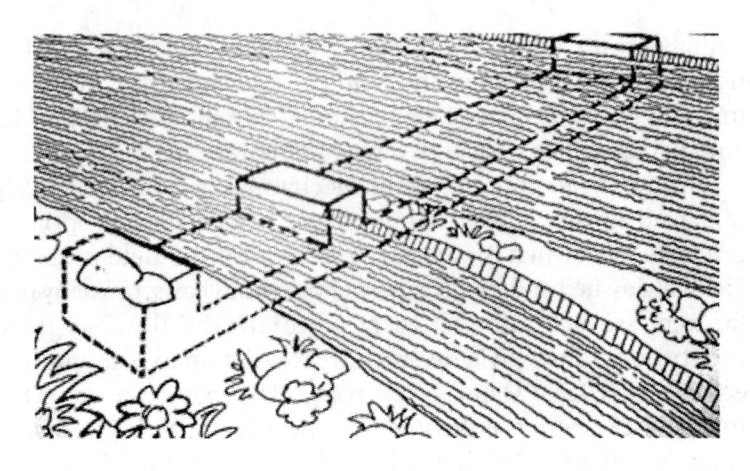

Figure 12.3: Hand-notched Log used as Flow Divider

Rules Related to Management of Water

The general maintenance of the irrigation system requires constant attention and a series of mutual obligations as the allocation of water is strictly determined by customary rules.

Most important among them is the rule stipulating that the flow of water must remain undisturbed from the source to the drainage channels. Hence repairs accompanied by the complete evacuation of water from one pond-field call for an irrigation channel to be dug which encircles the cultivated parcel in order to maintain an undisrupted flow of water. This very simple rule gives the farmers the flexibility to deal with problems related to irrigation water on a day-to-day basis, as illustrated in Figure 12.4.

If a dike collapses and is not repaired within days, large areas can be lost, therefore the owner of an irrigated parcel is held responsible for all damage caused by runoff, silting, and slippage occasioned in the field situated immediately below his own parcel, regardless of whether the former depends on the latter for his water supply. In the event of neglect, a fine in grain may be given to the owner of the damaged field as compensation for the estimated grain loss. For the same reason no one is allowed to retain water in his field or divert water from his field if it

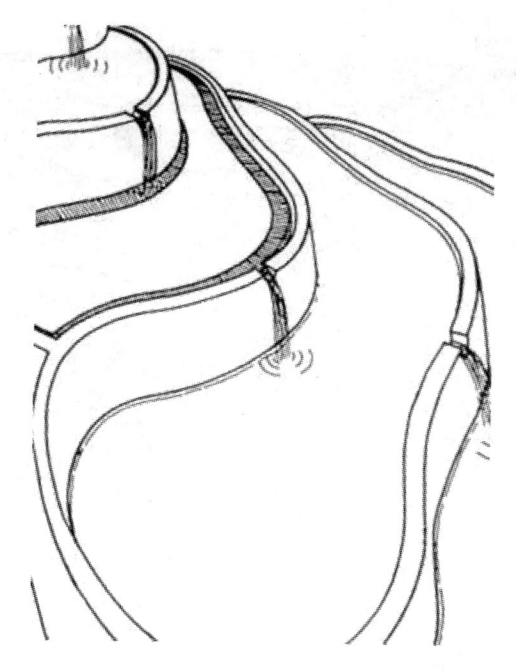

Figure 12.4: Method Adopted for a Temporary Drying Out of Field without Interrupting the Irrigation Flow

modifies the flow normally poured into the parcels situated downslope. In particular, any attempt during the dry season to reduce the amount of water flowing downwards is considered 'water stealing' (*utshü-ko*) and leads to a substantial fine. Similarly any attempt to expand the water inlet by enlarging the spillway intake located immediately above one's fields is punished by a fine in grain or cash imposed by the village council. Damage may occur as well during the rainy season if a dike happens to overflow and the excess water falls heavily under the crops of the parcel located immediately downhill. For that reason, owners are held responsible for their ability to contain the regular flow in their pond-field, that is to control a proper transfer of the flow in excess to the drainage canal, and therefore any attempt to enlarge one's own outflow spillway at that time is also liable to a fine.

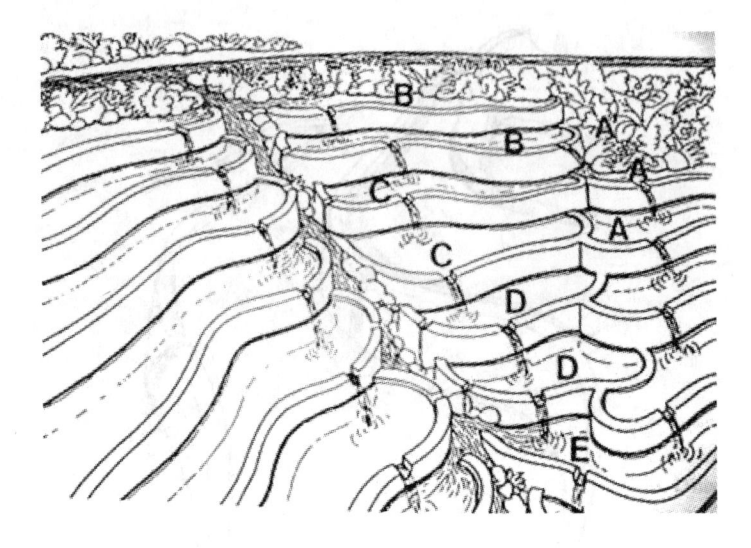

Figure 12.5: Social Constraints Related to the Expansion of Terraced Fields

The second basic constraint is that any modification of the water system due to an extension of the irrigated surface requires consent from all field owners whose water supply may be affected by the change. Figure 12.5 gives an example of such situations that may involve complex negotiations.

The owner of fields A wishing to dig up new irrigated terraces in A' and draw water from B would first have to obtain an agreement from the owners of C and D parcels, as their fields do not have direct access to an irrigation channel and only depend for their own supply on water flowing from B. Permission is usually given without compensation if the amount of water proves to be sufficient during the dry season, otherwise it may be obtained in exchange for an annual payment in grain or cash, or simply refused. As a last resort, the case would be handled at an assembly by the village headman assisted by village representatives *(abo-tsomo)*. In some cases where access to the irrigation network is physically possible, drawing water from a channel is only authorized during the rainy season and prohibited in the fallow season when water is scarce (Shimpei, 2007: 180). A general reorganization of the irrigation network is a normal process in village life due to population growth and does take place from time to time, but this matter can only be decided by common agreement on the part of village representatives.

As an extension to this general rule, no new human settlement is allowed above an already existing village if it has to depend for its supply on water flowing from one of the sources owned by this village. This can lead to serious disputes, especially with regard to non-Hani groups such as Miao or Yao who, by tradition, tend to occupy upland areas.

The set of constraints and rules related to the management of water implies an almost daily check on pond-fields, a time-consuming activity whenever those fields are located some distance from the village. In order to minimize the risk of conflicts, fields owners always wish to have direct access to both a secondary irrigation channel and a drainage canal. However this ideal situation, represented in Figure 12.5 by the location of parcels B, constitutes the exception rather than the rule. Regarding terrace expansion, people also have to balance their wish to acquire fields having direct access to the irrigation channels—often low yielding as they tend to be located on higher slopes—and their wish to obtain better yields from fields located at lower altitudes, i.e. also situated at the end of the irrigation network and therefore more exposed to water shortage during the dry season.

Cosmological Interpretation of the Environment

Since the pioneering works of sinologists such as Granet (1929, 1934) and Stein (1987) and also some more recent studies on Southeast Asia (e.g. Hutterer, 1985; Macdonald, 1999) we know that the concept of 'nature' in various agrarian societies of Southern China and its periphery is not based on a vague instinct or a sense of harmony, but on a constructed view of the environment rooted in religious beliefs. The local environment of farmers is rather conceived as a reduction of the macrocosm, a miniature universe which furthermore is not static but suggests movement. The Hani conception conforms to this general pattern. The Hanis consider their proximate environment as crossed by invisible energies or powers that emanate from spiritual entities. Not the revered gods of their celestial pantheon, but a myriad of terrestrial divinities mostly associated with some salient features of their surrounding landscapes such as mountains, cliffs, rocks, streams, lakes, caves as well as remarkable trees. Among them, spirits associated with mountains and water sources constitute a distinct category in the sense that they are not only supposed to use the element of landscape as their abode, but also to circulate along specific routes (*gama*) which are defined according to the local topography and hydrography. Besides, this general circulation of spiritual energy is conceived as a fertilizing flow which has the capability to concentrate at certain spots, where human beings attempt to capture them and use them to their own advantage.

Considering the mountains, the energy emanates from what the Hanis simply call an 'owner/master of the mountain' (*labo-yoso*), and flows through a 'mountain vein' (*mitsa-migu-mu*) that precisely matches the corresponding ridge line. The summit of the mountain is simply viewed as the abode of the divinity, the vein is said to be its road (*gama*) and is called *dzaela-khala-böla-gama*, literally the 'road from which cattle, crops and humans come'. Therefore it is seen as a channel, a way, through which flows non-material fertilizing power, a kind of vital principle. They also speak of a 'road of prosperity' (*dzala-gama*); originating from the mountain top it reaches the bottom of the valley following one of several ridges through a series of bifurcations depending on the local topography. As every mountain ridge is interconnected to a culminating summit in a given area, every god associated with a minor summit is connected to the mountain god of the culminating one and is conceived as dependent on this paramount master, helping him as an assistant in various ways. Thus the energy emanating from a major mountain peak flows from top to bottom, bifurcates into several branches according to the number of minor mountains that it encompasses, generating a pyramidal network. In a very similar way water sources are conceived as the abode of as many 'water owners' (*utshü-yoso*).

From the springs their powers circulate downwards to the valley bottom, following the lines of the hydrographic network, be it natural or human made in the case of an irrigation system. Thus mountain ridge lines and watercourses constitute the two main channels for the circulation of telluric flows.

There is a common perception amongst the Hanis that humans and their living dependants (domesticated animals, crops) can benefit from lengthy contact with these fertilizing energies, and so they seek to locate their settlements on the 'roads of gods'. By doing so, they believe that humans (*bï*), cattle (*dzae*) and crops (*kha*) will multiply in a very natural way, but if they choose to settle their villages or houses some distance from these routes they have little chance of prospering. Several configurations are said to be auspicious, as shown in Figure 12.6:

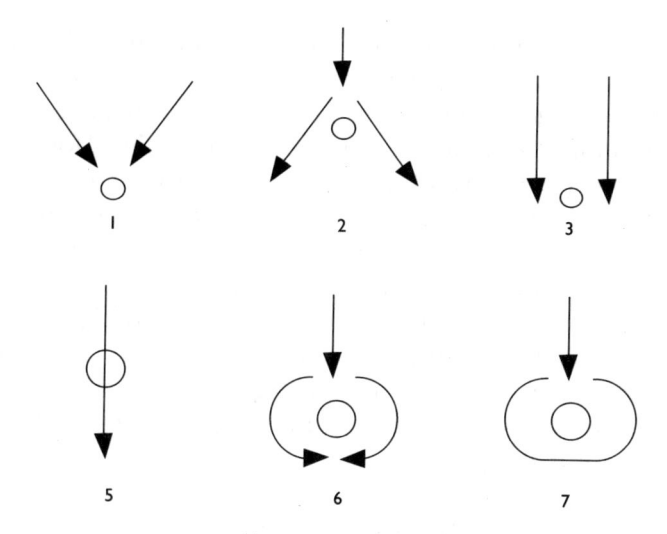

Figure 12.6: Various Auspicious Village Settings in Relation to Ridge Line Configurations

One of the best ones is on a relatively flat area, backed by the mountain, where one 'vein' ends (*mitsamigu-zayela-po*) or, even better, at a place where two veins converge. The Hanis imagine these flat grounds as '*a rest area for the gods*' and say that it evokes

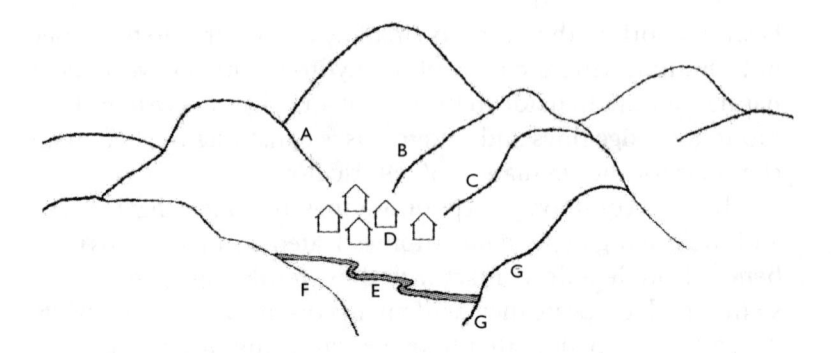

Figure 12.7: An Ideal Village Setting.
Located at the junction between several veins (A, B, C), just above a flat area (D) crossed by a slow-flowing stream (E) and surrounded on all sides by mountains (A, B, C, F, G).

a table with plenty of food on it, because in such areas the energy concentrates and accumulates. The greater the number of mountain ridges that converge or are directly connected to the major summit, the more valuable the site is considered for human settlement (Figure 12.7). Similarly, the site is believed to be particularly auspicious if it includes a depression where water accumulates, such as a natural pond or a channel in which the water flow is very slow, for it helps to establish contact with the fertilizing flow coming down from the mountain peak. The Hanis will not hesitate to artificially create such a channel, as the paved one that passes through Pukha village in the Shencun Circle, which is of no use in their irrigation system and has only been dug out for that purpose.

But nearness to a fast-running source of water is considered inauspicious, especially if it flows directly down towards the valley bottom, for it is believed that it may divert the flow emanating from the mountain vein and drive it off. In Phuka, for example, a bamboo hedgerow has been planted to obscure a nearby fast-flowing stream leading straight down to the valley. This was considered a preventive measure against any possible outflow of the fertilizing energy into that stream. The Hanis say that access to the valley has been 'blocked by the clump' (*hamae-adzo-shatsö*).

Similar measures will be taken to conceal a rock with a shape that evocates some feared animal such as a tiger, especially if its mouth faces the village. One of the best configurations for a surrounding landscape is a small mountain cirque, for it also helps to prevent energies from running off. In such a case, all roads of prosperity emanating from mountain peaks and springs ultimately converge towards the village and the fields. The Hanis apply the same principles to locating cemeteries which must be situated on the same vein as the village, some distance upslope. The protection that the living expect from their ancestors also partly depends on the ability of the latter to first capture for themselves the vital principles emanating from mountain gods.

However ideal the village setting may be, this remains the case provided that the general circuit is not disrupted, or, as the Hanis say, that the 'roads of prosperity are not blocked' (*dzala-gama-matotsö*). The flow emanating from the mountain is supposed to circulate under the ground at such a depth that ordinary agricultural activities (including slope terracing) will not affect it. But other excavating works, such as road building, are believed to intercept the flow and to sluice it into their own circuits. In 1956, the villagers of Pukha opposed a government project of opening an unpaved road just above their village, for fear that it would 'cut' their main vein and hence drive away a major source of prosperity for the village. The digging of a large artificial canal around the mountain such as those built during the Great Leap Forward (1958–1960) are reported to have had the same devastating effect by capturing and diverting the telluric flows in an unexpected way. For the same reason, Hani villagers strongly oppose the establishment of human settlements upslope on one of the ridge lines to which their villages are connected. Nowadays the problem most often arises with Miao and Yao immigrants who traditionally favour the higher uplands for establishing their dwellings and practising dry land cultivation.

Clearly, this general system of orientations based on local topography and a religious interpretation of the landscape brings to mind the Chinese theory of earth winds or telluric breaths (qi) serving as a foundation for a set of beliefs which have come to be called 'geomancy' (*fengshui*, literally 'wind and water'). A similar set of ideas underlies the general relationship between man and nature: humans are not thought of as separate from the landscape in which they live, and the landscape is seen and used as a medium between men and natural or cosmological forces. As in the Chinese model, the whole physical environment is an expression of hidden forces, of a cosmology, and the surrounding landscape is a microcosm centred upon a central spot, which constitutes the site as a miniature universe. This universe is in flux, in continuous change, but patterns of change are discernable to knowledgeable people, and various types of knowledge about topomantic or geomantic nature help men to situate themselves in the landscape where they may most benefit from natural forces. As in the Chinese tradition, the salient features of a landscape are those that can be traced as lines—mountain ridges, water courses and thoroughfares—and those that have definite shapes and outlines, such as mountain peaks, boulders, ponds and pools. By observing these patterns and by understanding the natural laws which they manifest, people can diagnose the prevalence of good and bad influences at any spot on the ground. Therefore great store is set by placing landscape features correctly around the site at appropriate points, like the proper placing of areas of human 'dwellings' (villages, cemeteries, houses, beds, etc.). Common landscape features and symbols (networks of veins or lines of influence, plant or animal symbolism, interpretations of shapes based on resemblances) constitute a common way of making geomantic diagnosis according to the lie of the land, indicating an eminently visual way of thinking that also constitutes the virtual basis of geomancy elsewhere in China.

Although undoubtedly influenced to some extent by the Han system, the topomancy developed by the Hanis nevertheless exhibits some striking differences which are worth noting here:

First it completely lacks any reference to some most basic elements of the Chinese tradition such as the life-breaths conception (*qi*), the theory of Five Elements (*wuxing*), the yin/

yang principles, the Eight Trigrams, the use of a compass or even such a basic concept as the north-south cardinal axis.

Second, in this universe in motion the Hanis, unlike the Hans, do not conceive this energy as a mere natural force but as an individualized power associated with some specific divinity. Nor do they conceive the circulating flows as 'breaths' but as 'roads' or 'ways' (*gama*).

Third, some basic principles associated with these energies in movement do not so much evoke the Chinese system of geomancy and the associated notion of telluric breaths as their most familiar environment, i.e. the rice-cropping sphere.

And though the Hanis do not explicitly say that these flows are liquid flows, some of their beliefs or practices tend to indicate this:

As water, the vital principle is always conceived as flowing from top to bottom and faster on steep slopes. And like water, wherever the ground is flat it stagnates and accumulates.

On a symbolic level, mountain peaks play a role analogous to springs in the irrigation system, both being considered as sources of fertility. Just as Hani settlements are invariably located downhill from a major irrigation water source, the site encircled by a channel network stemming from that source, for their village settlements, the Hanis seek a place located below a major mountain peak to which they are nevertheless connected through the ridge line, and surrounding mountains that constitute a similar network connected to the main ridge line. The village sites are then connected both materially to a water source and symbolically to the mountain top through a topographical 'vein'. The similarity between mountains and rivers or channels is very well exemplified by the mythology where mountain caves, as well as sub-water levels, are inhabited by ophidian-looking creatures watching over treasures. Even the mythical abode of the ancestors, from where primeval humanity is said to have emerged, is conceived as a mountain cave.

One may also note that the structure of this network of vital principles is reminiscent of the basic structure of an irrigation network. In both cases, lines stemming from one point diverge through a series of bifurcations, and in the interpretation of the local topography, each minor summit is conceived as a branch point, as represented in Figure 12.8:

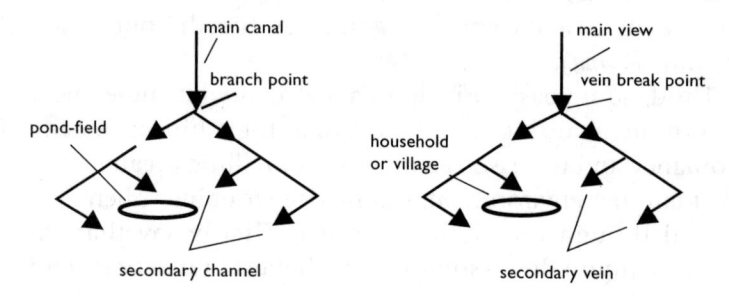

Figure 12.8: Irrigation and Vital Influx Networks

As a matter of fact, by observing and interpreting the landscape around them the Hanis mentally extract from the contours the terrain's skeleton lines just as a cartographer would do to produce a topographic map; on the one hand, the valley lines that connect the deepest point of valleys, on the other hand the ridge-lines that connect the highest points of ridges. Whether extracted from a natural drainage network (streams), an artificial drainage network (irrigation channels) or a mountain topographic network (ridge-lines), the required geometric structure is the same and corresponds to the general model of a simple tree structure; a node-link diagram that connect nodes together with line segments as represented above.

Besides, the way the energy of the mountain flows through a network of lines and dispatches its fertilizing power among living creatures by prolonged contact parallels the popular belief of the fertilizing power of water in the context of rice-cropping. For the Hanis traditionally believe that water—not the nutriments contained in the soil—is responsible for plant growth. This assumption is partly true if we consider soil pedogenic processes, such as podzolization (bleaching), which are likely to occur in permanently inundated soils and result in partial auto-regeneration of nutrients derived from soil.[7] One must also remember that the only traditional method of fertilizing pond-fields is to mix water with animal and green manure, i.e., to drag a fertilizing flow towards the parcel by using the irrigation network. Similarly, water in the rice-ponds is almost stagnant, and fast-running water is said to impoverish the yield; another assumption confirmed by agricultural empirism, especially at planting and transplanting when running water is said to not be conducive to the growth of rice. Thus the religious idea of benefiting from a continuous and slow fertilizing flow appears to be rooted in the agricultural sphere.

The same remark can be made if one considers that the Hanis establish their villages in conformity with some of the general principles that also prevail in their agricultural practices, in the sense that they select flat ground connected to a network of supposedly fertilizing power situated uphill. Flat areas are valued in their symbolic system in the same way that terraced-fields are always more valued than sloping fields in which a level of fertility does not accumulate and is rapidly washed away by rains. For the Hanis, a good field is always a parcel which is both a terraced plot (*shahao*) and an inundated plot (*ösha*); a low, flat ridge of earth built across the slope in which fertilizing elements from water, vegetal and animal manure can concentrate. In a similar manner, a good location for a human settlement on the mountain slope is on a relatively flat area encircled by mountains towards which fertilizing flows converge and accumulate. Also, just as every pond-field has an inlet to draw the water into the plots from the irrigation channel, every Hani village has an upper gate

---

[7]Water also provides nutrients by circulating through the fields and by permitting small aquatic animals to live in it, as decaying aquatic life is an additional source of soil nutrients. See also Geertz (1963), who argues that the stability and the productivity of the wet rice-cropping systems lie in water management. According to him, the most 'striking feature of the [wet rice] ecosystem (...) is its extraordinary stability or durability, the degree to which it can produce, year after year, and often twice in one year, a virtually undiminished yield (...) The answer to this puzzle almost certainly lies in the paramount role played by water in the dynamics of the rice terrace.'

erected across one of the main paths leading to the village, at which annual rituals for village welfare are performed. Conversely, reminiscent of the function of the rice-field outlet used for a regulated removal of runoff water, a yearly ritual purification is performed at the village lower gate, which consists in throwing ashes collected from each household over the wooden porch. At both levels—agricultural and symbolic—measures are taken to prevent fast-flowing water, overflow and unwanted derivations. And in the same way, as inlets and outlets are repaired each year before paddy is sowed, the upper village gate is ritually renewed on a yearly basis at the time of the *Hamatu* festival, which also takes place just before—and actually gives the signal for—sowing activities.

Lastly, the rule that forbids any human settlement on the same mountain vein above an existing village clearly parallels the customary rule forbidding anyone to draw water from a channel without getting prior consent from all owners of the fields located downslope which depend on the same channel for their water supply. Here also vital influxes, such as water, tend to be assimilated with goods over which individuals or groups claim specific rights.

Thus the Hani geo-dynamic conception of the local environment and their interpretation of the landscape stem from a series of identifications forming a system in which religious and technical conceptions of space management are closely related. The irrigation system, its logical workings as well as the social rules associated with it, provide both a conceptual framework and a set of principles that give a specific religious sense to the perception of the local environment. In the symbolic sphere the village functions as a rice-pond, mountain peaks as water sources, and mountain ridges on the model of a giant irrigation network. In this particular case, symbolism operates by means of analogical transfers from both the technological and social domain associated with wet rice-cropping, in order to elaborate a coherent system in the religious sphere. More specifically, it uses a simple mental scheme—the irrigation network scheme and its tree structure—to classify and organize the divinities associated with the two most culturally salient features of their local environment, i.e. mountains and springs. At the same time the tree structure provides an organizing principle by which the hierarchical relationships between them are defined. This case-study focuses on the fact that we are not merely contemplating a society giving shape to its environment according to its own set of already established cultural values. Here we are also witnessing the reverse process by which a subsistence technique serves as a model for elaborating a specific core of religious beliefs applied to landscape interpretation.

References

Bouchery Pascal. 1996. 'The Rice-Terraces System of the Hani of Yuanyang: A Preliminary Survey'. Unpublished paper, presented at the 2nd International Conference on Hani/Akha Culture, Chiangmai.

Formoso, Bernard. 2006 'A Terraced World for an Armored Body: The symbolism of women costumes among the Yi of Yuanyang'. *Research in Anthropology and Aesthetics* 37: 89–106.

Geertz, Clifford. 1963. *Agricultural Involution: The Process of Agricultural Change in Indonesia.* Berkeley: University of California Press.

Granet, Marcel. 1968 [First edition 1929]. *La Civilisation chinoise. La vie publique et la vie privée.* Paris: Albin Michel.

_____ 1968 [First edition 1934]. *La Pensée chinoise.* Paris: Albin Michel.

Huang, Shaowen. 2000. 'Lun Hani Titian de Kechixu Fazhan' [Sustainable Development of the Hani Rice Terrace Cultivation]. In Li Qibo ed., *Hanizu Titian Wenhua Lunji* [*Collected Papers on the Hani Rice Terrace Culture*], Kunming: Yunnan Minzu Chubanshe [Yunnan Minorities Press].

Hutterer, Karl L. ed. 1985. *Cultural Values and Human Ecology in Southeast Asia.* Michigan Papers on South and Southeast Asia, Ann Arbor: University of Michigan Center for South and Southeast Asian Studies.

Li, Qibo, 2000. 'Lun Hani Titian Daozuo Wenhua' [The Hani Culture of Rice Terrace Cultivation]. In Li Qibo ed., *Lun Hani Titian Daozuo Wenhua* [*Collected Papers on the Hani Culture of Rice Terrace Culture*]. Kunming: Yunnan Minzu Chubanshe [Yunnan Minorities Press].

Li, Qibo ed. 2000. *Lun Hani Titian Daozuo Wenhua* [*Collected Papers on the Hani Culture of Rice Terrace Culture*]. Kunming: Yunnan Minzu Chubanshe [Yunnan Minorities Press].

Li, Baoze and Chen, Woniang. 2000. 'Hani Titian Jiqi Gengzuojishu de Yanbian' [Changes in the Cultivation Technologies of the Hani Rice Terrace Agriculture]. In Li Qibo ed. *Lun Hani Titian Daozuo Wenhua* [*Collected Papers on the Hani Culture of Rice Terrace Culture*]. Kunming: Yunnan Minzu Chubanshe [Yunnan Minorities Press].

Macdonald, Charles. 1999. 'Le Jardin Cosmique. Considérations anthropologiques sur le paysage en Asie'. *Aséanie* 3: 13–26.

Mao, Youquan. 1991. 'Hani Titian Wenhua Lun' [The Hani Terrace Culture]. *Nongye Kaogu* [*Agricultural Archeology*], Kunming: Yunnan Daxue Chubanshe [Yunnan University Press].

Shimpei, Adachi. 2007. 'Agricultural Technologies of Terraced Rice Cultivation in the Ailao Mountains, Yunnan, China'. *Asian and African Area Studies* 6 (2): 173–96.

Stein, Rolph A. 1987. *Le monde en petit. Jardins en miniature et habitations dans la pensée religieuse d'Extrême Orient*. Paris: Flammarion.

Wang, Qinghua. 1999. *Titian Wenhualun* [*The Rice Terrace Culture*]. Kunming: Yunnan Daxue Chubanshe [Yunnan University Press].

Yuanyang Xianzhi Bianxie Weiyuanhui [Editorial Committee of General Gazetteer of Yuanyang County]. 2000. *Yuanyang Xianzhi* [*Gazetteer of Yuanyang County*], Guiyang: Guizhou Minzu Chubanshe [Guizhou Minorities Press].

The Sacred Confluence, Between Nature and Culture

Chiara Letizia

A Brahman boy undergoes the *vratabandha* initiation at the confluence of the Kālī Gaṇḍakī and Trisulī Gaṇḍakī rivers in Dev Ghāṭ, Tanahun District, Nepal (Photo: Chiara Letizia)

I wish to thank Silvia Vignato and Nicola Gasbarro for reading a previous version of this chapter, and Marie Lecomte-Tilouine for giving me the opportunity to contribute to this volume.

In India as well as in Nepal, holy sites (*tīrtha*: literally 'ford')[1] are typically located at a source of water, along the bank or at the confluence of rivers.

At these *tīrthas*, great pilgrimages, called *melā*, take place. Pilgrims bathe in a holy river not only to obtain purification from sins or to acquire merits in the hope of having a better rebirth, but also to cross the ocean of existence and to free themselves forever from the chain of rebirths.

Among the *tīrthas*, the confluence of rivers is deemed to be particularly significant; in general, scholars state that it has additional power.[2] J. Ensink (1974: 62) remarks:

> It may be said that bathing at the meeting point of two rivers is believed to be much more meritorious than at just any point in the course of river. The confluence seems more than to double the effect of the bath.

Others scholars have noted in the same way that, as rivers are considered holy entities, at the meeting point of two streams, the 'sacredness' of the first river adds to that of the second one. The confluence seems to have a sort of 'additive fame' or 'cumulative nature' because it gives pilgrims the opportunity to bathe in two rivers at the same time.[3]

Some years ago,[4] I studied holy sites located at the confluence of rivers in Nepal. In particular, I conducted fieldwork by spending short periods on several occasions at three famous pilgrimage sites: Dev Ghāṭ at the confluence of the Kālī Gaṇḍakī

---

[1] On *tīrthas*, see Eck (1981).
[2] Jacques (1960: 165, 178) writes that the sacredness of each adds up and two *tīrtha* are more sacred than one. According to him, this is the reason why confluences of rivers are particularly 'sacred': they accumulate the 'purifying power' of the two rivers.
[3] See Spera (1977), Bharati (1963) and Eck (1983: 293-4).
[4] This chapter is based on fieldwork conducted between 2001-03 for a doctoral research in History of Religions dealing with sacred confluences of rivers in Nepal, funded by the Department of History of Religions at the University of Rome La Sapienza.

and the Trisulī in Tanahun District; Ridī Ghāṭ at the confluence of the Kālī Gaṇḍakī and the Riḍī Kholā in Gulmi District; and Varāhakṣetra, at the confluence of the Kośi and the Kokā in Sunsari District (Letizia 2003).

Pilgrimages at these confluences consist of a large gathering of different castes and ethnic groups. Each group is connected to the site through specific myths, by worshipping different deities or by performing a ritual that differs from others in terms of its timing, the officiating persons or the type of offering made.

These places are not only charged with symbolic significance, but also have political and economic importance: they are also centres for trade and exchanges. A pilgrimage is also a fair (*melā*) where people come to buy and sell their products. Indeed, in the past, the most important rivers in Nepal were trading routes connecting Tibet and India. In addition, the rivers of the three confluences that I have studied form the administrative boundaries of current Nepalese districts; rivers were formerly used to divide the land, and confluences often used as the boundaries of ancient kingdoms and sites where kings met to sign treaties.[5]

During my fieldwork, I interviewed pilgrims from different castes and groups who had gathered at the *melā* celebrated at the confluence, as well as the ascetics and renouncers living on these holy sites, and the Brahmans officiating at the temple located near the confluence. I recorded various local stories and mythologies establishing the importance of the sites, as well as the beliefs associated with particular locations at the *tīrthas*. I also took into account the local pilgrimage guides and ritual handbooks, which included local stories but also linked themselves to the Great Tradition present in Indian epics and in the Puranas.

Far from being only a Nepalese phenomenon, these holy places take their inspiration from the great *tīrthas* celebrated in Hindu texts. For example, in the list of sacred sites enumerated

---

[5]The Dev Ghāṭ confluence served as a boundary to Makwanpur and the Tanahun kingdoms, and Riḍī's confluence was at the intersection between three ancient territories: Palpa, Gulmi and Grahon (Lecomte-Tilouine 2003: 175).

in the *Mahābhārata*, river confluences (*sangama*) are constantly mentioned. Among them, the most important is the confluence between the Gaṅgā and Yamunā rivers in Prayāga. This site is also called *triveṇī* ('three braids'); the third river is the mythical and invisible Sarasvatī, which flows underground into the Gaṅgā and the Yamunā. The merits obtained by bathing in this *triveṇī* are said to be even greater than those obtained from the performance of a Vedic ritual.[6]

Sacred places are especially celebrated in the texts called *Māhātmya* (literally 'glorifications'), which are part of the *Purāṇas*. The *Māhātmyas* tell the origin of pilgrimage, the manifestation of a God and the miracles that occurred. They provide a list of sites to visit, of the auspicious dates and of the merits to be earned. The *Māhātmyas* describe the benefits of making a pilgrimage: even the worst sins are cleansed at the same speed as a cotton bale catches fire; it is possible to earn a place in the deities' heaven; by performing certain rites, one's ancestors and descendants are saved and those who die in the *tīrthas* are never reborn.

The analysis of these texts and the data resulting from the fieldwork I conducted in Nepal have allowed me to consider sacred places from different perspectives which can be summarized as follows: the confluence of rivers, and in fact every *tīrtha*, appears to be a place of intersection and exchange between the different components of the universe, and thus a place of continuous cultural construction through the ritual. In this chapter, I will attempt to describe some general features of these 'sacred' sites and will try to look at these features from a nature/culture-category perspective.

My considerations start from the premise that Western categories of nature and culture are not easily generalized. An analysis of the features of the *tīrthas* reveals a complex network of correspondences (connecting the human life cycle, the human

---

[6]'The man that bathes at the confluence of the Gaṅgā and the Yamunā, obtains the merit of ten horse-sacrifices, and also rescues his race' *Mahābhārata, Vana Parva* I–LXXXIV (trans. Ganguli 1970: 185).

and divine body, and the physical and imagined landscape) which blurs the nature/culture opposition. The study of *tirthas* entails a third pole situated between nature and culture, that is 'sacredness', which I consider here as a mediating concept between nature and culture, i.e. a way—a Western culture's way—of emphasizing the intersection between natural and cultural space.

In this chapter, I try to focus on the construction process of what is referred to as 'sacred', and this allows me to reflect on some categories used in religious studies.

The general remarks on *tīrthas* that follow may appear more like a survey of the common features one can find in the *śāstras* than a presentation of the local practices observed during fieldwork. This should not be misconstrued as disregard for empirical observation. Indeed, I agree with Axel Michaels (1990: 136) when he writes that the pilgrims' degree of familiarity with Sanskrit myths, which are meant to explain the holiness of a particular temple, tends to be limited. According to him, what is important in the veneration of the sacred sanctuary is 'the element of ritual: i.e., the formalized performance of acts by means of which the divine order is quite literally given concrete embodiment, without there being any necessity that the individual himself is aware of the inner mythological meaning of those acts'. For this reason, he affirms:

> it is necessary to examine not only the esoteric laudatory glorifications of the grandeur of a temple, but also the associated performative aspects, i.e. the pilgrims themselves, the priests who guide them and the ritual specialists, as well the sites which these individuals seek out and the rituals they celebrate there. All this affords more conclusive empirical data on the religious and social axioms of a place of pilgrimage than the often so uniform *Māhātmya*s and *Sthala Purāṇa*s.

Moreover, during my fieldwork, I noticed that local rituals and explanations were often more meaningful to pilgrims (that is, bearing more influence on their practices) than the parallel references to the so-called Great Tradition one could find in ritual handbooks.[7]

Thus, I do not believe that an analysis of a sacred place should rely simply on transcendental and non-empirical categories. On the contrary, I agree with William Sax (2003: 193) that 'sacred' aspects of central Himalayan religious cults cannot be understood without taking practices into account and that the sacred has to be understood in terms of society, politics, kinship and territory.

In fact, my attempt here is to propose, in the field of religious studies, a perspective that does not ignore the specifically religious dimension of sacred places, but at the same time, avoids considering 'the sacred' as an ontological category; seeing it rather like the results of a construction process. Although this is now considered to be a common assumption for the anthropologist when referring to the Durkheimian notion of the sacred, in human and social sciences both concepts of 'religion' and 'sacred' are still used (sometimes unconsciously) in their theological and reified sense; the danger of such usage has been demonstrated by Strenski (1993) and Fitzgerald (2000).[8]

Let me now turn to the description of the distinct, yet interrelated general features of the *tīrthas* I studied.

Holy Sites: A Symbolic Net

Since a confluence of rivers is more meaningful for the pilgrim than a simple river, it is common for a *tīrtha* to be said to have

---

[7] As Daniela Berti (2003) also argues, people tend to see their past much more through local markers than is sometimes assumed, given their will to refer also to pan-Indian epics.

[8] It seems difficult to generalize a category by analyzing a culture where a corresponding term is not found. As Axel Michaels (2003:13) points out 'in Sanskrit, "sacred" does not correspond to a single term. Equivalents of "sacred" could be *punya, pavitra* (as well as *śuddha* or *śuci*), *mangala, daiva, pūjya/pūjārha* or *vaidika*, all denoting sacredness plus other aspects: merit, purity, auspiciousness, divinity, worship or the Veda'.

an underground secret river that flows into it when there is no confluence, in order to enhance its holiness. This also happens when there is already a confluence, in order to further increase its value. Not all confluences are sacred, but almost all holy places tend to proclaim the existence of confluences thanks to an underground river-net. Therefore, the Indian and Nepalese geography is considerably transformed and the Ganges can be found in the most unexpected places, even at the smallest most remote pilgrimage places in Nepal.

In Nepal, confluences are a special category characterized by specific effective action. However, this efficacy is not linked to its natural aspect, because every *tīrtha* can easily become a confluence, as is recounted in many stories.[9] According to the Nepalese water cosmology, all the *tīrthas* are connected through a net of terrestrial, celestial and mythical channels; not only are the different rivers in the Kathmandu Valley connected to each other, but they also join the most well-known Indian rivers (Slusser 1982: 350–54).

Thanks to this system of connections, each single stream can turn into a sacred confluence and be extolled by local tradition in its wider grandeur, linking it with the sacred geography of high tradition. For example, Paśupatināth, the most important *tīrtha* in the Kathmandu Valley, is said to be a confluence of three rivers (*triveṇī*) on the pattern of the Indian Prayāga. People in Deopatan say that three rivers converge at the eastern stairs of Paśupatināth at the Āryaghāt: the Bāgmatī, the holy water of the temple itself and the subterraneous Sarasvatī (Michaels 1990: 134).

The river net is conceived as an underground system that links every *tīrtha* into an immense confluence. The existence of this underground net explains why the texts assert that millions of

[9]For instance, it is said that an underground and invisible river is 'invited', or created by a Goddess to make the confluence. See for example Barré *et al.* (1981: 48–53).

other *tīrthas* flow into a single *tīrtha* and that to bathe in it allows the pilgrim to bathe in all of them.[10] For instance, Varanasi is considered to be the confluence of all Indian *tīrthas*. According to some *Purāṇas*, all Indian *tīrthas* have two forms: a gross and tangible form in their own physical location and a subtle and invisible form in Varanasi (Eck 1983: 283 and 1991: 294).

This concentration of rivers is not of great importance *per se*; what is important is the positive effect it has on the pilgrims, the great amount of merit it grants them.

If all rivers can become a confluence, the natural place called 'confluence' loses its clear and definable borders; however, apart from its natural *objectivity*, the idea of confluence is well defined and has a clear function: it is a concept that creates sacredness, that is able to confer meaning to some places and to situate them in relation to time and to connect them with other aspects of culture (life-cycle rites, death, relationships with ancestors and so on).

Tīrthas are not isolated; even those found in the most remote area of the Himalayas are conceived as part of a whole frame of reference and meaning that constitutes an interconnected landscape based on invisible but no less actual connections. As Eck (1998) has shown, the landscape of pilgrimage places has been used in order to create a complex system of reference at local, regional and national levels. The recognition of *tīrthas* in pilgrimage places is one of the models of meaning that has produced the Indian and Nepalese symbolic landscape. The landscape is conceived as a thick net of intertwining lines; *tīrthas* are the most visible points on this net: like knots of the threads that make this net. In my opinion, the importance of the confluences of rivers stems from the fact that they are the natural and tangible expressions of this symbolic net.

[10] In the Aranyaka Parvan of the Mahābhārata, it is said: 'In Prayāga there are hundred million and ten thousand *tīrthas*' (LXXXIII, trans Ganguli: 79) and: 'All the *tīrthas* of the world are found in Naimisha' (LXXXII, idem: 55).

The notion of landscape mentioned above seems to have the features of what J. Bonnemaison (1990), in a remarkable article on the social and territorial organization of the Melanesian island of Tanna, calls a 'reticulate space', a networked territorial system perceived as a composite of centres each of which relates to the other. This space is not structured by limits, but rather by knots that are tied to form a tissue of nexus. Each knot can be seen as a fraction of the whole, and at the same time, reflects the whole; in a certain way, each part is also a centre, an absolute but not limited place. In Tanna mythology, this kind of space originates from the pieces of a giant's corpse which were thrown away and, wherever they fell, gave birth to a centre or, to use a Melanesian expression, a 'heart'. The 'organic ontology' or the body metaphor is also found in the case of Indian and Nepalese sacred places.

Tīrthas and the Body

During my fieldwork in Prayaga, I recorded the words of an Indian pilgrim, as follows: 'India is like a body and *tīrthas* are its *cakra*', he said. 'The pilgrims who move from one *tīrtha* to the other allow energy to flow within this body.'

Pilgrimage guides, when describing the ritual journey from one *tīrtha* to the other, use the metaphor of the body to express the interrelationship between all the *tīrthas*. They describe the *tīrthas* as the head, the heart and the feet of a huge divine body extending horizontally. For example, Parry (1981) reports that the region of Eastern Uttar Pradesh and Bihar is represented as a body with its head in the holy confluence of Prayāga, its chest in Varanasi and its feet in Gaya.

Nepal itself is symbolically conceived as the space between the holy rivers Sapta Gaṇḍakī in the West and Sapta Kośi in the East; a myth recounts that these rivers originated respectively from the sweat of the right and left side of the body of the Goddess Pārvatī while she was practising a very hard ascesis.[11] As M.

[11] *Himavant khaṇḍa* 44, pp. 1–80 quoted in Lecomte-Tilouine (2003: 174).

Lecomte-Tilouine (2003: 174) points out, this myth evokes the image of a huge Goddess standing over the Nepalese land, one of her legs extending towards the East and the other one towards the West. During her ascesis, her sweat creates the Nepalese river system.

One myth concerning the origin of the confluence of Ridī says that Viṣṇu, impressed by the penitence of the young Ruru, promised her that her body would become the most important pilgrimage place in the world and would be named after her: Ruru Kṣetra.[12] As the *pūjāri* of Hrishikesh temple told me, Ridī's confluence is also conceived as Viṣṇu's body. The valley is surrounded by high hills; for 'those who are able to see', these hills are actually the heads of the mythic Snake *Śeṣa Nāga*, holding Viṣṇu's sleeping body in the cosmic ocean.

The holy places on the Kālī Gaṇḍakī River are also often described in the texts as parts of Viṣṇu's body in his four-armed form: his head is Muktināth (Kālī Gaṇḍakī's source), his heart is Ridī and the feet of the God are Dev Ghāṭ.[13]

The most meaningful example of the use of the body metaphor is the tantric notion of pilgrimage place called *pīṭha*, the seat of the Goddess (Sircar 1973; Tiwari 1985). The myth that links all the *pīṭhas* together tells us that Śiva, in despair after the death of his wife Satī, starts a furious dance across the universe, carrying Satī's body on his back. In order to prevent the destruction of the universe, Viṣṇu throws his *cakra* and dismembers Satī's corpse; the *pīṭhas* are the places where the limbs of the goddess's body fell on the ground.

This myth echoes deeply in Nepal, where temples and pilgrimage places that define themselves as the tooth, the foot or the *yonī* of Satī are found everywhere. The notion of a set of sacred sites distributed over a territory and related one to one to the parts of the body of a supernatural being is not only limited to the *pīṭhas*: throughout my fieldwork, I encountered the

---

[12] I have been told this myth by pilgrims and *pūjāris*; it is also cited by the local ritual handbook, the *Ridīkṣetra Māhātmya* (Saraswati 2045 VS).

[13] See *Devghāṭ Māhātmya* (Paudel 2055 VS; Mudral 2055 VS).

mythological and ritual theme of the body (of a king, of an ascetic) becoming a stone and then embedding itself in the landscape to constitute the sacred place.[14]

According to Bharati (1965), the equation between pilgrimage and the mystic body is due to the influence of tantrism. He describes the homology of the geographical site with an 'organ' in the mystical body of the tantric devotee. D. White (1996) noted that a number of tantric works present the subtle body in the form of pilgrimage guides; these guides are all the more remarkable for the fact that the pilgrim in question is a Goddess, and the sites are at once the sacred *pīthas* of India (identified with the body parts of the Goddess herself) and loci *within* the Goddess's body. The nature of such pilgrimages, of a being within its own body, which is at the same time the body of the (Hindu sacred) universe, seems to be taken for granted in many texts. What are at first sight geographical locations in the 'real world' turn out to be sites within the subtle body.

The references to rivers and to natural places are meaningful only if looked at from the perspective of the subtle body and vice versa. From this perspective, the confluence of rivers takes on a new meaning. According to a common place in Hatha yoga and Tantras, the subtle body has subtle channels of vital energy (*nādī*) and nodal points (*cakra*).[15] These are situated along the spine and the energy of *prāṇā* and *kuṇḍalini* flows through them. The three main subtle channels of vital energy (*pingala*, *īḍā* and central *suṣumnā*), are identified as the three rivers of the famous

---

[14]In Riḍī Ghāṭ and Dev Ghāṭ, people tell many stories about King Mani Mukunda Sen who turned himself into stone after his death; I also observed the cult of stones kept in temples and believed to be pieces of the body of this king (See also Lecomte-Tilouine 2003: 182). Here, the corpse of a king, made of *śāligrām*—the stones representing Viṣṇu itself—replaces the corpse of Satī. Nick Allen (1981) reports the Thulung Rai myth narrating how the pieces of the body of Mapa Raja, having fallen on the ground, turned into stone and then became sacred Bhume places; he compares this myth to the Indian myth of Satī.

[15]See S. Gupta, J.D. Hoens and T. Goudriaan (1979); Padoux 2002.

confluence of Prayāga: *pingala* is Yamuna, *īḍā* is Ganga, and *suṣumnā* is identified as the invisible Sarasvati.[16] The inner journey is described as a pilgrimage of the ascetic and his own breath, *prāṇā*, is his vehicle. The channels through which the air flows are conceived as rivers each with its own *tīrthas*. As Varenne (1976: 198-199) writes: 'The breath is conceived as making a pilgrimage from *tīrtha* to *tīrtha* just as worshippers do on earth. And just as those worshippers bathe themselves in the waters of the sacred fords, so the breath is bathed in the water of the inward *tīrthas*'.

The Confluence: Reality versus Illusion

When I asked the ascetics who live at Dev Ghāṭ about the importance of the holy site they had elected as their residence, they told me that the actual reality of the confluence does not appear to the bodily eyes: only 'those who do not know' limit themselves to the natural aspect of reality. They said that during the festival of Māgh sankrānti, Gods come to Dev Ghāṭ with their bodies of wind and fire, bathe and then go back to heaven. Some ascetics are able to listen to the sound of the Gods as they come to bathe: it is as light and sweet as music. There are three kinds of eyes, those of the body, those of *dharma* and the celestial ones (*dibya*), without the last two eyes, it is impossible to grasp the reality of the confluence and to see that when the two rivers meet at the confluence of Dev Ghāṭ, an underground river is created. This vision of *tīrthas* is based on the concept that the natural world is *Māyā*, a simple illusion; it is impossible to grasp reality with the body's eyes; as the ascetics of Dev Ghāṭ say, in order to reach the reality behind the veil of *Māyā* and to investigate this mystery, one has to dig into the sacred texts and to practice ascesis and meditation.

[16]This identification is found in the Śiva Samhitā. The confluence of the three rivers in Prayāga is considered in this text as a place in the human body (Morinis 1984: 294). For the *nādīs*, see Briggs (1982: chap. 15).

According to the Buddhist Tantra, mention of the names of places called *kṣetra*, *pīṭha* and *tīrtha* is only intended for foolish people who wander across the country. Actually, they are places within the body or, rather, they are the outer (exterior) equivalent of the body's inner reality.[17]

The Relationship between *Tīrthas* and Death

The *tīrthas* are connected to death in the broadest sense of the word. First of all, the *tīrthas* are ideal places to go and die; death, which is feared everywhere else, is welcomed there as a long-expected guest, because dying there brings liberation. Many old devotees stay in the sacred places and await their death. They look after the temples and the *ghāṭs*; they are convinced that whoever dies there will be free from rebirth.

Since dying in these places is considered to be good fortune, it is easy to understand that one of the ways to ensure that death will come there is to come to terms with it personally. In the *Mahābhārata*, it is explicitly said: 'O child, let not the texts of the Veda, nor the opinions of men dissuade thy mind from the desire of dying at Prayāga.'[18] Suicide in the sacred waters at the confluence of Prayāga has been practised in India since as early as the 7th century AD.[19]

The *tīrthas* are also the right sites for funerals and for rites to be performed for one's ancestors. The dead are cremated there. They offer themselves as offerings of the last sacrifice in the cremation fire—thanks to which they start their journey towards the world of ancestors. This sacrifice will be completely fulfilled through another rite that takes place at the *tīrtha*: the *śrāddha*. The *śrāddha* aims at transforming the wandering 'bad' spirit of

---

[17]Saraswati (1983: 50) and Snellgrove (1959: chapter X, 2–5).
[18]*Mahābhārata, Vana Parva*, LXXXV (trans. Ganguli 1970: 194–5).
[19]See Chattopadhyaya (1937: 65–79); Watters (1904, I: 362); Beal (1906, I: 232–4).

the dead (*preta*) into a 'father', a benevolent ancestor who lives among other ancestors in the world devoted to them. To achieve this transformation, the dead have to acquire a body and need food, which is offered to them during the rite.[20] Thus, the *tīrtha* is not only the place to go and die, but also the site for ritually communicating with and for breaking away from the world of the dead; on the one hand, the dead are nourished and worshipped, in a mutual exchange of favours, and on the other hand, they are accompanied and given over forever to the place they deserve. There they lose their individuality to become benevolent ancestors; the dead are abandoned to the river in a symbolic and material sense: their families bid them farewell by abandoning their clothes to the river.

Relationship to Auspicious Astrological Dates

At every pilgrimage centre, there is a privileged moment that is more beneficial than any other and a date in particular is constantly repeated in the texts: the *makara sankrānti*. *Sankrānti* is the name given to the entry of the sun in any sign or constellation of the zodiac (*rāśi*). The *makara sankrānti* (or *māgh sankranti*) marks the entry of the sun in the *makara*, the sign that is equivalent to our Capricorn, which marks the beginning of the winter.[21] The passage of the sun from one sign (*rāśi*) to the other is the most auspicious moment to bathe in the *tīrtha*, which is the crossing *par excellence*, since *tīrtha* in Sanskrit literally means 'ford'. It is noteworthy that, in this way, bathing in the *tīrtha* is an act of passage, of crossing through the river, which repeats or emphasizes the celestial passages. The exact moment the sun leaves a *rāśi* and enters into the following one is said to be infinitesimally small and impossible to perceive with 'eyes of flesh' (ordinary human eyes). The great attention given to precisely calculating this moment in order to situate it on the

[20]See Kane (1953: section III chapter IX).
[21]Kane (1962: section I, chapter XI).

calendar reveals the major importance given to the coincidence of the terrestrial passage with the celestial one.

As previously pointed out, the *tīrtha* is a 'good place to die', and the date of the *makara saṅkrānti* is a 'good time to die' there. This date marks the beginning of the journey of the sun northwards, in the auspicious direction (*uttarāyana*),[22] and in the *Mahābhārata* (Bhīṣma *Parva*), the *uttarāyana* is called the best moment to leave life. Bhīṣma, wounded by Arjuna's arrows, notices that the sun is still pursuing its southwards journey (*dakṣiṇāyana*). He decides not to die in this unfavourable moment, but to remain on his bed of arrows until the sun changes its direction towards the north.

Space and Time in *Tīrtha*

The space of the *tīrtha*, called *kṣetra*, has a unique set of qualities. By entering it, the pilgrim reaches a place where the rules are different: castes can mix without contamination, monstrous crimes such as the killing of a Brahman can be forgiven, suicide is not a sin and death does not bring rebirth.[23] Any action conducted here is greatly enhanced: pure actions produce larger fruits than anywhere else and the effects of sins are amplified and become unforgivable.[24]

The space of the *tīrtha* is the space for ritual action *par excellence* and particularly for rituals marking the stages of life: at the

[22] For the two halves of the year, see Gaborieau (1982: 11–29).

[23] At holy places, the ground is not contaminated by incurring contact with untouchable persons and there is no question of untouchables and contamination when bathing in holy waters, says the *Brihaspati Purāṇa* (Kane 1953: 570); in the *Kūrma Purāṇa* and *Liṅga Purāṇa* it is said that by merely residing in a *tīrtha* not only does a man become free from the great sin of a brāhmaṇa murder, but from the never-ending cycle of births and deaths and he is not born again (*ibid.* 566); while the Dharmaśāstra generally condemn suicide as a great sin, religious suicide is allowed at the confluence of the two great rivers Gaṅgā and Yamunā and at some other *tīrthas* (*ibid.* 604).

[24] Parry (1981: 346).

three river confluences I visited, devotees of all castes and groups gather not only for cremations and rituals associated with their ancestors, as I have already mentioned, but also for the celebration of initiation rituals of young boys, like the tonsure ceremony celebrated by the Rais, or the *Vratabandha* celebrated by all 'twice-born' Hindus.

Entering into the *tīrtha* entails a shift to a non-conventional timeframe, a non-historical time. In fact, it is believed that the *tīrtha* will survive the universal dissolution that occurs at the end of each cosmic cycle. Some texts provide a concrete image of this, stating for example that the *tīrthas* of Varanasi and Prayāga will be lifted upwards, like an umbrella, above the universal conflagration.[25] Even the origins of Varanasi and Prayāga are situated before the beginning of time. The *tīrtha* is a natural place suspended in time and space, free from the historical cycles and of the never-ending cycles of death and rebirth, creation and cosmic dissolution.

Bathing in a *Tīrtha* as a Multiple Action

If we take into account all the features mentioned above, the pilgrim who goes to bathe on Māgh *sankrānti* in a *tīrtha*, performs a multiple action: he travels, simultaneously, within himself and along a path inside an immense divine body lying on the land; he is also bathing himself in many other *tīrthas* which are mystically present in the place where he actually finds himself. Moreover, he bathes during the passage of the sun to a different zodiacal sign, which also marks the passage to the auspicious half of the year. This will allow him to ford from human existence to liberation. The entire path of the man, the relationship between life and death, the relationship between the living and his ancestors, the spatial and temporal recognition of a place through a ritual act: all these levels of signification are involved by

---

[25]See Parry (1981) and Dubey (2000: 4), quoting the *Matsya Purāṇa* 110.3–4.

immersion in the *tīrtha*. By dying (literally, passing away) in this place, and thus enacting in his personal existence a perfect connection between a spatial passage (*tīrtha*=ford) and a temporal passage (*sankrānti* = passage of the sun), the pilgrim will complete the circle and, after the last life-cycle ritual, he will ford the river of *samsara* to the far shore beyond birth and death.

Reflections on Nature and Culture

I would like to now propose some reflections on the characteristics of the sacred places that I have just described. These considerations originate from an attempt to understand what kind of relation exists between the Western 'nature versus culture' opposition and the Nepali *prakritik-samskritik* opposition.

Comparative history of religions prompts us to think over our nature/culture categories and the possibility of generalizing them especially in connection with sacredness. The study of river confluences in Nepal has shown—in total opposition to the epiphany of the sacred proposed by Mircea Eliade—that a quality of *a priori* sacredness does not exist.[26] The sacredness of confluences in Nepal does not appear to me as something intrinsic to the place, but rather as a product of ritual actions performed there.[27]

---

[26] For a historical perspective on 'the sacred', see de Martino (1957) and Massenzio (1994). As Sax (2003:193) pointed out, if the sacred is an important dimension of cults and processions to sacred places, the term 'sacred' can and must be understood in the context of human practice, rather then as a transcendental category.

[27] During my fieldwork in Ridī, I did not find any intrinsic sacredness in the confluence. What I found instead was a place *made sacred*, or better, made special by the ritual actions and the meditation of some mythical actors, actions that are repeated by ascetics living in the place and who continue to make this place sacred. In a similar way, Michaels writes: 'Likewise holy places, including mountains, are generally discovered in that they show or make visible, where a miracle has happened or where a holy person has settled down. If I'm not mistaken, there is not even a word for holy

Leaving aside these considerations, it seems more important to understand the process of constructing sacredness itself. When I speak of the sacredness of a confluence, I mean a place which receives significance and value thanks to a series of rules and prescriptions and, in particular, thanks to the performance of a precise ritual in a given space and at a given time. As a result of these ritual prescriptions, this place is no longer just any section of space, but one that is specifically marked.

Of course, if a given confluence can be more sacred than another given space, it is because such a confluence is a meeting point, a particular intersection of a landscape. It serves as a reference point, which helps to define a given space because its natural characteristics immediately lend themselves to signify a series of semantic oppositions, which refer to a humanized milieu and to its separateness with respect to different realities (opposition such as heavenly-earthly, ground-underground, land-water, and so on) ... and so on[28]: a space interrupted by a confluence (or by a crossroads, phenomenologically similar to confluence) can be organized.

The same can also be said for time: constellations are reference points in the sky just as confluences are reference points on Earth. In the course of my fieldwork, I observed that one bathes at the confluences just when the sun enters a new constellation; before being a religious act, it is a cultural act—it is the spatial-temporal organization of a territory.

When I say that an *a priori* intrinsic quality of sacredness does not exist, I do not deny the fact that in the Nepalese conception of landscape, Gods inhabit rivers and the peaks of mountains, and that each place is divinized and assumes a meaning thanks

---

mountain in Tibetan (Dollfus 1996). The two terms in question, *yul lha* and *gnas ri*, indicate more: *gnas ri* means "power place" in general, on which especially a holy person has worked and which therefore attracts a lot of pilgrims; *yul lha* means literally "God (*lha*) of the country (*yul*)". Yul can be compared with the range of meanings the Sanskrit word *kṣetra* has, which denotes not only a country or region, but also a nation, state, area or field'(2003: 17). Here again, it is the action that produces the holy place.

[28] See Taviani (1990: 37–45).

to a myth of origin. The issue I am addressing here is the problem of the category of 'the sacred' that we use in order to define a natural space marked in a specific way, what I have defined above as a mediating concept between nature and culture, a Western culture's way of emphasizing the intersection between natural and cultural space. Above all, I intend to examine the problem of the construction process of what we call 'sacred space', which blurs the notion of nature, culture, and the notion of sacred itself.

My view is that, in the Nepalese and Indian context, this process takes place through ritual in three phases, as follows:

- The starting point is an empirical and natural base, a place that naturally marks a discontinuity in the landscape. A confluence is from a natural point of view a specific point in the flow of rivers, where such flow is perceived as the flow of existence; what I would call an 'empirical starting point'.
- Ritual, whose function is to give order to existence, confers symbolic values on this specific spatial base. Ritual therefore creates a visible social order, perceivable in nature.
- The spatial reference point is therefore also an existential reference point; I would say that it is the place of ritual rules. Ritual governs the flow of existence and projects the ritually-defined social order (caste, life-cycle rituals, kinship, politics, etc.) onto nature, inscribing such order in an immutable cosmology. Thus, social order becomes unchangeable.[29]

In the Western view, nature is the basis of culture, which transforms nature in order to build civilization.[30] It seems to

[29] Rules are not imagined or theorized, but rather *inscribed* in and then *practised* on the territory. I refer the reader again to the Melanesian Island of Tanna described by Bonnemaison (1990). It is not possible here to relate the complex system described by the author. I will limit myself to pointing out that the notion of kinship and the rules of marriage in Tanna are not understood in the abstract, but rather, lived and inscribed in the landscape. The very term used to indicate a lineage is 'traces on the road' and their marriage strategy is summarized in a very simple way by local people: one marries following one's road. Kinship classifications do not have a concrete meaning for them. Inhabitants of Tanna Island do not follow rules, but roads.

[30] As Staszak (1996) points out, the opposition between nature and culture (*phusis* vs. *nomos*) plays a crucial role in Greek thought. This opposition

me that in India and in Nepal, on the contrary, nature is the goal of a ritual dynamic,[31] which aims at the final legitimization of the signifying rules of culture. These rules are immutable because they are inscribed in nature, in the cosmic order in mythology and even in the physical body, both divine and human.

What I earlier called the 'empirical starting point' is therefore nullified by a *surplus* of meaning established by ritual rules. Instead of speaking of 'sacredness inscribed in nature', as phenomenological studies of religion have done, I would propose that we speak of a process which makes an order immutable.

Here, we do not actually see a static natural-visible versus cultural-invisible opposition, but a three-phase process that starts from the natural-empiric, that is funnelled through the cultural and then comes back to the natural. The process makes visible the invisible-cultural and immutable the order of culture.

Nature becomes what is meta-cultural and meta-historical, and ritually established. One cannot modify culturally and historically what ritual has made coincident with nature. Rather than sacredness inherent to nature, I would speak of a super-cultural and super-historical nature.

This order, which transcends nature and which, at the same time, is made natural and therefore immutable through the ritual,

---

was already well established around 430 BC. In the Hippocratic treaty 'Of air, of waters and of places' the word *phusis* is opposed to *nomos*. The term *phusis* can be defined in the negative: it indicates the power of what is not made by humans, what is external to and not dependent on them. *Phusis* is what is fixed, innate, given, anterior to and transcends humans. *Phusis* is the external world. On the other hand, *nomos* indicate what is built, made, and provisory; it is the result of human action, posterior and immanent to men.

[31] In this respect, I draw a parallel with Malamoud's discussion in this volume, about the (sacrificial) rite which precedes nature and society and determines them both. In his words, 'man does not perform sacrifice but rather deploys it: by performing certain ritual actions, one reveals an implicit sacrifice, and in doing so, prolongs and repeats an initial sacrifice, which corresponds in Vedic cosmology to the very act of creation of the world. ... *The rite reveals and deploys nature which is itself already pre-instituted by the founding sacrifice*' (italics are mine).

is appropriately expressed by the concept of dharma. Dharma is simultaneously the Universal Law, the cosmic order, and also just the single natural phenomenon and any non-descriptive, existing object. With the concept of Dharma, our distinction between nature and culture vanishes. Dharma is a meta-cultural and meta-historical ritually established nature, which not only cannot be modified, but with which any single living being must harmonize itself, following his personal dharma.

By equating Dharma with religion, we give it a cultural value, thus certainly not the meaning of 'nature'; but while I was translating teachings from a Nepalese Buddhist monk, I happened to write: 'What is the red chilli pepper's *dharma*? 'The red chilli pepper's *dharma* is being hot'. Dharma is a general principle; it is the 'ought' of everything. In the case of an object, it is its functioning and its function in teleological terms. This is also valid for men (culture) and the cosmic order (nature): the 'super naturalization' of meanings affects any order and level, even the chilli pepper. This structure, which for Western culture is natural, here is supernatural (*dharma*), because all ritual rules which give meaning and perspective to human action and natural events have become natural (or rather so deeply sunk in nature, that they identify with nature itself). Therefore, these rules become permanent and eternal from a ritual standpoint.

In Nepal and in India, nature has no value *per se*, because what is empirical and biological is included in cultural values through the concept of Dharma.[32] Empirical nature therefore is a veil, which hides what men have made of nature, i.e., its Dharma.

I am attempting here to see the notion of ritual as an identifying instrument of a thought that places the 'ought to be' ahead of the 'be' and makes the first the dimension of the second; just the opposite of western metaphysics. Ritual, first of all, establishes what ought to be done and what ought not to be done. Pilgrimage is a ritual tracking of the space of

---

[32] Das (1985) writes: 'Bodily experiences are themselves culturally defined and derive their meanings as *human* experiences from the cultural definition given to them. In this sense one may say that, at least for some purposes, nature is itself a construct of culture'.

existence and is therefore the paradigm of the ritual 'ought to be'.[33]

To conclude, let me come back to the case of river confluences and to the structure of the visible and invisible networks mentioned at the beginning. The pilgrimage to a sacred confluence is a consequence of the three-phase process stated above: the pilgrim goes to places which signify ritual rules until he transforms his own body in a sort of microcosm conceived as an image of the macrocosm. Without this transformation, there is no purification.[34] The real purification is to impress in one's own body the social order's structure, which has become a natural order.[35]

I would add as a final comment, that if there is a geography of sacred sites, this happens not because nature is sacred *per se*, but because ritual, at least here, transforms it into the perfect social and cosmic order, thus inventing an original geography of meaning to make the social sense of history unalterable.

---

[33] It is perhaps for this reason that pilgrimage is often used to fix or to reassert some points that the community or the subject feels to be crucial. I am thinking, for example, of the patriotic pilgrimages organized by the militant Hindu right-wing—and the video of propaganda that followed—in order to create, elaborate and visualize their idea of *'hindutva'* (hinduness), as described by Brosius (2004). I am also thinking of the pilgrimages of the divine kings of Rawain to Kedarnath and Badrinath described by William Sax. He remarks that 'pilgrimage is a declaration of orthopraxy, in effect an undertaking to renounce certain objectionable practices. It also functions as a means of encouraging orthopraxy'(2003: 193).

[34] Amado (1971: 197–215) writes that during the ritual bath in the Ganges (*snāna*), the devotee immerses himself in the water thrice: the first time, he recites a *mantra* to leave his physical body; the second time he recites another *mantra* to leave his subtle body; during the third immersion he will feel in his mind the sound of a *bīja* (the seed syllable of a *mantra*) and he shall be free of his causal body. In some way, he 'dies' in the water, or in the terms I propose here, integrates himself in the Order inscribed in the 'holy' river.

[35] Similarly, in Ridī, devotees believe that the ashes thrown in the water of the holy confluence after cremation will turn into *śaligrāms*, the black stones inside some fossils, usually ammonites, seen as the manifestation of *Viṣṇu's cakra*. Here the powerful effect of the confluence seems to transform the body in the (sacred) nature.

Thus, instead of talking of natural places made sacred by culture, I propose that we should think of such places as being full of meaning given by ritual action intended to bring order to the flow of existence.

References

Allen, N. 1981. 'The Thulung Myth of the Bhume Sites and some Indo-Tibetan Comparisons'. In C. Von Fürer-Haimendorf ed. *Asian Highlands Societies in anthropological perspective.* New Delhi:Sterling. pp. 168–82.

Amado, P. 1971. 'Le bain dans le Gange: sa signification'. *Bulletin de l'École Française d'Extrême-Orient* LVIII: 197–212.

Barré, V. et al. 1981. *Panauti, une ville au Népal.* Paris: Berger-Levrault Architectures.

Beal, S. 1906. *Si-Yu-Ki, Buddhist Records of the Western World, translated from the Chinese of Hiuen Tsiang.* London: Kegan Paul, 2 vols.

Berti, D. 2003. 'Epics, Local History and Electoral Politics in the Indian Himalayas'. Paper presented at the international meeting 'Past as the Present. A Discourse on South Asian Society', organized by C. Servan-Schreiber and B. Narayan, 29–30 October in Paris, EHESS.

Bhandari, K. 2058 VS (2001). *Śrī Varāhakṣetra Darśan.* Varahakshetra Dham.

Bharati, A. 1963. 'Pilgrimage in the Indian Tradition'. *History of Religions* 3(1): 135–67.

____ 1965. *The Tantric Tradition.* Delhi: B.I. Publications.

Bonnemaison, J. 1989. 'L'espace réticulé. Commentaires sur l'idéologie géographique'. In *Tropiques, Lieux et liens. Florilège offert à Gilles Sauter et Paul Pélissier.* Paris: ORSTOM. pp. 500–10.

Briggs, G.W. 1982 [First edition 1938]. *Gorakhnāth and the Kānphata Yogīs.* Delhi: Motilal Banarsidass.

Brosius, C. 2003. 'Mappare il corpo della nazione. Le processioni territoriali nei video di propaganda della destra indù'. In D. Berti and G. Tarabout eds. *Terra, Territorio e Società nel Mondo Indiano, Etnosistemi* 10: 130–44.

Chattopadhyaya, K.C. 1937. 'Religious Suicide at Prayaga'. *Journal of the Uttar Pradesh Historical Society* 10: 65–79.

Das, V. 1985. 'Paradigms of Body Symbolism: An Analysis of Selected Themes in Hindu Culture'. In R. Burghart and A. Cantlie eds. *Indian Religion*. London: Curzon Press. pp. 180–207.

De Martino, E. 1957. 'Storicismo ed irrazionalismo nella storia delle religioni'. *Studi e Materiali di Storia delle Religioni* 28 (1): 89–107.

Dubey, D.P. ed. 2000. *Pilgrimage Studies. The Power of Sacred Places.* Allahabad: The Society of Pilgrimage Studies.

Dollfus, P. 1996. 'No sacred mountains in Central Ladakh?' In A.M. Blondeau and E. Steinkellner eds. *Reflections of the Mountain. Essays on the History and Social Meaning of the Mountain Cult in Tibet and the Himalaya*. Vienna: Verlag der Österreichischen Akademie der Wissenschaften. pp. 2–17.

Eck, D.L. 1981. 'Indian Tīrthas. Crossings in Sacred Geography'. *History of Religions* 20 (4): 323–44.

_____ 1983. *Banaras, City of Light*. New Delhi: Penguin Books India.

_____ 1991. 'Kashi: City of all India'. In T.N. Madan ed. *Religion in India*. New Delhi: Oxford University Press. pp. 138–55.

_____ 1998. 'The Imagined Landscape. Patterns in the Constructions of Hindu Sacred Geography'. In V. Das, D. Gupta and P. Uberoi eds. *Tradition, Pluralism and Identity. In Honour of T.N. Madan. Contributions to Indian Sociology Occasional Studies* 8: 23–45.

Ensink, J. 1974. 'Problems of the Study of Pilgrimage in India'. *Indologica Taurinensia* 2: 57–79.

Fitzgerald, T. 2000. *The Ideology of Religious Studies*. New York, Oxford: OUP.

Gaborieau, M. 1982. 'Les fêtes, les temps et l'espace: Structure du calendrier hindou dans sa version indo-népalaise'. *L'Homme* 22 (3): 11–29.

Gupta, S.D., J. Hoens, and T. Goudriaan. 1979. *Hindu Tantrism*. Leiden: Brill.

Jacques, C. 1960. 'Les pèlerinages en Inde'. In *Les pèlerinages: Égypte ancienne, Israël, Islam, Perse, Inde, Tibet, Indonésie, Madagascar, Chine, Japon*. Collection Sources Orientales 3. Paris: Seuil. pp. 157–97.

Kane, P.V. 1953. *History of Dharmaśāstra: Ancient and Mediaeval Religious and Civil Law in India*, vol. IV, Poona: Bhandarkar Oriental Research Institute.

_____ 1962. *History of Dharmaśāstra: Ancient and Mediaeval Religious and Civil Law in India*, vol. V, Poona: Bhandarkar Oriental Research Institute.

Letizia, C. 2003. 'Le confluenze sacre dei fiumi in Nepal' [The sacred river confluences in Nepal]. PhD. thesis, Rome University.
Lecomte-Tilouine, M. 2003. 'Le paysage népalais, exégèse et appropriation du pays'. In J. Smadja ed. *Histoire et devenir des paysages en Himalaya*. Paris: CNRS Éditions. pp. 165-92.
Massenzio, M. 1994. *Sacro ed identità etnica. Senso del mondo e linea di confine*. Milano: FrancoAngeli.
The Mahābhārata, K.M. Ganguli trans. 1970 [First edition 1883-1896]. New Delhi: Munshiram Manoharlal, 12 vols.
Michaels, A. 1990. 'Pilgrimage and Priesthood at the Paśupatinātha temple of Deopatan (Nepal)'. In H. Bakker ed. *The History of Sacred Places in India as Reflected in Traditional Literature*. Leiden: E.J. Brill. pp. 131-59.
_____ 2003. 'The Sacredness of (Himalayan) Landscapes'. In N. Gutschow, A. Michaels, C. Ramble, E. Steinkellner eds. *Sacred Landscape of the Himalaya*. Vienna: Austrian Academy of Sciences Press. pp. 13-18.
Morinis, A. 1984. *Pilgrimage in the Hindu Tradition: A Case Study of West Bengal*. New Delhi: Oxford University Press.
Mudral, B.P. 2055 VS (1998). 'Sapta Gandakī ksetrako mahatīrthasthan Dev Ghāt dham'. *Devavāni, A half yearly research oriented magazine of Devghat Vaidic Adhyatmic Sewa Parishad* I (1): 6-23.
Paudel, A. ed. 2055 VS (1998). *Devghāt Māhātmya*, Devghat.
Padoux, A. 2002. 'Corps et Cosmos. L'image du corps du yogin tantrique'. In V. Bouillier and G. Tarabout eds. *Images du corps dans le monde hindou*. Paris: CNRS Éditions. pp. 163-87.
Parry, J.P. 1981. 'Death and Cosmogony in Kashi'. *Contributions to Indian Sociology* 15 (1-2): 337-65.
Saraswati, B. 1983. 'Traditions of Tirthas (Sacred Sites) in India'. *Man in India* 63 (1): 40-81.
Saraswati, G. 2045 VS (1989). *Ridīkśetra Māhātmya*. Ridi (Gulmi, Nepal): Ridikshetra Pracharak Samiti.
Sax, W.S. 2003. 'Divine Kingdoms in the Central Himalayas'. In N. Gutschow *et al.* eds. *Sacred Landscape of the Himalaya*. Vienna: Austrian Academy of Sciences Press. pp. 177-94.
Sircar, D. 1973 [First edition 1950]. *The Śākta Pīthas*. Banaras: Motilal Banarsidass.
Slusser, M. 1982. *Nepal Mandala. A Cultural Study of the Kathmandu Valley*. Princeton: Princeton University Press.

Snellgrove, D.L. 1959. *The Hevajra Tantra: A Critical Study.* London: Oxford University Press, 2 vols.

Spera, G. 1977. 'Some Notes on Prayāga-māhātmya'. *Indologica Taurinensia* V: 179-89.

Staszak, J. 1996. 'Nature et Culture: des origines du "déterminisme géographique"'. *Géographie et Cultures* 19: 95-115.

Strenski, I. 1993. *Religion in Relation: Method, Application and Moral Location.* University of South Carolina Press.

Taviani, P. 1990. 'Soglie dell'aldilà nell'Irlanda medioevale'. In S. Boesch and L. Scaraffia eds. *Luoghi sacri e spazi della santità.* Torino: Rosenberg & Sellier. pp. 37-45.

Tiwari, N. 1985. *Goddess Cults in Ancient India.* New Delhi: Sundeep Prakash.

Varenne, J. 1976. *Yoga and the Hindu Tradition.* Chicago and London: University of Chicago Press.

Watters, T. 1904. *On Yuan Chwang's Travels in India 625-645 CE.* London: Royal Asiatic Society, 2 vols.

White, D.G. 1996. *The Alchemical Body.* Chicago: University of Chicago Press.

List of Contributors

STÉPHANE ARGUILLÈRE is Agrégé professor in Philosophy, doctor in the History of Religions and Religious Anthropology, and habilitated to direct researches. He is a Fellow Member of the Observatoire du Religieux [Observatory of Religious Facts] of the Institute of Political Studies (IEP) of Aix-en-Provence, France and of the UMR 8155 (CNRS/EPHE).

PASCAL BOUCHERY is lecturer in Anthropology at the University of Poitiers, where he teaches Political Anthropology and Environmental Anthropology. He has a Ph.D. in Social Anthropology from the University of Paris X. From 1994 to 1998 he conducted several fieldworks in Southern Yunnan, China, mainly among the Hani and Yi ethnic minorities. He is currently conducting research in Northeast India, where he first travelled in 1979 and 1980. More specifically, he is carrying out comparative research into kinship and is also involved in a project to help preserve the Apatani language of Arunachal Pradesh.

BEN CAMPBELL is lecturer in Anthropology, and coordinator of the Anthropology in Development research group at Durham University, UK. He has worked in Rasuwa District, Northern Nepal since 1989, and his book on Tamang environmental relations 'Living Between Juniper and Palm: Nature, Culture and Power in the Himalayas' is forthcoming. His film 'The Way of the Road' looks at the impact of road connection to the Tibetan border.

SUBHADRA MITRA CHANNA is professor in Anthropology at the University of Delhi. She was a Charles Wallace Fellow and a visiting professor to MSH, Paris, Fulbright visiting lecturer to

USA and a visiting professor in 2008-09 to USC, USA. She has written about fifty scholarly papers and four books. She was the president of the Indian Anthropological Association and is currently editor of the *Indian Anthropologist;* also Chair of the Commission on the Anthropology of Women (IUAES).

MARC GABORIEAU is emeritus research scholar at the CNRS and honorary professor at the EHESS, Paris. In the 1960s and 1970s, he conducted ethnographical and historical research among the Muslims and the Hindus of Nepal and Kumaon, producing several books and many articles on the place of Muslims in the caste society, spirit possession and folk literature. He then specialized in the historical anthropology of the Muslim commmunities of the Indian subcontinent, particularly India and Pakistan; he wrote about caste among South Asian Muslims, Sufi brotherhoods, Islamic reform movements and the relation of Islam and politics. He summarized his findings in his last book, *Un autre islam: Inde, Pakistan, Bangladesh.*

MARTIN GAENSZLE is professor in Cultural and Intellectual History of Modern South Asia at the Institute of South Asian, Tibetan and Buddhist Studies, University of Vienna, Austria. His research interests include ethnicity, local history, oral traditions and religious pluralism in North India and Nepal. He is the author of *Origins and Migrations: Kinship, Mythology and Ethnic Identity Among the Mewahang Rai* (Mandala Book Point, 2000) and *Ancestral Voices: Oral Ritual Texts and their Social Contexts among the Mewahang Rai of East Nepal* (LIT Verlag, 2002), and has co-authored *Rai Mythology: Kiranti Oral Texts* (with Karen Ebert, Harvard Oriental Series, 2008). His edited volumes are *Himalayan Space: Cultural Horizons and Practices* (with B. Bickel, Völkerkundemuseum der Universität Zürich, 1999), *Visualizing Space in Banaras: Images, Maps, and the Practice of Representation* (with J. Gengnagel, Harrassowitz, 2006), *The Power of Discourse in Ritual Performance* (with U. Demmer, LIT Verlag, 2007).

RACHEL GUIDONI has a Ph.D. in Social Anthropology from Université Paris-X, Nanterre, France (2006). She is associated with the CNRS Team (Etudes Himalayennes), Villejuif and teaches at the Institut de Langues Orientales, Paris.

ROBERTE N. HAMAYON is professor emerita, Ecole Pratique des Hautes Etudes, Paris, member of the Groupe Sociétés, Religions, Laïcité (CNRS). Trained in Linguistics and Anthropology, she conducted fieldwork in Mongolia and Buryatia since the late 1960s. Her main publications concern shamanism, epics, rituals and the notion of playing.

MARIE LECOMTE-TILOUINE is senior researcher in Social Anthropology at CNRS, France, and teaches at the Institut National des Langues Orientales, Paris. Her latest publications include: *Hindu Kingship, Ethnic Revival, and Maoist Rebellion in Nepal* (Collected Essays), New Delhi: OUP, 2009 and (ed.) *Bards and Mediums: History, Culture and Politics in the Central Himalayan Kingdoms*, Almora: Almora Book Depot, 2009.

CHIARA LETIZIA is researcher in Cultural Anthropology at the University of Milano-Bicocca and a Newton Fellow at the Institute of Social and Cultural Anthropology, University of Oxford. Her main interest is the religious anthropology of Nepal. She has carried out fieldworks on Newar Buddhist cults and initiation rituals, mythology and religious practices related to the confluence of rivers, and conversions to Buddhism among Magars and Tharus in the context of post-1990 ethnic claims. Following the 2007 declaration of Nepal as a secular state, she is currently studying the understandings of and reactions to secularism in Terai, as well as the religious and political debates around secularism in a time of constitution making.

CHARLES MALAMOUD is honorary directeur d'Etudes des religions de l'Inde at the École Pratique des Hautes Etudes (EPHE), Paris. He is the author of: *Cuire le monde, Rite et pensée dans l'Inde ancienne*, Paris, La Découverte, 1989 (*Cooking the World: Ritual and Thought in Ancient India*, OUP, 1997), *Le jumeau solaire*, Paris, Seuil, 2002; *Féminité de la parole, Études sur l'Inde ancienne*, Paris,

Albin Michel 2005 ; *La danse des pierres, Études sur la scène sacrificielle dans l'Inde ancienne*, Paris, Seuil, 2005.

ANDREAS WILKES has worked on indigenous knowledge and natural resource management in China since 1997. He has a Ph.D. in Environmental Anthropology from University of Kent, UK, and is currently deputy country representative for the World Agroforestry Centre's China Programme.

CLAUS PETER ZOLLER is professor of Hindi at the University of Oslo, Norway. His Ph.D. (1980) deals with the language of the Rang-pas, Garhwal Himalayas, and his Habilitation (1997) on the grammar and poetry of an oral Mahabharata epic from the Garhwal Himalayas. Research fellow in the Pakistan-German project *Culture Area Karakorum* 1997–2001, his special fields of research are: linguistics of West Himalayan and Dardic languages, North Indian folk traditions and epics.

Index

acculturation 123, 139, 142
Adibasi 119
agency 69, 79, 161, 181
agriculture 68, 69, 71, 93, 151, 174, 175, 191, 210, 245, 252, 285, 287, 319, 320, 324, 328, 330
alliance 14, 98, 99, 101, 105, 106, 107, 123, 141, 164, 166, 167, 184, 232
altitude 10, 17, 119, 167, 223, 233, 236, 237, 241, 287, 331
ancestor 110, 111, 112, 123, 124, 125, 144, 148, 149, 150, 192, 200, 205, 210, 216, 335, 337, 347, 351, 356, 357, 359
animal 3, 11, 13, 14, 15, 18, 22, 23, 24, 36, 37, 39, 44, 50, 51, 65, 69, 87, 89, 92, 95, 99, 100, 101, 102, 103, 104, 106, 108, 111, 112, 130,, 132, 137, 138, 139, 145, 147, 150, 151, 152, 157, 163, 164, 165, 166, 168, 178, 196, 209, 212, 214, 215, 229, 230, 231, 232, 233, 235, 241, 276, 277, 285, 287, 291, 293, 294, 296, 297, 299, 302, 304, 307, 308, 311, 312, 313, 323, 324, 327, 333, 335, 336, 339
animism 127, 158, 159, 160, 167, 178, 184, 185, 186, 187

apologetic theology 13, 62, 66
Arabic 13, 248
Arabic philosophy 13
Aristotle 52
artifice 18, 42, 149, 266, 279, 280, 334, 335, 338
Arya 119, 136, 137, 138, 141, 145
ascetics 11, 21, 28, 129, 134, 213, 238, 270, 346, 354, 355, 360
Atheism 54
austerities 35, 38, 39, 40 ; 131, 132
autonomy 6, 126, 128, 157, 160, 174, 176, 195

Bahun-Chetri 119
bamboo 38, 122, 192, 202, 334, bangle-makers 70, 75, 77
bark 39, 40, 41, 45, 102
bear 95, 171, 172, 173, 174, 175, 177, 184, 185, 192, 231
beer 186, 194, 198, 199, 200, 201, 202, 203, 205, 206, 208, 212, 233, 303, 304, 312
Bhutan 269
biodiversity 6, 129, 150, 152, 153, 157, 304
bird 102, 203, 208
blood 103, 123, 141, 191, 194, 203, 208, 212, 232, 235, 245, 252, 268, 269, 298
boar 22, 25, 142, 143, 177

body 12, 15, 16, 18, 23, 39, 41, 45, 46, 102, 106, 136, 140, 164, 173, 203, 230, 261–71, 273, 274, 275, 276, 300, 301, 302, 347, 352, 353, 354, 355, 356, 357, 359, 363, 365
Bon 55, 56, 57, 127, 261, 281
bone 14, 102, 103, 164, 167, 264, 266, 267, 268, 269, 275, 279, 296, 297, 302, 303, 312
Buddha 55, 56, 125, 134, 262, 263, 273, 275, 280
Buddhism 10, 12, 13, 17, 18, 50, 51, 52, 53, 54, 58, 124, 125, 127, 133, 134, 140, 144, 145, 185, 223, 224, 226, 227, 228, 229, 239, 241, 261, 263, 286, 355, 364
buffalo 122, 137, 166, 171, 175, 213, 323, 324
Buryat 14, 93, 98

Catholic tradition 76, 261, 262, 266
cattle 19, 93, 122, 123, 171, 172, 173, 184, 253, 285, 287–94, 296–300, 303, 308–313, 332, 333
causality 54, 64
cave 132, 267, 279, 333, 337
chicken 22, 25, 137, 138, 141, 199, 204, 205, 206, 207, 208
China 10, 176, 285, 319, 320, 322, 332, 335, 336, 338, 341
Christianity 62, 93
civilization 3, 22,, 23, 24, 121, 133, 145, 223, 236, 237, 238, 242, 363
civilizing force 191
civilizing process 16, 215

climate 10
colonial models 160
colonial period 8, 224, 228, 234
colonization 5, 8, 93, 136, 137,
colonizing ideologies 9
contingency 10
cosmos 18, 19, 45, 64, 68, 69, 70, 72, 79, 80, 165
cow 19, 45, 46, 122, 146, 171, 232, 292, 293, 296, 298–302, 309, 310, 312
cremation 145, 266, 269, 275, 280, 356, 359
cultural act 361
cultural choice 112
cultural construction 348
cultural disposition 165
cultural model 285, 286
cultural preconceptions 319
cultural space 348
cultural understandings 313
cultural values 341
culture 3, 5, 7, 14, 16, 17, 23–24, 25, 26, 28, 49, 61, 91, 94, 123, 130, 133, 134, 135, 136, 137, 139, 144, 150, 151, 152, 158, 178, 192, 223, 242, 245, 246, 247, 248, 251, 253, 347, 348, 362
   cumulative progress of 49
   material 319
   shared 182

deer 27, 36, 37, 39
demon 51, 213
Deoband 63
   Deobandi school 70
desire 11, 13, 167, 183, 257, 356
dharma 34, 80, 127, 133, 140, 144, 145, 225, 238, 355, 358, 364

Diderot 6
dichotomy 5, 6, 143, 210, 223, 226, 230, 312, 313, 319,
domestic 91, 92, 96, 110, 111, 137, 138, 173, 174, 177, 184, 186, 200, 201, 202, 206, 233, 234, 235, 238
domesticated 10, 11, 138, 232, 290, 321, 333
domestication 138, 286, 290
drainage 322, 323, 325, 326, 327, 328, 329, 331, 338
duality 10, 149, 185, 209, 210
duck 291

earth 19, 25, 42, 44, 123, 144, 147, 186, 230, 262, 272, 323, 324, 326, 335, 339, 355, 361
earth-god 15, 16, 120
Ehirit-Bulagat 14, 92, 112
energy 18, 19, 332, 334, 337, 338, 352
vital 300–305, 354
Enlightenment 52, 53, 55, 56, 57
Age of 49
environment 3, 4, 8, 10, 14, 15, 19, 24, 25, 27, 29, 94, 119, 121, 123, 130, 137, 138, 141, 148, 150, 152, 157, 159, 160, 162, 163, 165, 225, 227, 234, 240, 319, 331, 332, 336, 337, 340, 340
environmental conservation 157, 158, 184, 186
environmental knowledge 162, 164, 176, 180, 181, 183, 184, 185, 186
environmental subjectivity 15, 157, 159, 160, 162, 163, 177, 180, 183, 184, 185, 186, 187

environmentalism 157
environmentality 15
epics 14, 17, 96, 98, 251, 346, 349
ethnicity 9
Ethnography 10, 157, 158, 159, 161, 162, 164
Evenk 89, 92, 98
Yenissei Evenk 107

fairy 17, 245, 249, 250, 251, 252, 254, 255, 256
fairy tale 249, 250, 254, 256,
father-in-law 14, 94, 96, 170, 172, 173
fertility 19, 26, 27, 69, 71, 72, 191, 192, 213, 218, 300, 301 337, 339
fertilizer 323, 324
field 22, 26, 119, 121, 122, 167, 170, 172, 175, 177, 195, 197, 203, 205, 207, 223, 232, 233, 287, 321–31, 335, 339, 340
fish 95, 100, 102, 147, 203, 205, 276
fitra 61, 65, 73–76, 79, 80
fodder 19, 122, 231, 233, 285–88, 297, 298, 305, 308–311, 313, 314
forest 4, 11, 14, 17, 22, 25, 28, 33, 35, 36, 37, 38, 41, 89, 90, 93, 94, 95, 101, 105, 106, 112, 122, 129, 130, 135, 138–42, 158–62, 165, 166, 168, 169, 170, 172, 174, 175, 178–184, 186, 203, 230, 231, 233–238, 241, 252, 323
fruits 69, 70, 142, 143

gas 294, 296, 301, 306, 312
Ghale 167, 168, 175, 176
Ghâzî Miyân 71, 72

globalization 4, 9, 120
goat 122, 141, 168, 186, 232, 235, 291, 298, 299, 303,
grass 39, 41 45, 229, 285, 287, 292, 295-300, 308-311, 313
guinea pig 291
Gurung 126, 134, 137, 139, 142, 168, 191, 209

Hani 19, 319-25, 331-40
harvest 70, 71, 196, 203, 287, 310, 324, 327
Hegel 50, 51, 52
Heraclitus 11
herders 14, 89-90, 92, 93, 94, 98, 110, 112, 166, 167, 285, 287, 293, 298, 305, 309
hermit 36, 37, 41, 238
hermitage 33, 36, 39, 41
Hindu 11, 15, 17, 20, 22, 24, 25, 28, 119, 120, 121, 122, 123, 124, 125, 128, 129, 130, 131, 132, 135, 136, 139, 140, 141, 142, 143, 144, 145, 146, 147, 152, 153, 157, 176, 191, 193, 212, 215, 217, 223, 224, 225, 226, 227, 228, 229, 231, 237, 238, 239, 240, 241, 242, 347, 354
Hinduism 10, 124, 127, 128, 129, 140, 143, 144, 145, 146, 147, 223, 224, 226, 227, 228, 238, 241, 345-366
history 10, 13, 49, 53, 125, 131, 133, 135, 139, 140, 162, 179, 180, 195, 223, 229, 249, 250, 253, 254, 256, 266, 359, 360, 363
Hobbes 58
horse 92, 93, 96, 232, 310

humanization 53, 361
hunter 14, 21, 22, 25, 27, 90, 92, 93, 94, 95, 98, 104, 110, 111, 112, 145, 146, 166, 231, 238
hunting 14, 27, 90, 91, 92, 95, 98, 99, 102, 109, 112, 138, 152, 157, 166, 205
season 14, 96, 98

India 123, 127, 136, 158, 210, 224, 225, 227, 228, 229, 239, 345, 346, 349, 350, 352, 354, 356, 362, 363, 364
Indigenous Peoples 4-6, 7, 8, 9, 15, 16, 20, 27, 28, 119, 120, 123, 124, 126, 128, 136, 137, 138, 141, 144, 145, 148, 150, 151, 152, 153, 157, 163, 315
irrigation 19, 69, 119, 121, 122, 167, 177, 319, 320, 324-28, 328, 330, 331, 333, 334, 337-40,
Islam 10, 13, 61, 72, 245, 250, 251, 252
Islamization 17

Jad 16, 223, 224, 225, 226, 227, 228, 229, 230, 231, 232, 234, 235, 236, 237, 238, 239, 240, 241, 242
Janajati 119, 120, 121, 122, 123, 124, 125, 127, 128, 129, 130, 132, 134, 136, 137, 138, 139, 140, 141, 142, 143, 144, 145, 146, 147, 148, 149, 150, 151, 152, 157, 159, 163, 177

Kant 53
king 21, 22, 26, 46, 121, 123, 129, 132, 165, 196, 213, 217, 346, 353

kingdom 25, 121, 129, 213, 346
kingship 21, 46, 106
Kirant 124, 127, 131, 132, 133, 134, 135, 145, 195
Kulung/e Rai 105, 191, 194, 195, 197, 199, 200, 202, 208, 212

lake 14, 175, 332
landscape 3, 17, 164, 165, 224, 225, 246, 251, 257, 293, 319, 320, 322, 332, 335, 336, 338, 341, 351, 361, 362
 imagined landscape 348
 organic landscape 8
 symbolic landscape 351
 technoscape 8
law 10, 27, 53, 66, 73, 74, 80, 126, 249, 253, 258, 336, 364
legislation 13, 119
liberation 11, 13, 35, 52, 144, 356, 359
Limbu 122, 127, 131, 142
linearity 6
Lisu 286, 289, 294, 298, 304
Lohorung Rai 201
love 17, 36, 98, 100, 106, 245, 246, 247, 248, 249, 251, 252, 253, 254, 255, 256, 257, 258
 maternal 22
lovers 17, 246, 247, 248, 249, 250, 251, 252, 253, 255, 256, 257, 258,

Magar 122, 125, 126, 134, 135, 137, 138, 139, 140, 141, 142, 145, 146, 191, 209
marriage 99, 100, 101, 105, 106, 109, 138, 167, 169, 176, 179, 223, 232, 236, 237, 238, 256, 258, 286

meadows 17, 19, 252, 255, 289, 292, 298, 303
meat 19, 24, 111, 147, 160, 203, 205, 206, 209, 212, 214, 285, 293, 296–304, 311–314
meditation 35, 38, 130, 355, 360
meta-culture 363, 364
metamorphosis 51
metaphor 14, 27, 41, 57, 73, 97–100, 107, 121, 142, 147, 177, 178, 253, 289, 312, 352, 353
Mewahang Rai 16, 191–194, 196, 198, 205, 206, 208–210, 212–215, 218
miracle 66, 67, 68, 262, 267, 268, 274, 347
Mongol 93, 124, 146
Mongolia 93, 185
monkey 24, 142, 143, 192,
mountain 17, 19, 22, 24, 37, 109, 139, 140, 162, 166, 169, 224, 225, 227, 228, 229, 231, 232, 234, 235, 236, 240, 241, 245, 252, 267, 285, 287, 300, 302, 304, 305, 311, 319, 321–25, 332–40, 361
mummification 268, 275, 276
myth 92, 135, 165, 166, 168, 169, 173, 174, 175, 176, 177, 178, 184, 185, 191–194, 198, 210, 215, 215, 225, 337, 346, 347, 348, 350, 352, 353, 354, 362, 363

naturalization 38, 109, 364
nature culture opposition 4, 5, 15, 17, 25, 49, 50, 56, 59, 61, 80, 164, 245, 256, 312, 348, 360
nature
 appropriation of 6

as an implicit category 92
becoming of 52
Children of 5, 14, 87, 91, 101, 112
closeness to 159, 177
concept of 11, 157, 312, 331
conception of 20, 91, 215, 312, 336, 363
conservation 164
cumulative 346
distance from 15
exploiters of 120
forces of 191, 215
good will of 37
harmony with 14, 15, 88, 90, 91, 113, 146
human 78, 89
idea of 93
intact 37
laws of 67, 313
love for 6
non-intervention in 15, 146, 152,
oneness with 163
osmosis with 11, 38
preservation of 6
primordial 65, 75, 78
protection of 157, 164, 186
proximity to 88
raw 53
relations to 91, 109, 113
relationship with 8, 10, 11, 119, 120, 128
religion of 125, 127, 138, 140, 144, 145, 146, 147
respect for 11, 128, 129, 143
sacredness of 226, 240
single 158
socialisation of 94, 112
state of 49
second 52, 50
struggle with 88
transformation of 15, 27, 120
unspoiled 17, 26, 242
untouched 28
natural resources 14, 119, 137, 140, 150, 151, 158, 159, 160, 164, 182, 184, 186, 223, 285, 287, 289, 290, 305
Naturism 125, 127
Neoplatonism 50, 53
nettles 170, 173, 174
network 18, 19, 176, 326, 327, 330, 331, 332, 333, 336, 337, 338, 339, 340, 347, 352, 366
Nirvana 13, 53, 55, 56, 57
Nepal 9, 15, 16, 20, 21, 24, 25, 26, 27, 29, 63, 71, 72, 122, 123, 127, 134, 135, 136, 137, 138, 142, 149, 151, 152, 157, 167, 176, 182, 184, 185, 186, 191, 195, 214, 224, 266, 270, 319, 345–47, 350–53, 361–64
Nepali 9, 22, 25, 70, 121, 138, 178, 191, 360
Newar 167, 168, 169, 176, 177, 184
Nu 286, 288, 296, 297, 298, 300, 301, 302, 303, 304

paddy 321, 322, 324, 325, 340
Pakistan 10, 17, 245, 246, 250, 252, 253, 257
Parvati 38, 41
pastoralist 18, 223, 226, 286, 311, 315
pasture 17, 109, 166, 168, 171, 172, 191, 195, 197, 212, 223, 224, 231, 232, 233, 234, 236, 237, 245, 252, 287, 293, 299, 306

pheasant 137
pig 22, 25, 142, 198, 208, 209, 276, 288, 296, 299, 303, 309
pilgrimage 19, 175, 240, 345-48, 349-54, 356, 365
plants 18, 26, 28, 45, 50, 51, 69, 89, 145, 152, 157, 163, 164, 165, 168, 192, 280, 285, 287-292, 294-97, 299, 305, 307
Plato 58
poetry 33, 36, 88, 248, 249, 256, 257
porcupine 177
pork 204, 207, 298, 301, 303, 304
practices 6, 8, 11, 17, 18, 21, 24, 119, 120, 121, 122, 124, 125, 126, 127, 129, 130, 134, 138, 139, 140, 141, 145, 150, 152, 157, 161, 163, 165, 175, 176, 178, 184, 201, 202, 204, 207, 208, 211, 245, 257, 285, 293, 294, 298, 300, 314, 323, 337, 339, 348, 349
prakriti 11, 25, 26, 127, 136, 137, 145, 360
perspectivism 15, 158, 178, 185
poultry 25
pyre 40, 266, 275

rabbit 291
Rai 127, 131, 142, 147, 191, 192, 202, 206, 212, 213, 217
rain 71, 191, 192, 199, 209, 210, 213, 229, 311, 329, 330, 339
raw 10, 23, 233
refined 10, 25
regularity 68, 72, 329
reindeer 91, 92, 95, 98, 100
relics 18, 261-81

renouncer 35, 36, 38, 346
rice 119, 120, 122, 169, 196, 200, 202-208, 214, 319-22, 337-40
rite 11, 12, 34, 35, 37, 38, 41, 42, 44, 46, 47, 72, 146, 198-210, 212, 213, 226, 347, 351, 356, 357
ritual 9, 11 14, 16, 17, 20, 21, 23, 24, 25, 28, 43, 92, 96, 98, 99, 100, 101, 105, 106, 107, 119, 120, 121, 129, 138, 166, 168, 175, 191-93, 198-202, 205-08, 210-18, 226, 227, 230, 231, 234, 235, 238, 240, 340, 346,-49, 352, 353, 358-64
river 19, 38, 90, 175, 223, 225, 227, 245, 267, 268, 286, 289, 319, 320, 322, 337, 345-47, 349-55, 357-61
Rousseau 58, 61
Russia 93
Russian 14, 88, 91

sacred places 18, 225, 231, 235, 237, 240, 267, 268, 271, 272, 273, 275, 276, 345-66
sacrifice 12, 34, 37, 41, 42, 43, 44 45, 47, 71, 111, 139, 141, 147, 157, 175, 187, 235, 356, 363
saint 13, 70, 71, 245, 261, 262, 263, 265, 266, 267, 268, 271, 275, 277
Sampange Rai 16, 193, 194
samsara 13, 52, 54, 55, 56, 57, 58, 360
samskara 23, 24, 25, 28
samskriti 11, 23, 24, 53, 360
Sanskrit 11, 348, 349, 358, 362